All that glitters...

Even the stars

All things precious...

Even your life

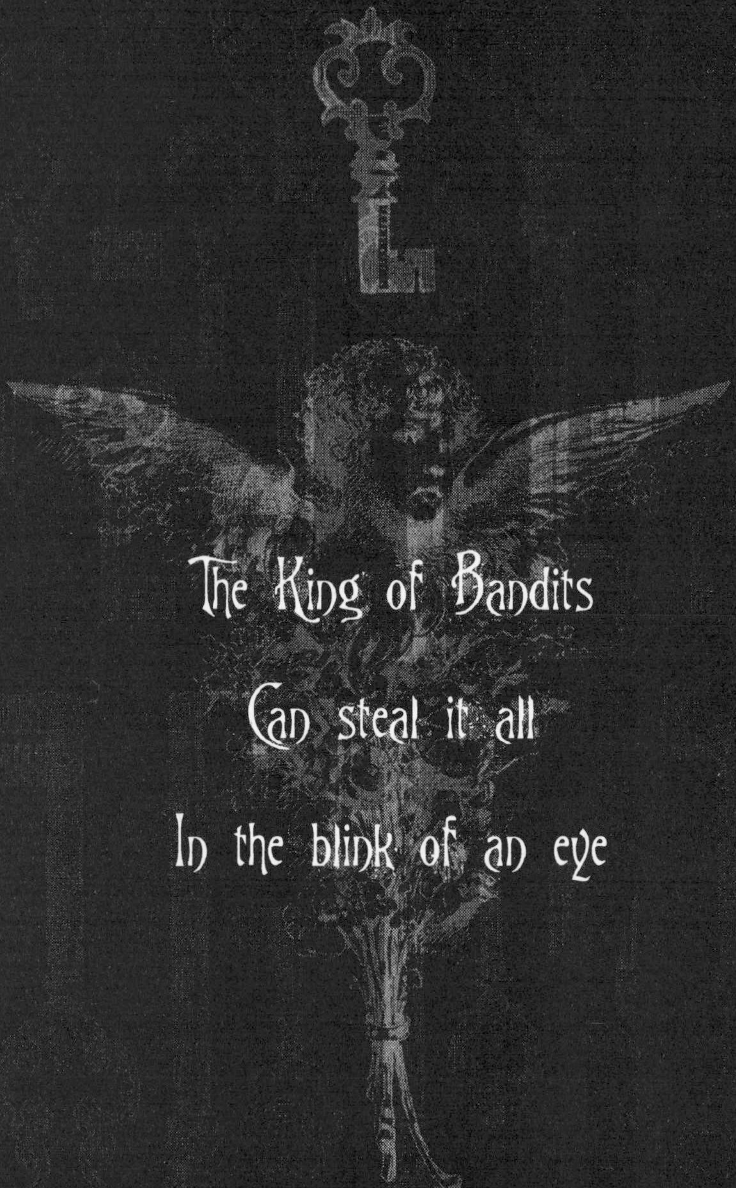
The King of Bandits
Can steal it all
In the blink of an eye

王ドロボウ
JING
新装版
THREE

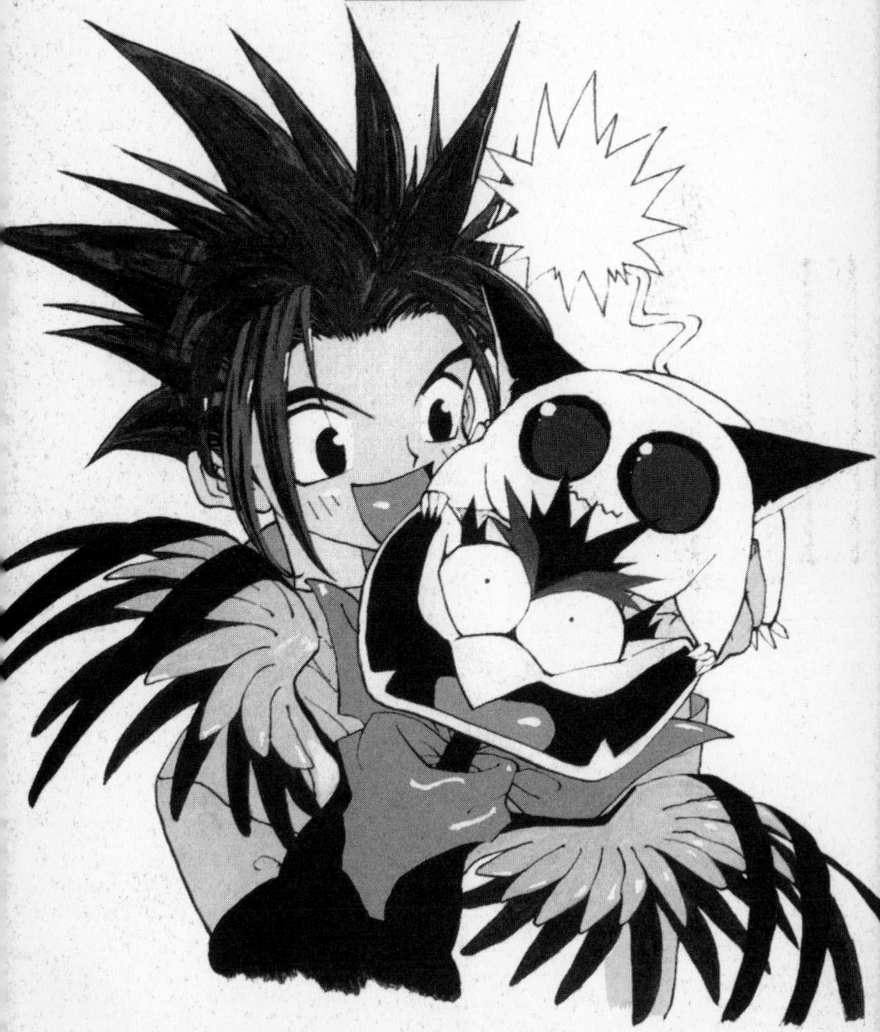

jing&kir&porvora

ALSO AVAILABLE FROM TOKYOPOP®

MANGA

.HACK//LEGEND OF THE TWILIGHT
@LARGE (December 2003)
ANGELIC LAYER*
BABY BIRTH*
BATTLE ROYALE*
BRAIN POWERED*
BRIGADOON*
CARDCAPTOR SAKURA
CARDCAPTOR SAKURA: MASTER OF THE CLOW*
CHOBITS*
CHRONICLES OF THE CURSED SWORD
CLAMP SCHOOL DETECTIVES*
CLOVER
CONFIDENTIAL CONFESSIONS*
CORRECTOR YUI
COWBOY BEBOP*
COWBOY BEBOP: SHOOTING STAR*
CYBORG 009*
DEMON DIARY
DIGIMON*
DRAGON HUNTER
DRAGON KNIGHTS*
DUKLYON: CLAMP SCHOOL DEFENDERS*
ERICA SAKURAZAWA*
FAKE*
FLCL*
FORBIDDEN DANCE*
GATE KEEPERS*
G GUNDAM*
GRAVITATION*
GTO*
GUNDAM WING
GUNDAM WING: BATTLEFIELD OF PACIFISTS
GUNDAM WING: ENDLESS WALTZ*
GUNDAM WING: THE LAST OUTPOST*
HAPPY MANIA*
HARLEM BEAT
I.N.V.U.
INITIAL D*
ISLAND
JING: KING OF BANDITS*
JULINE
KARE KANO*
KINDAICHI CASE FILES, THE*
KING OF HELL
KODOCHA: SANA'S STAGE*
LOVE HINA*
LUPIN III*
MAGIC KNIGHT RAYEARTH*

MAGIC KNIGHT RAYEARTH II* (COMING SOON)
MAN OF MANY FACES*
MARMALADE BOY*
MARS*
MIRACLE GIRLS
MIYUKI-CHAN IN WONDERLAND*
MONSTERS, INC.
PARADISE KISS*
PARASYTE
PEACH GIRL
PEACH GIRL: CHANGE OF HEART*
PET SHOP OF HORRORS*
PLANET LADDER*
PLANETES*
PRIEST
RAGNAROK
RAVE MASTER*
REALITY CHECK
REBIRTH
REBOUND*
RISING STARS OF MANGA
SABER MARIONETTE J*
SAILOR MOON
SAINT TAIL
SAMURAI DEEPER KYO*
SAMURAI GIRL: REAL BOUT HIGH SCHOOL*
SCRYED*
SHAOLIN SISTERS*
SHIRAHIME-SYO: SNOW GODDESS TALES* (Dec. 2003)
SHUTTERBOX
SORCERER HUNTERS
THE SKULL MAN*
THE VISION OF ESCAFLOWNE
TOKYO MEW MEW*
UNDER THE GLASS MOON
VAMPIRE GAME*
WILD ACT*
WISH*
WORLD OF HARTZ (November 2003)
X-DAY*
ZODIAC P.I. *

For more information visit www.TOKYOPOP.com

*INDICATES 100% AUTHENTIC MANGA (RIGHT-TO-LEFT FORMAT)

CINE-MANGA™

CARDCAPTORS
JACKIE CHAN ADVENTURES (November 2003)
JIMMY NEUTRON
KIM POSSIBLE
LIZZIE MCGUIRE
POWER RANGERS: NINJA STORM
SPONGEBOB SQUAREPANTS
SPY KIDS 2

NOVELS

KARMA CLUB (April 2004)
SAILOR MOON

TOKYOPOP KIDS

STRAY SHEEP

ART BOOKS

CARDCAPTOR SAKURA*
MAGIC KNIGHT RAYEARTH*

ANIME GUIDES

COWBOY BEBOP ANIME GUIDES
GUNDAM TECHNICAL MANUALS
SAILOR MOON SCOUT GUIDES

080103

KING OF BANDITS

王ドロボウ JING

VOLUME 3 OF 7

Story and Art by
Yuichi Kumakura

Los Angeles • Tokyo • London

Translator - Kong Chang
English Adaptation - Carol Fox
Copy Editor - Tim Beedle
Retouch and Lettering - Deron Bennett
Cover Layout - Gary Shum

Editor - Jake Forbes
Managing Editor - Jill Freshney
Production Coordinator - Antonio DePietro
Production Manager - Jennifer Miller
Art Director - Matt Alford
Editorial Director - Jeremy Ross
VP of Production - Ron Klamert
President & C.O.O. - John Parker
Publisher & C.E.O. - Stuart Levy

Email: editor@TOKYOPOP.com
Come visit us online at www.TOKYOPOP.com

A  Manga

TOKYOPOP Inc.
5900 Wilshire Blvd. Suite 2000
Los Angeles, CA 90036

Jing: King of Bandits Vol. 3

ISBN: 1-59182-178-9

First TOKYOPOP® printing: December 2003

10 9 8 7 6 5 4 3 2 1

Printed in USA

JING: KING OF BANDITS
THREE

CONTENTS

The Story so Far...

You wonder what our Jing is doing tonight?
What merriments is Jing pursuing tonight?
The glimmer in his eyes has never burned as bright
You wonder what our Jing is up to tonight?
He's escorting a Porvora
with a babe that Kir adores
over treacherous and lecherous terrains.
The same Jing who stole a clockwork grape
now hopes to steal the Milky Way,
or at least the biggest star gem
in the night.
Right?
So lets go back to our tale
of Jing's latest plight.
I'm sure you want to know
if he gets off all right.
Well this is what
our hero Jing is
doing tonight--!

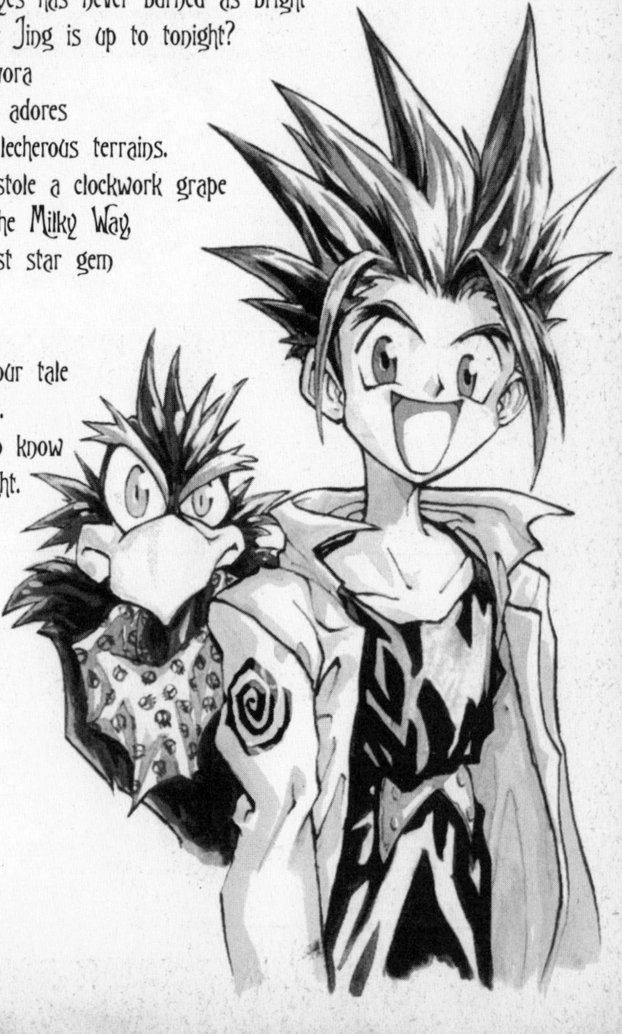

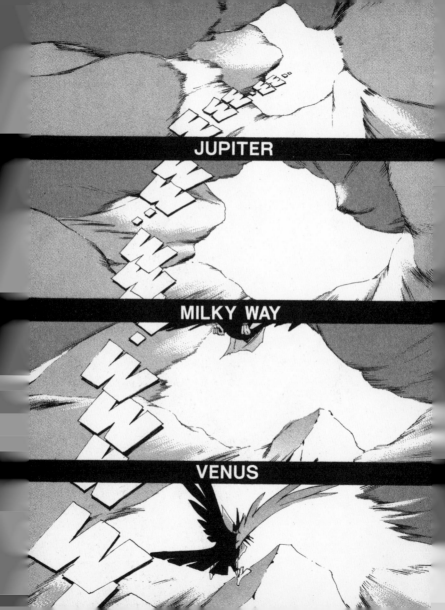

JUPITER

MILKY WAY

VENUS

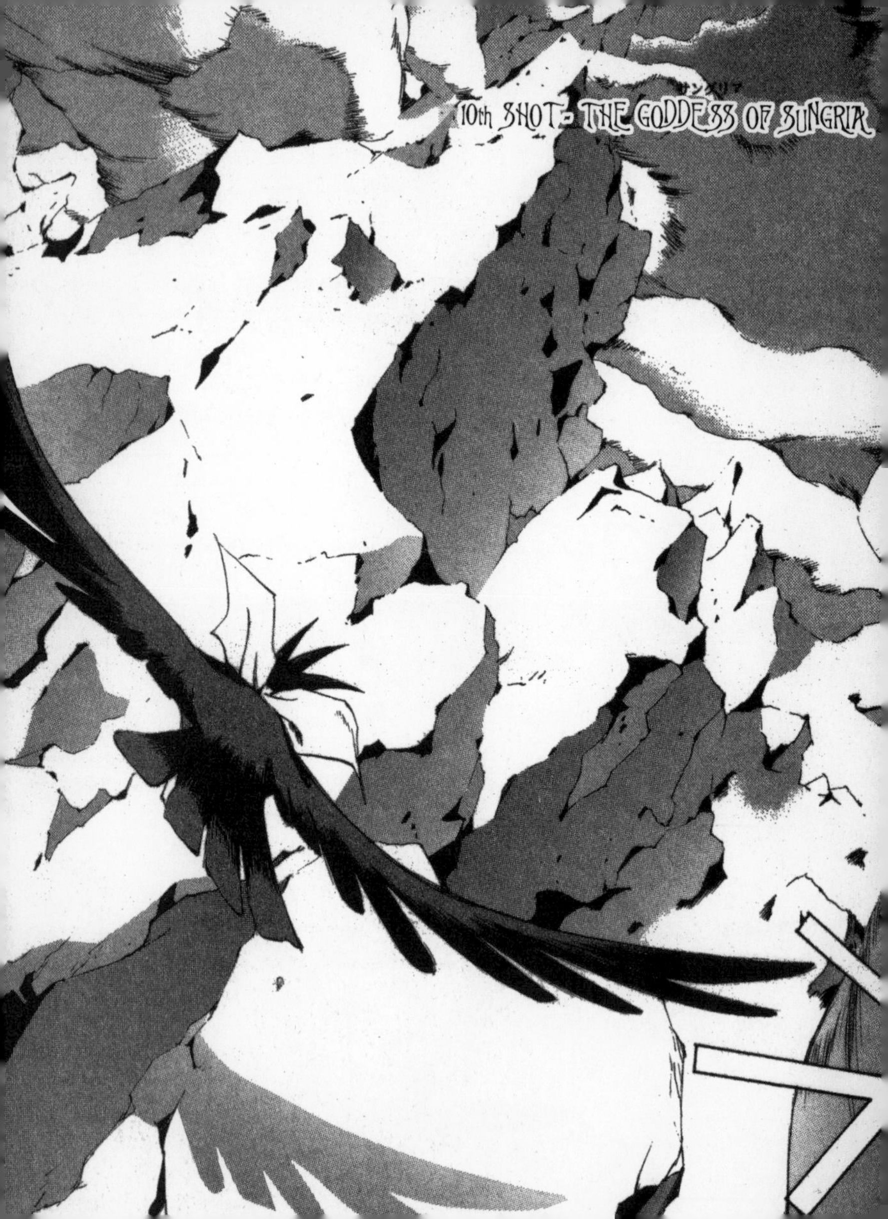
サングリア
10th SHOT - THE GODDESS OF SUNGRIA

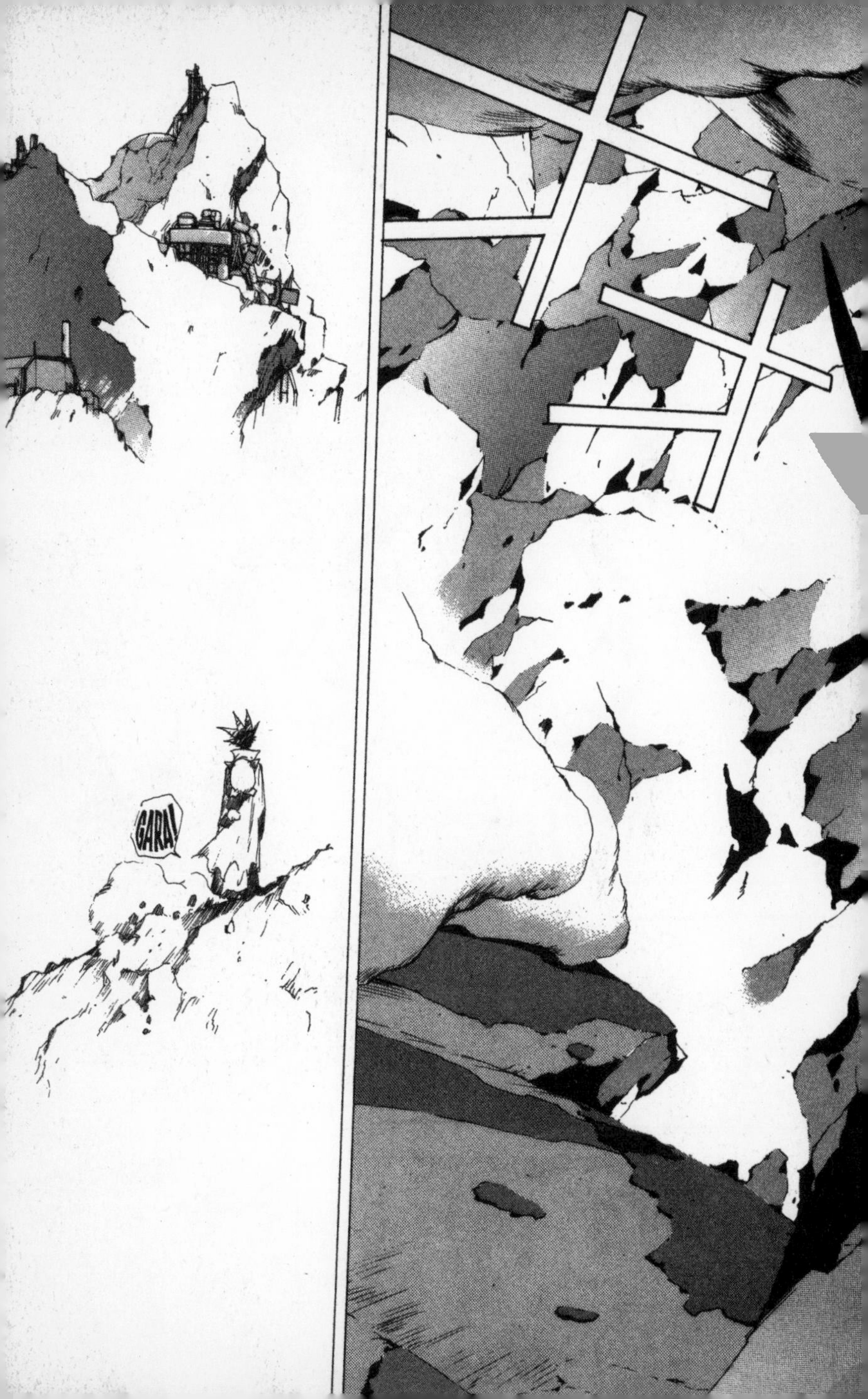
GARA!

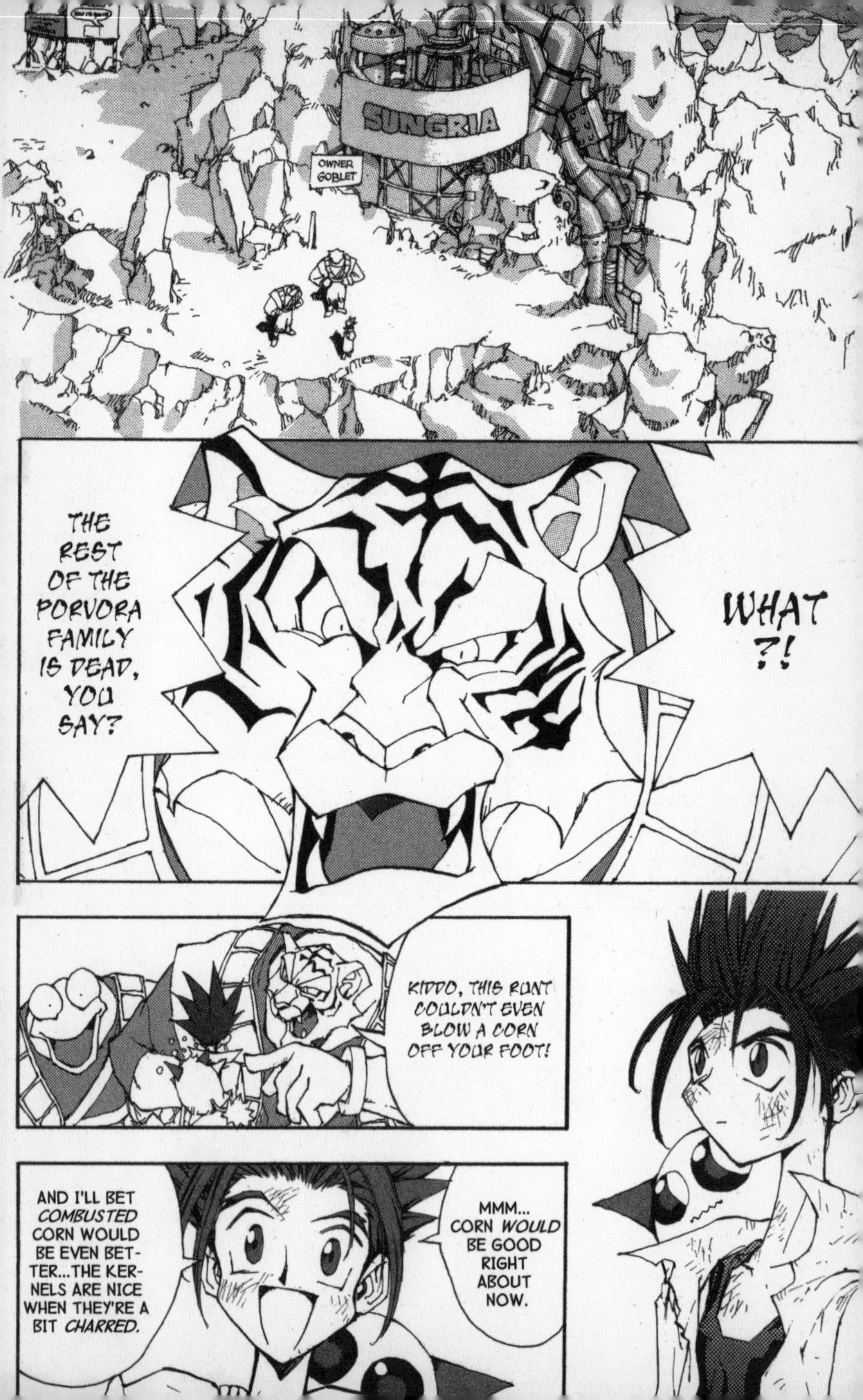
SUNGRIA
OWNER GOBLET
WHAT ?!
THE REST OF THE PORVORA FAMILY IS DEAD, YOU SAY?
KIDDO, THIS RUNT COULDN'T EVEN BLOW A CORN OFF YOUR FOOT!
MMM... CORN *WOULD* BE GOOD RIGHT ABOUT NOW.
AND I'LL BET *COMBUSTED* CORN WOULD BE EVEN BETTER...THE KERNELS ARE NICE WHEN THEY'RE A BIT *CHARRED.*

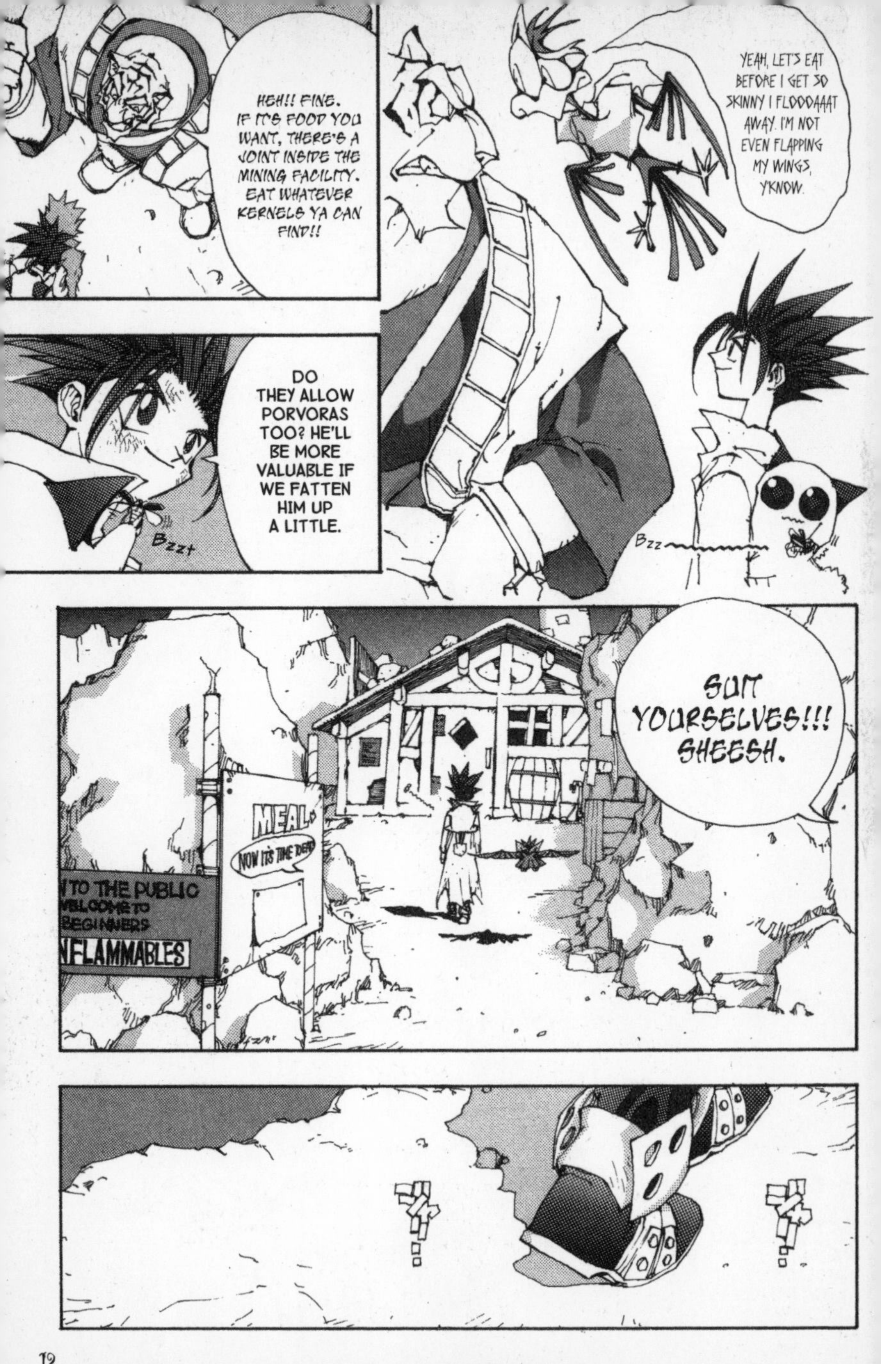
YEAH, LET'S EAT BEFORE I GET SO SKINNY I FLOOOAAAT AWAY. I'M NOT EVEN FLAPPING MY WINGS, Y'KNOW.
Bzz
HEH!! FINE. IF IT'S FOOD YOU WANT, THERE'S A JOINT INSIDE THE MINING FACILITY. EAT WHATEVER KERNELS YA CAN FIND!!
DO THEY ALLOW PORVORAS TOO? HE'LL BE MORE VALUABLE IF WE FATTEN HIM UP A LITTLE.
Bzzt
SUIT YOURSELVES!!! SHEESH.
MEAL
N TO THE PUBLIC
WELCOME TO
BEGINNERS
NFLAMMABLES

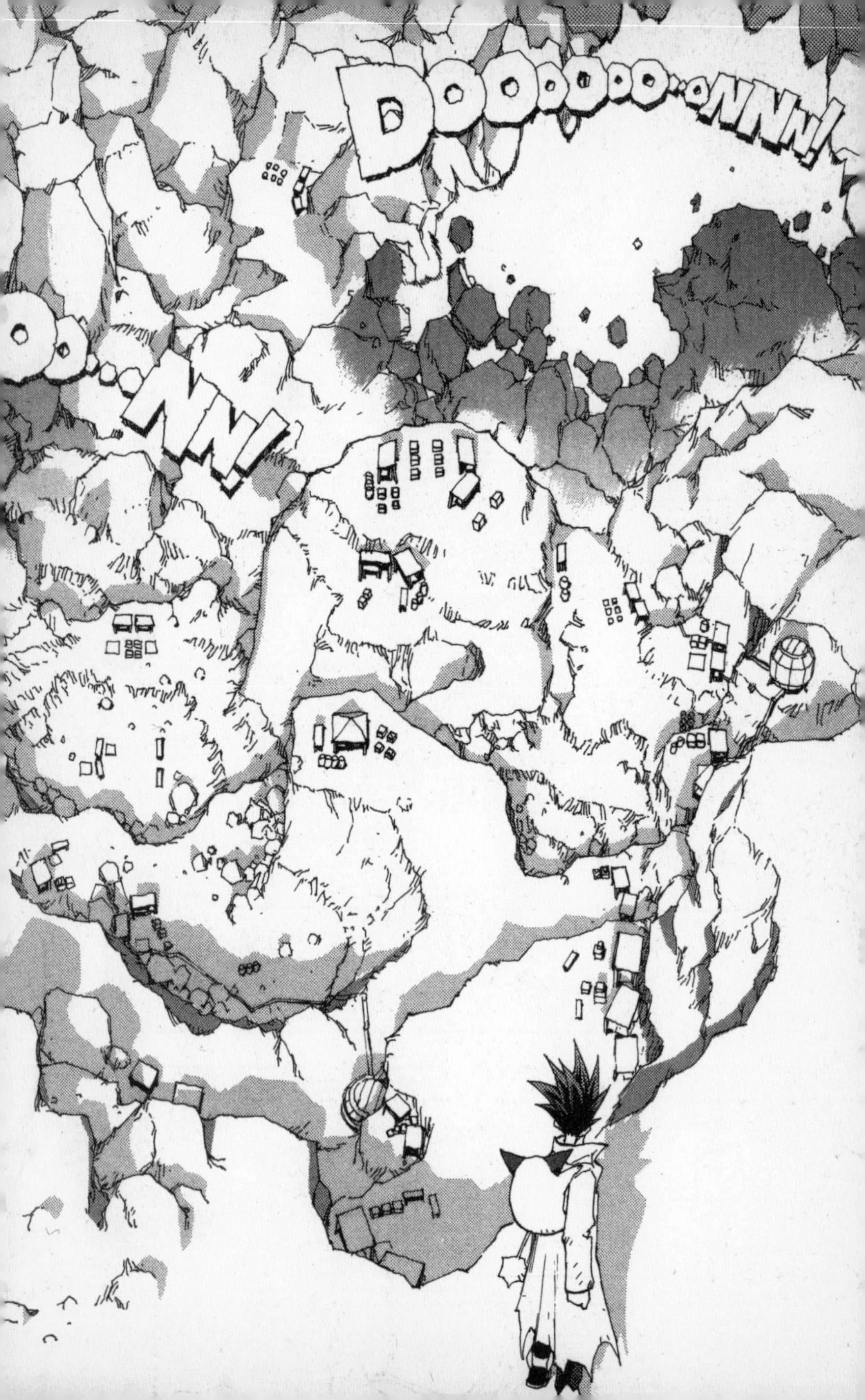
DOOOOOO..ONNNN!
OO..NN!

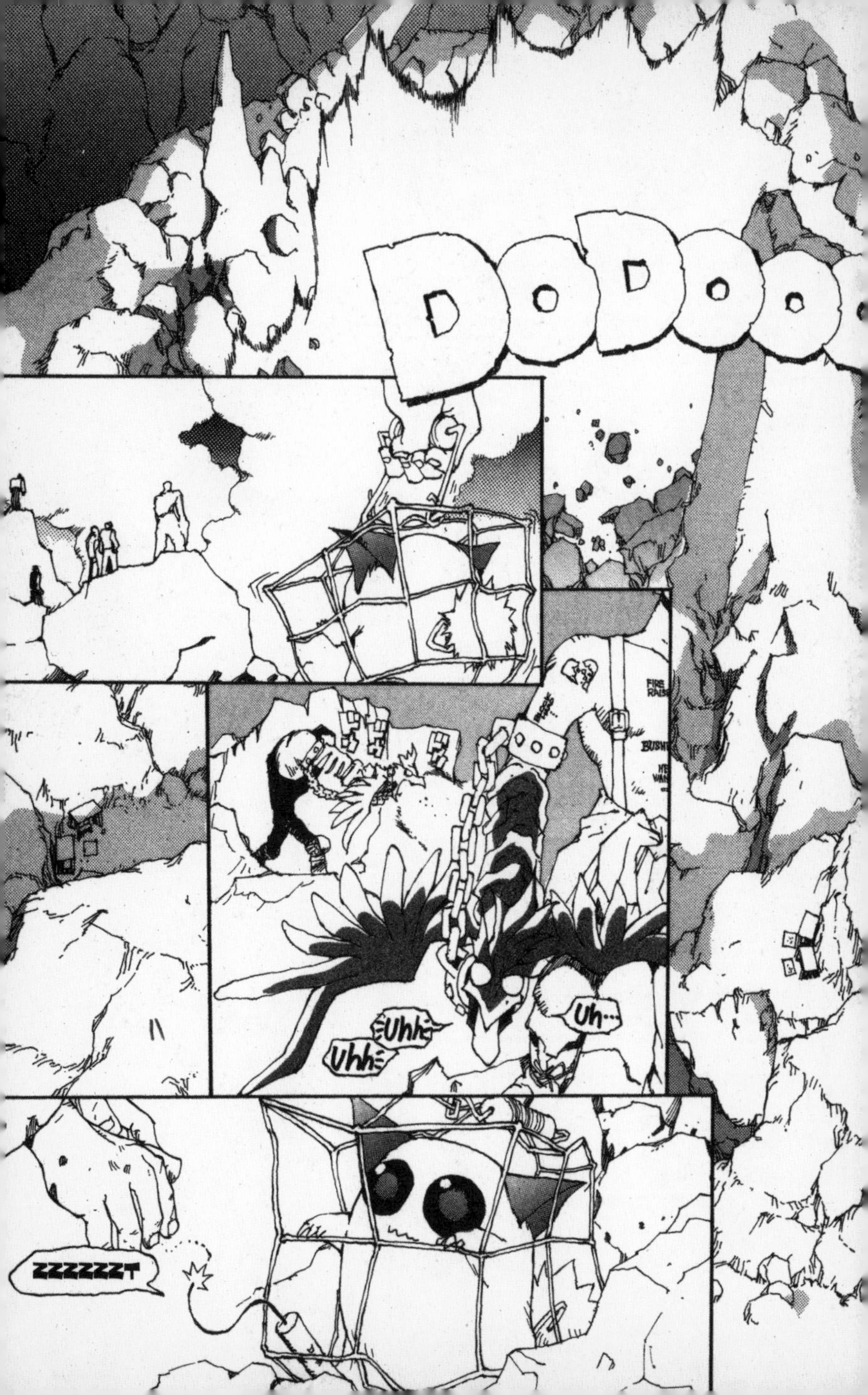
DODOO
Uh...
Uhh
Uhh
ZZZZZZT

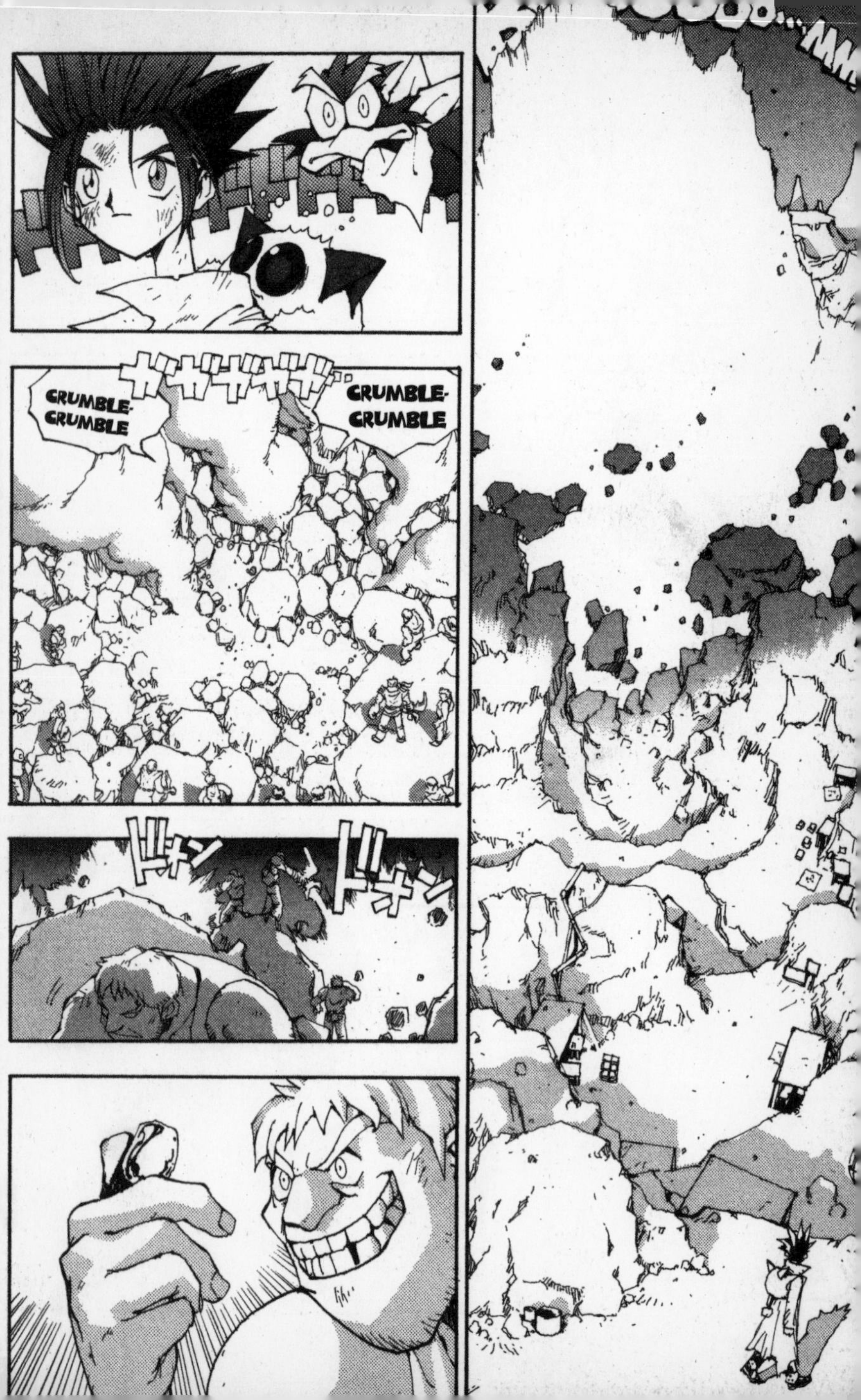
CRUMBLE-
CRUMBLE
CRUMBLE-
CRUMBLE

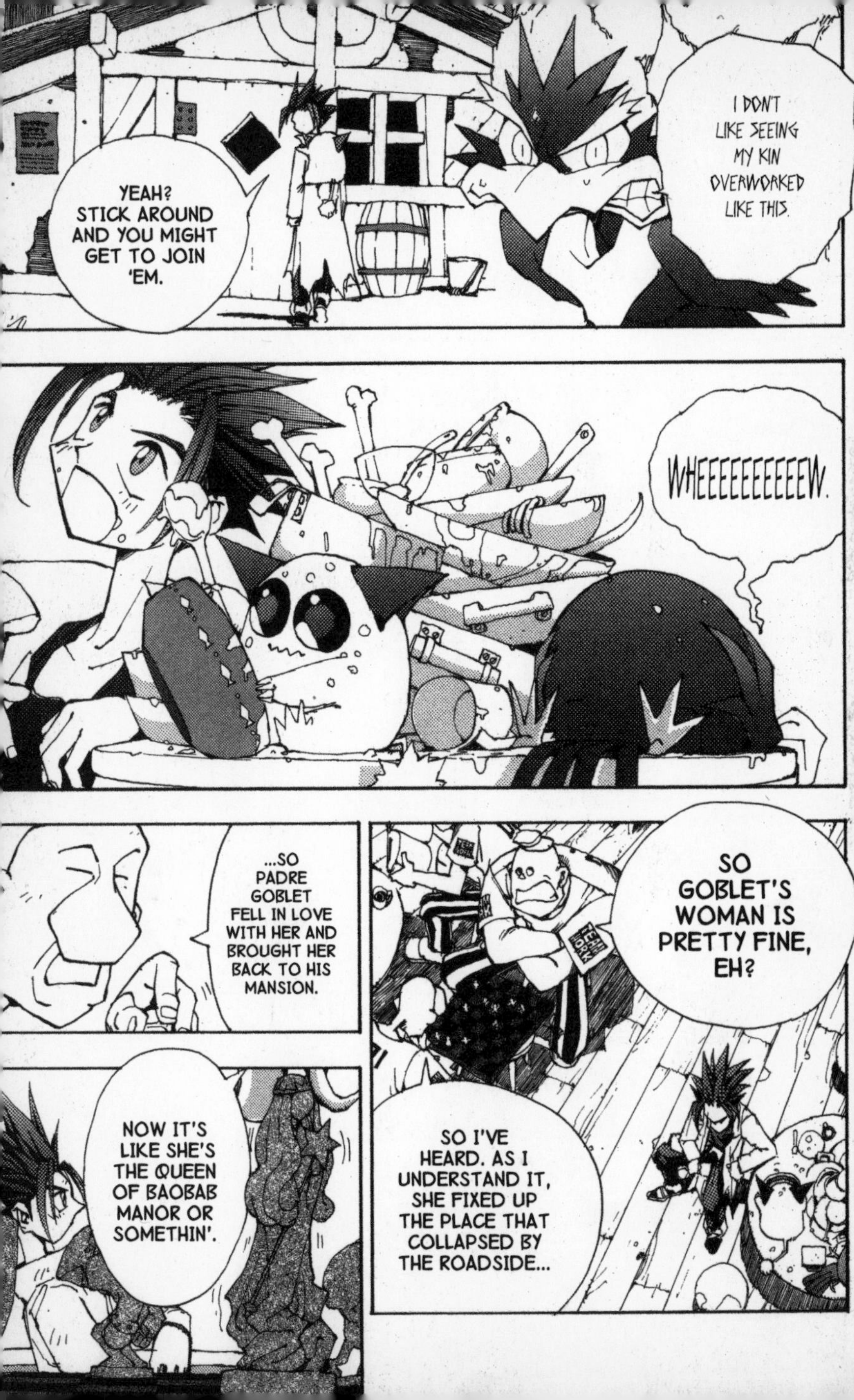
I DON'T LIKE SEEING MY KIN OVERWORKED LIKE THIS.
YEAH? STICK AROUND AND YOU MIGHT GET TO JOIN 'EM.
WHEEEEEEEEEEW.
SO GOBLET'S WOMAN IS PRETTY FINE, EH?
SO I'VE HEARD. AS I UNDERSTAND IT, SHE FIXED UP THE PLACE THAT COLLAPSED BY THE ROADSIDE...
...SO PADRE GOBLET FELL IN LOVE WITH HER AND BROUGHT HER BACK TO HIS MANSION.
NOW IT'S LIKE SHE'S THE QUEEN OF BAOBAB MANOR OR SOMETHIN'.

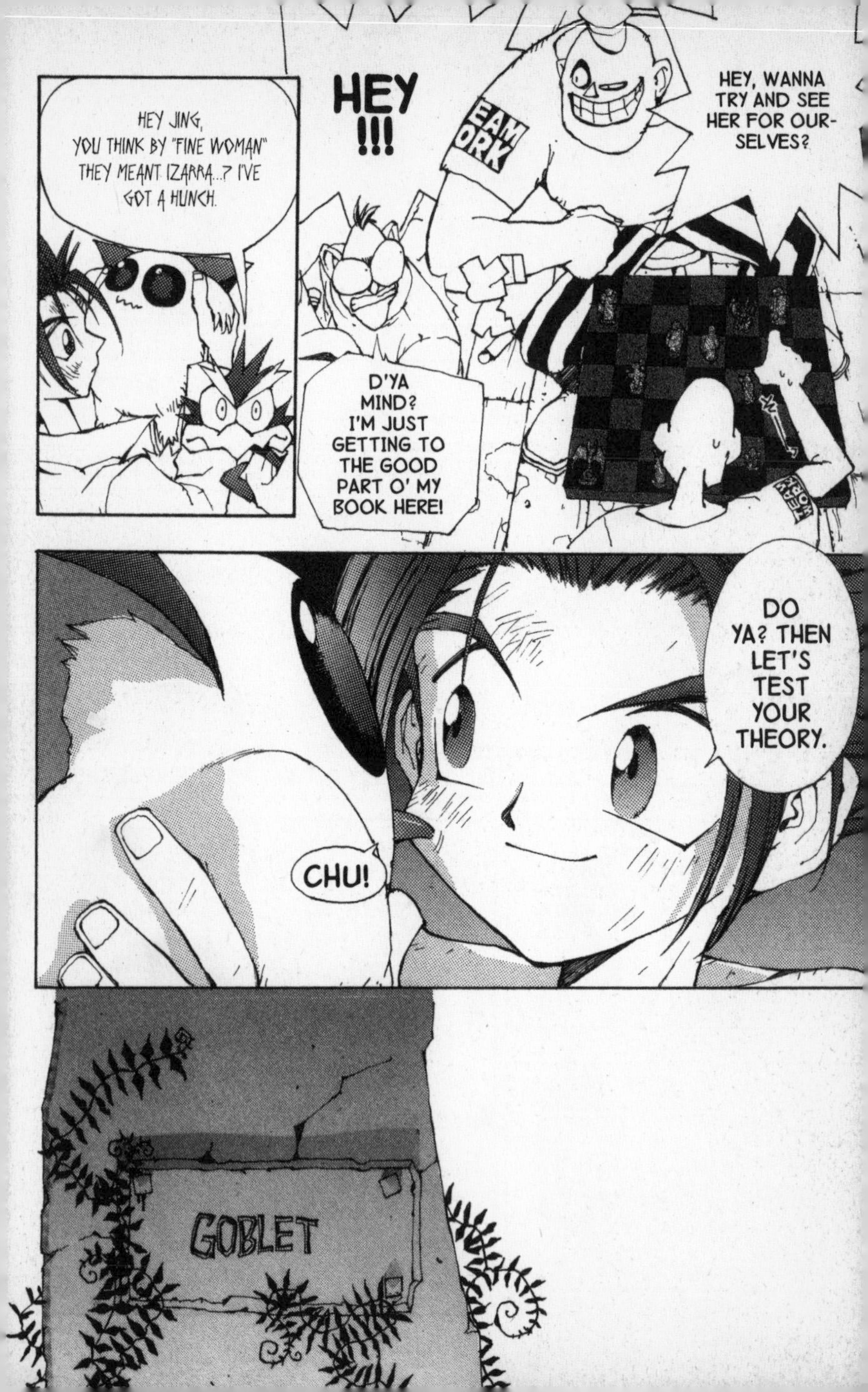
HEY, WANNA TRY AND SEE HER FOR OURSELVES?
HEY !!!
D'YA MIND? I'M JUST GETTING TO THE GOOD PART O' MY BOOK HERE!
HEY JING, YOU THINK BY "FINE WOMAN" THEY MEANT IZARRA...? I'VE GOT A HUNCH.
DO YA? THEN LET'S TEST YOUR THEORY.
CHU!
GOBLET

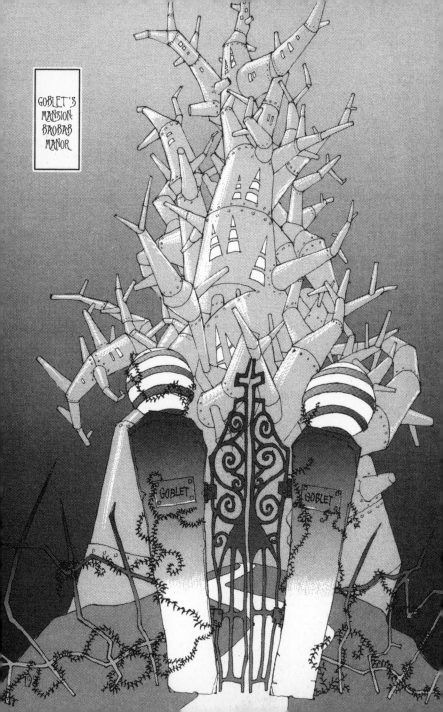

GOBLET'S
MANSION:
BAOBAB
MANOR

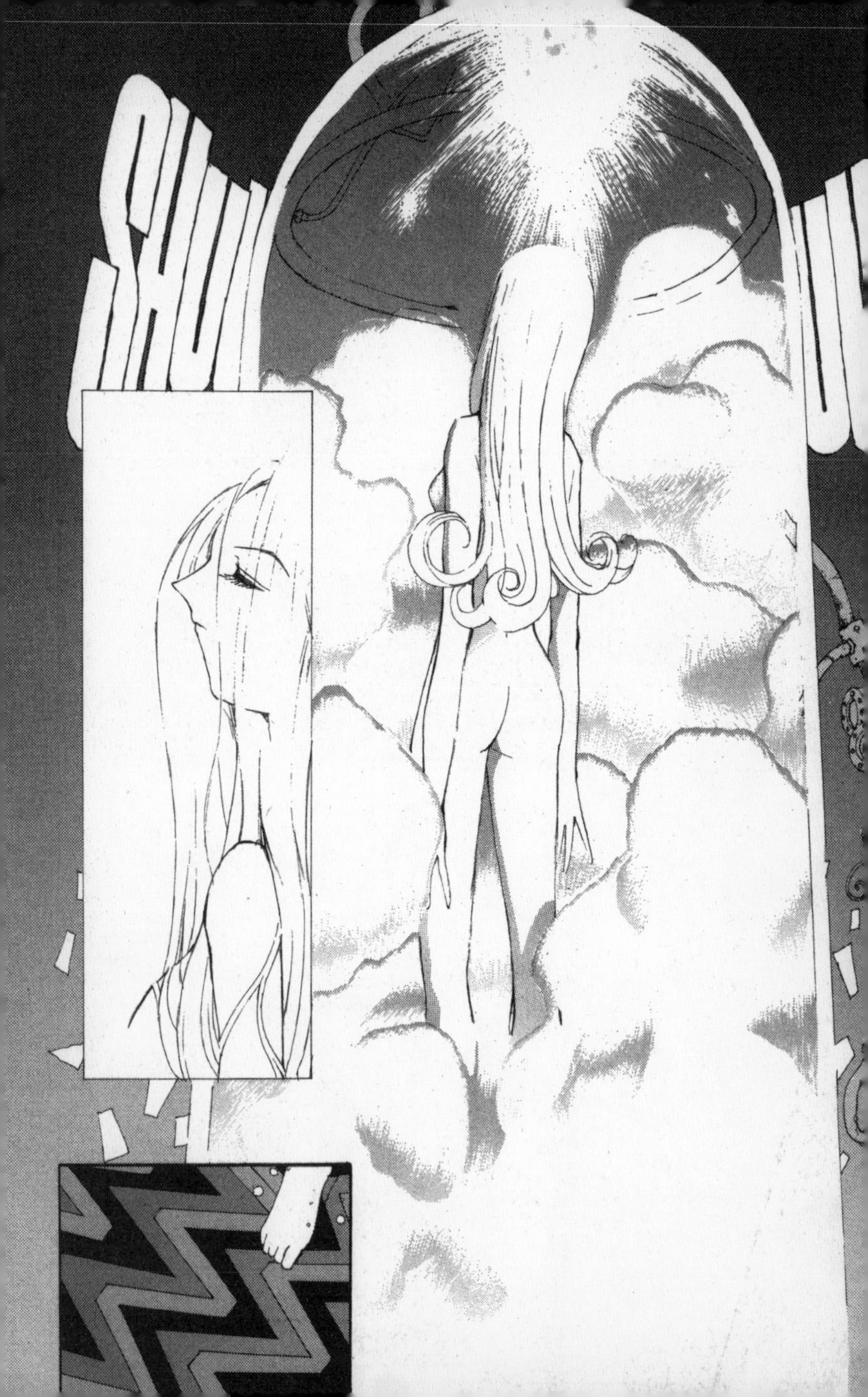
SHUU

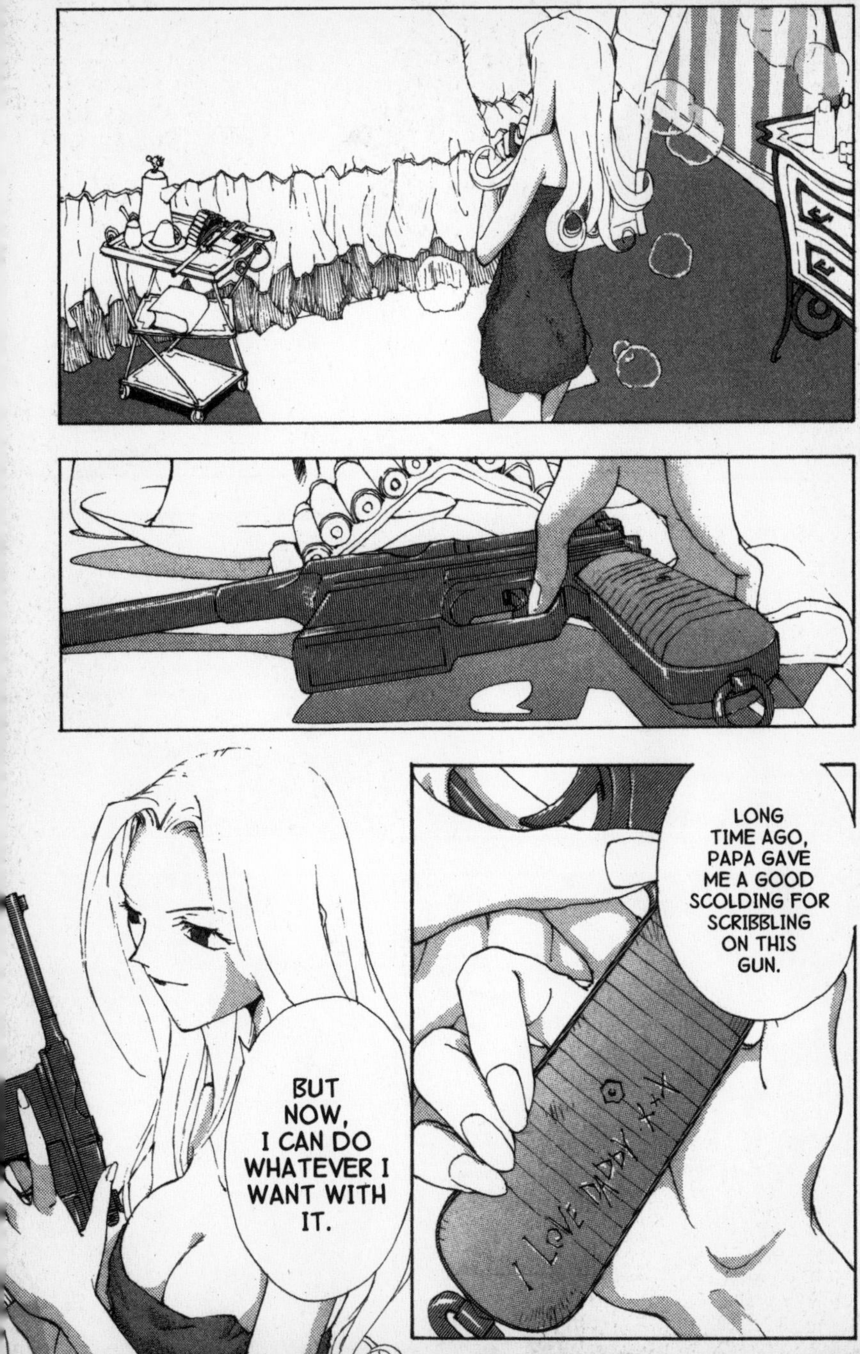
LONG TIME AGO, PAPA GAVE ME A GOOD SCOLDING FOR SCRIBBLING ON THIS GUN.
I LOVE DADDY x+x
BUT NOW, I CAN DO WHATEVER I WANT WITH IT.

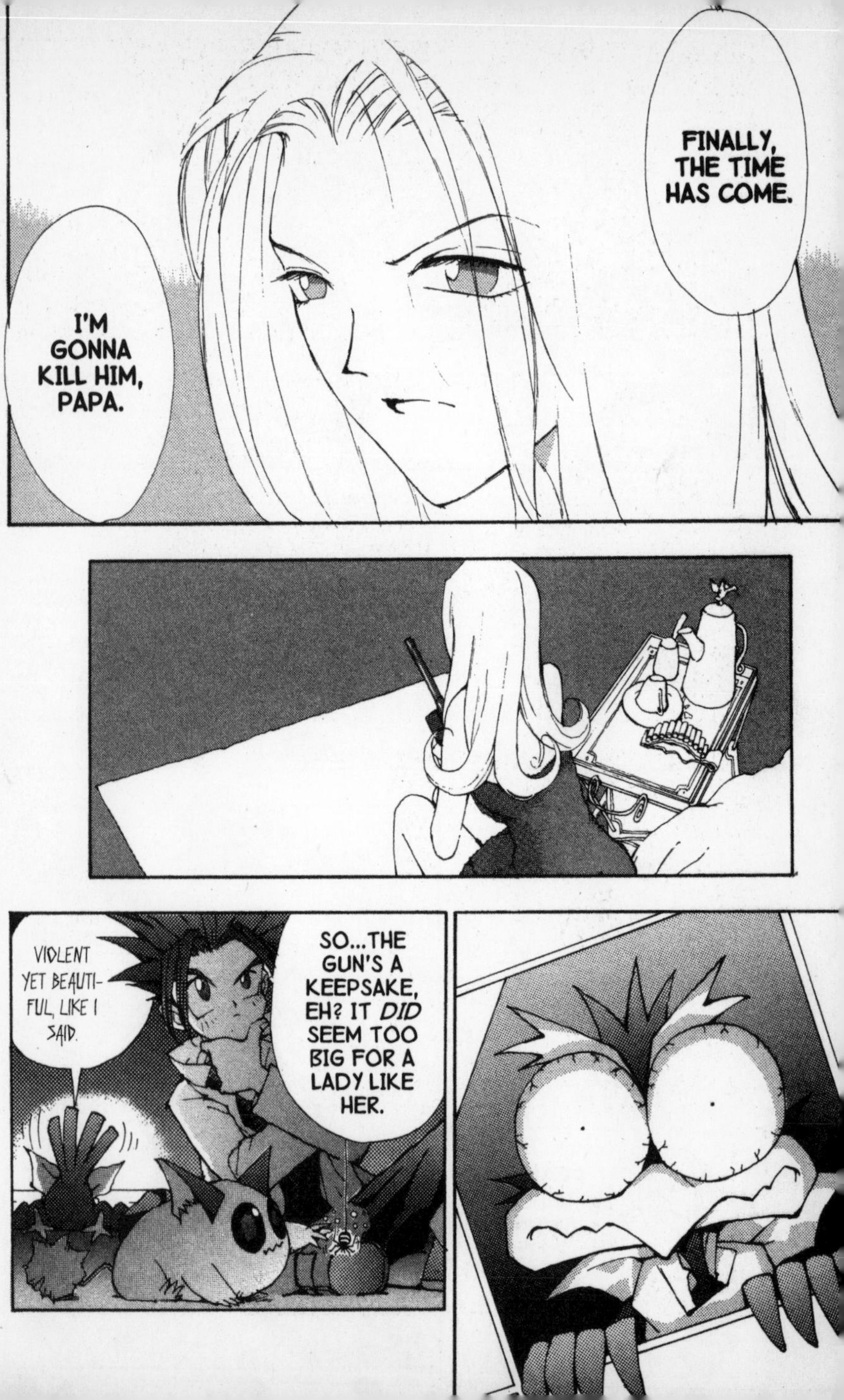
FINALLY, THE TIME HAS COME.
I'M GONNA KILL HIM, PAPA.
SO...THE GUN'S A KEEPSAKE, EH? IT *DID* SEEM TOO BIG FOR A LADY LIKE HER.
VIOLENT YET BEAUTI-FUL, LIKE I SAID.

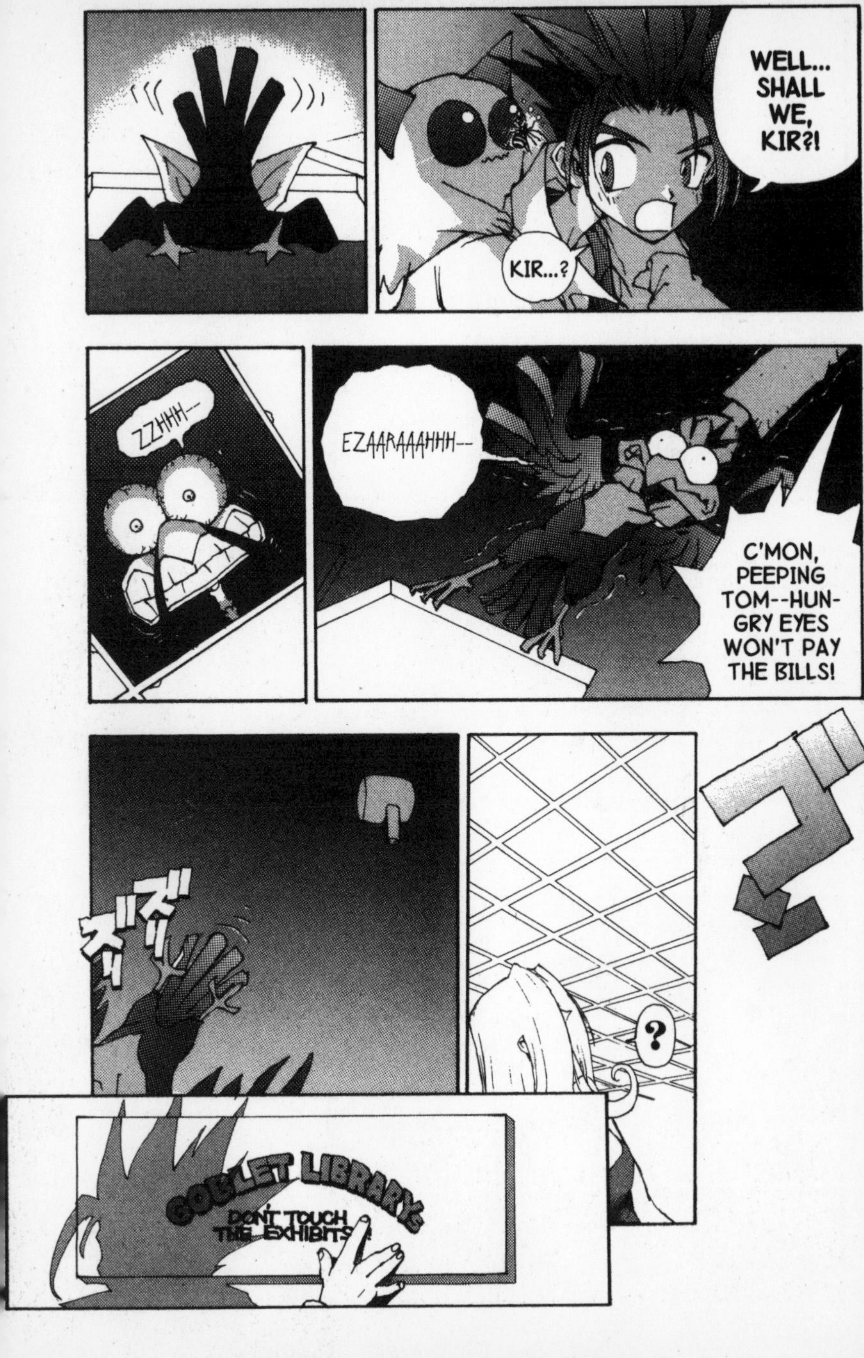
WELL... SHALL WE, KIR?!
KIR...?
EZAARAAAHHH--
C'MON, PEEPING TOM--HUNGRY EYES WON'T PAY THE BILLS!
ZZHHH--
?
GOBLET LIBRARY
DON'T TOUCH THE EXHIBITS

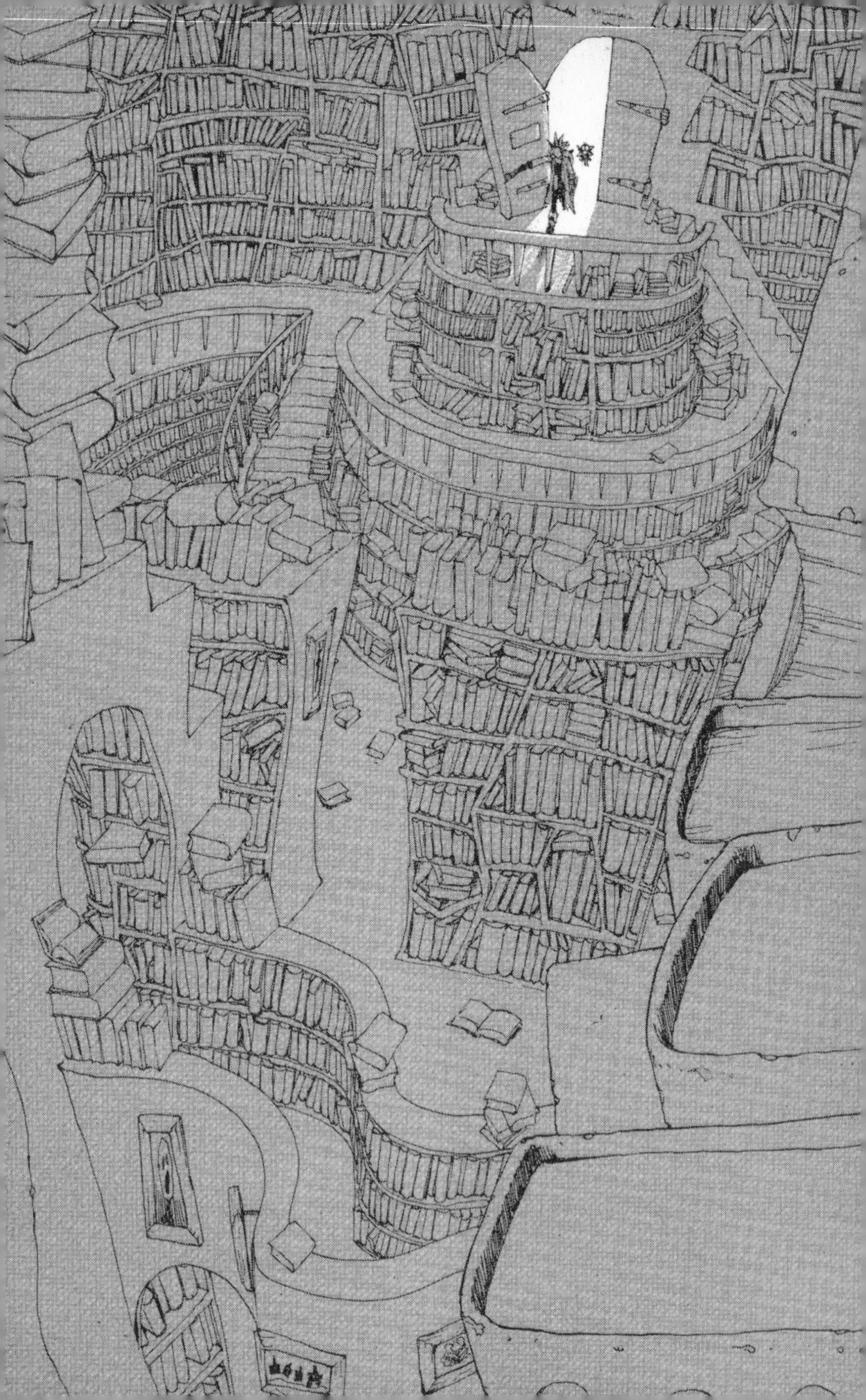

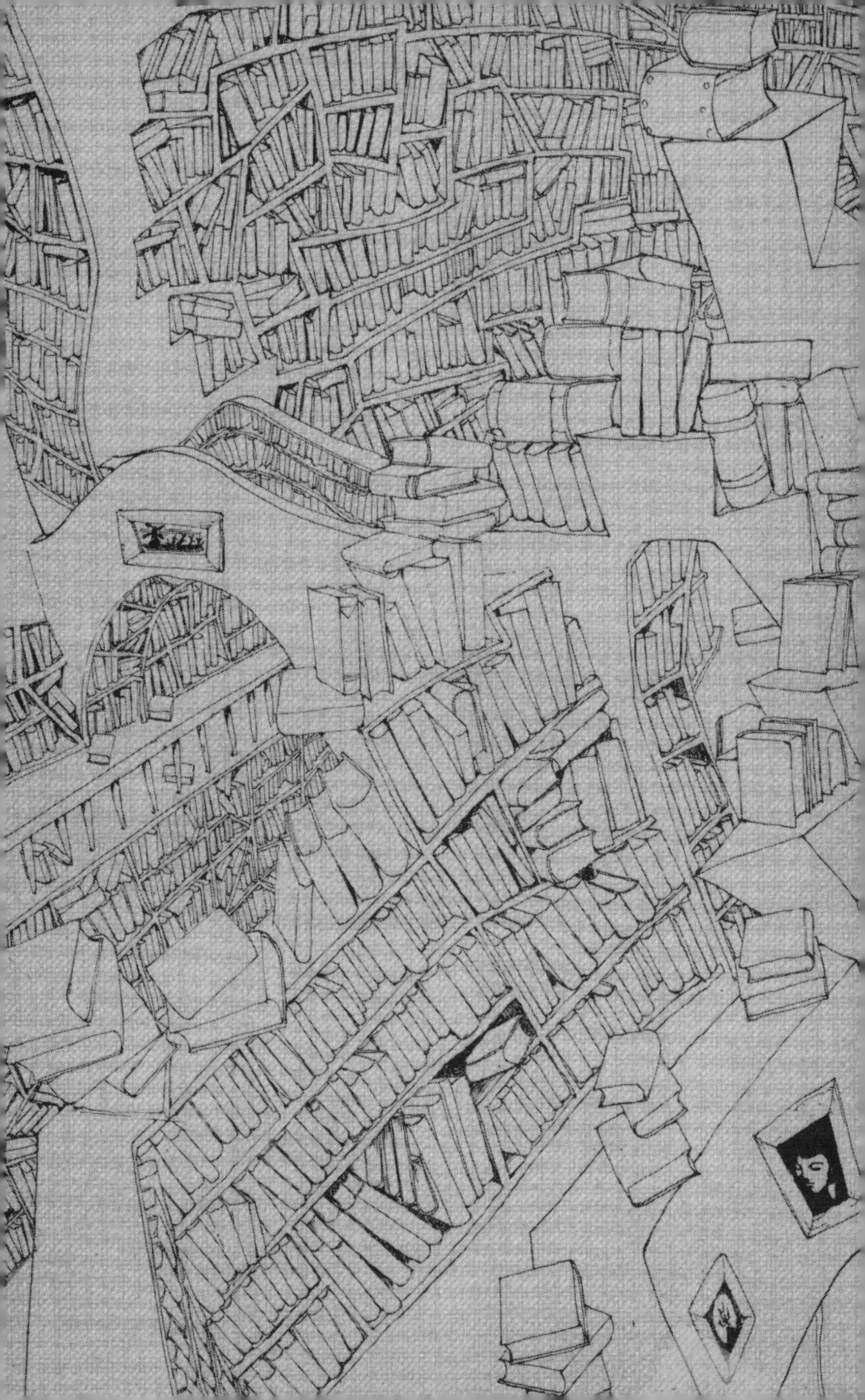

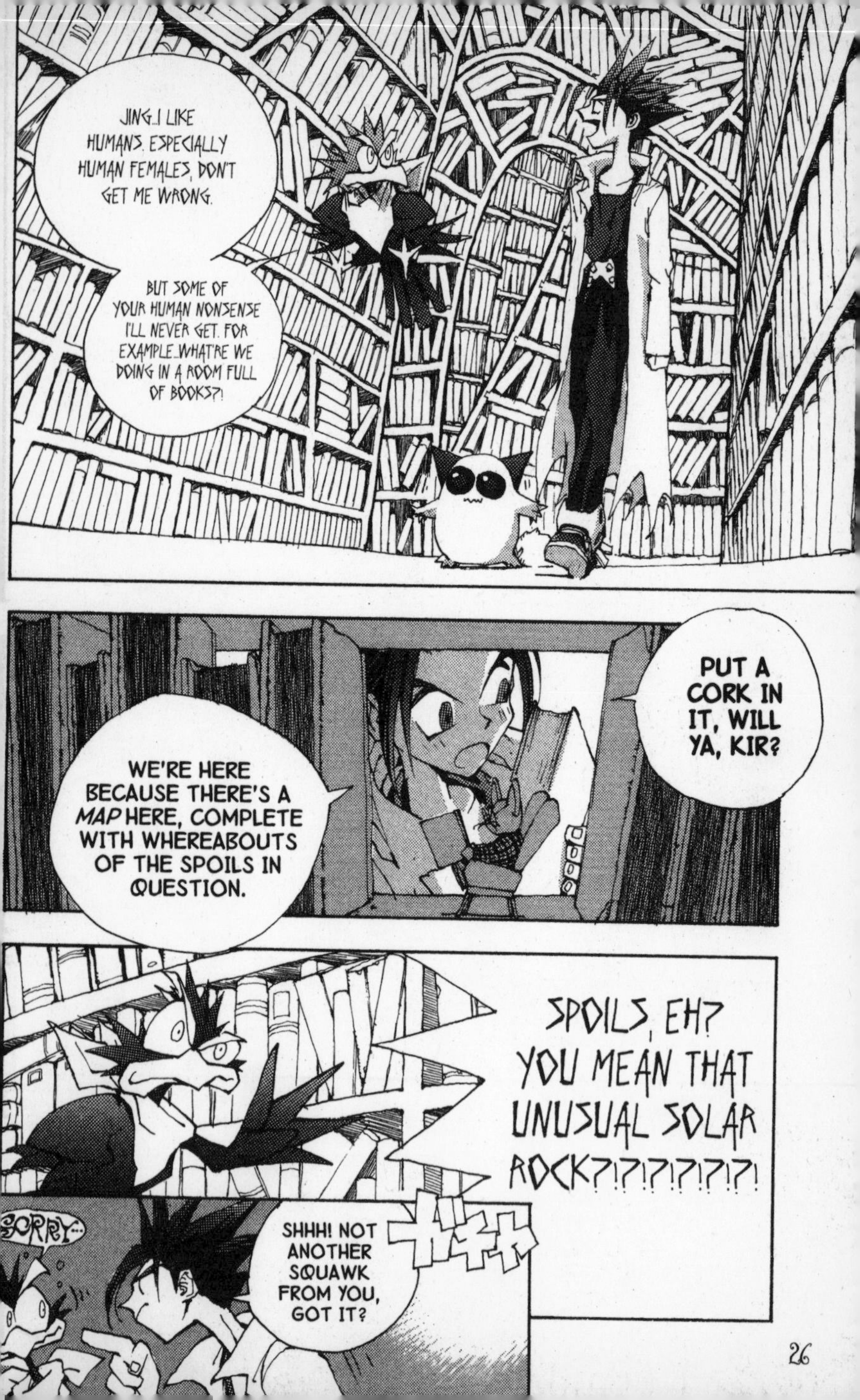
JING...I LIKE HUMANS. ESPECIALLY HUMAN FEMALES, DON'T GET ME WRONG.
BUT SOME OF YOUR HUMAN NONSENSE I'LL NEVER GET. FOR EXAMPLE...WHAT'RE WE DOING IN A ROOM FULL OF BOOKS?!
PUT A CORK IN IT, WILL YA, KIR?
WE'RE HERE BECAUSE THERE'S A *MAP* HERE, COMPLETE WITH WHEREABOUTS OF THE SPOILS IN QUESTION.
SPOILS, EH? YOU MEAN THAT UNUSUAL SOLAR ROCK?!?!?!?!?!?!
SHHH! NOT ANOTHER SQUAWK FROM YOU, GOT IT?
SORRY...

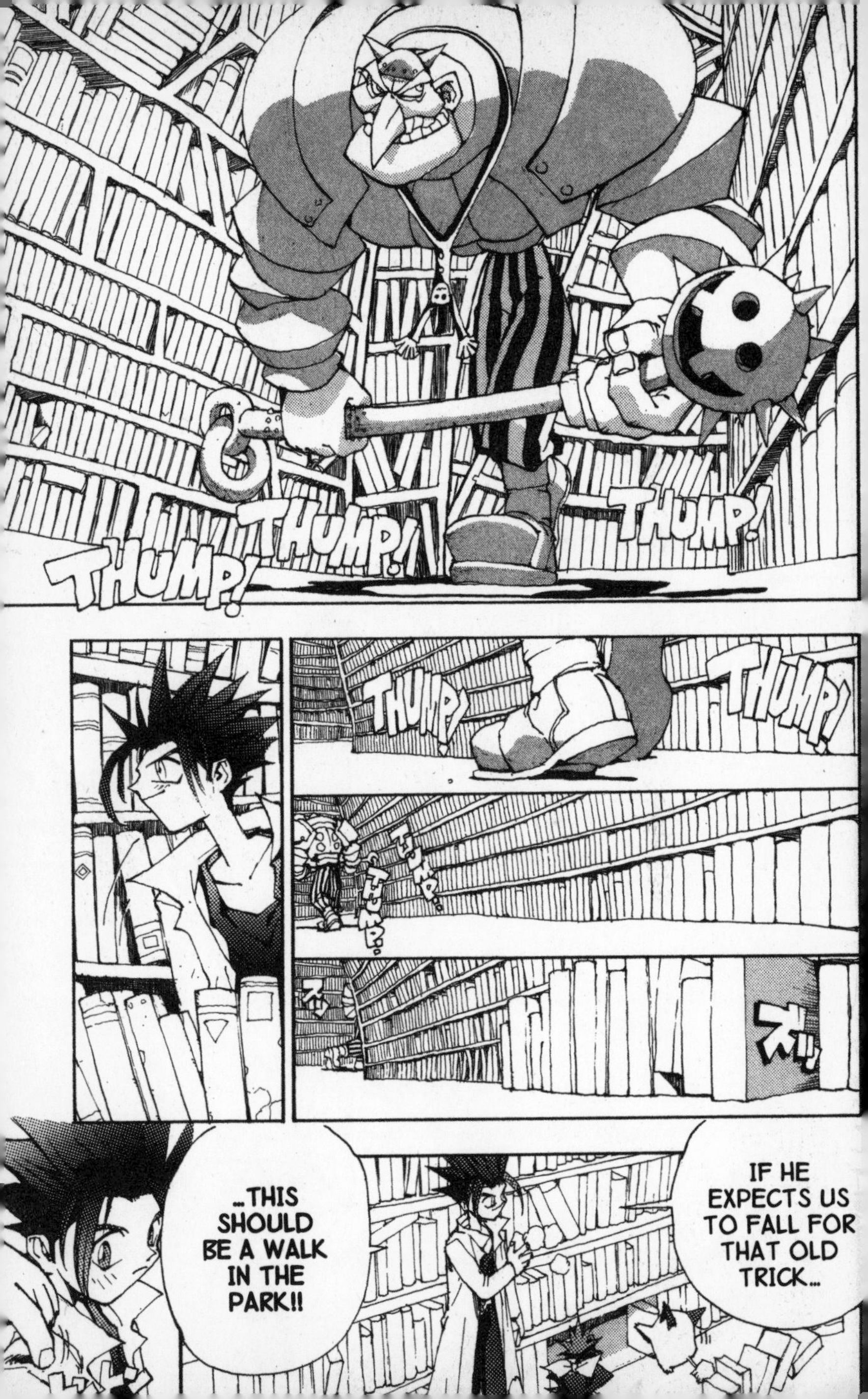
THUMP!
THUMP!
THUMP!
THUMP!
THUMP!
THUMP...
THUMP!
IF HE EXPECTS US TO FALL FOR THAT OLD TRICK...
...THIS SHOULD BE A WALK IN THE PARK!!

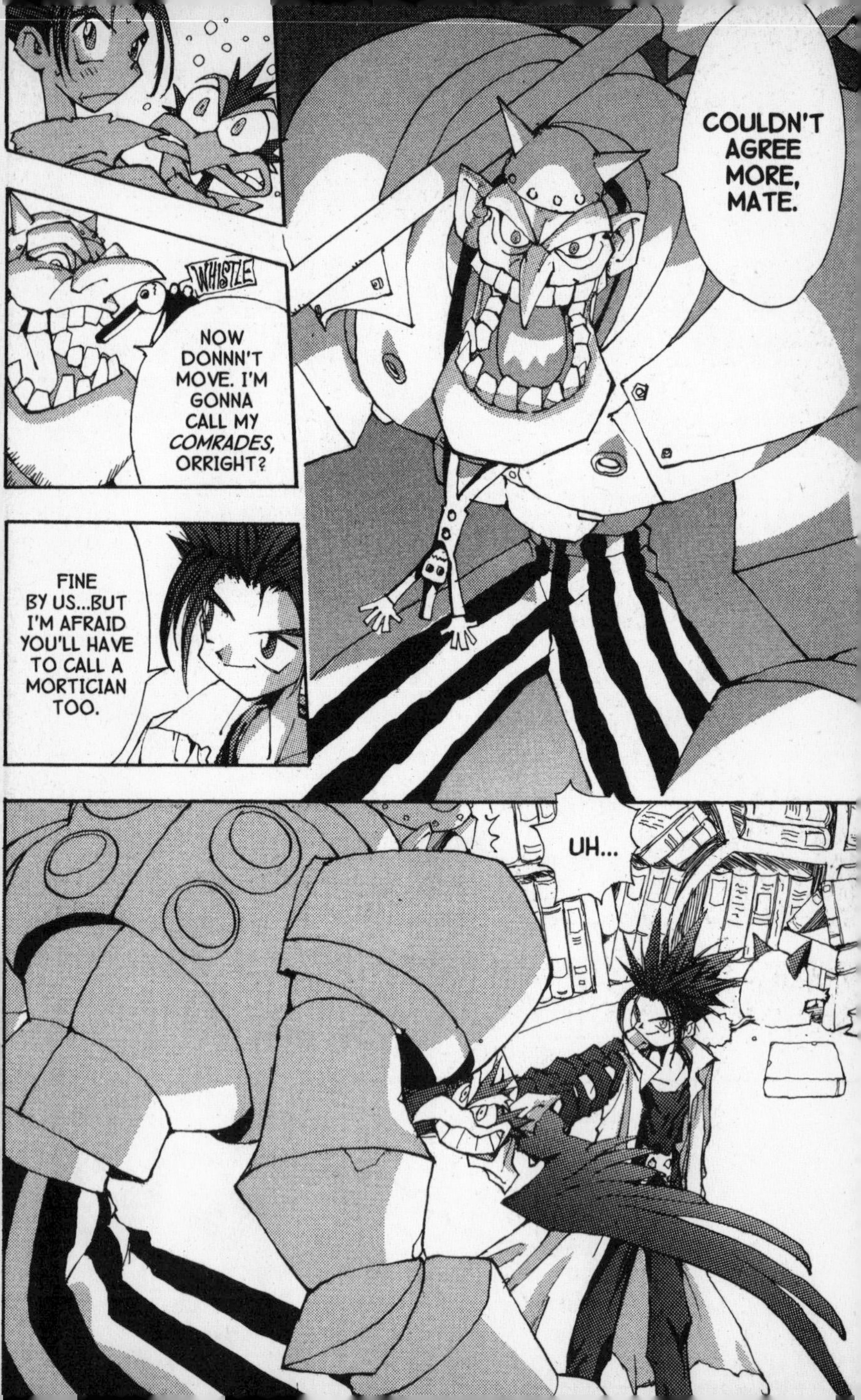
COULDN'T AGREE MORE, MATE.
WHISTLE
NOW DONNN'T MOVE. I'M GONNA CALL MY *COMRADES*, ORRIGHT?
FINE BY US...BUT I'M AFRAID YOU'LL HAVE TO CALL A MORTICIAN TOO.
UH...

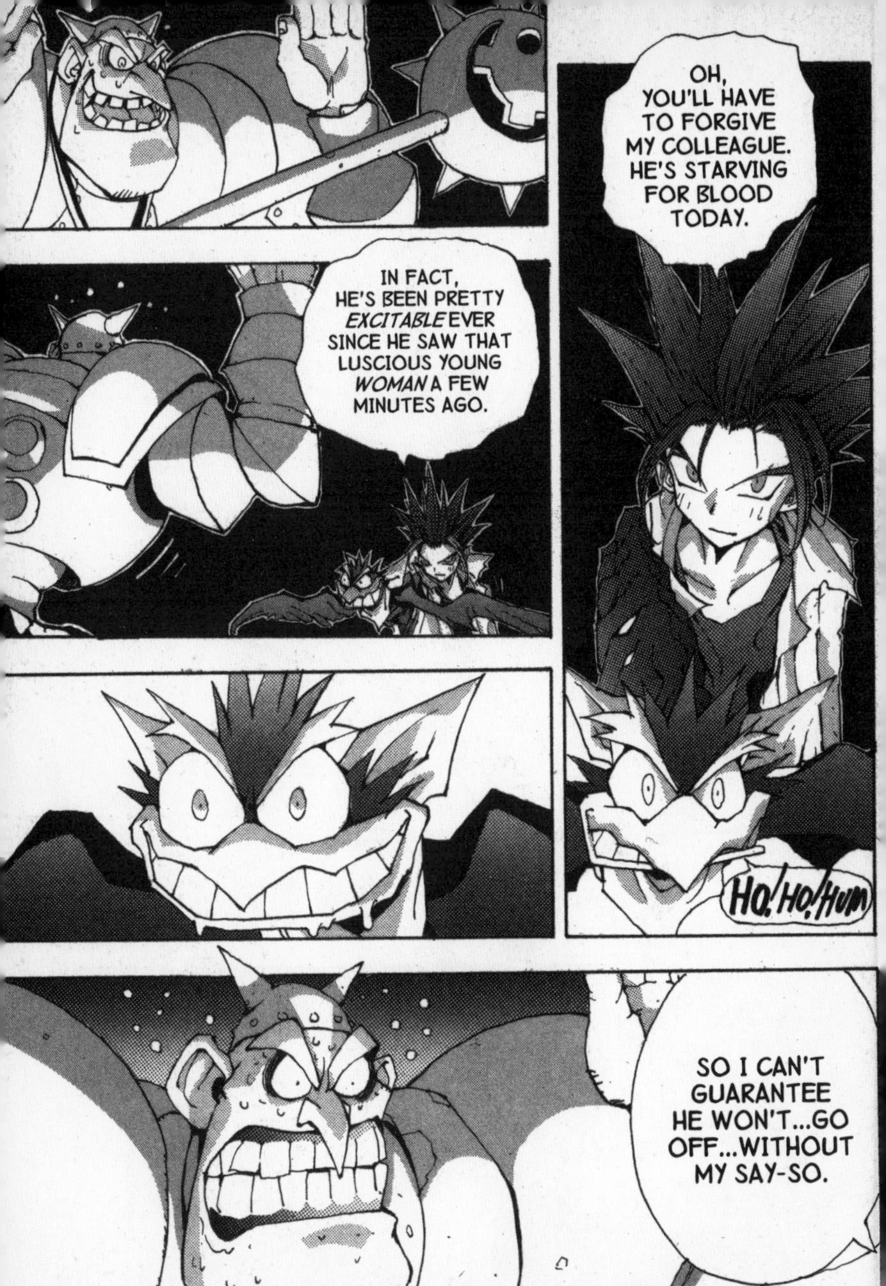
OH, YOU'LL HAVE TO FORGIVE MY COLLEAGUE. HE'S STARVING FOR BLOOD TODAY.
HA! HO! HUM
IN FACT, HE'S BEEN PRETTY *EXCITABLE* EVER SINCE HE SAW THAT LUSCIOUS YOUNG *WOMAN* A FEW MINUTES AGO.
SO I CAN'T GUARANTEE HE WON'T...GO OFF...WITHOUT MY SAY-SO.

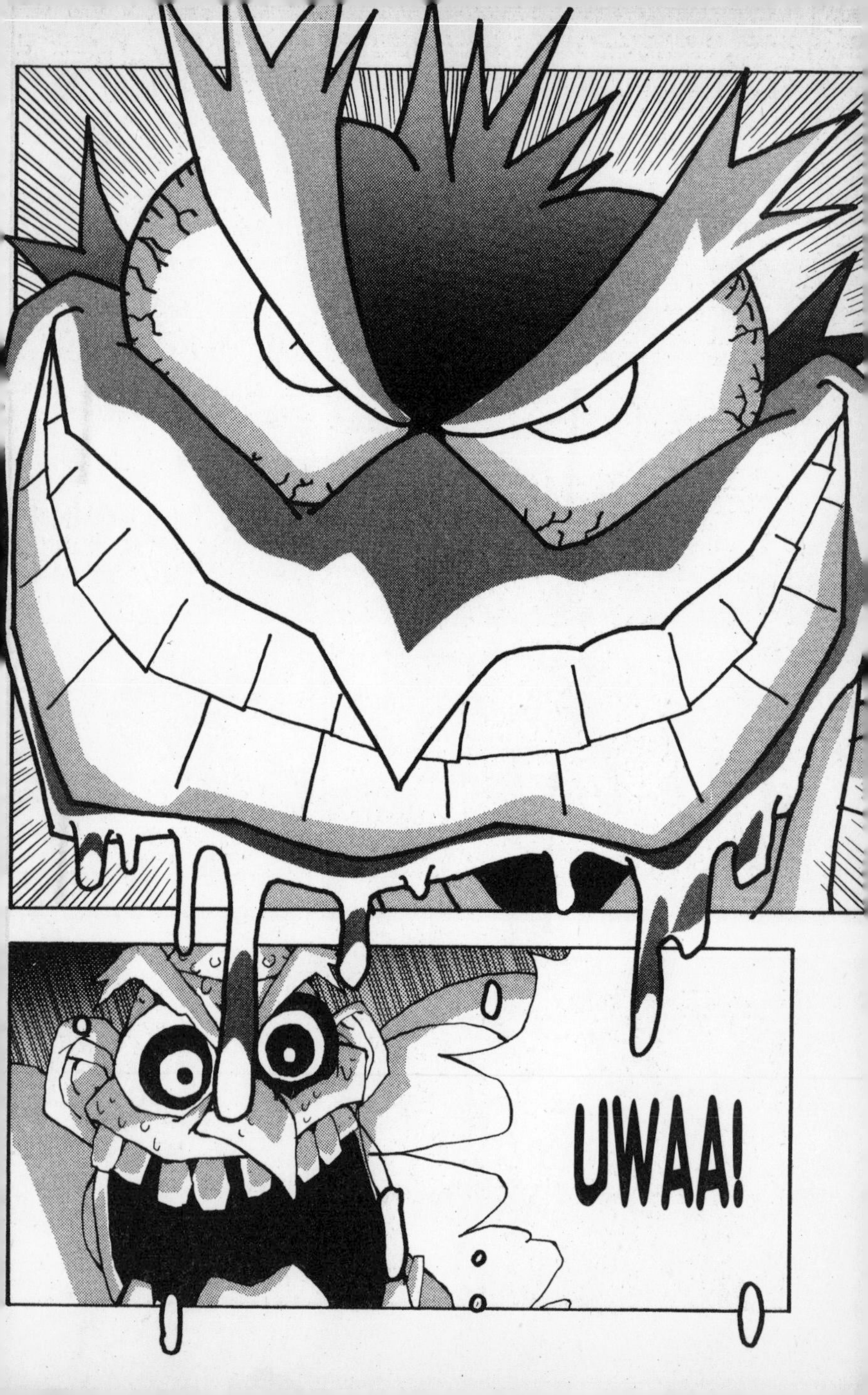
UWAA!

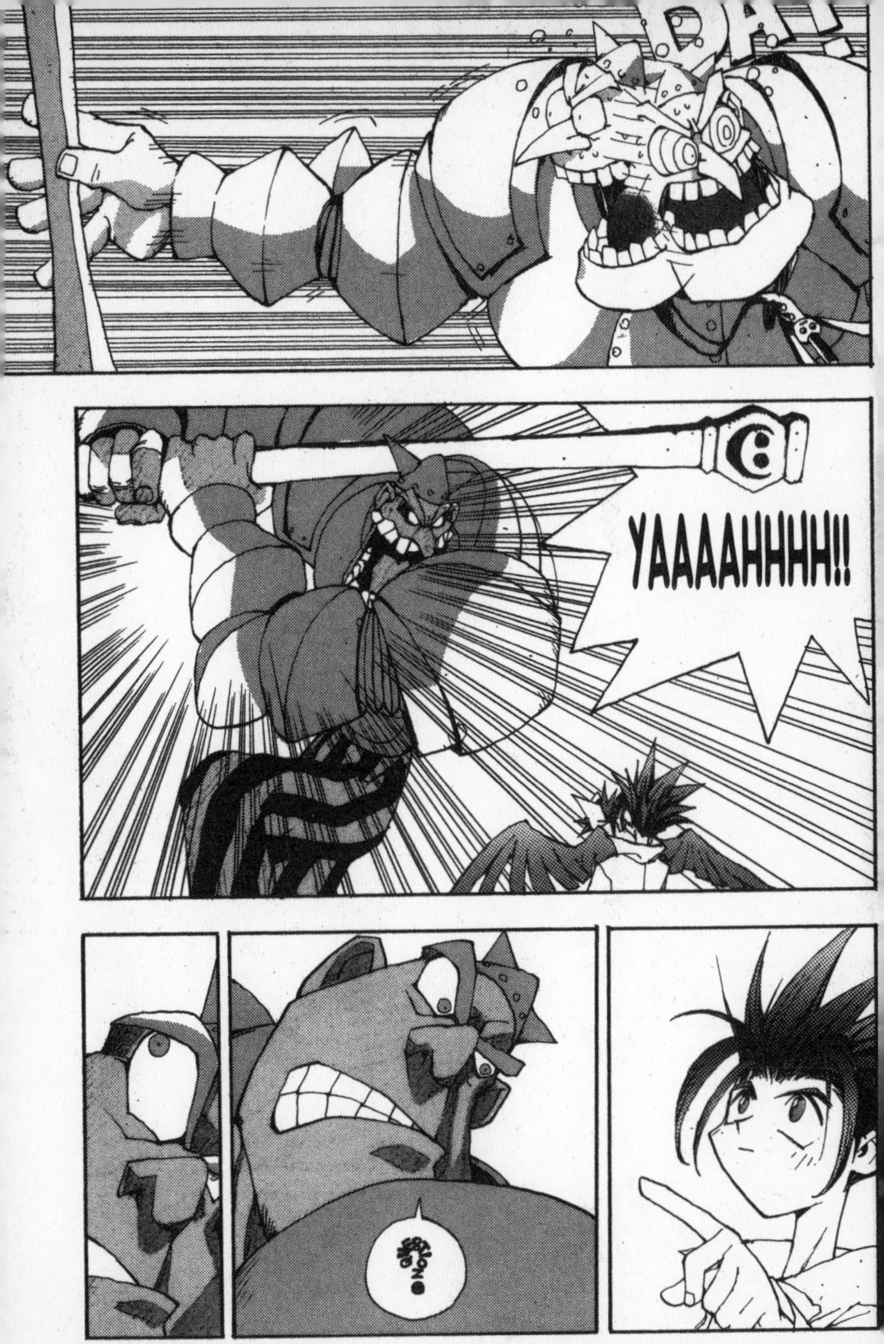
DA!!
YAAAAHHHH!!
QUESTION!

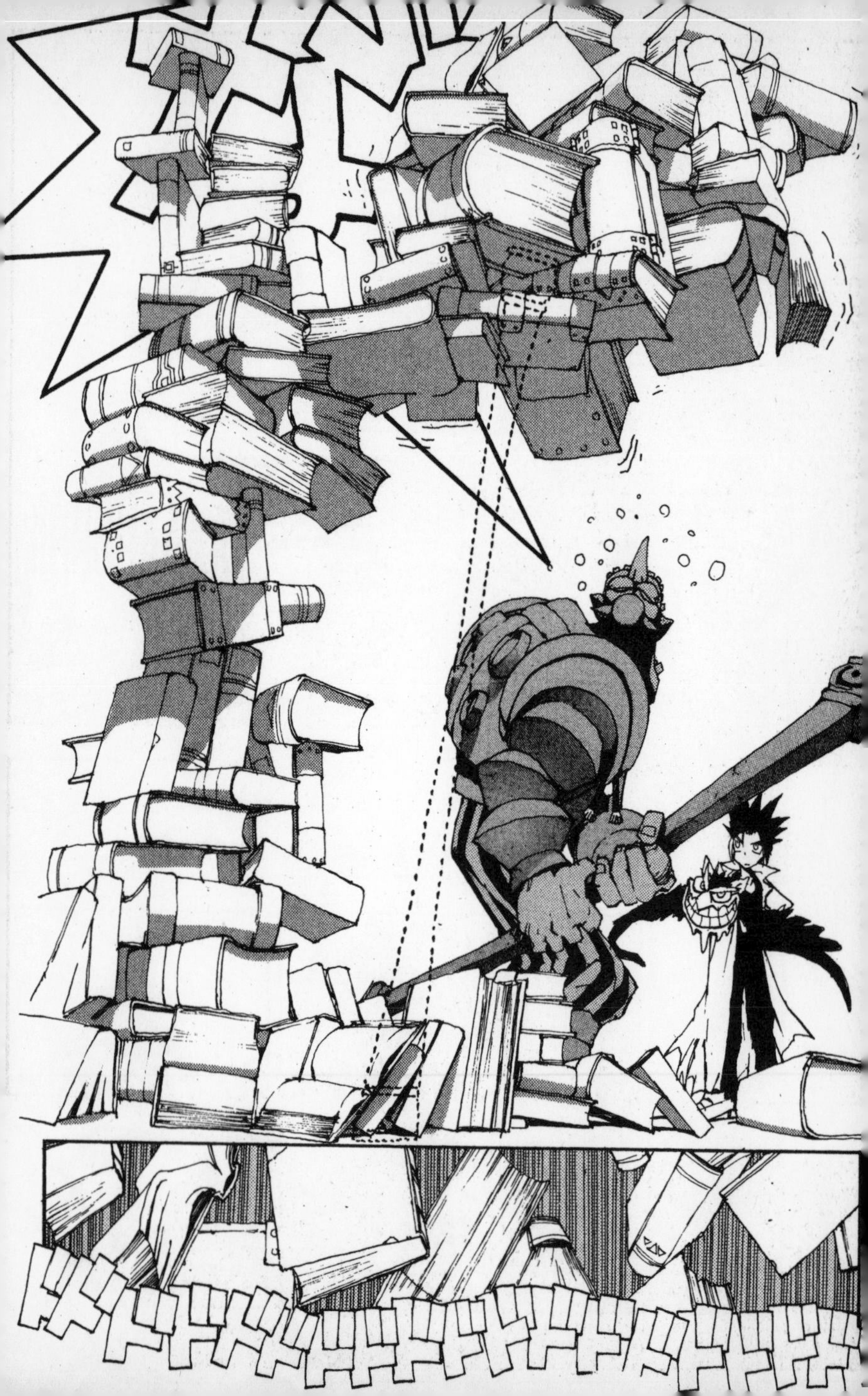

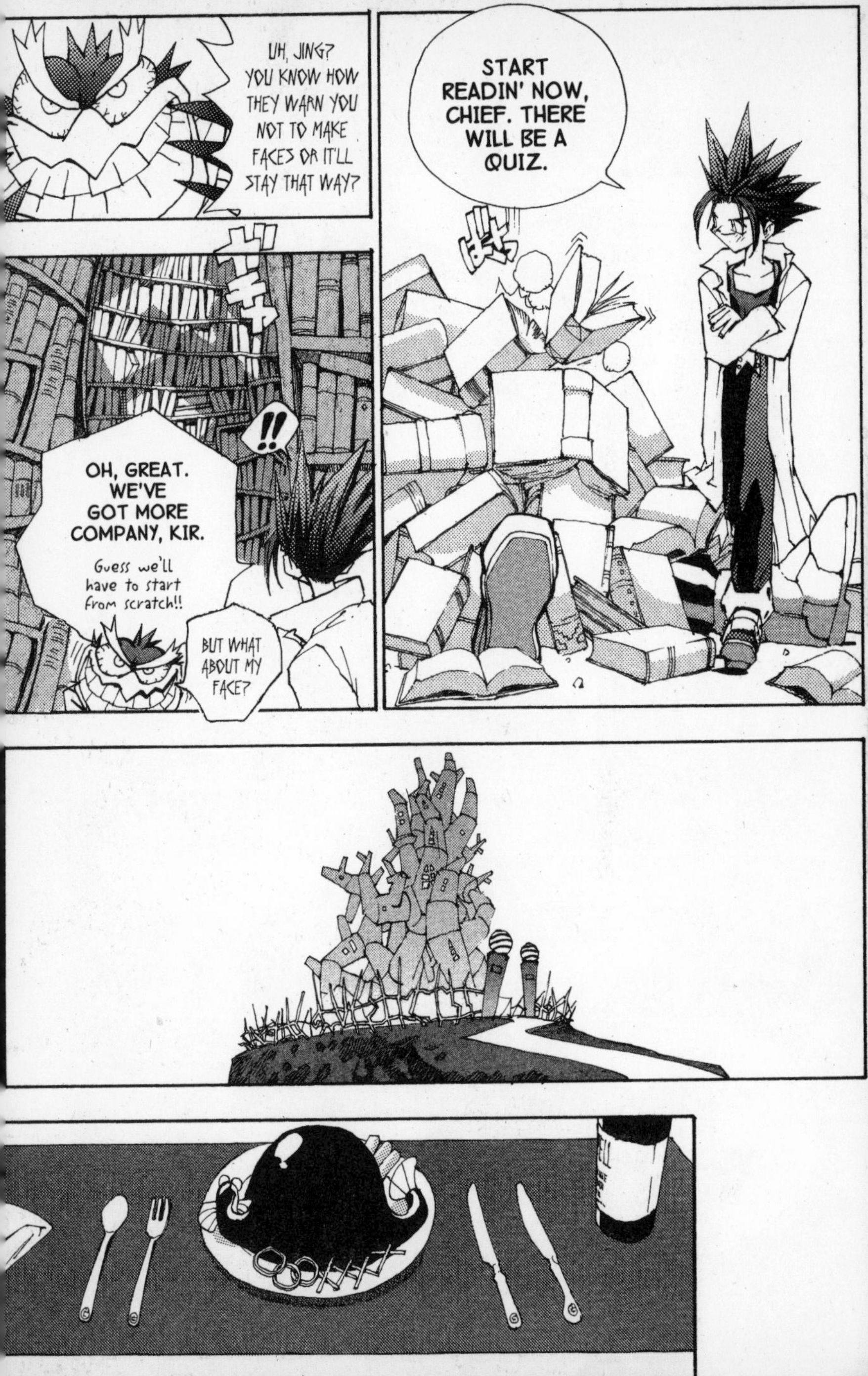
START READIN' NOW, CHIEF. THERE WILL BE A QUIZ.
UH, JING? YOU KNOW HOW THEY WARN YOU NOT TO MAKE FACES OR IT'LL STAY THAT WAY?
OH, GREAT. WE'VE GOT MORE COMPANY, KIR.
Guess we'll have to start from scratch!!
!!
BUT WHAT ABOUT MY FACE?

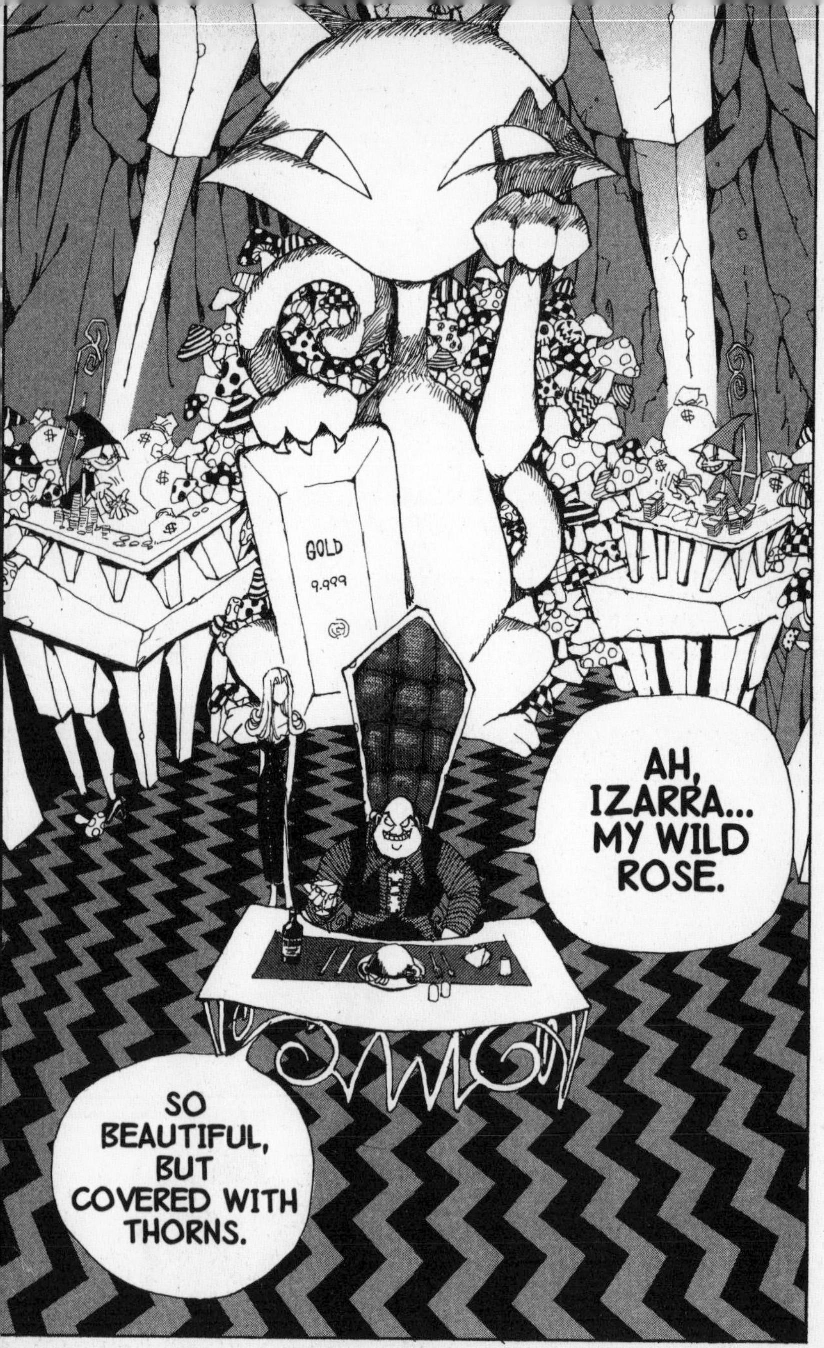
AH, IZARRA... MY WILD ROSE.
GOLD
9.999
SO BEAUTIFUL, BUT COVERED WITH THORNS.

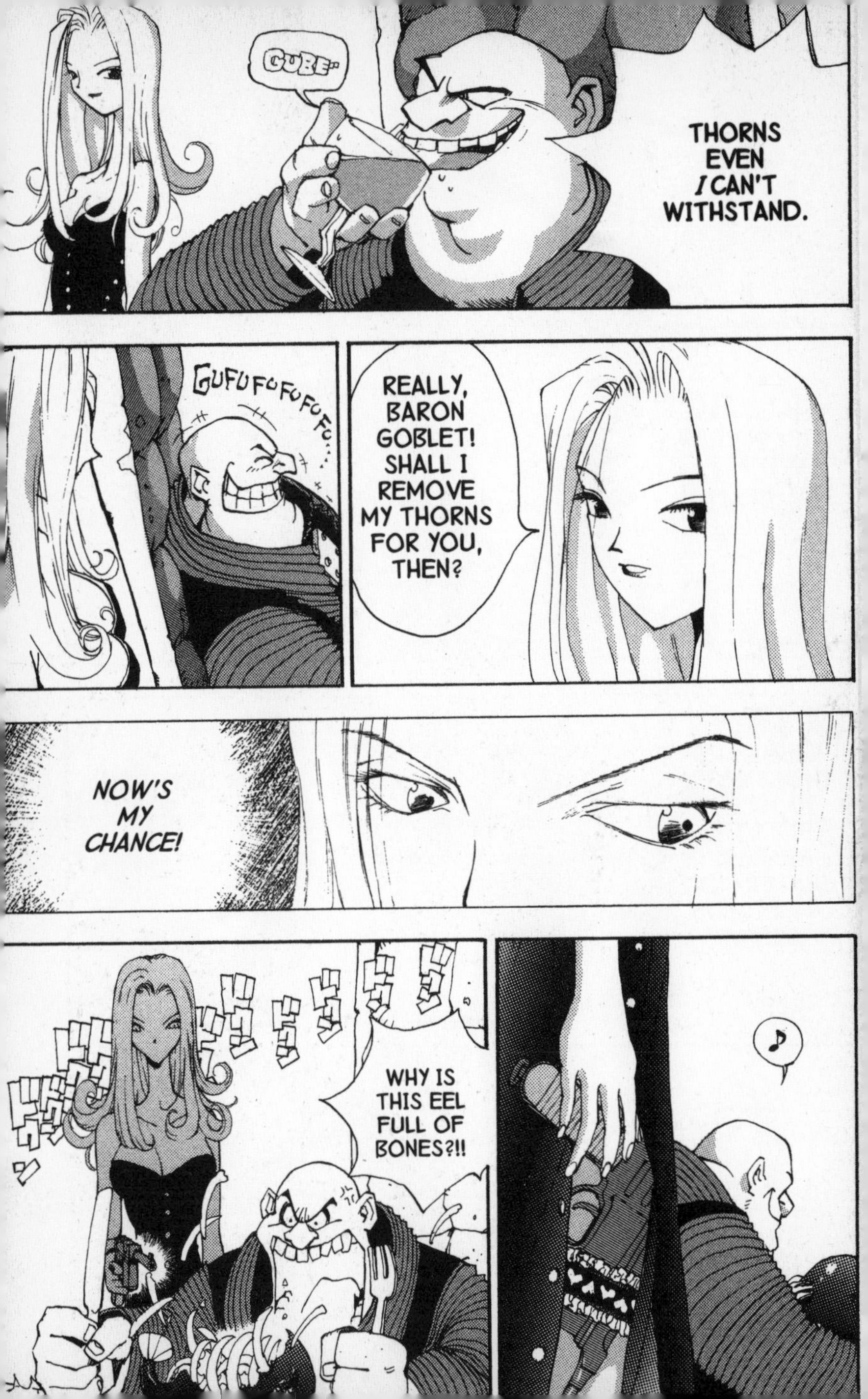

THORNS EVEN I CAN'T WITHSTAND.
GUBE"
REALLY, BARON GOBLET! SHALL I REMOVE MY THORNS FOR YOU, THEN?
GUFUFUFUFUFUFU...
NOW'S MY CHANCE!
♪
WHY IS THIS EEL FULL OF BONES?!!

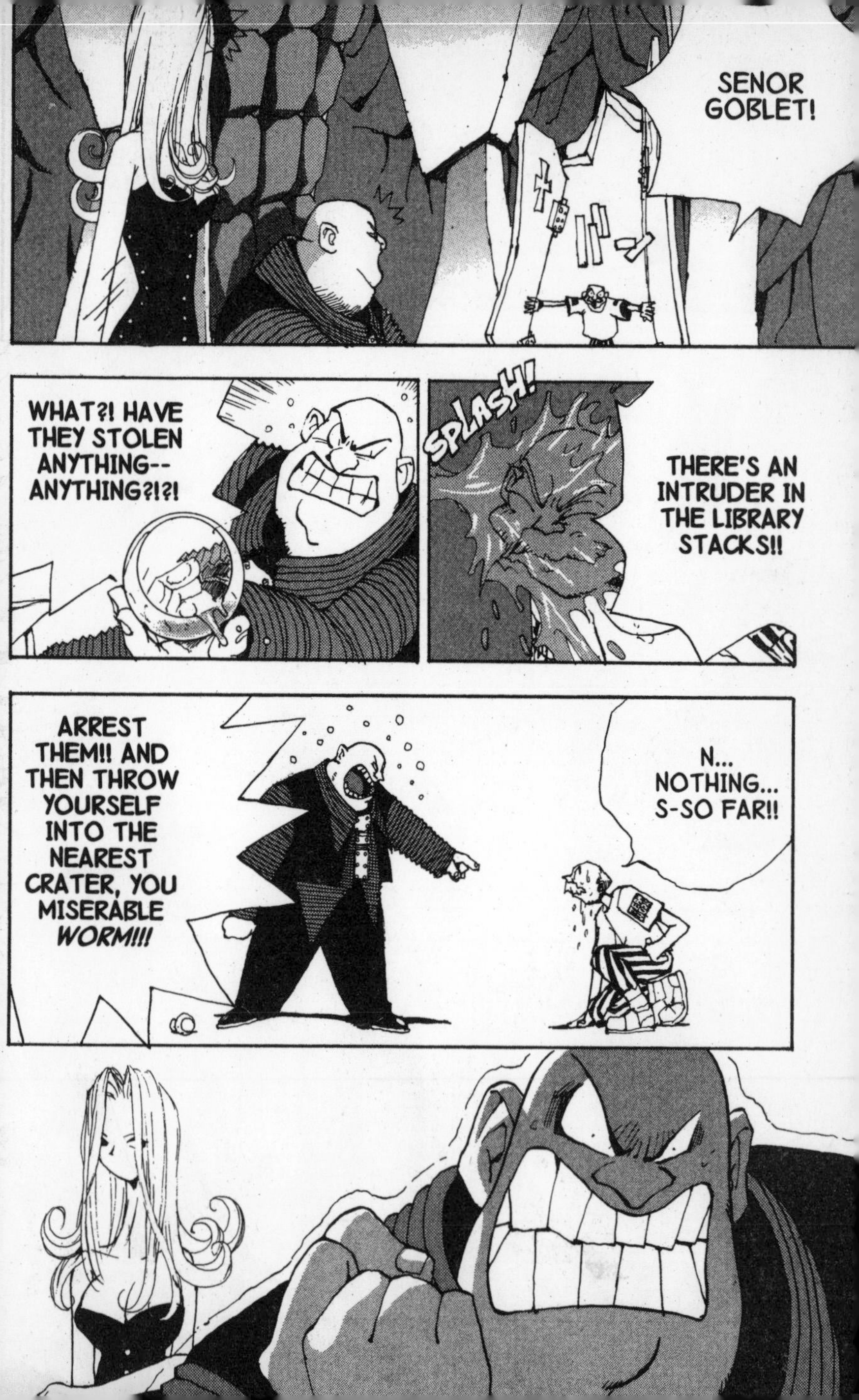
SENOR GOBLET!
SPLASH!
THERE'S AN INTRUDER IN THE LIBRARY STACKS!!
WHAT?! HAVE THEY STOLEN ANYTHING-- ANYTHING?!?!
N... NOTHING... S-SO FAR!!
ARREST THEM!! AND THEN THROW YOURSELF INTO THE NEAREST CRATER, YOU MISERABLE *WORM!!!*

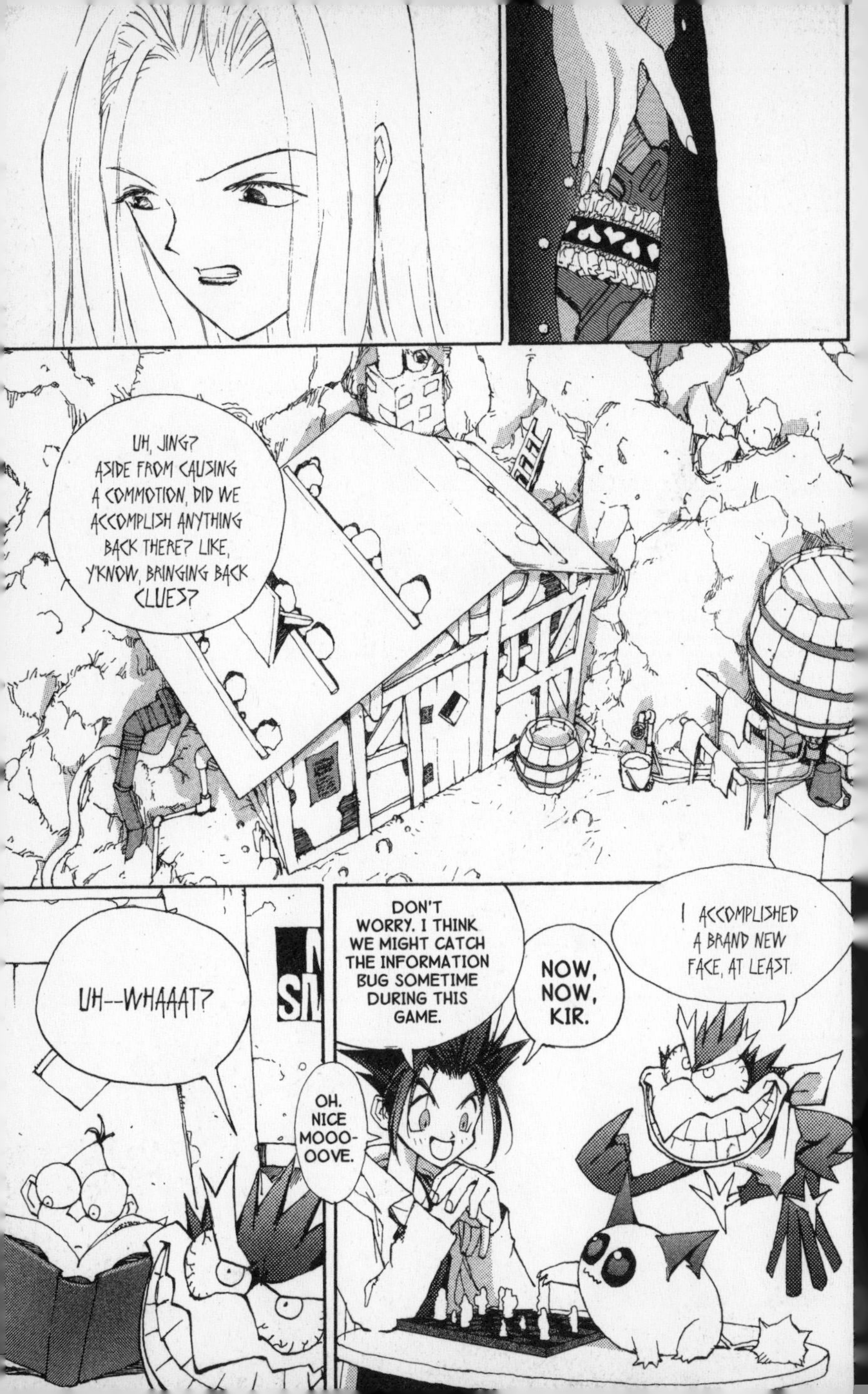
UH, JING? ASIDE FROM CAUSING A COMMOTION, DID WE ACCOMPLISH ANYTHING BACK THERE? LIKE, Y'KNOW, BRINGING BACK CLUES?
I ACCOMPLISHED A BRAND NEW FACE, AT LEAST.
NOW, NOW, KIR.
DON'T WORRY. I THINK WE MIGHT CATCH THE INFORMATION BUG SOMETIME DURING THIS GAME.
OH. NICE MOOOO-OOVE.
UH--WHAAAT?

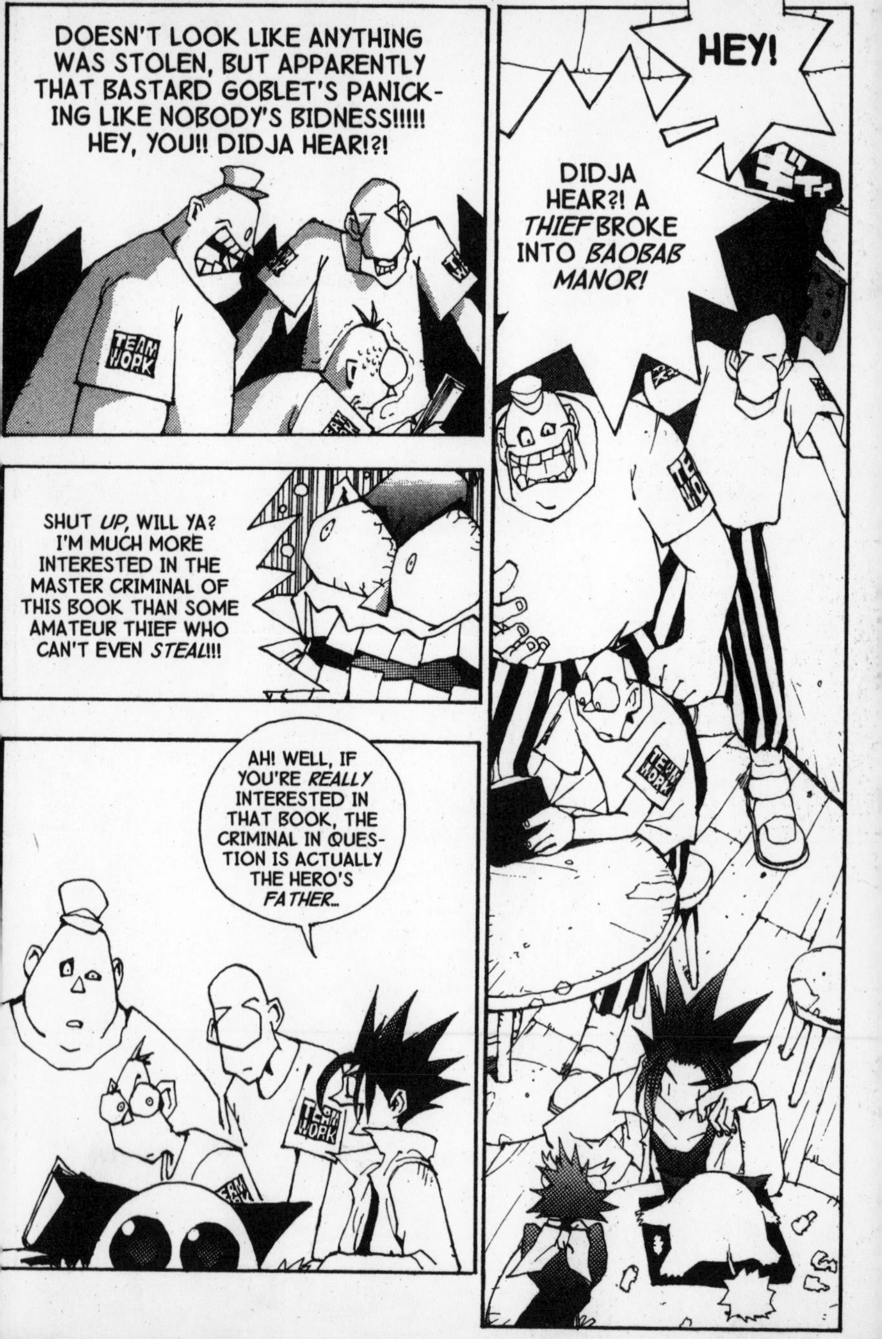
HEY!
DIDJA HEAR?! A *THIEF* BROKE INTO *BAOBAB MANOR!*
DOESN'T LOOK LIKE ANYTHING WAS STOLEN, BUT APPARENTLY THAT BASTARD GOBLET'S PANICK-ING LIKE NOBODY'S BIDNESS!!!!! HEY, YOU!! DIDJA HEAR!?!
SHUT *UP*, WILL YA? I'M MUCH MORE INTERESTED IN THE MASTER CRIMINAL OF THIS BOOK THAN SOME AMATEUR THIEF WHO CAN'T EVEN *STEAL*!!!
AH! WELL, IF YOU'RE *REALLY* INTERESTED IN THAT BOOK, THE CRIMINAL IN QUES-TION IS ACTUALLY THE HERO'S *FATHER*..

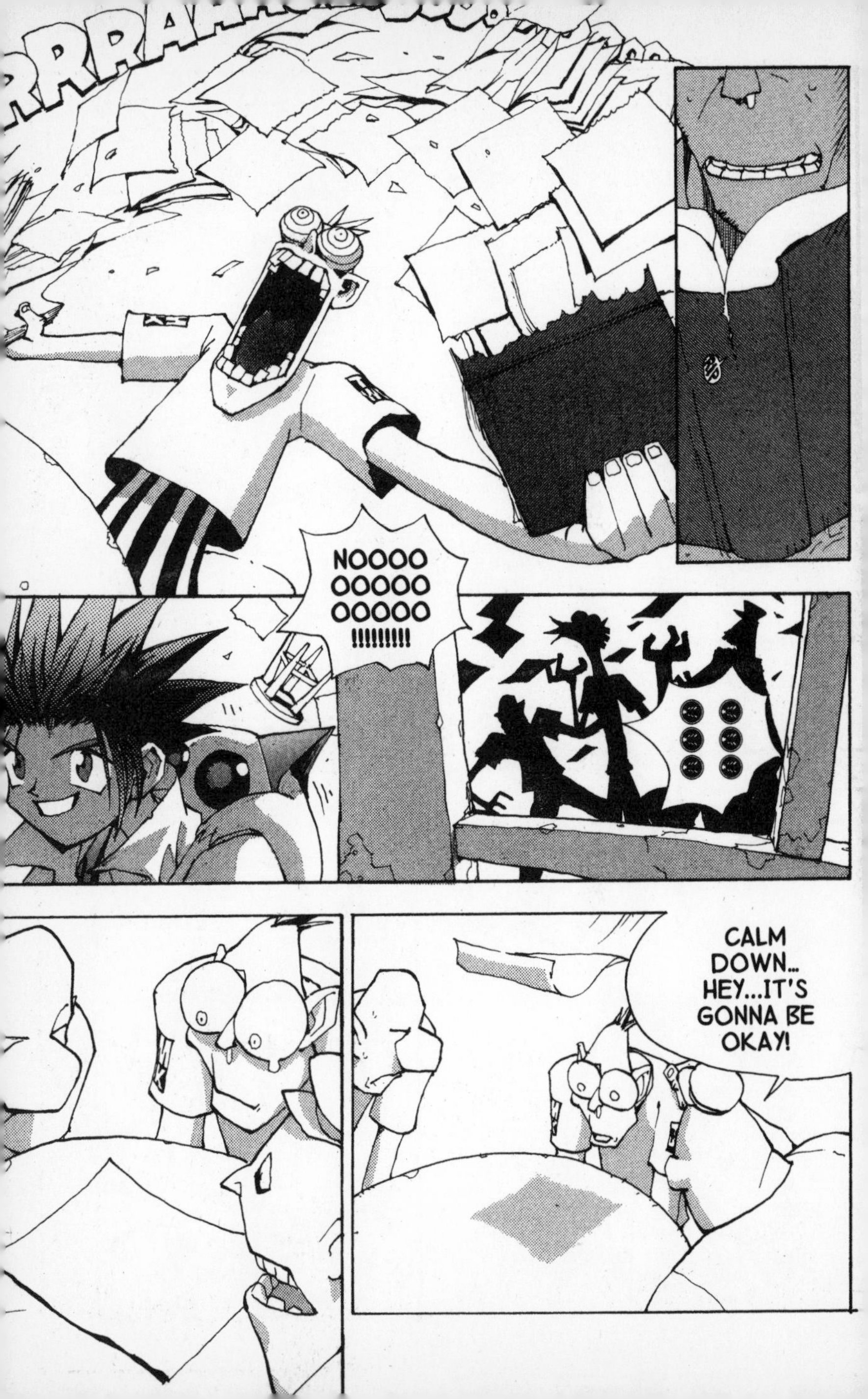
RRRA
NOOOOOOOOOOOOOOO!!!!!!!!!
CALM DOWN... HEY...IT'S GONNA BE OKAY!

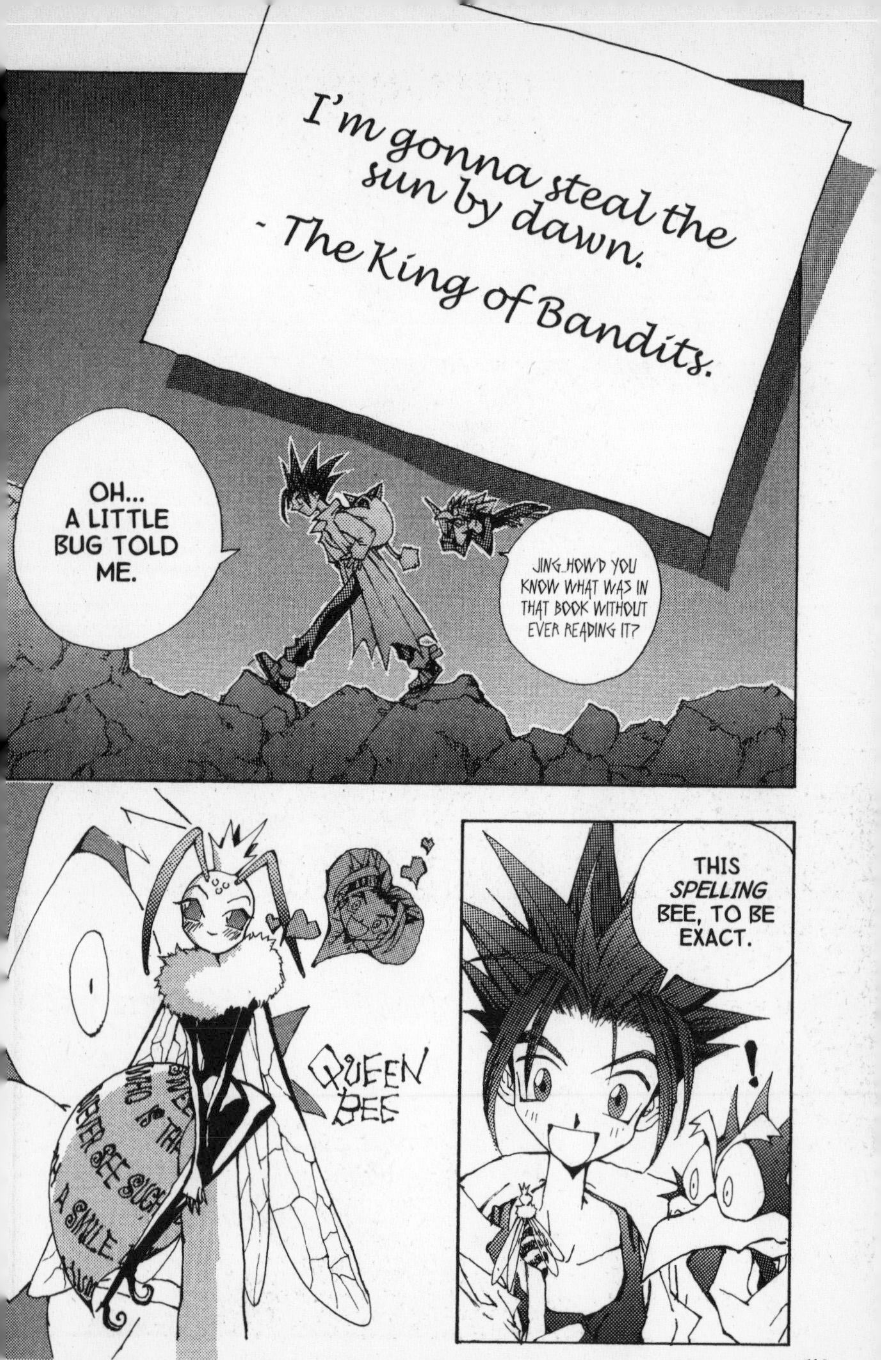
I'm gonna steal the sun by dawn.
- The King of Bandits.
JING..HOW'D YOU KNOW WHAT WAS IN THAT BOOK WITHOUT EVER READING IT?
OH... A LITTLE BUG TOLD ME.
THIS *SPELLING* BEE, TO BE EXACT.
!
QUEEN BEE

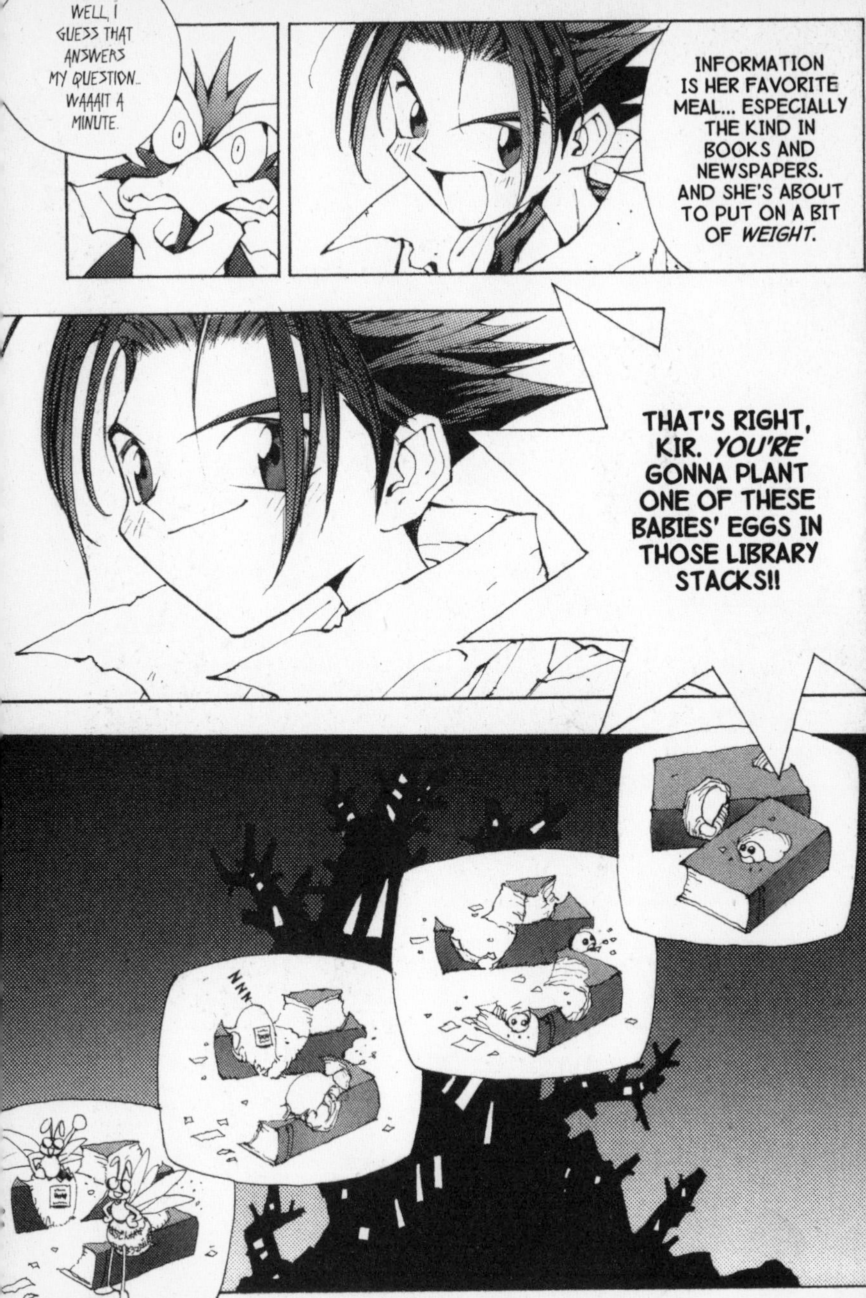
INFORMATION IS HER FAVORITE MEAL... ESPECIALLY THE KIND IN BOOKS AND NEWSPAPERS. AND SHE'S ABOUT TO PUT ON A BIT OF *WEIGHT*.
WELL, I GUESS THAT ANSWERS MY QUESTION... WAAAIT A MINUTE.
THAT'S RIGHT, KIR. *YOU'RE* GONNA PLANT ONE OF THESE BABIES' EGGS IN THOSE LIBRARY STACKS!!
NNN

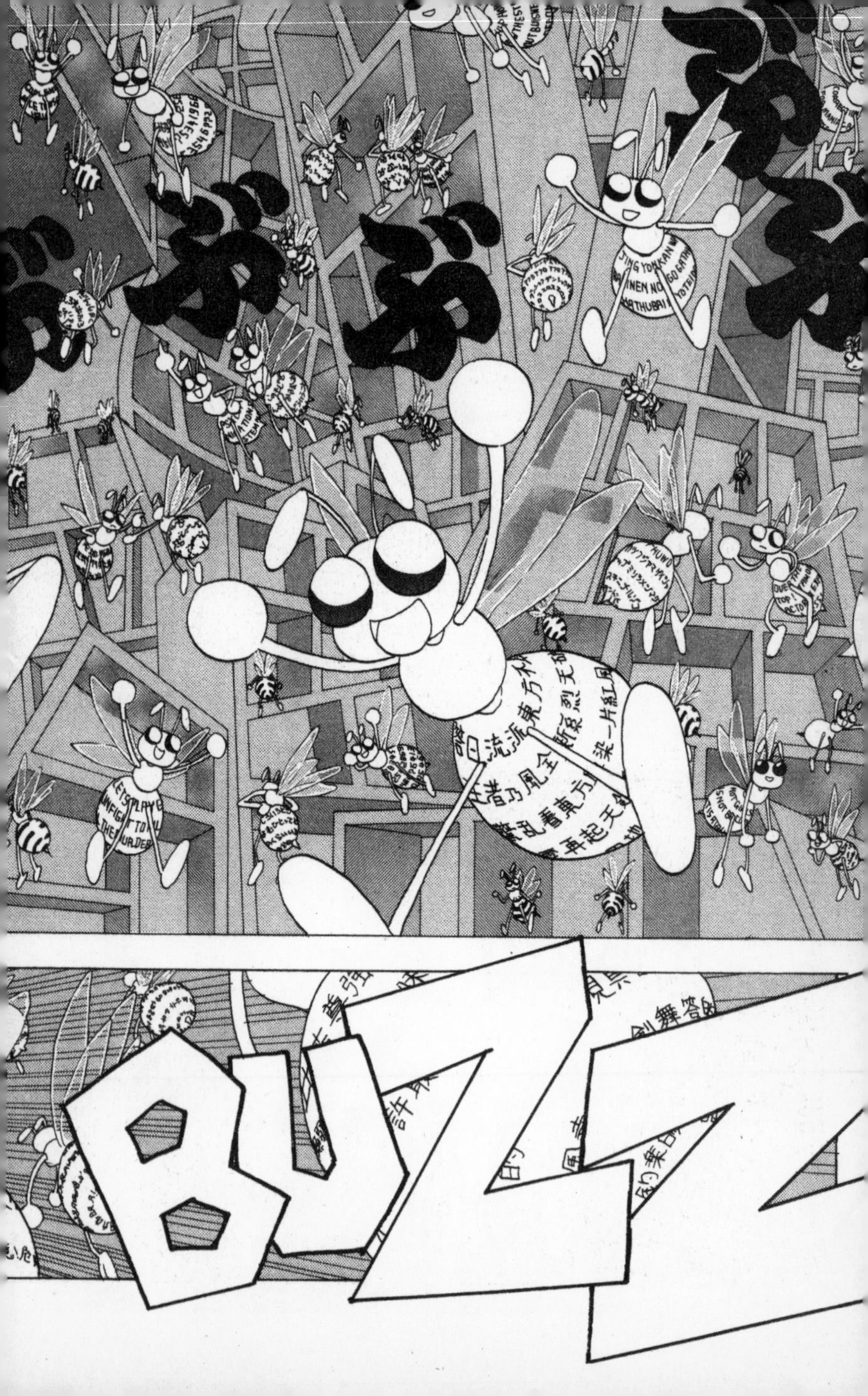
BUZZ

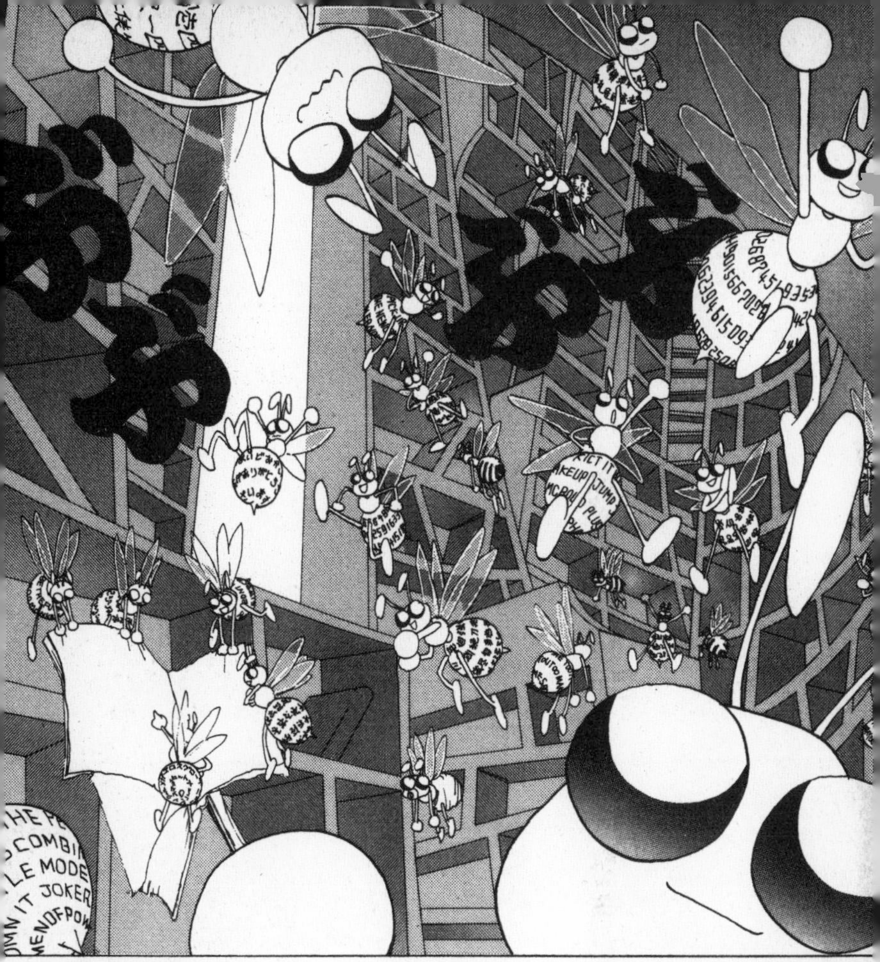
KICK IT
MAKEUP
JUMP
COMBI
LE MODE
IT JOKER
MENOFPOW

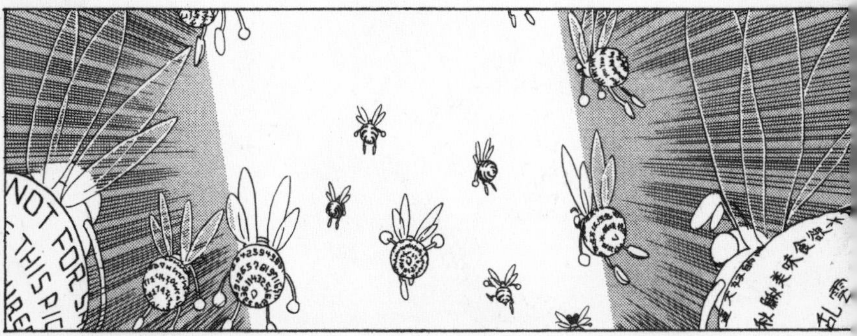
NOT FOR S
THIS PIC

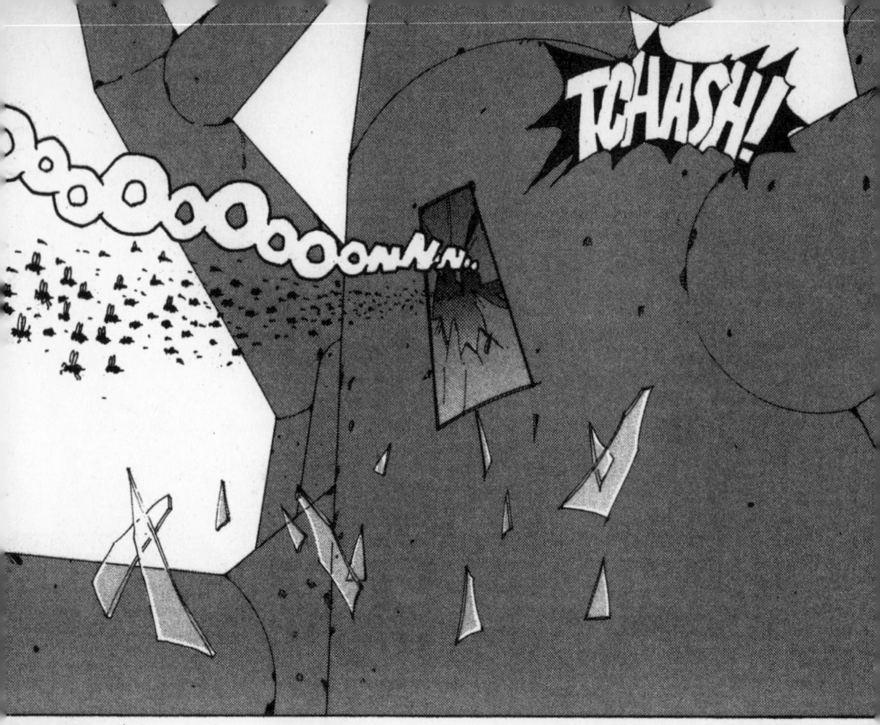
TCHASH!
OOOOOOOOOOOONNN..
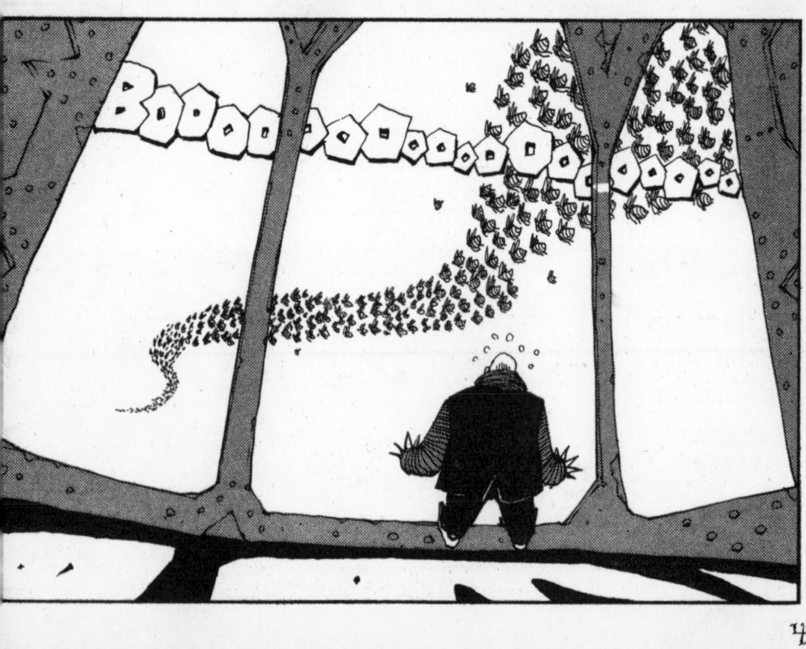
BOOOOOOOOOOOOOOOOO

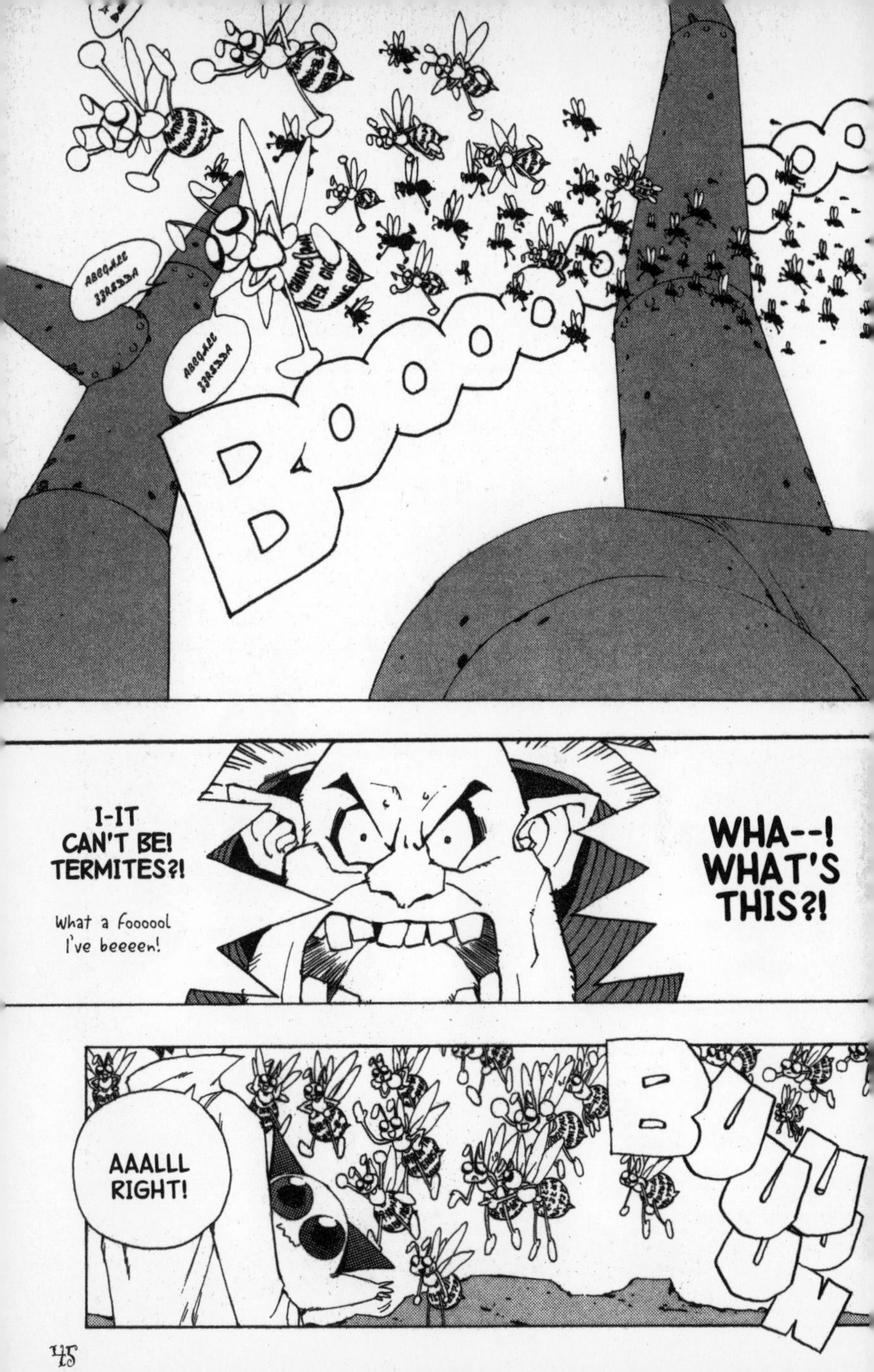

BOOOOOD
WHA--! WHAT'S THIS?!
I-IT CAN'T BE! TERMITES?!
What a foooool I've beeeen!
BUUUUN
AAALLL RIGHT!

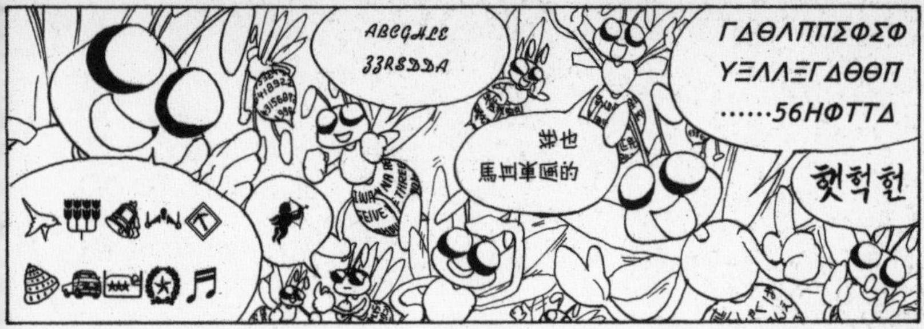
ΓΔΘΛΠΠΣΦΣΦ ΥΞΛΛΞΓΔΘΘΠ 56ΗΦΤΤΔ
ABCGALE 33RSDDA

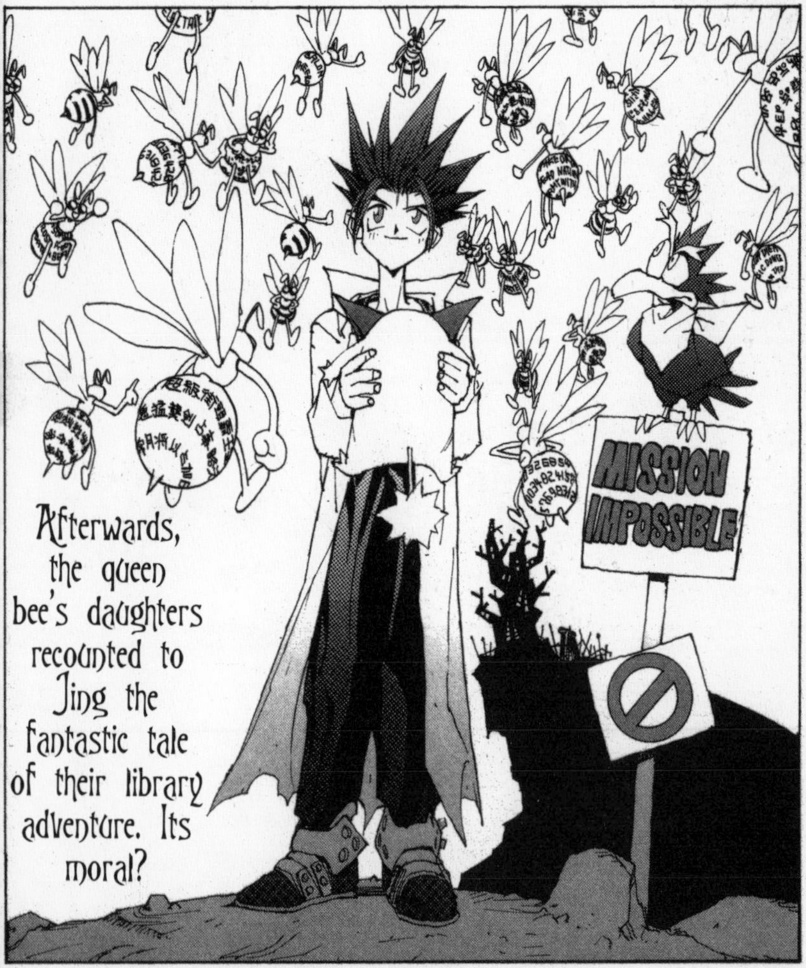
MISSION IMPOSSIBLE
Afterwards, the queen bee's daughters recounted to Jing the fantastic tale of their library adventure. Its moral?

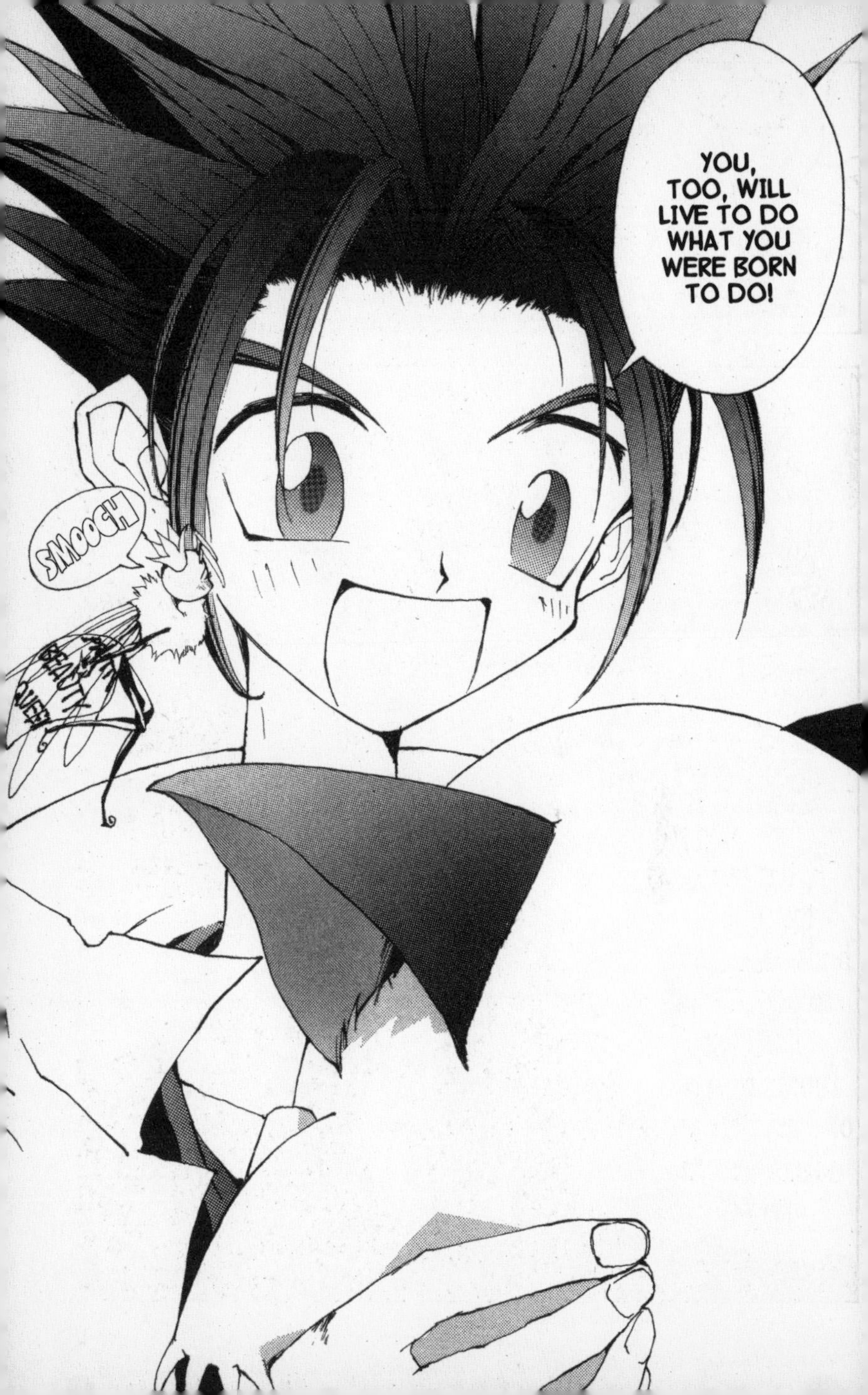
YOU, TOO, WILL LIVE TO DO WHAT YOU WERE BORN TO DO!
SMOOCH
BEAUTY

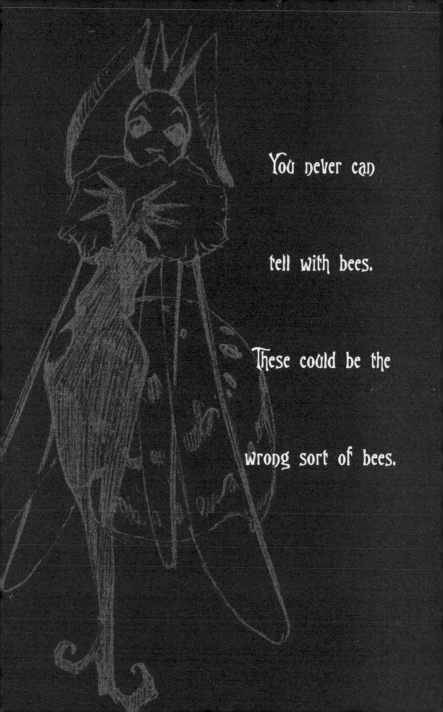

You never can

tell with bees.

These could be the

wrong sort of bees.

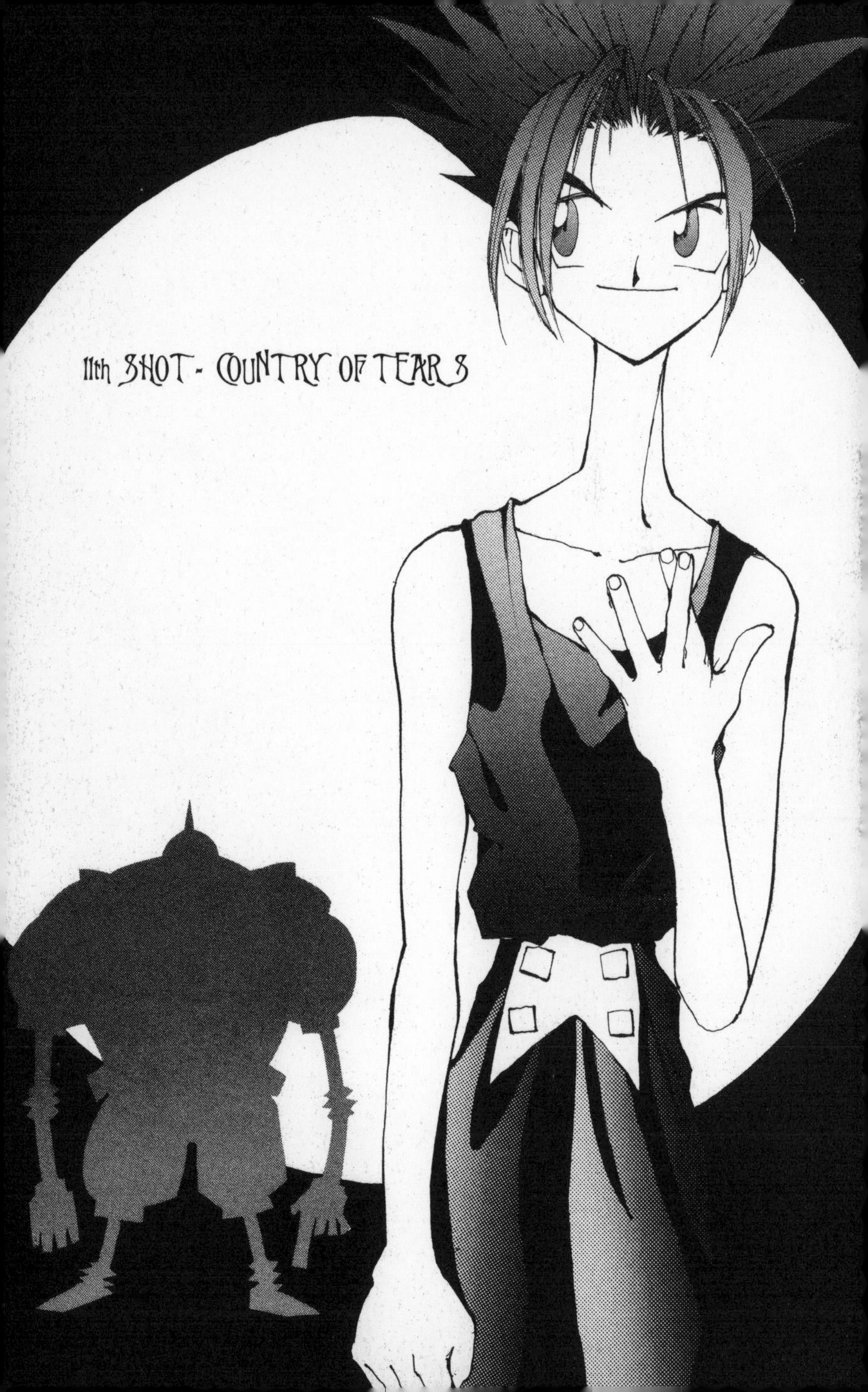
11th SHOT - COUNTRY OF TEARS

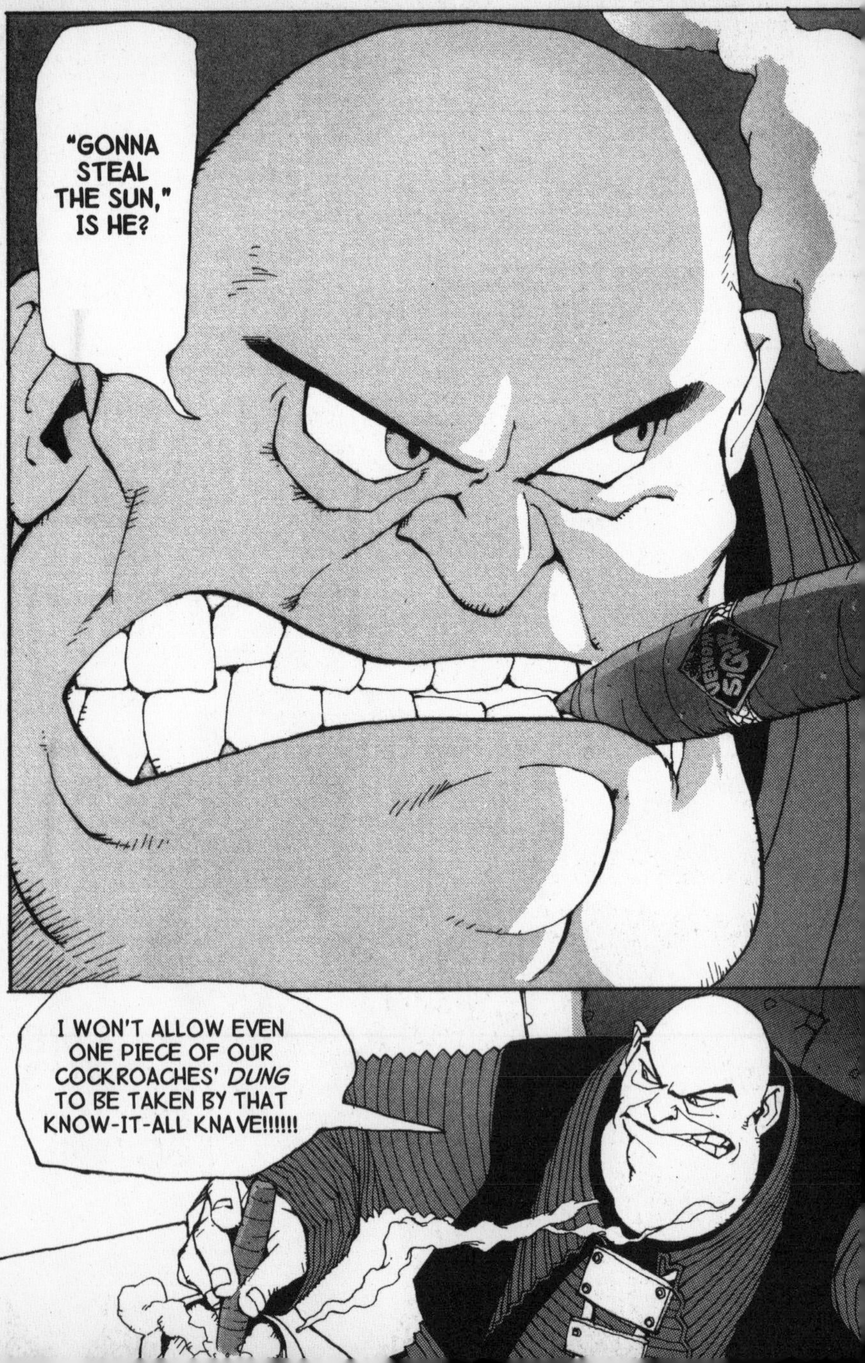
"GONNA STEAL THE SUN," IS HE?
I WON'T ALLOW EVEN ONE PIECE OF OUR COCKROACHES' *DUNG* TO BE TAKEN BY THAT KNOW-IT-ALL KNAVE!!!!!!

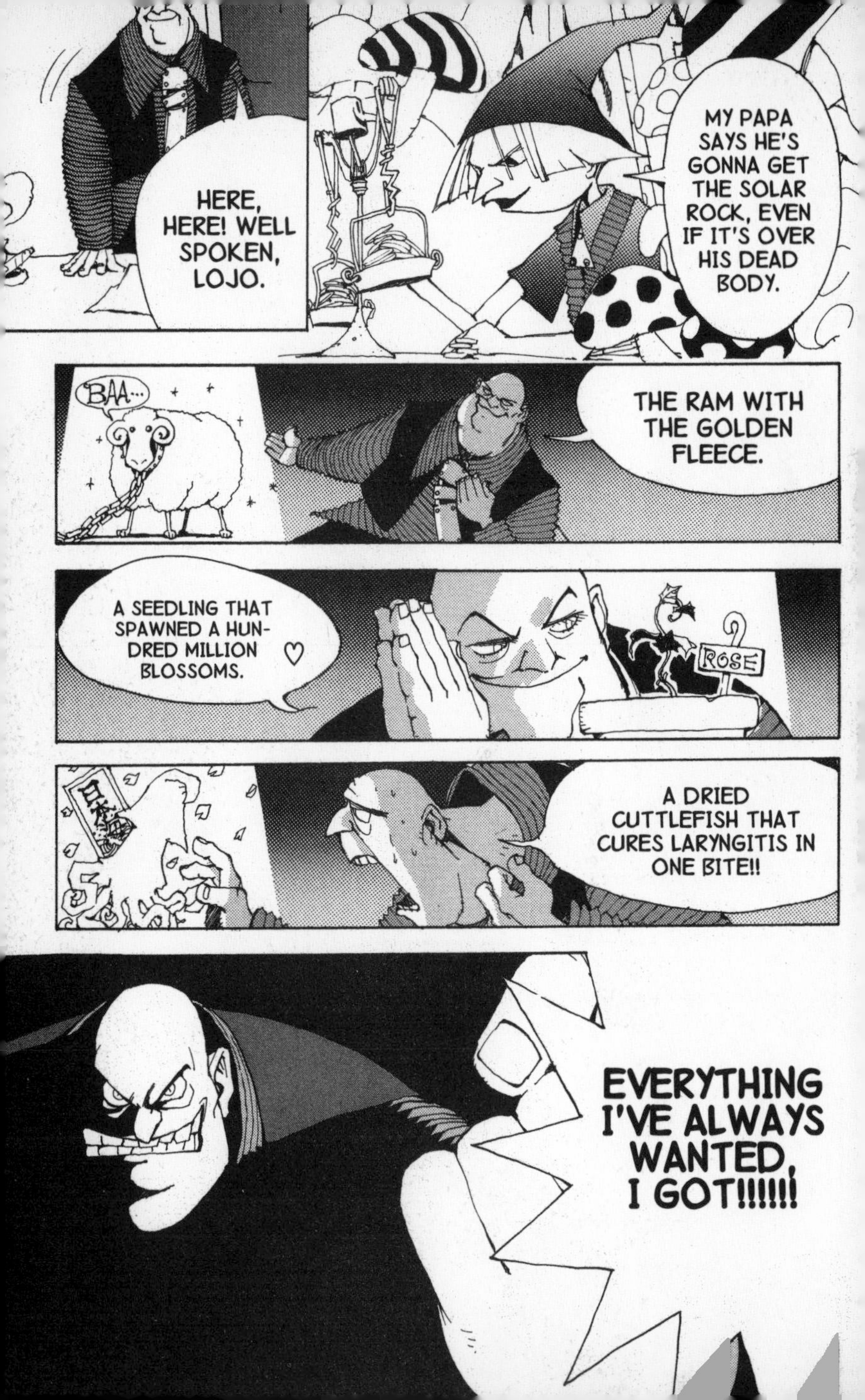
MY PAPA SAYS HE'S GONNA GET THE SOLAR ROCK, EVEN IF IT'S OVER HIS DEAD BODY.
HERE, HERE! WELL SPOKEN, LOJO.
THE RAM WITH THE GOLDEN FLEECE.
BAA...
ROSE
A SEEDLING THAT SPAWNED A HUNDRED MILLION BLOSSOMS. ♡
A DRIED CUTTLEFISH THAT CURES LARYNGITIS IN ONE BITE!!
EVERYTHING I'VE ALWAYS WANTED, I GOT!!!!!!

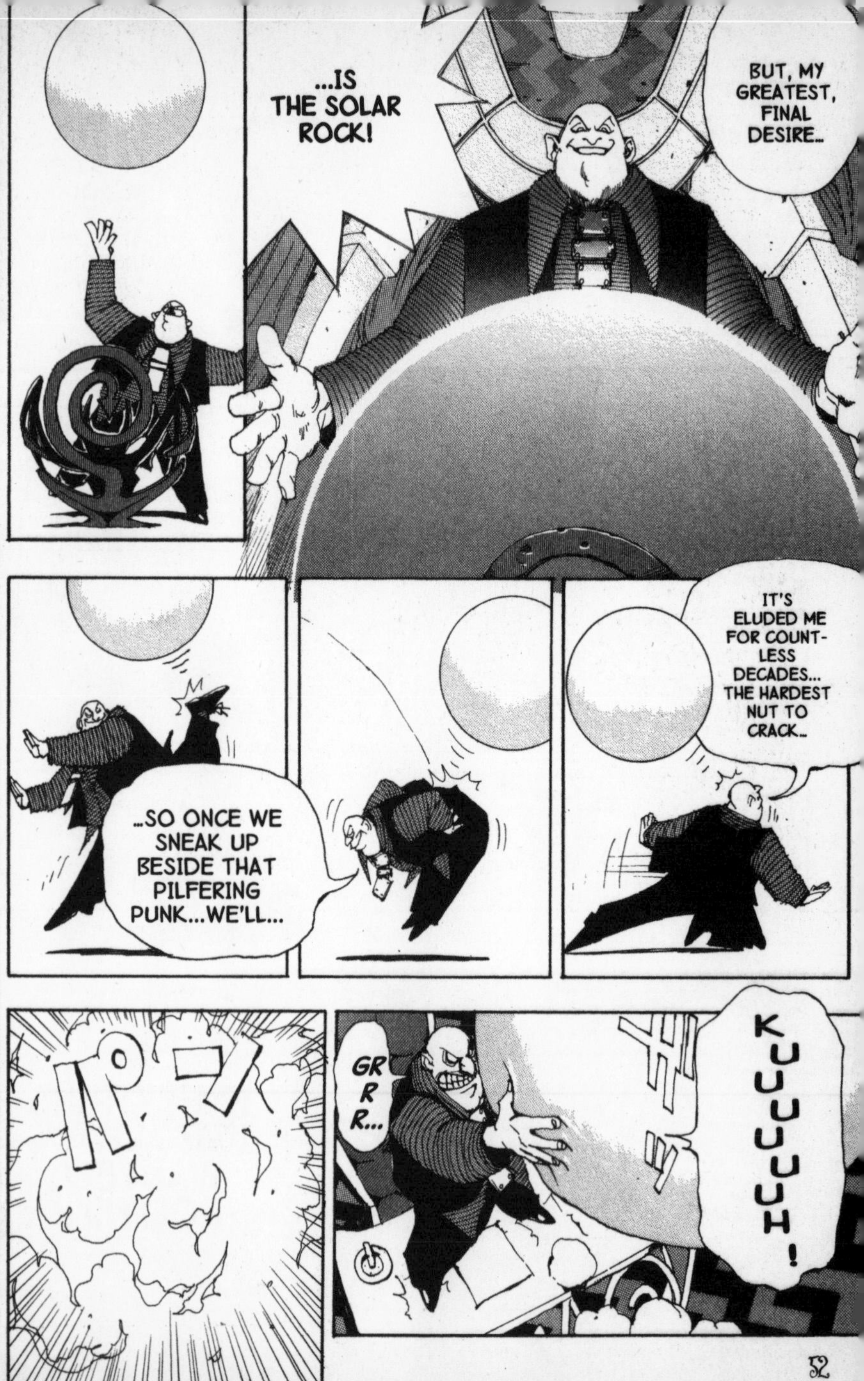
BUT, MY GREATEST, FINAL DESIRE...
...IS THE SOLAR ROCK!
IT'S ELUDED ME FOR COUNT-LESS DECADES... THE HARDEST NUT TO CRACK...
...SO ONCE WE SNEAK UP BESIDE THAT PILFERING PUNK...WE'LL...
KUUUUUUH!
GRRR...

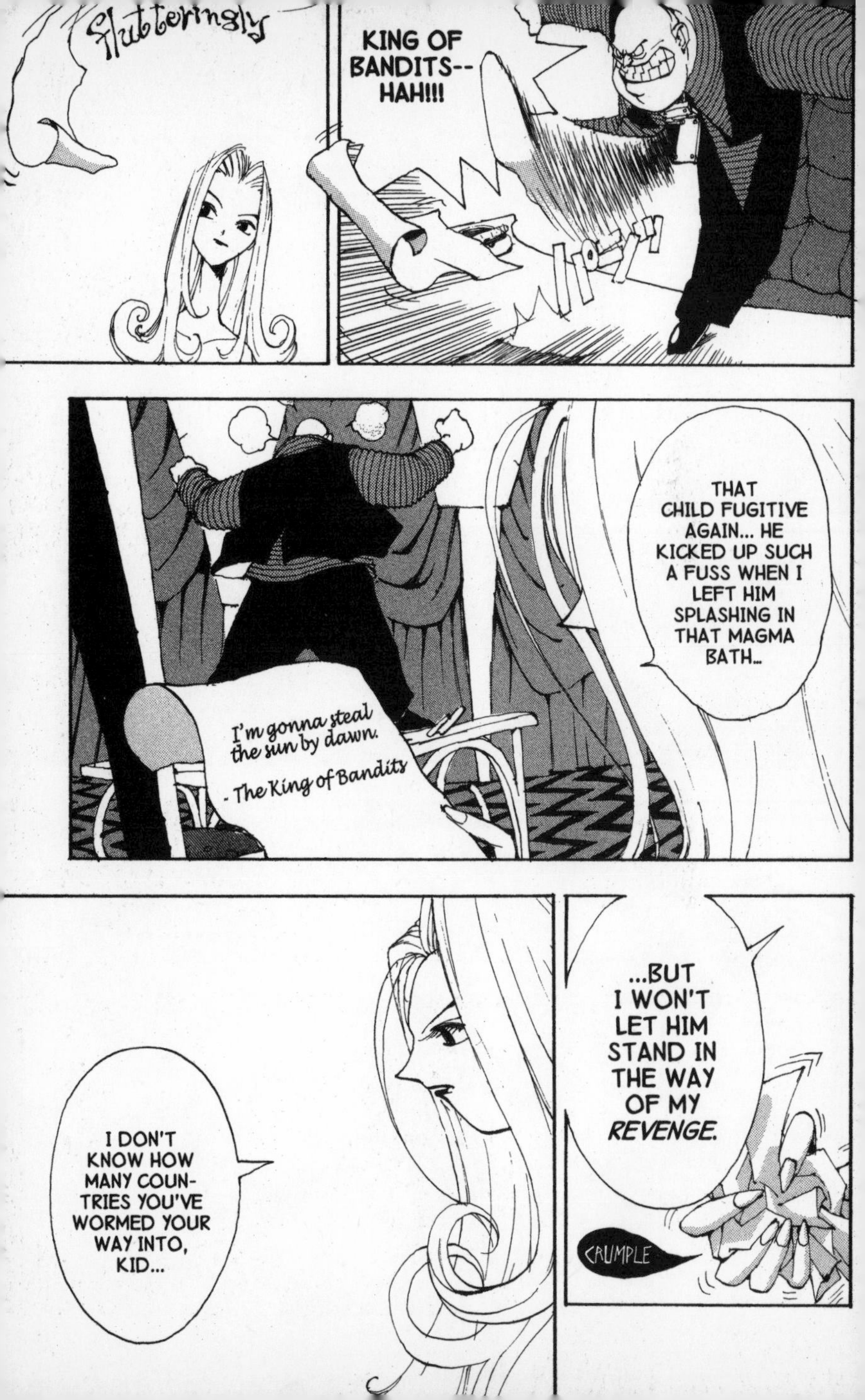
KING OF BANDITS-- HAH!!!
Flutteringly
THAT CHILD FUGITIVE AGAIN... HE KICKED UP SUCH A FUSS WHEN I LEFT HIM SPLASHING IN THAT MAGMA BATH...
I'm gonna steal the sun by dawn.
- The King of Bandits
...BUT I WON'T LET HIM STAND IN THE WAY OF MY *REVENGE*.
CRUMPLE
I DON'T KNOW HOW MANY COUNTRIES YOU'VE WORMED YOUR WAY INTO, KID...

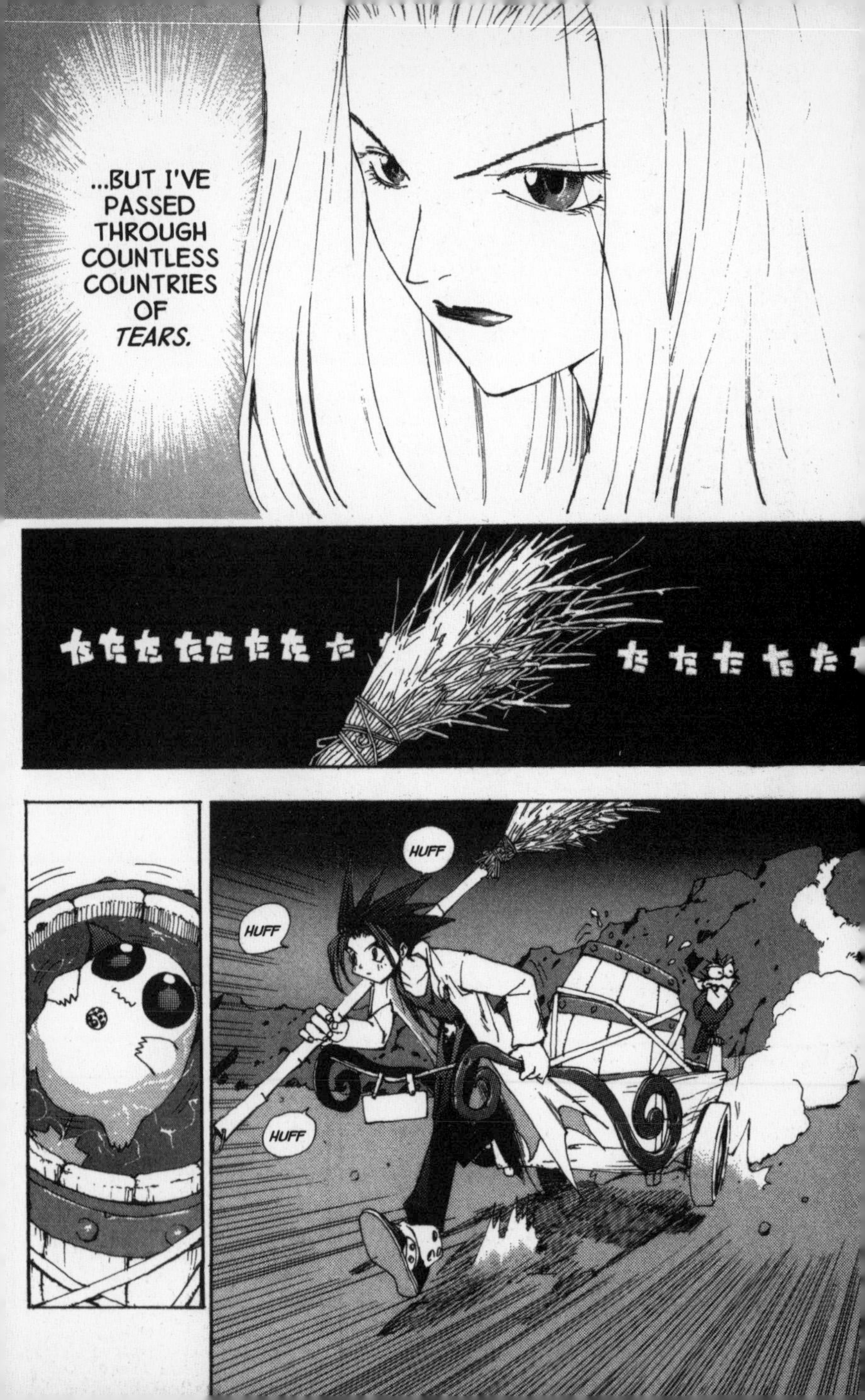
...BUT I'VE PASSED THROUGH COUNTLESS COUNTRIES OF TEARS.
たたたたた
たたたたたたた
HUFF
HUFF
HUFF

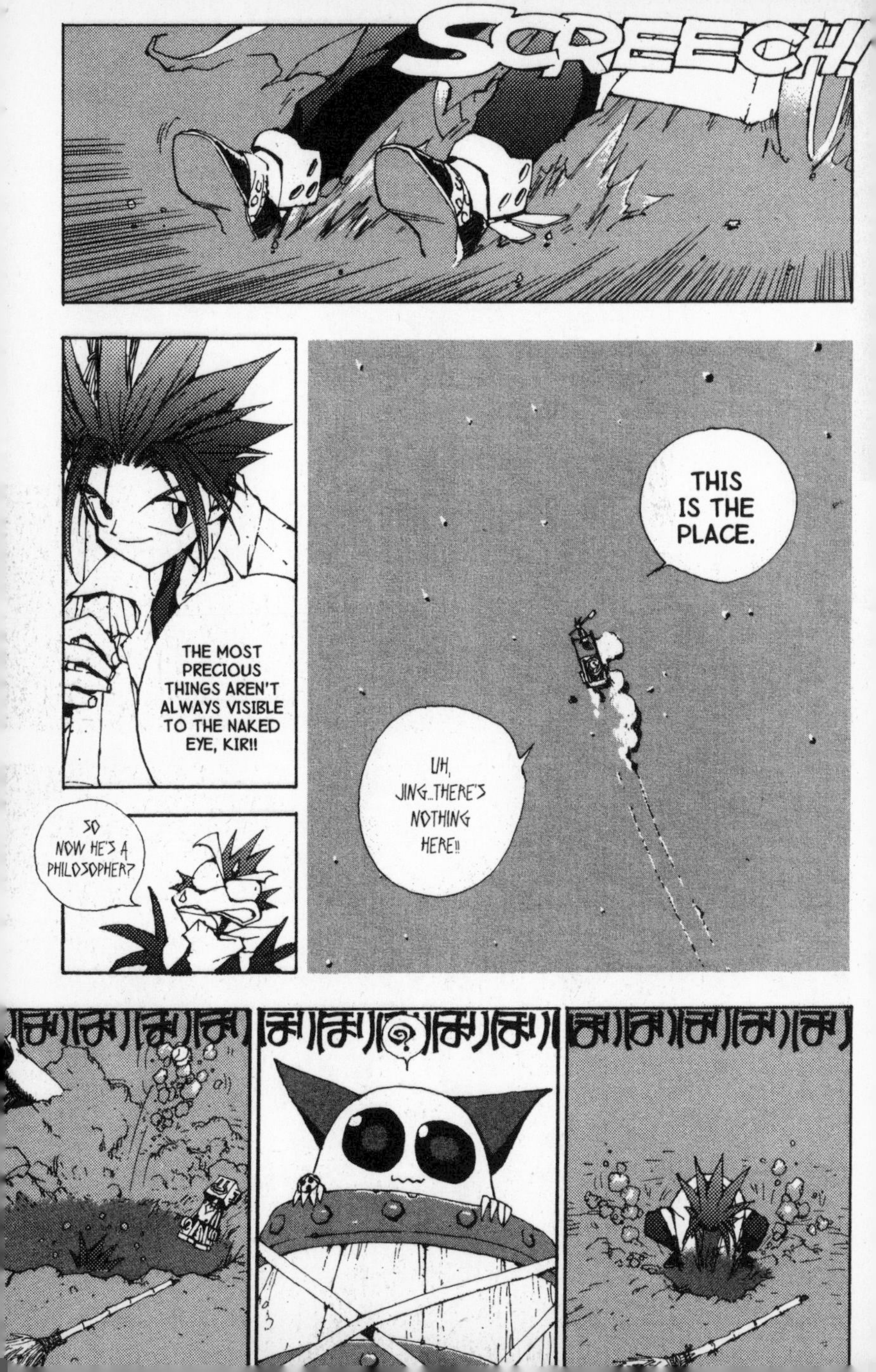
SCREECH!
THIS IS THE PLACE.
UH, JING...THERE'S NOTHING HERE!!
THE MOST PRECIOUS THINGS AREN'T ALWAYS VISIBLE TO THE NAKED EYE, KIR!!
SO NOW HE'S A PHILOSOPHER?

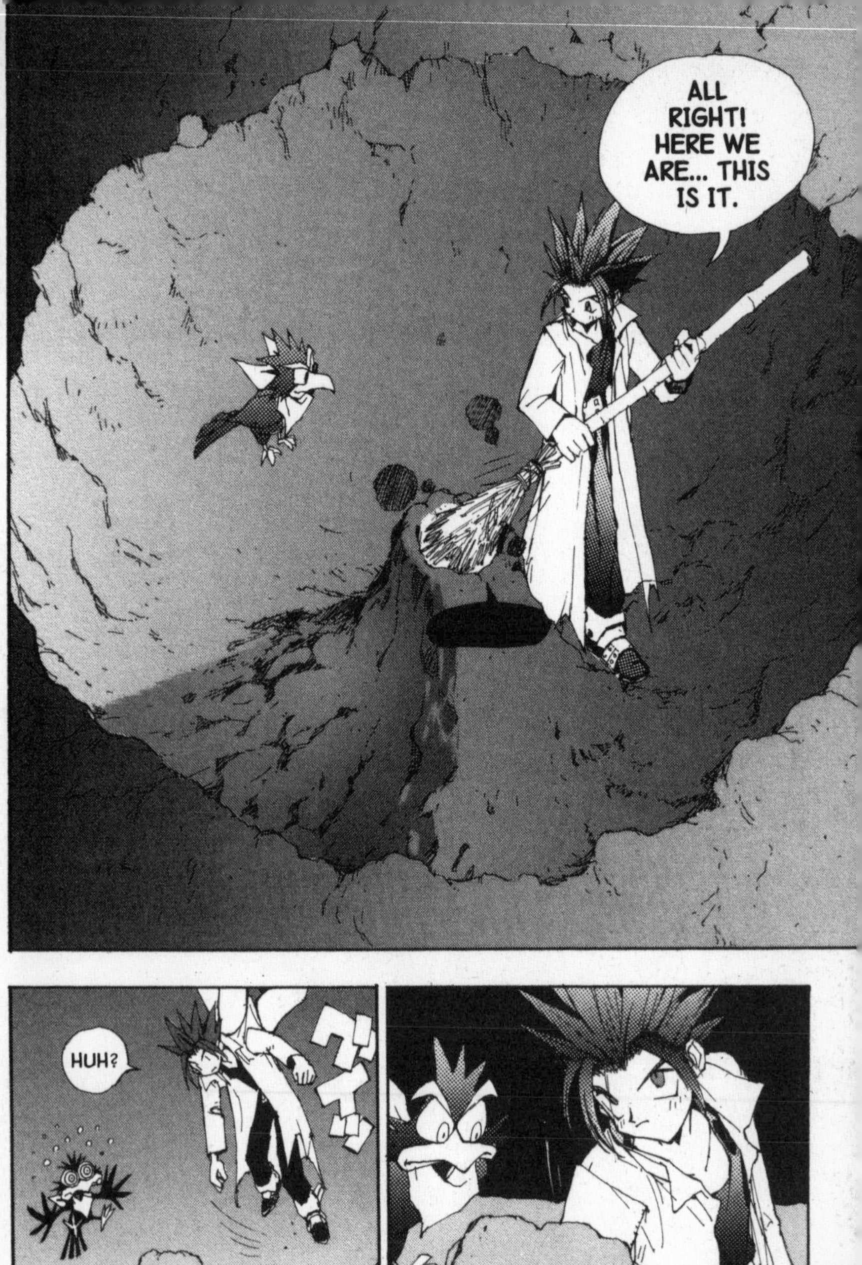
ALL RIGHT! HERE WE ARE... THIS IS IT.
HUH?

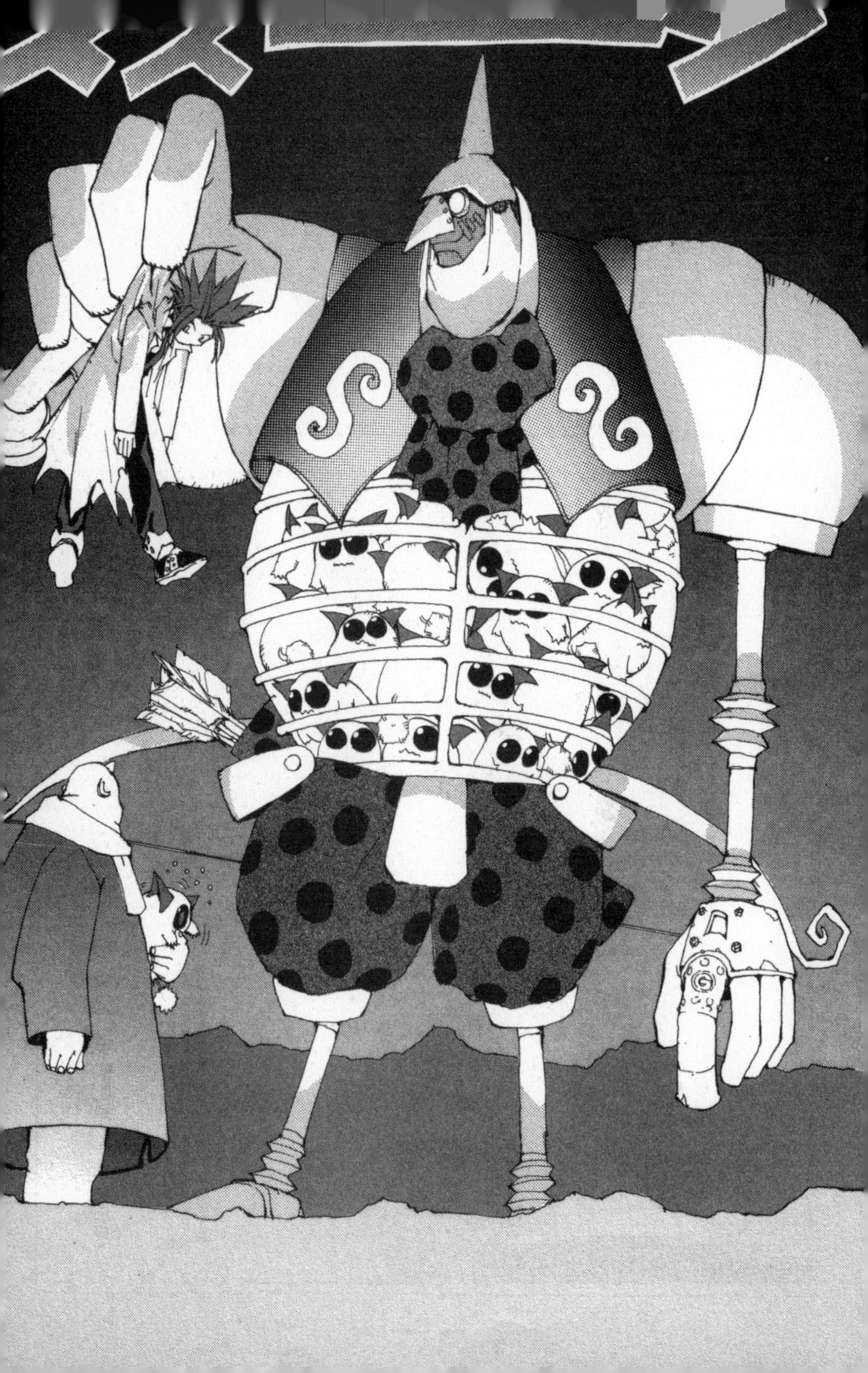

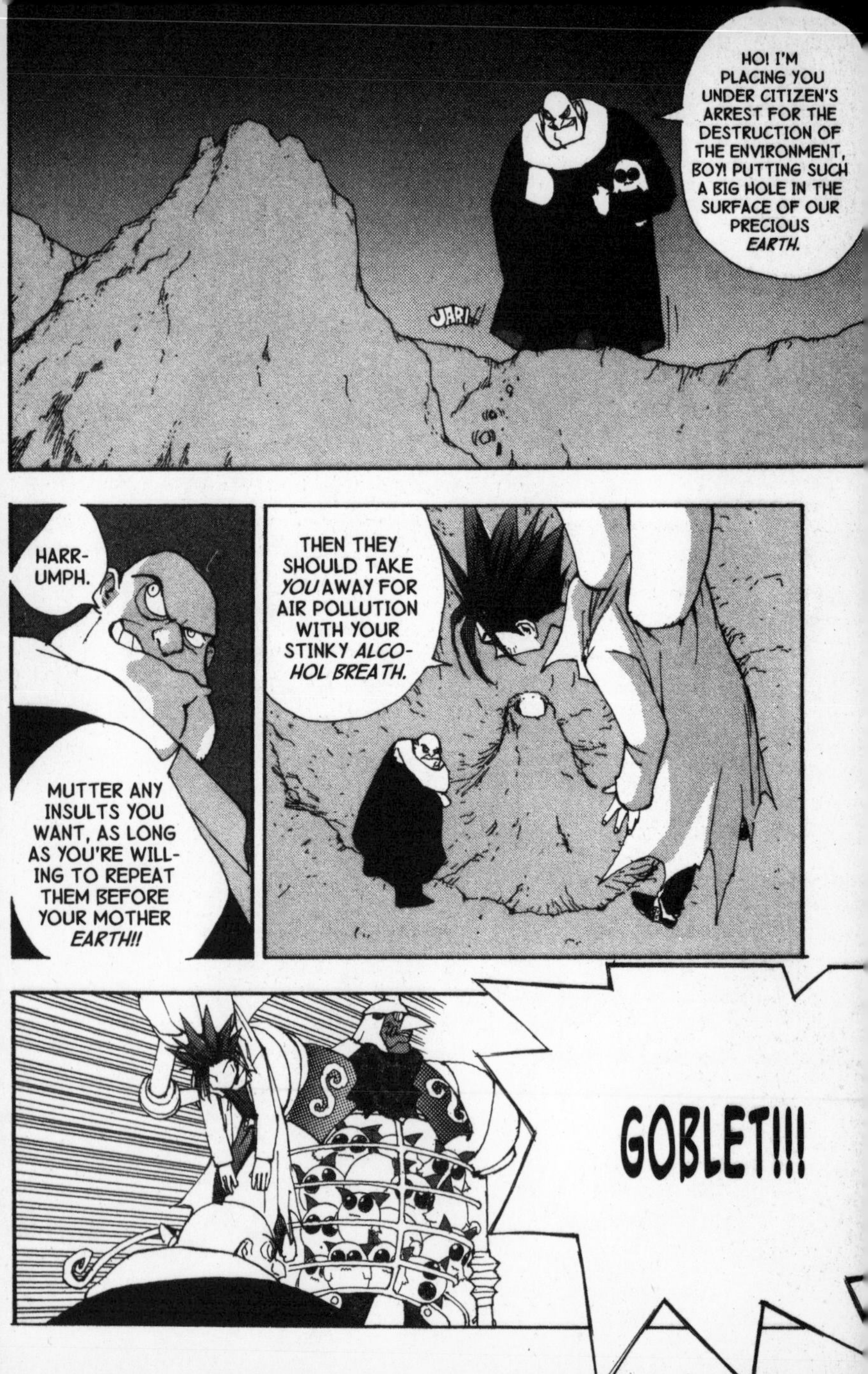
HO! I'M PLACING YOU UNDER CITIZEN'S ARREST FOR THE DESTRUCTION OF THE ENVIRONMENT, BOY! PUTTING SUCH A BIG HOLE IN THE SURFACE OF OUR PRECIOUS *EARTH.*
JARI
THEN THEY SHOULD TAKE *YOU* AWAY FOR AIR POLLUTION WITH YOUR STINKY *ALCOHOL BREATH.*
HARRUMPH.
MUTTER ANY INSULTS YOU WANT, AS LONG AS YOU'RE WILLING TO REPEAT THEM BEFORE YOUR MOTHER *EARTH!!*
GOBLET!!!

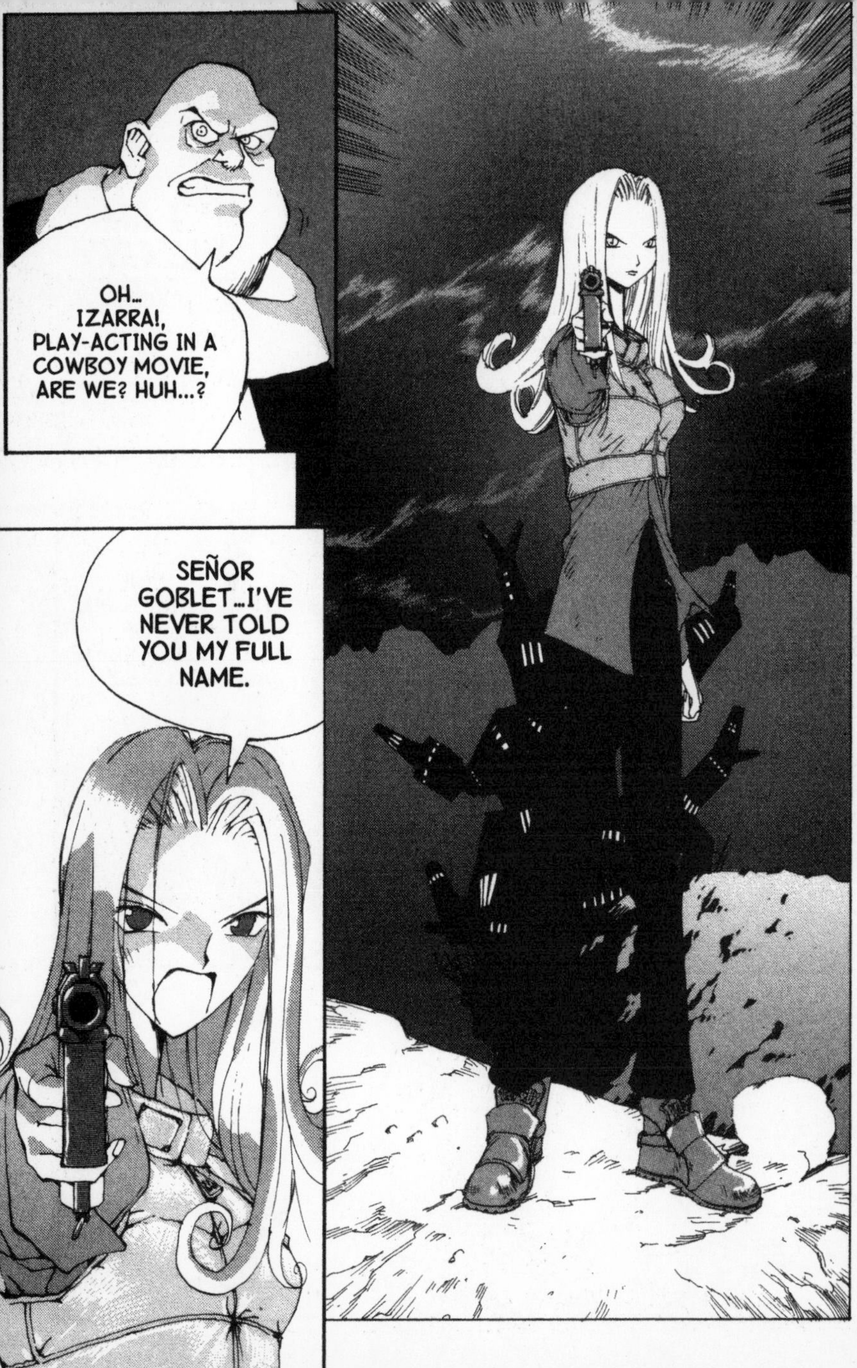
OH... IZARRA!, PLAY-ACTING IN A COWBOY MOVIE, ARE WE? HUH...?
SEÑOR GOBLET...I'VE NEVER TOLD YOU MY FULL NAME.

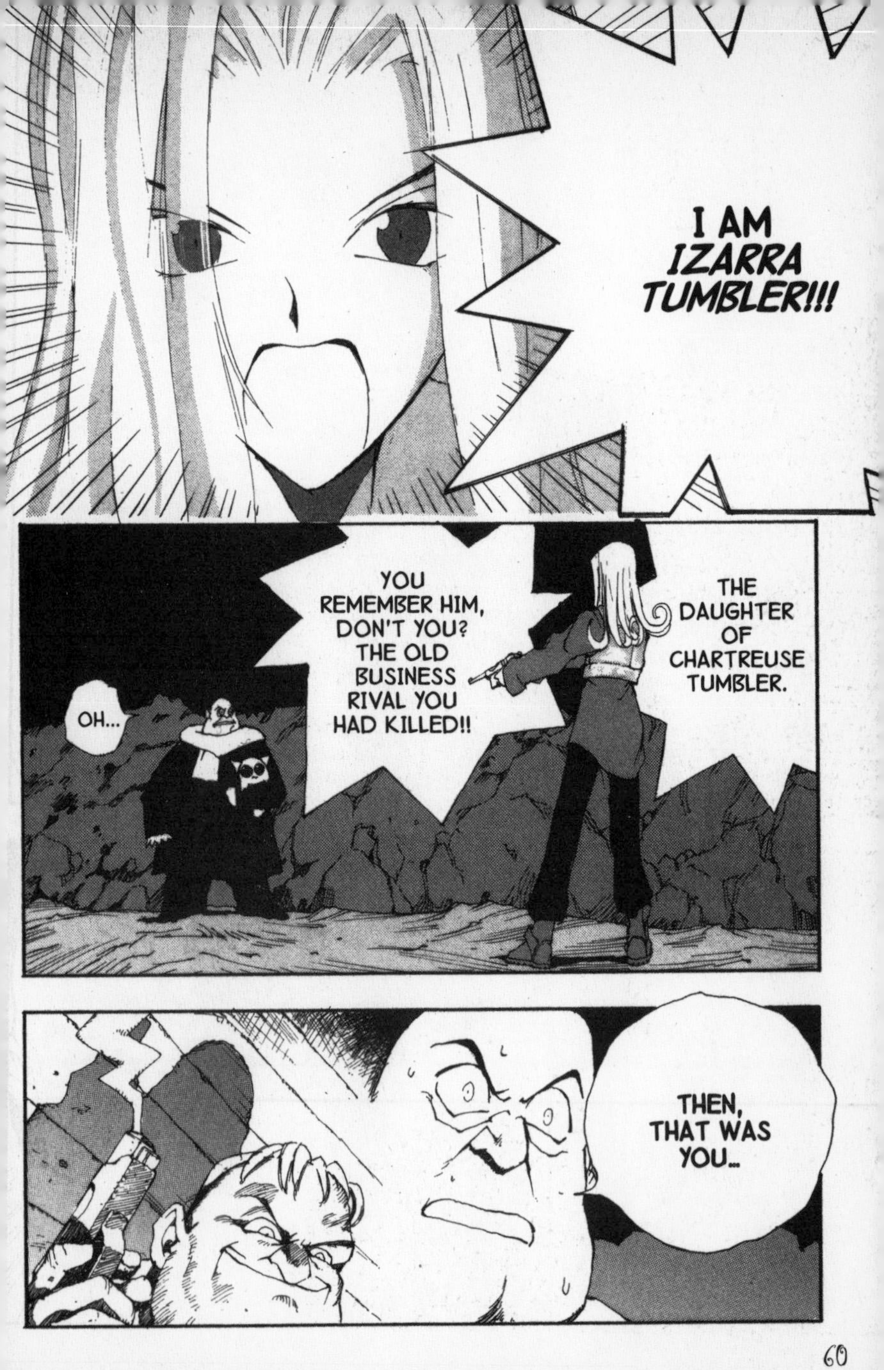
I AM IZARRA TUMBLER!!!
THE DAUGHTER OF CHARTREUSE TUMBLER.
YOU REMEMBER HIM, DON'T YOU? THE OLD BUSINESS RIVAL YOU HAD KILLED!!
OH...
THEN, THAT WAS YOU...

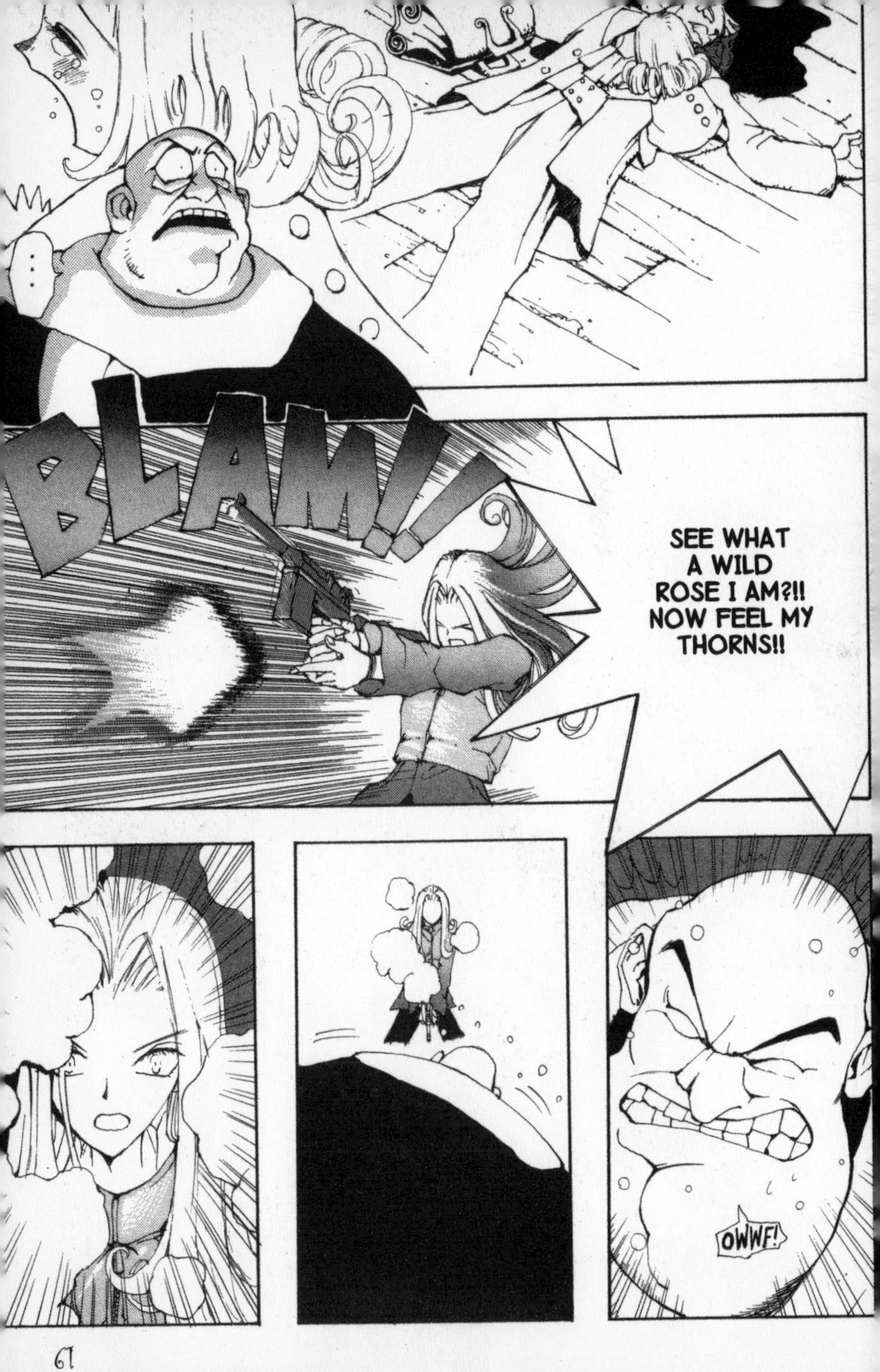
...
BLAM!!
SEE WHAT A WILD ROSE I AM?!! NOW FEEL MY THORNS!!
OWWF!

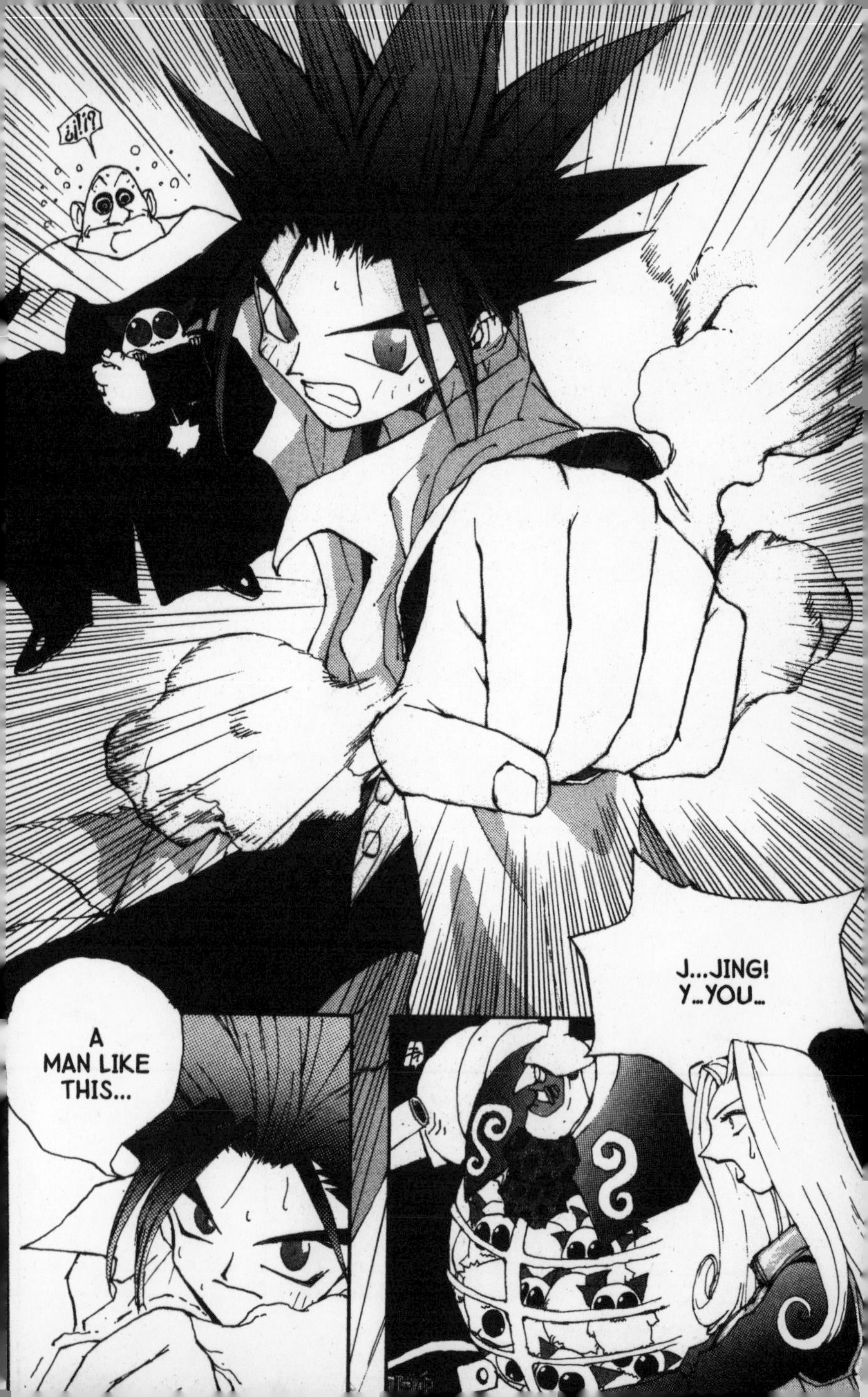
¿!!?
J...JING! Y...YOU...
A MAN LIKE THIS...

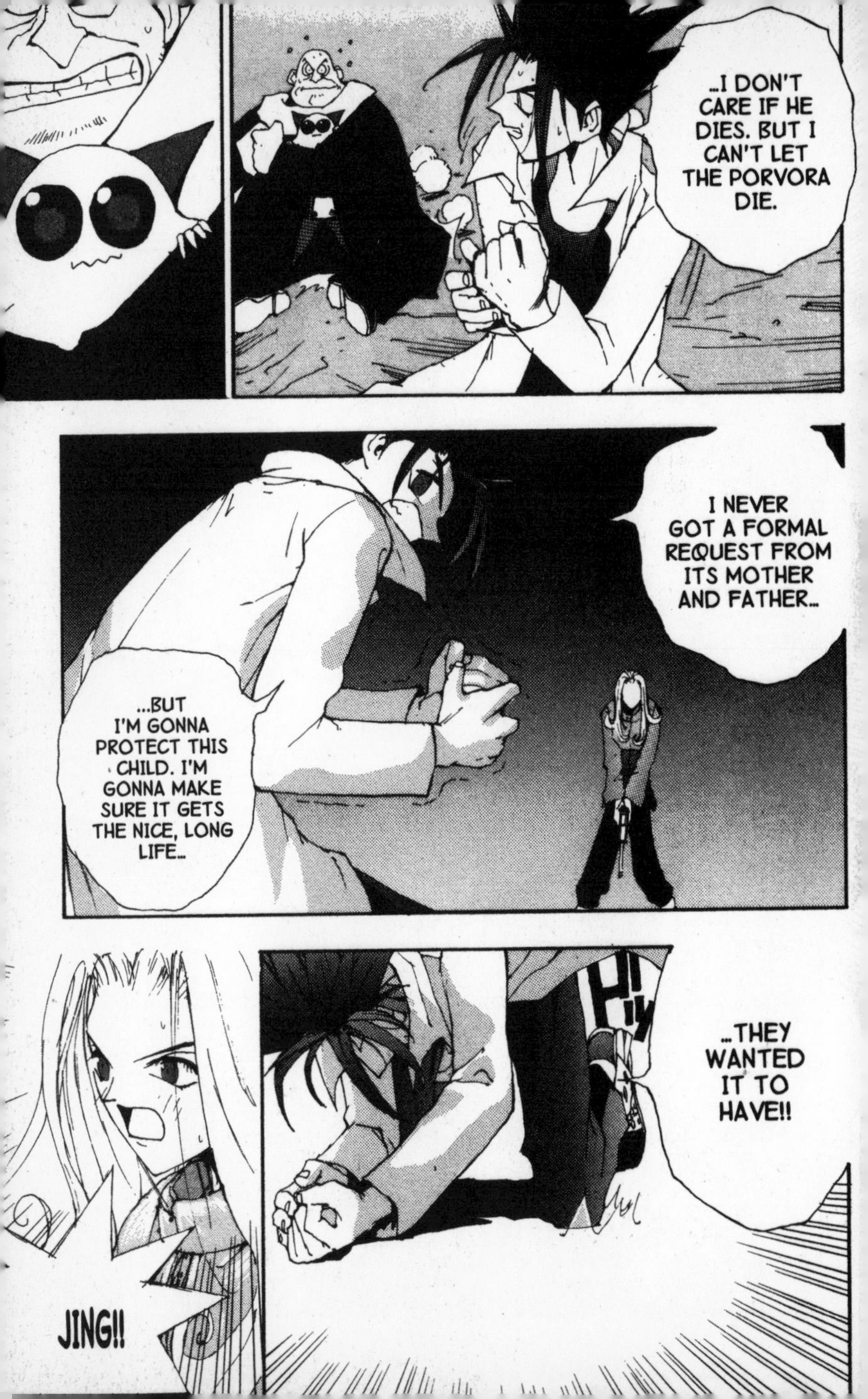
...I DON'T CARE IF HE DIES. BUT I CAN'T LET THE PORVORA DIE.
I NEVER GOT A FORMAL REQUEST FROM ITS MOTHER AND FATHER...
...BUT I'M GONNA PROTECT THIS CHILD. I'M GONNA MAKE SURE IT GETS THE NICE, LONG LIFE...
...THEY WANTED IT TO HAVE!!
JING!!

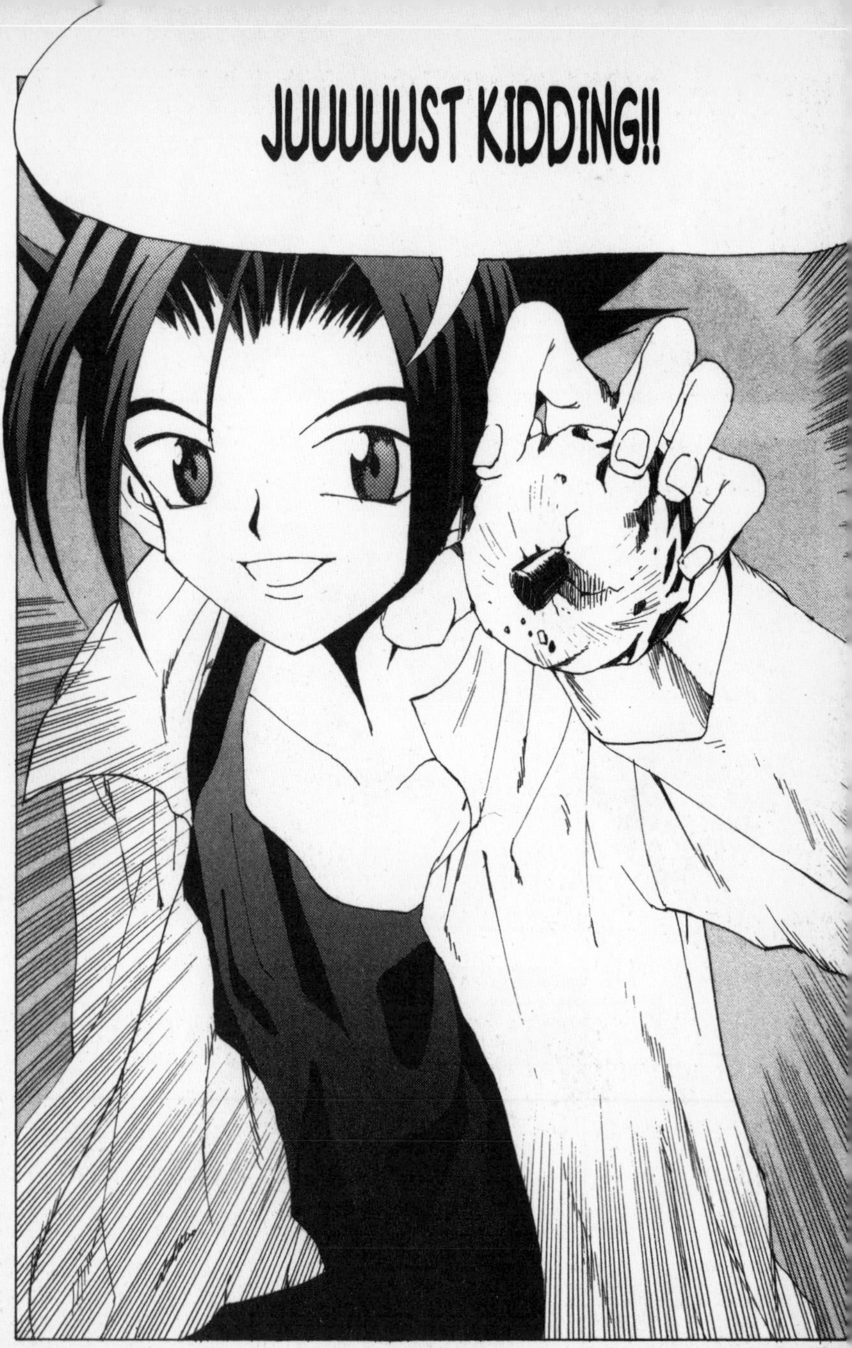
JUUUUUST KIDDING!!

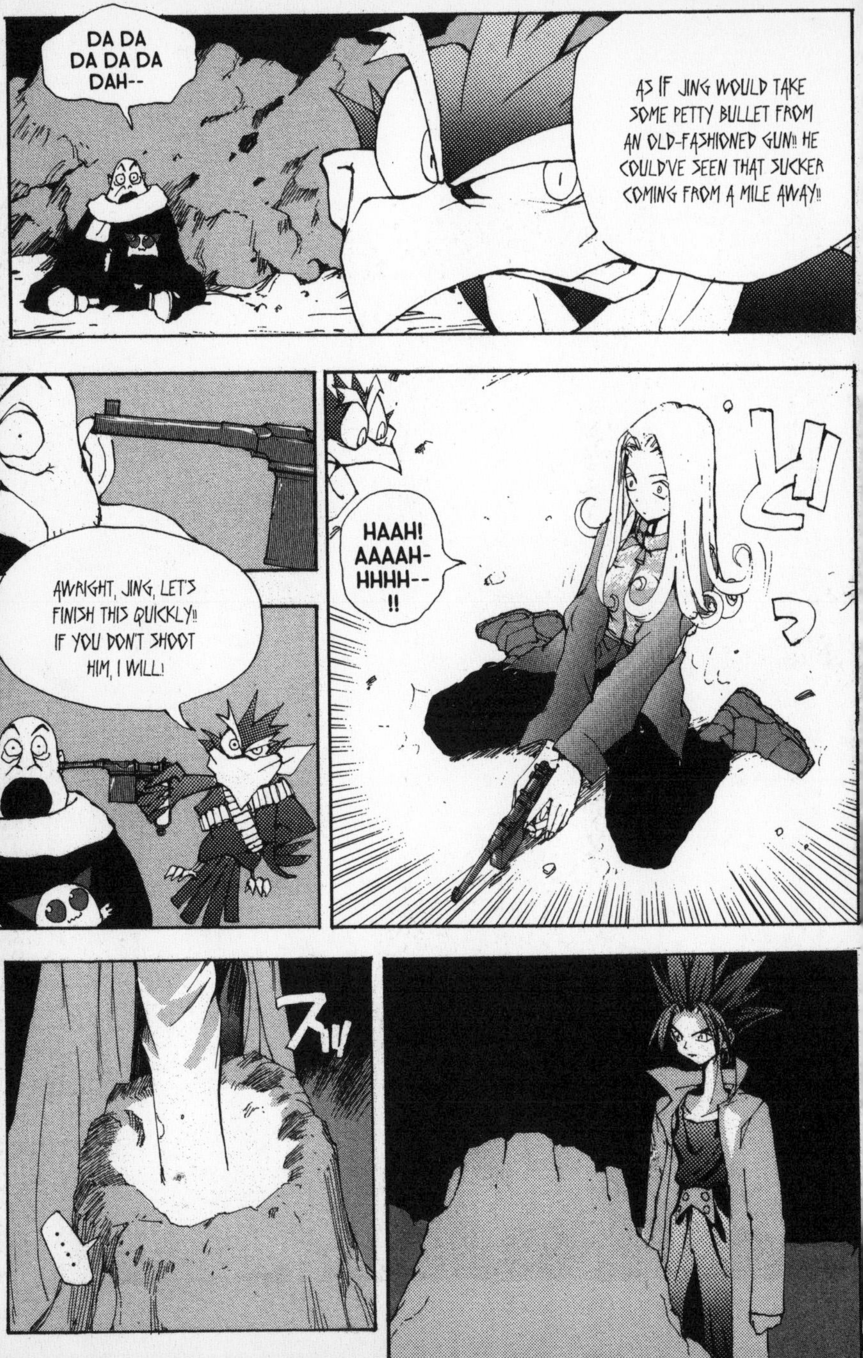
AS IF JING WOULD TAKE SOME PETTY BULLET FROM AN OLD-FASHIONED GUN!! HE COULD'VE SEEN THAT SUCKER COMING FROM A MILE AWAY!!
DA DA DA DA DA DAH--
HAAH! AAAAH-HHHH--!!
AWRIGHT, JING, LET'S FINISH THIS QUICKLY!! IF YOU DON'T SHOOT HIM, I WILL!
.....

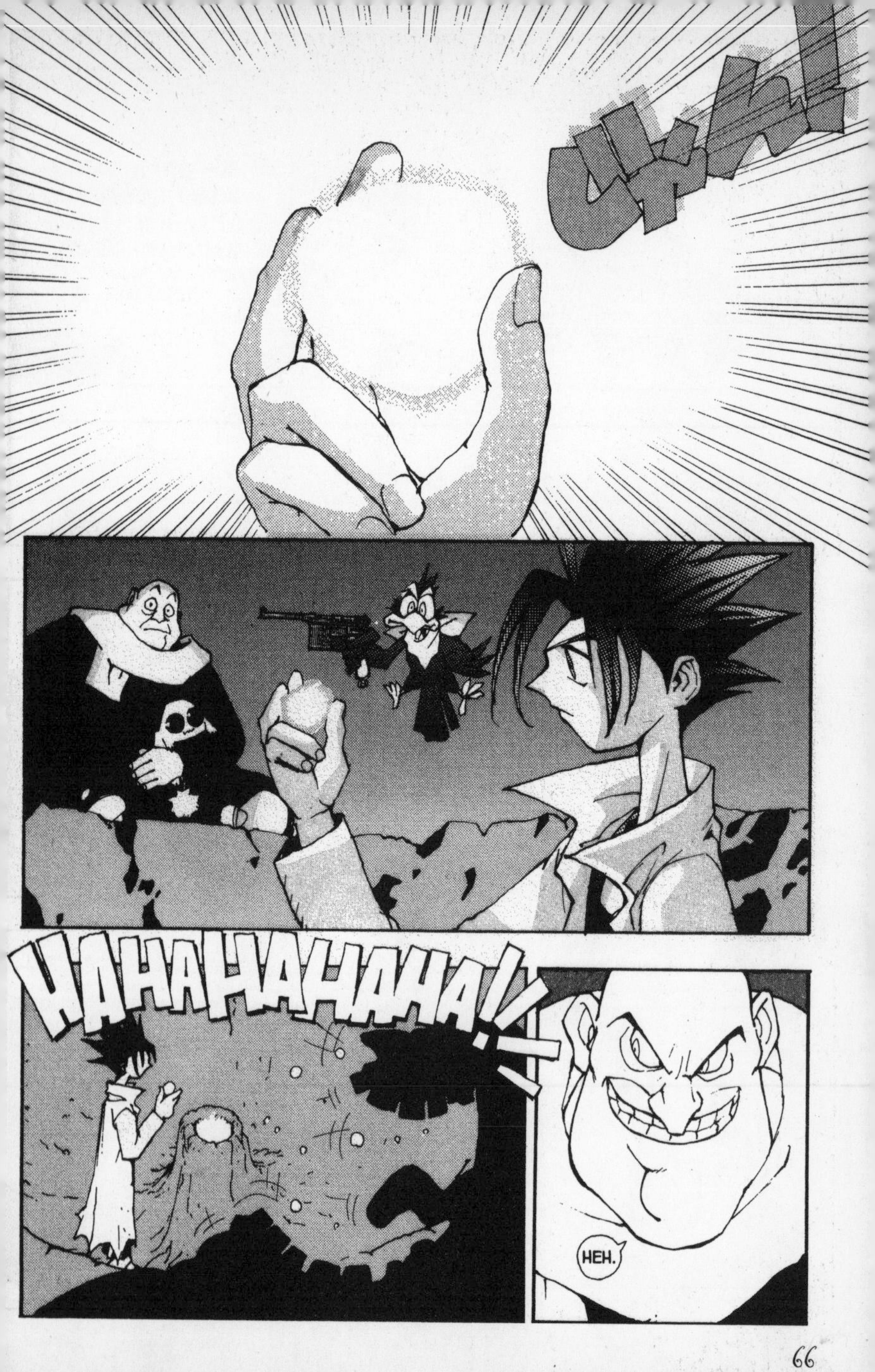
HEH.
HAHAHAHAHA!!

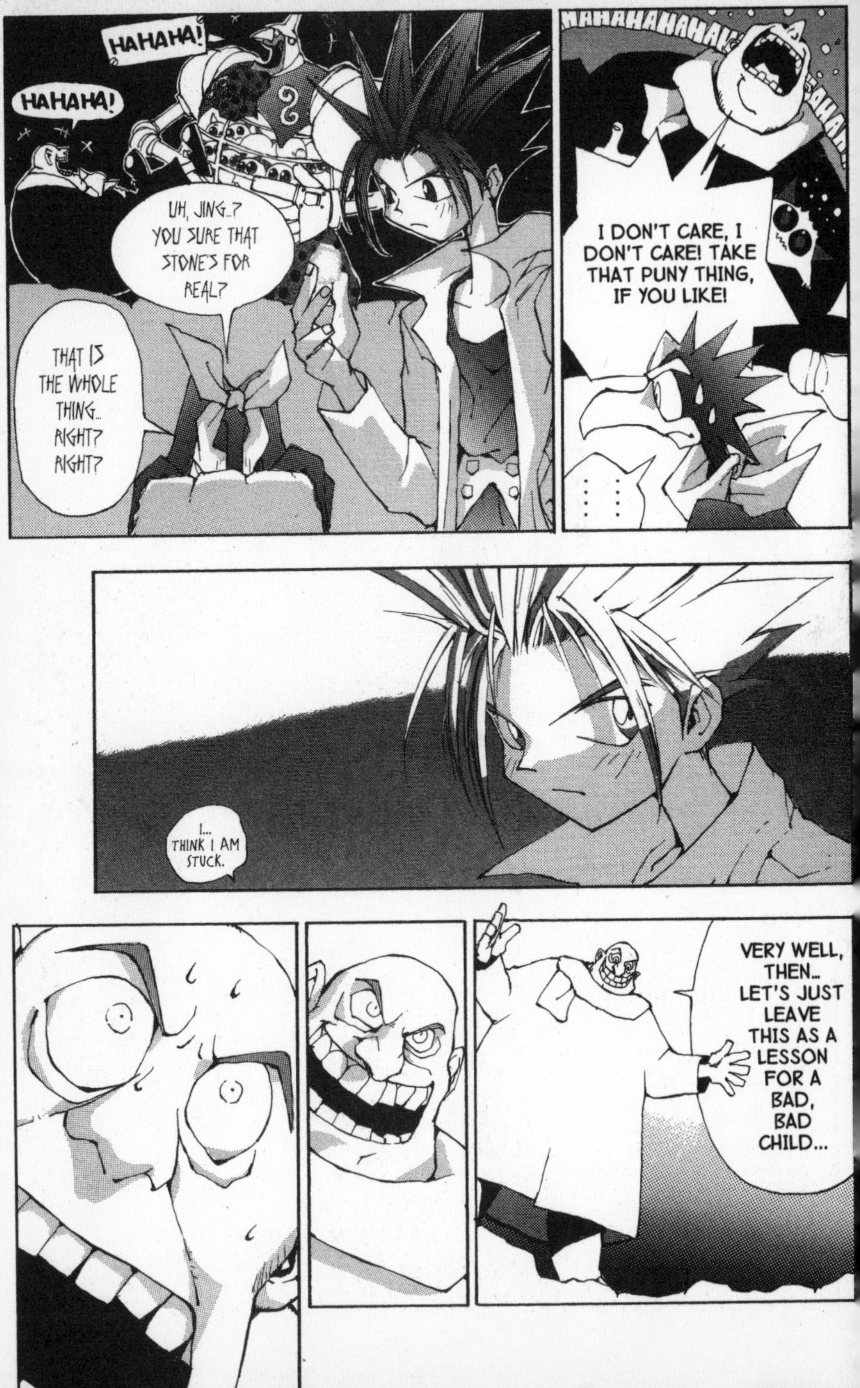
HAHAHAHAHAHA
HAHAHA
I DON'T CARE, I DON'T CARE! TAKE THAT PUNY THING, IF YOU LIKE!
......
HAHAHA!
HAHAHA!
UH, JING...? YOU SURE THAT STONE'S FOR REAL?
THAT IS THE WHOLE THING... RIGHT? RIGHT?
I... THINK I AM STUCK.
VERY WELL, THEN... LET'S JUST LEAVE THIS AS A LESSON FOR A BAD, BAD CHILD...

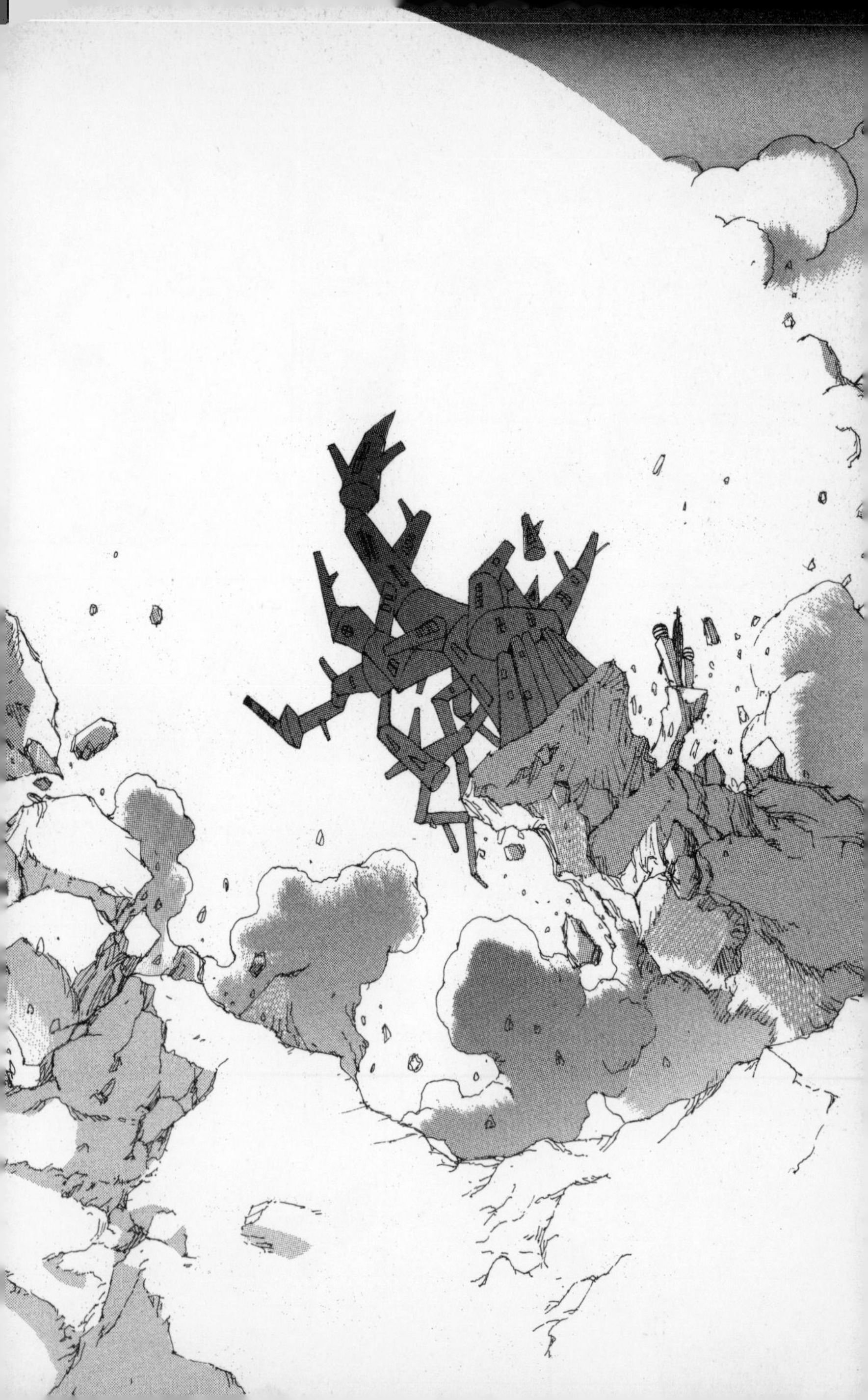

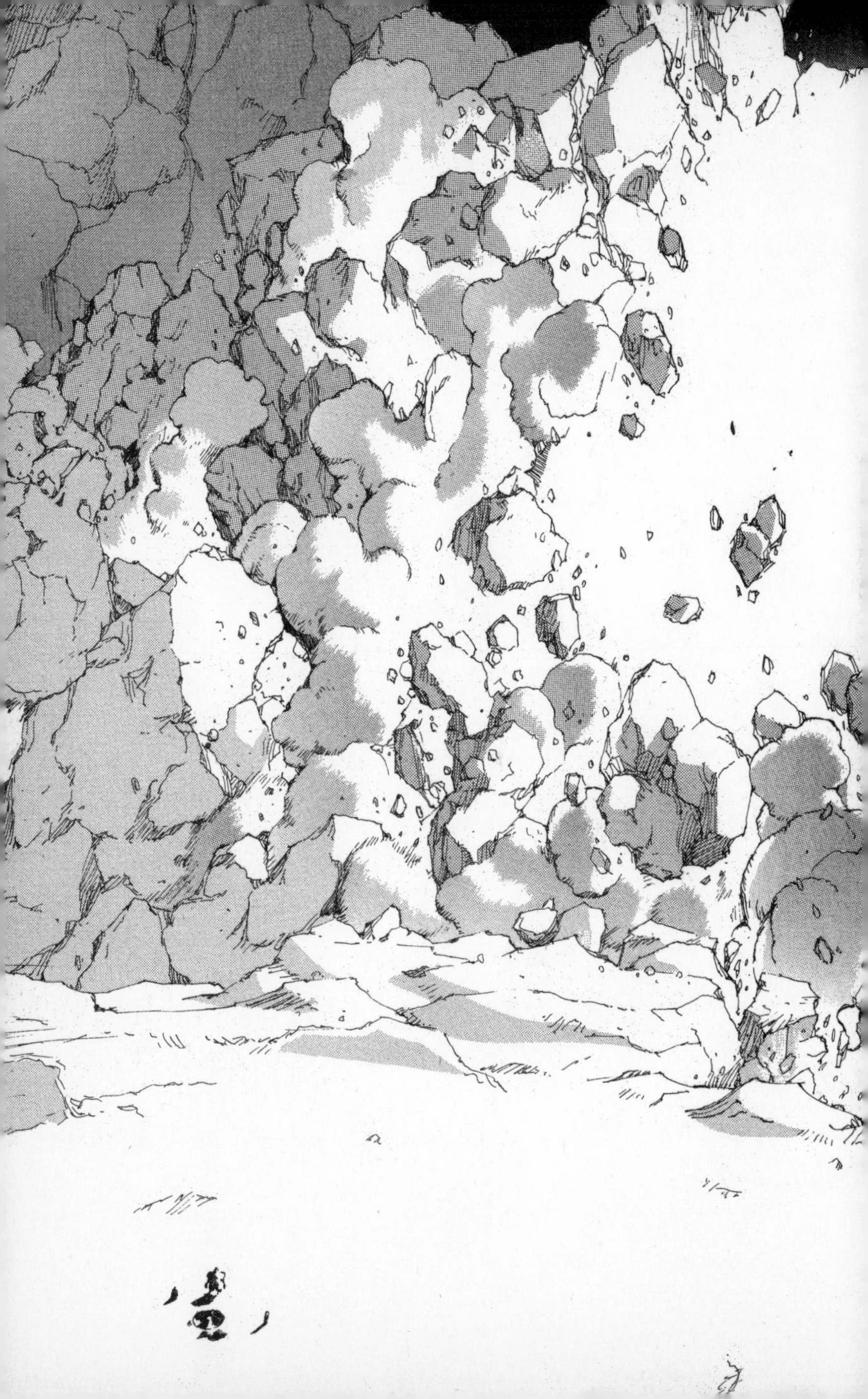

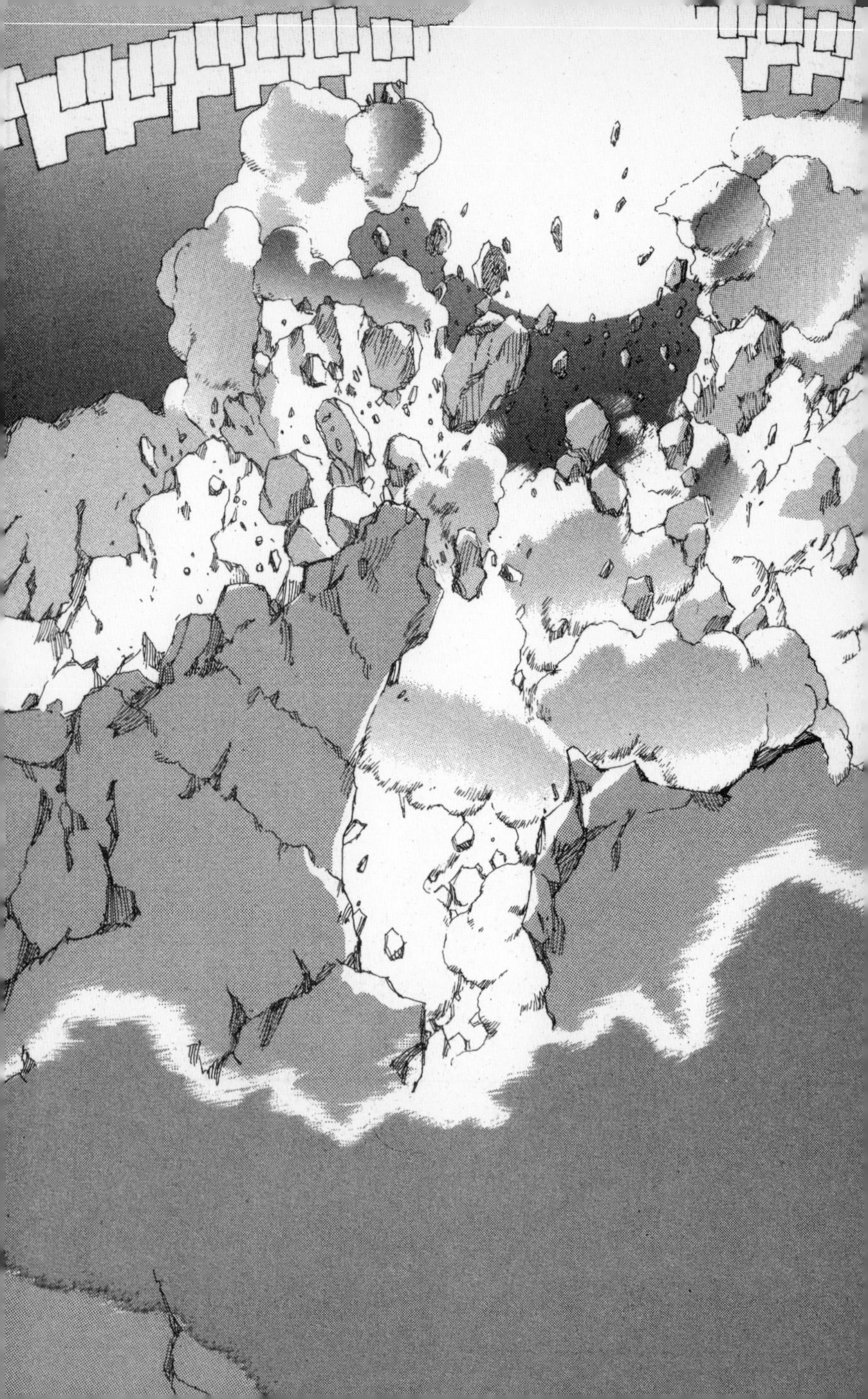

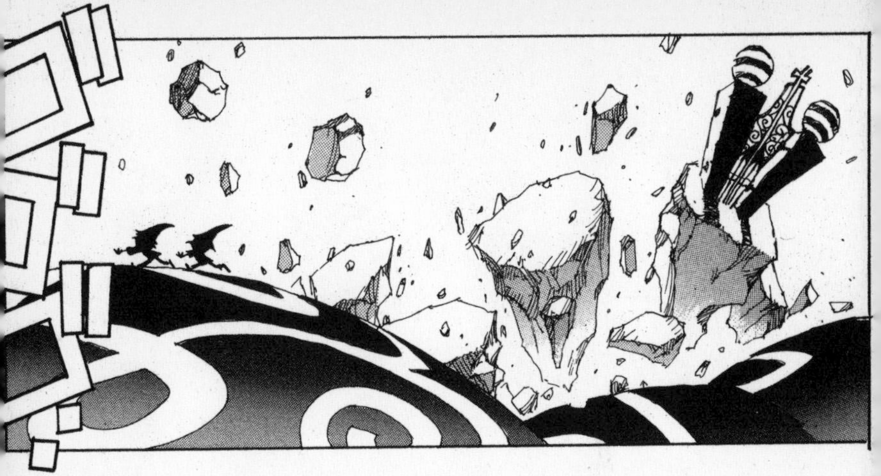
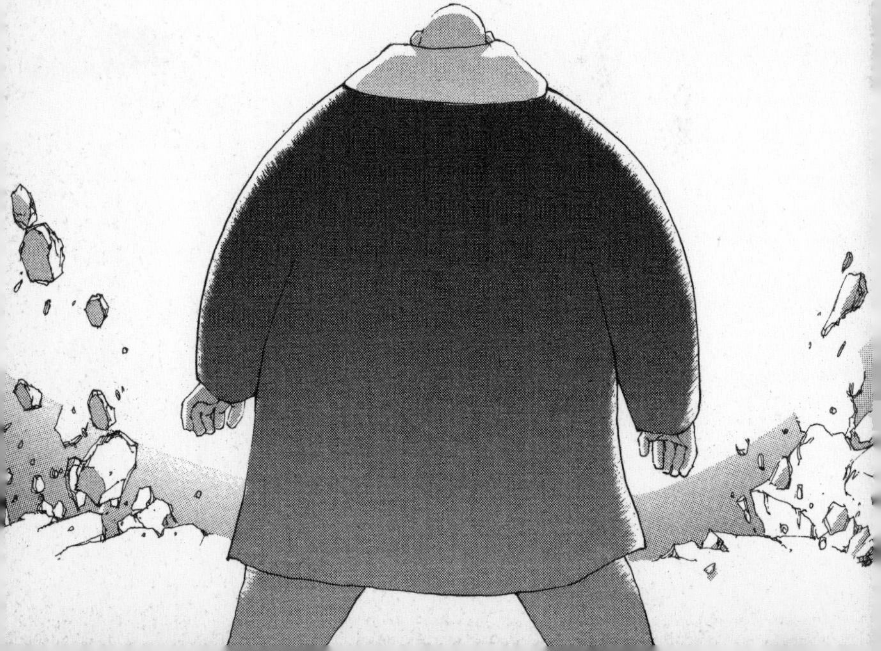

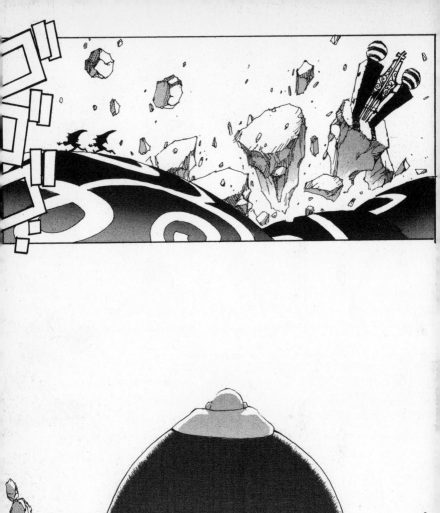

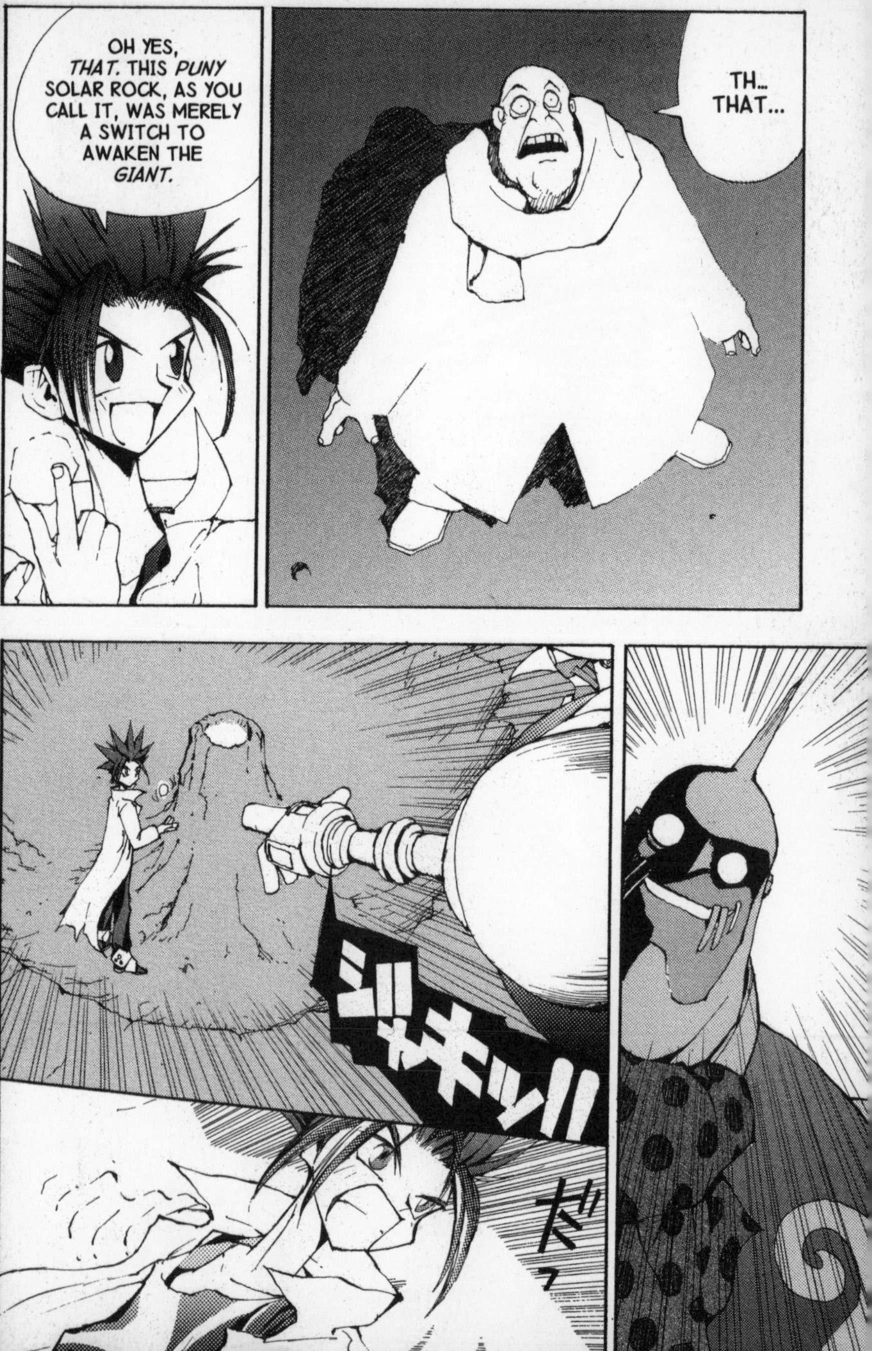
TH... THAT...
OH YES, THAT. THIS PUNY SOLAR ROCK, AS YOU CALL IT, WAS MERELY A SWITCH TO AWAKEN THE GIANT.

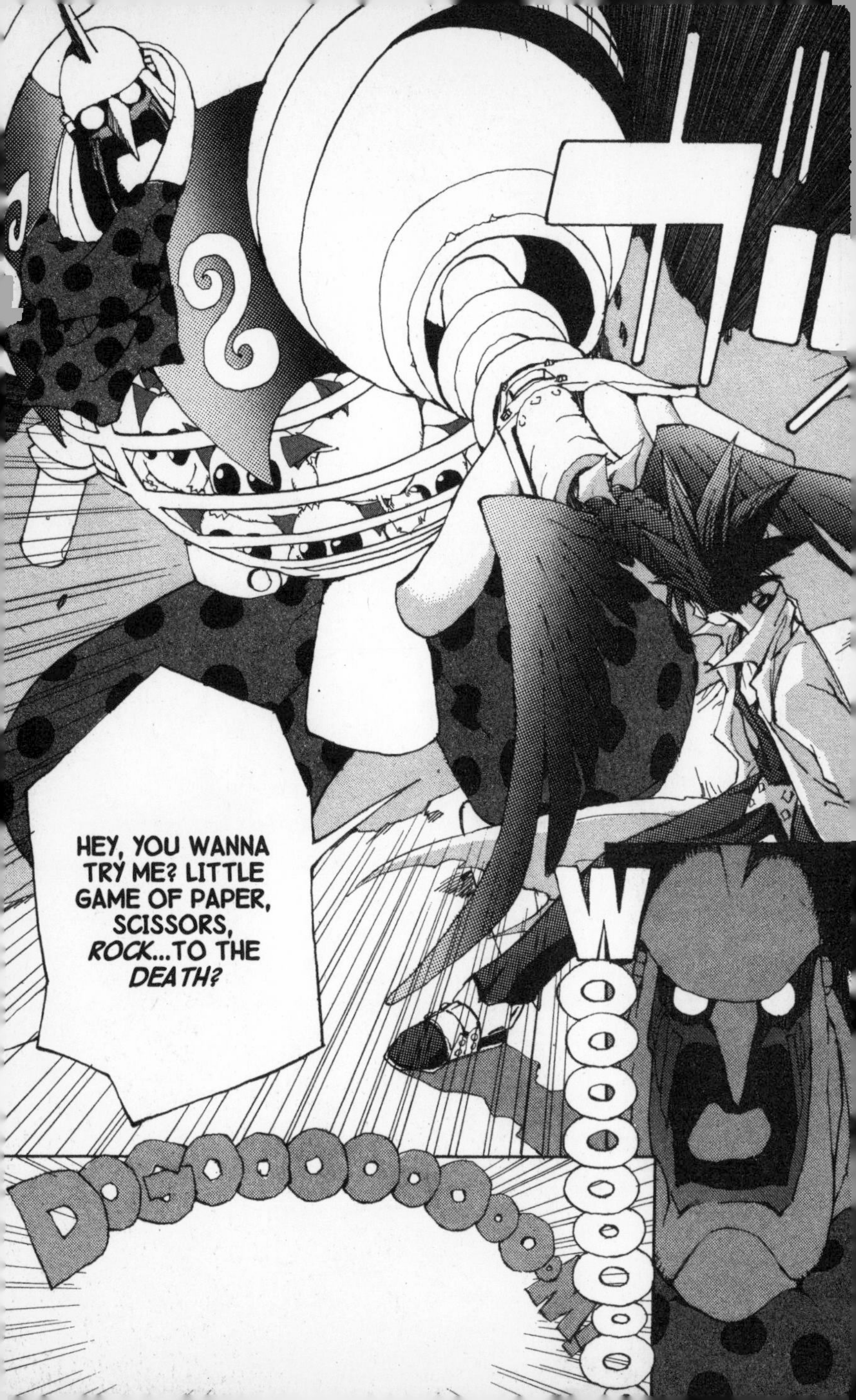
HEY, YOU WANNA TRY ME? LITTLE GAME OF PAPER, SCISSORS, *ROCK*...TO THE *DEATH*?
WOOOOOOOOOOO
DOGOOOOOOOOOOM

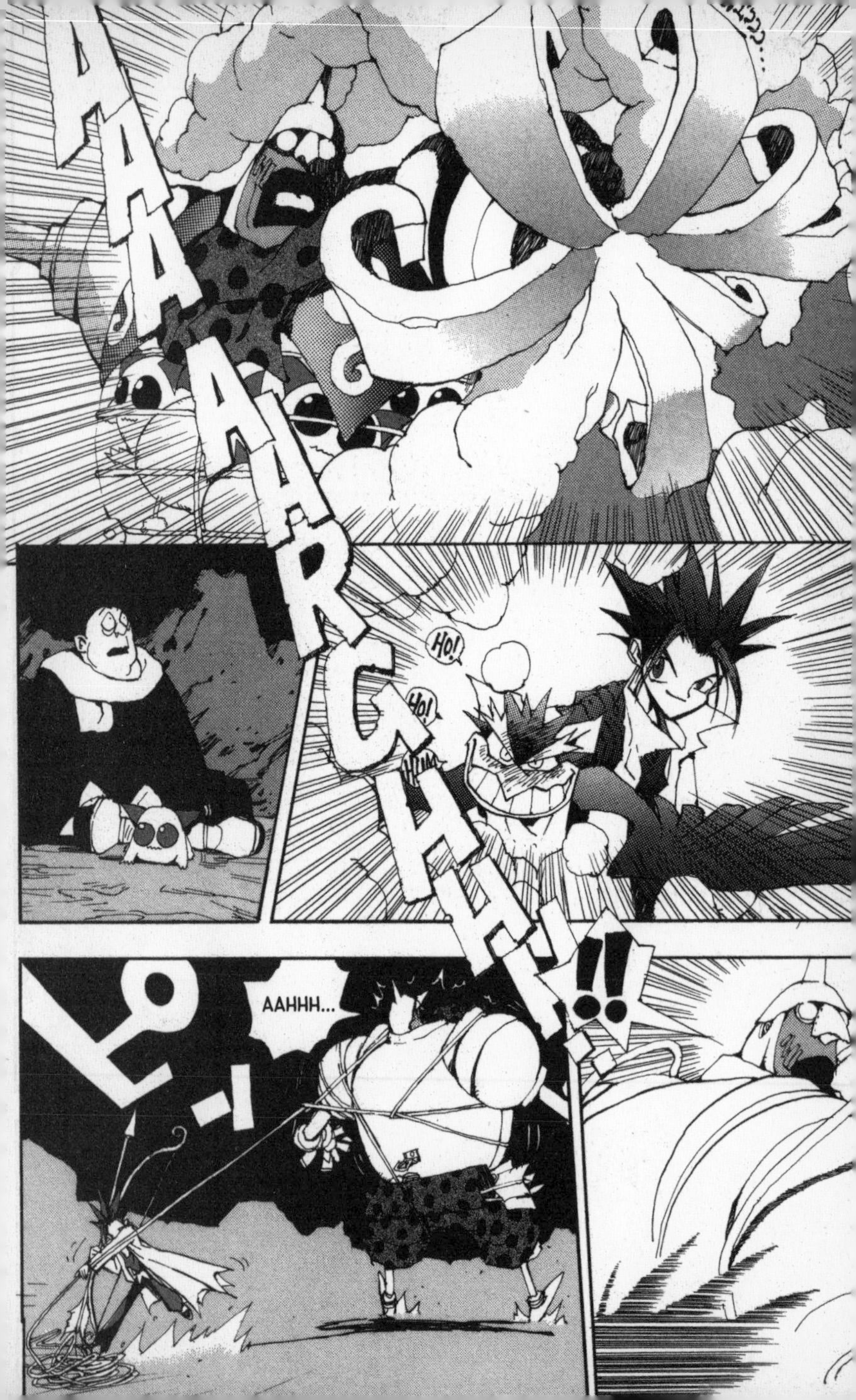
AAAARGCHH!!
HO!
HO!
AAHHH...
?!

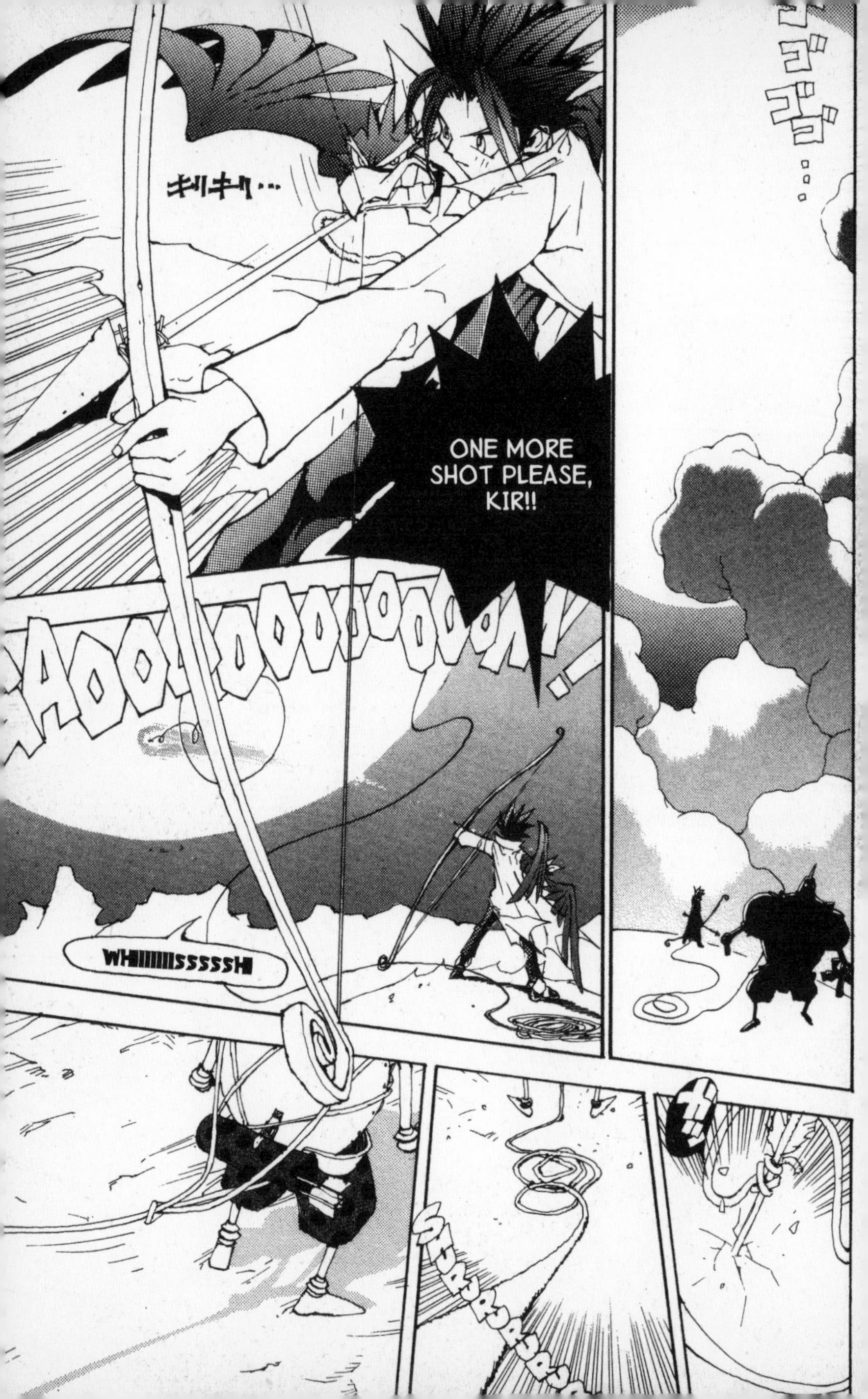
ゴゴゴ…
キリキリ…
ONE MORE SHOT PLEASE, KIR!!
AOOOOOOOOOON!!
WHIIIIISSSSSH
SHURURURU

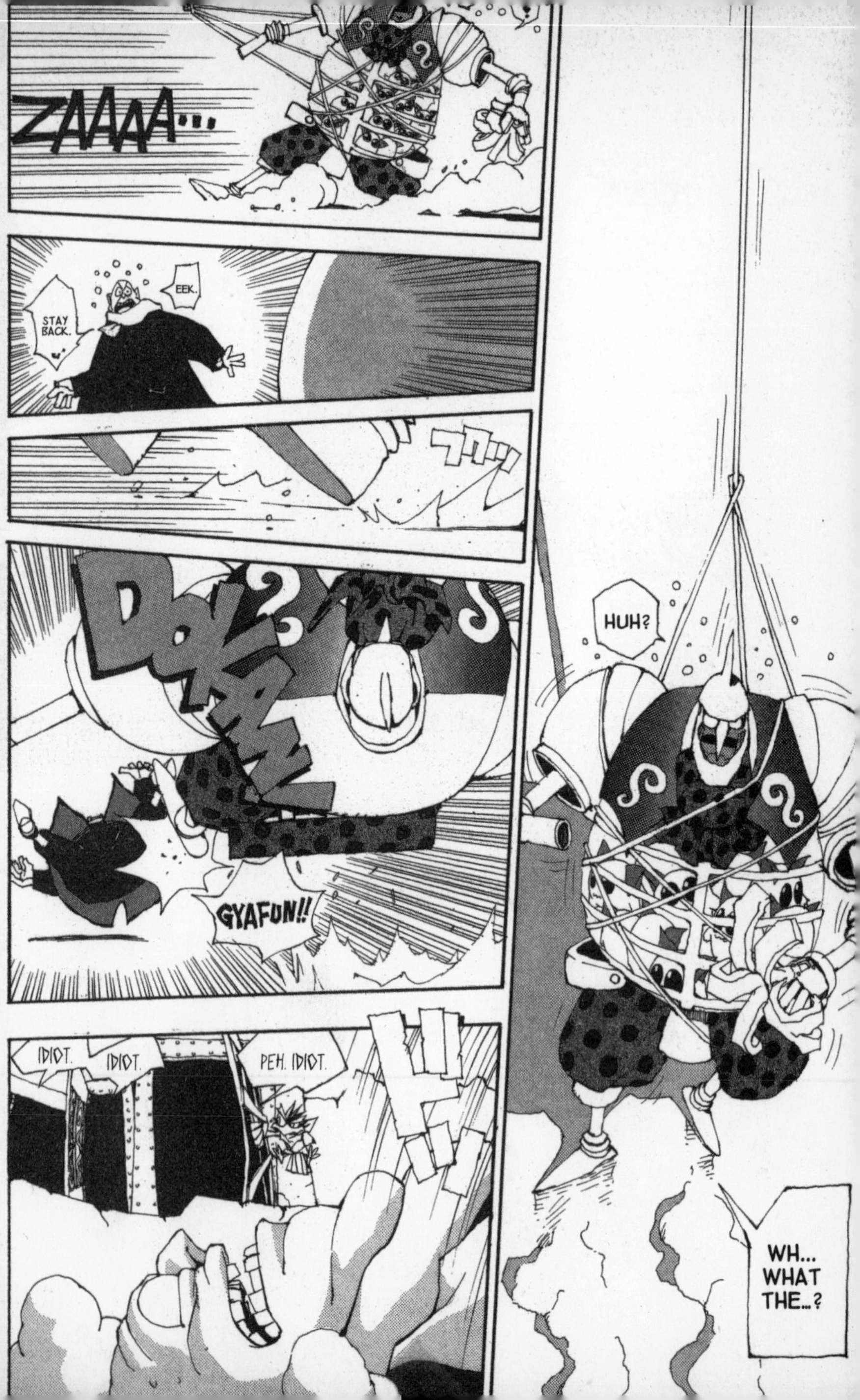
HUH?
WH... WHAT THE...?
ZAAAA...
EEK.
STAY BACK.
DOKAN
GYAFUN!!
PEH. IDIOT.
IDIOT.
IDIOT.

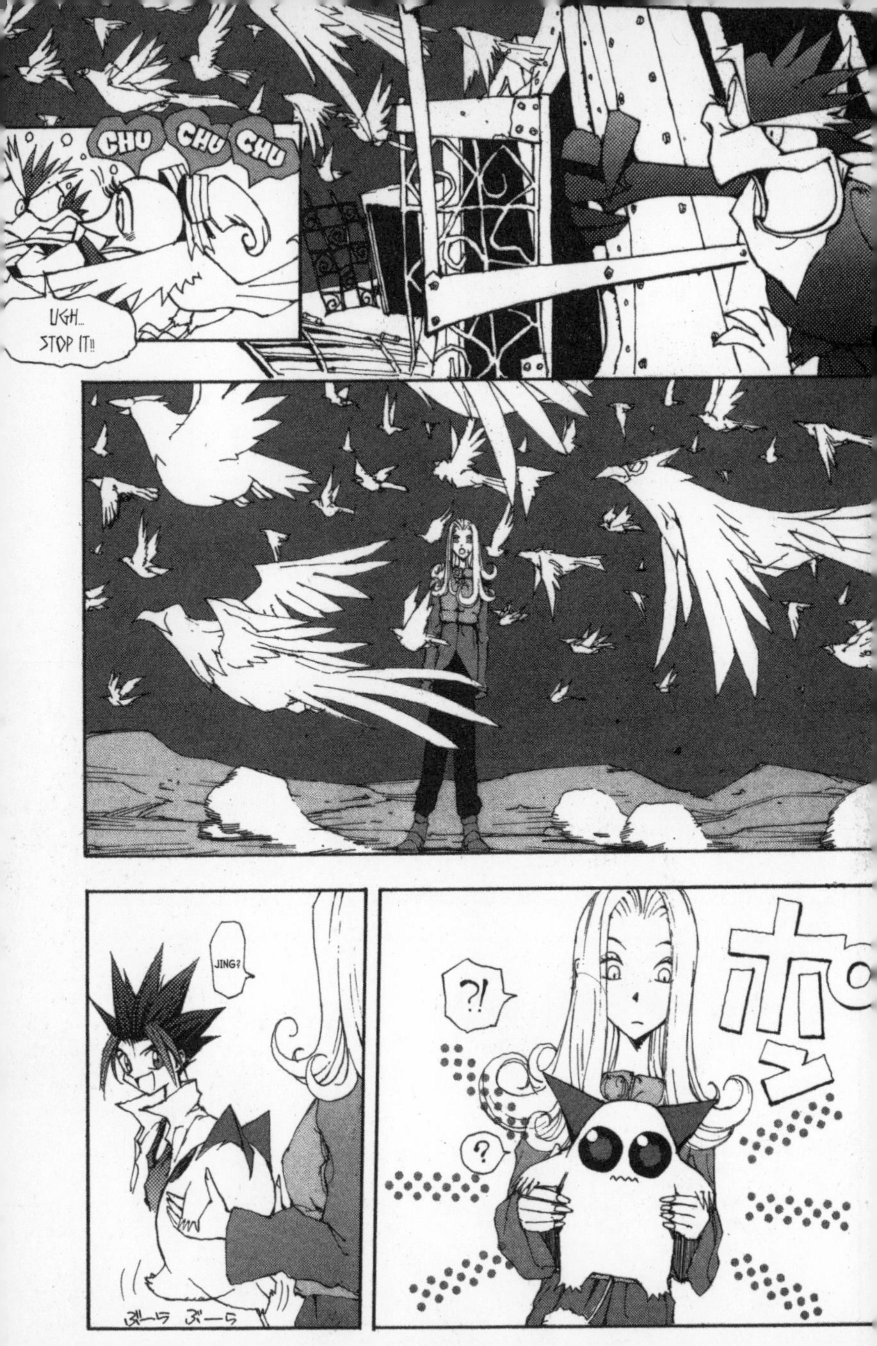
CHU CHU CHU
UGH... STOP IT!!
?!
?
ポッ
JING?
ぶーら ぶーら

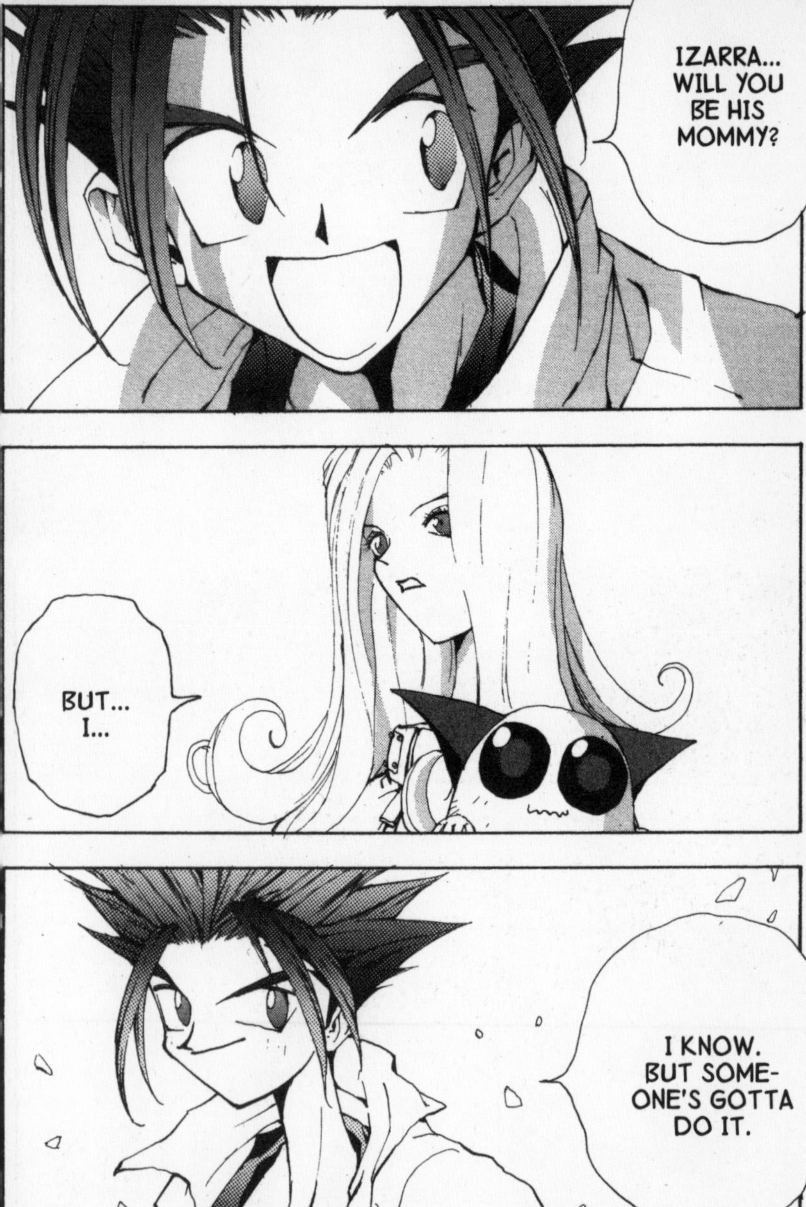
IZARRA... WILL YOU BE HIS MOMMY?
BUT... I...
I KNOW. BUT SOME-ONE'S GOTTA DO IT.

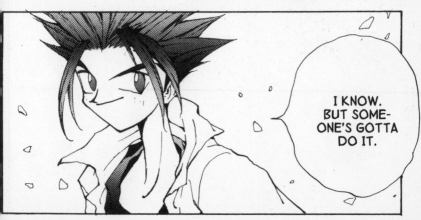

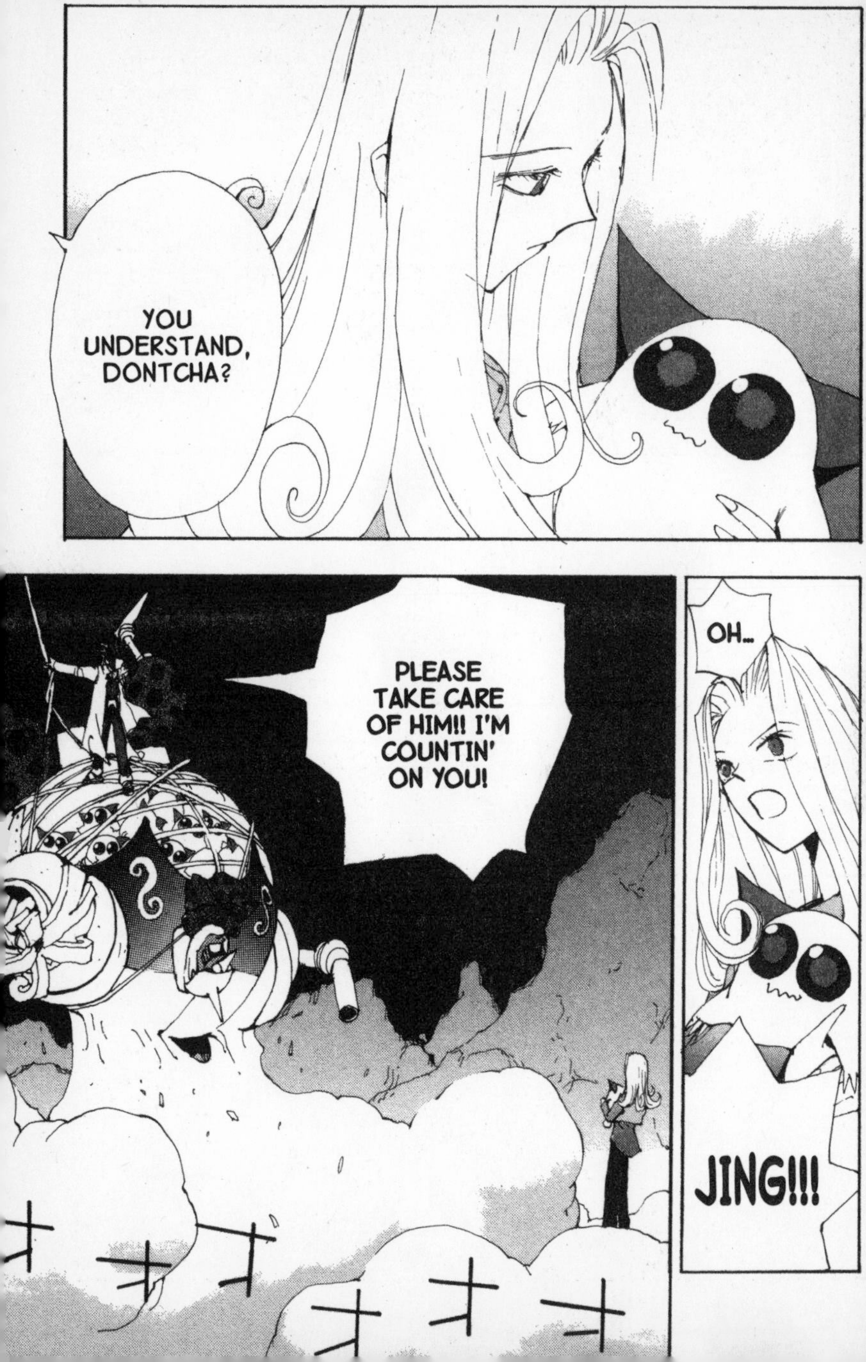
YOU UNDERSTAND, DONTCHA?
OH...
JING!!!
PLEASE TAKE CARE OF HIM!! I'M COUNTIN' ON YOU!

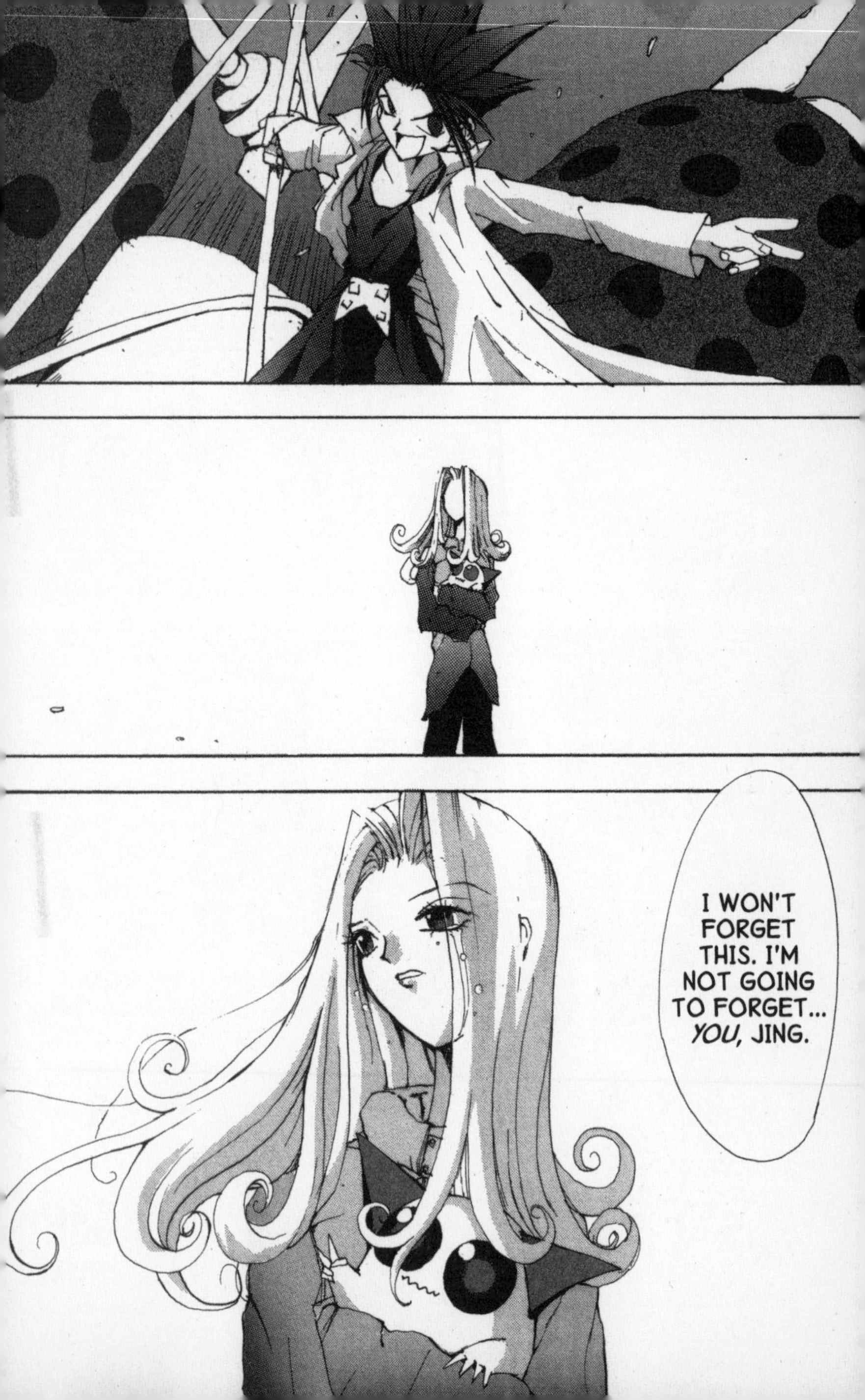
I WON'T FORGET THIS. I'M NOT GOING TO FORGET... *YOU*, JING.

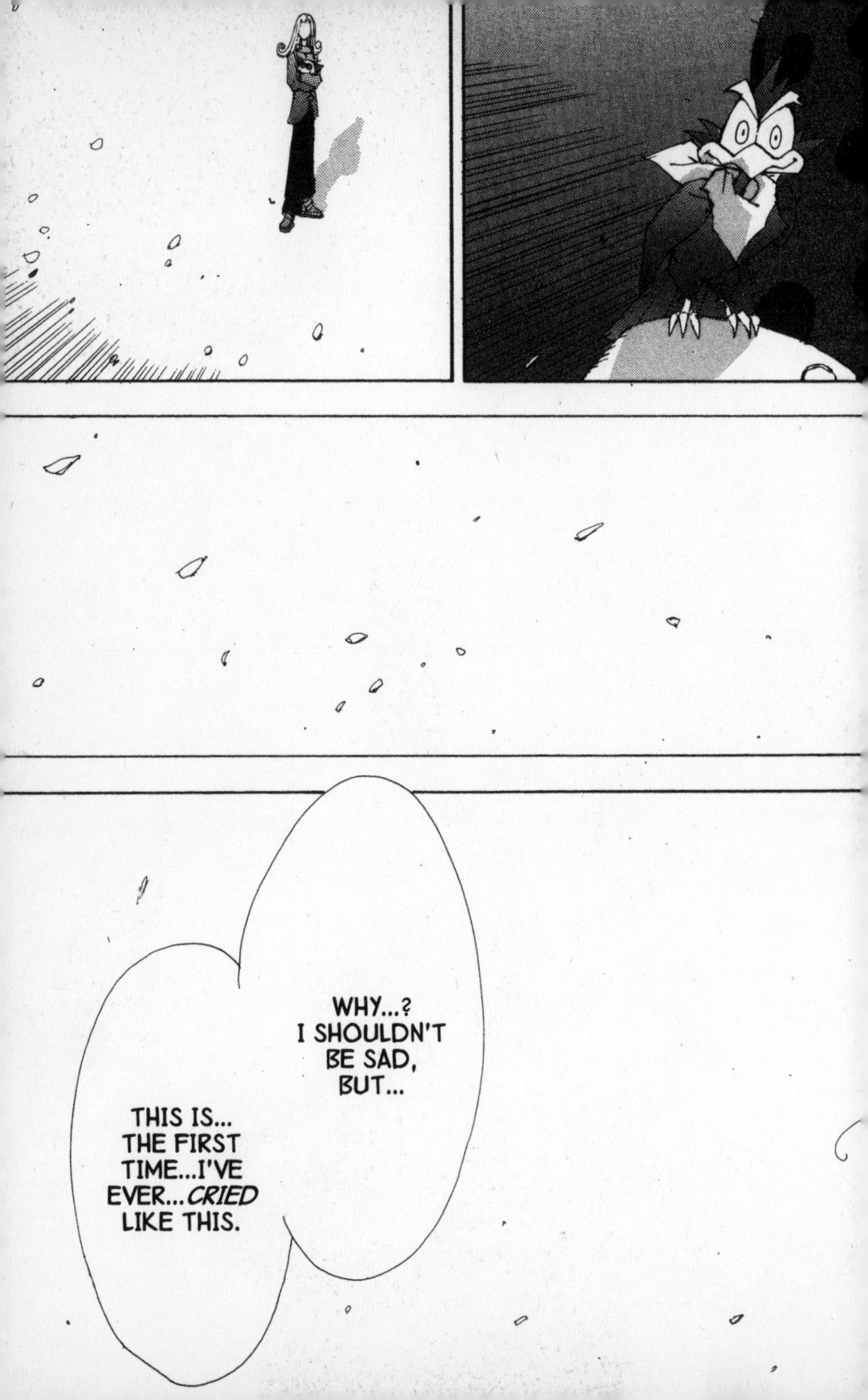
WHY...? I SHOULDN'T BE SAD, BUT...
THIS IS... THE FIRST TIME...I'VE EVER...*CRIED* LIKE THIS.

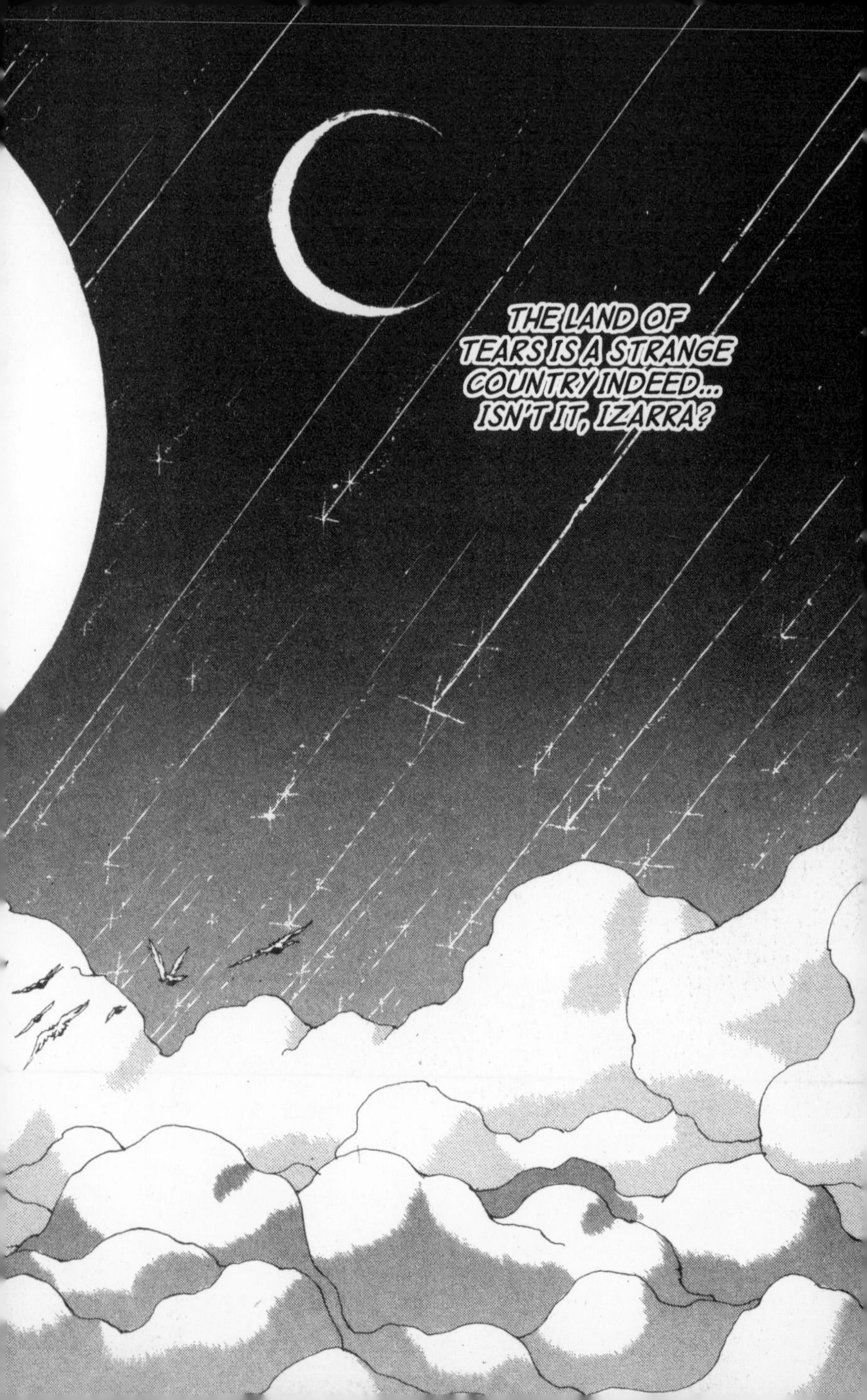
THE LAND OF TEARS IS A STRANGE COUNTRY INDEED... ISN'T IT, IZARRA?

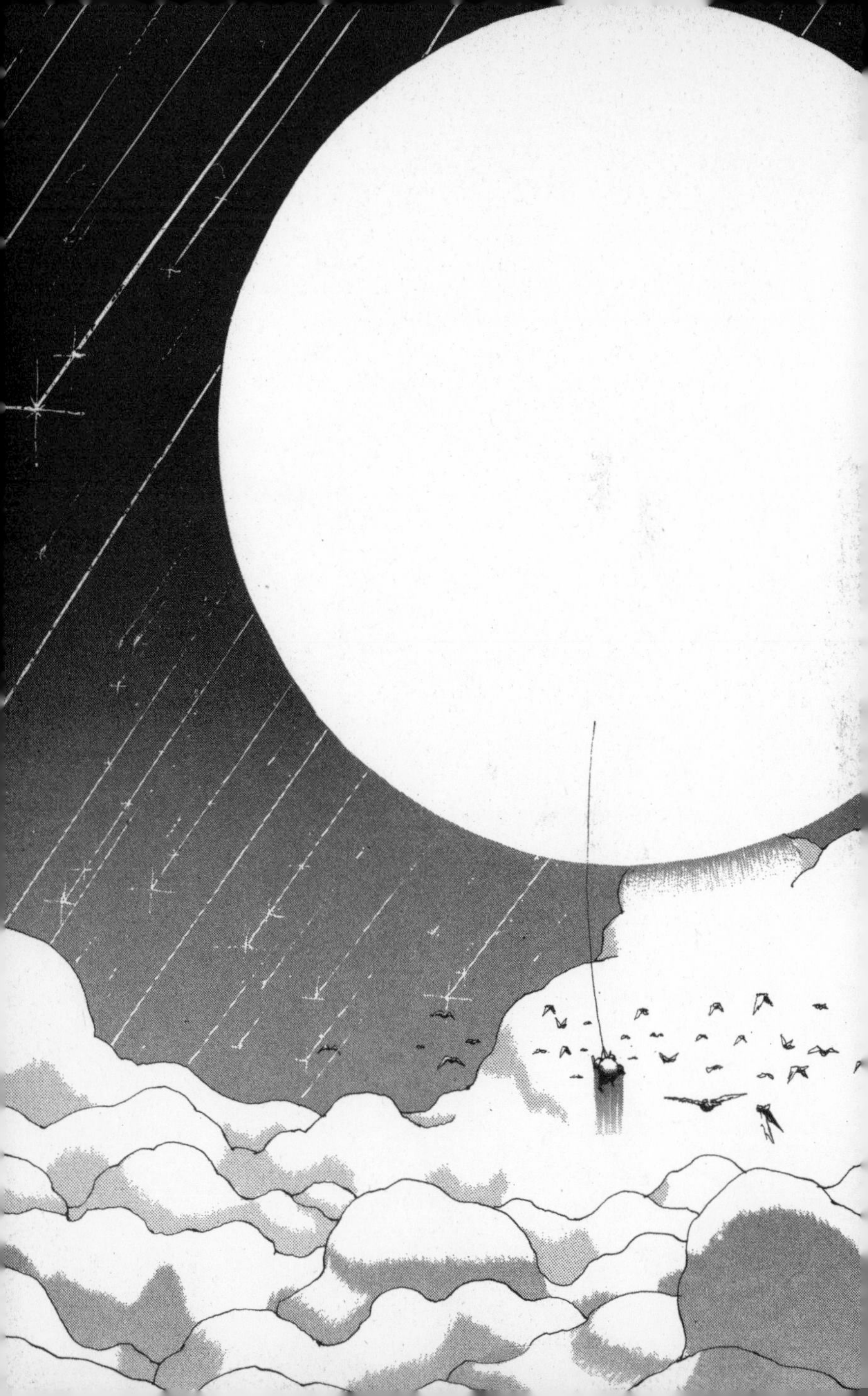

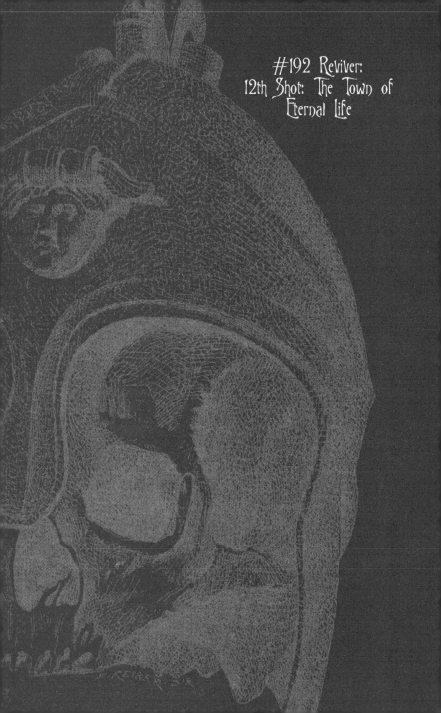

#192 Reviver:
12th Shot: The Town of
Eternal Life

Known as the everlasting ancient city, Reviver is thought to have originated as an artificial island built on the ocean for the Galabed Committee as a factory site for its famous perpetual motion machines. Before long, the machines' extremely delicate power was found to aid in the perpetuation of human life itself, finally casting light onto the mystery of eternal youth...mankind's biggest dream.

However, at the heart of this process were secrets not to be removed from the premises. This spawned the ironic custom of putting any who attempted to leave this island of eternal life...to death.

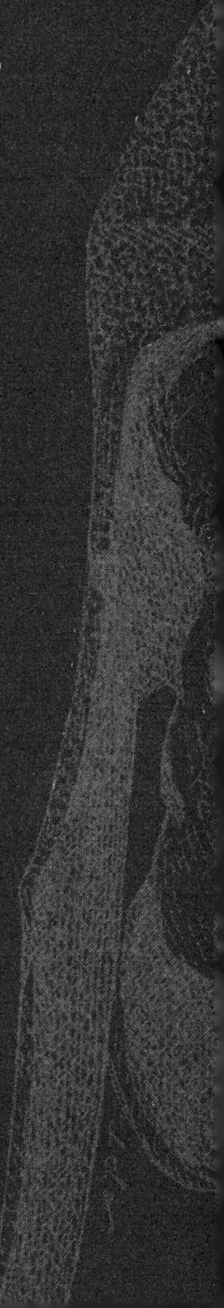

So the city's eternal life could exist only in a vacuum.

Accordingly, since all those who attempted to leave the island were killed, there is to this day no way to ascertain its whereabouts...presuming humanity should be allowed that knowledge at all.

(From Chapter 1 of All Walking Tour of Cities You'll Never See)

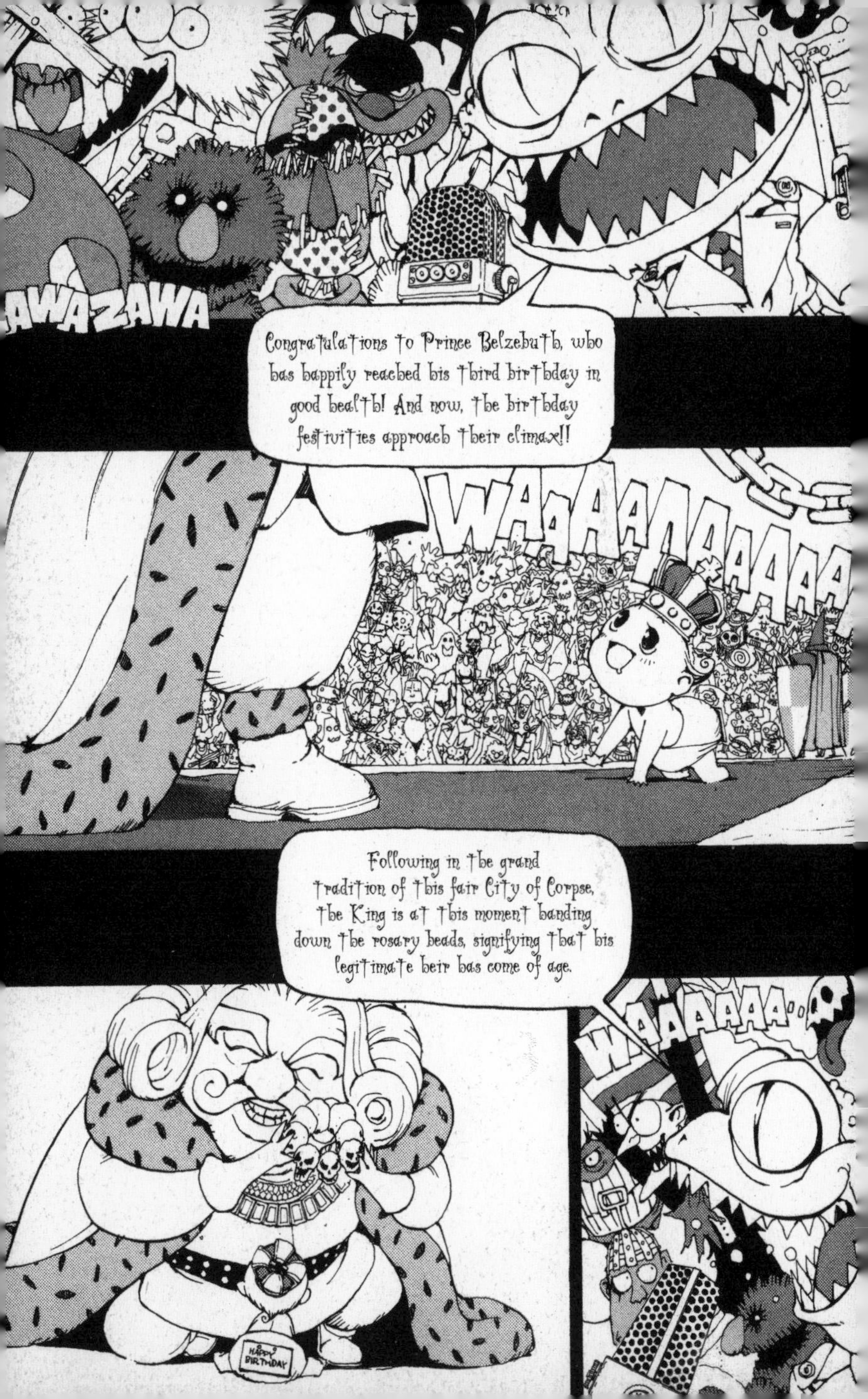
AWAZAWA
Congratulations to Prince Belzebuth, who has happily reached his third birthday in good health! And now, the birthday festivities approach their climax!!
WAAAAAAAAA
Following in the grand tradition of this fair City of Corpse, the King is at this moment handing down the rosary beads, signifying that his legitimate heir has come of age.
WAAAAAA..
HAPPY BIRTHDAY

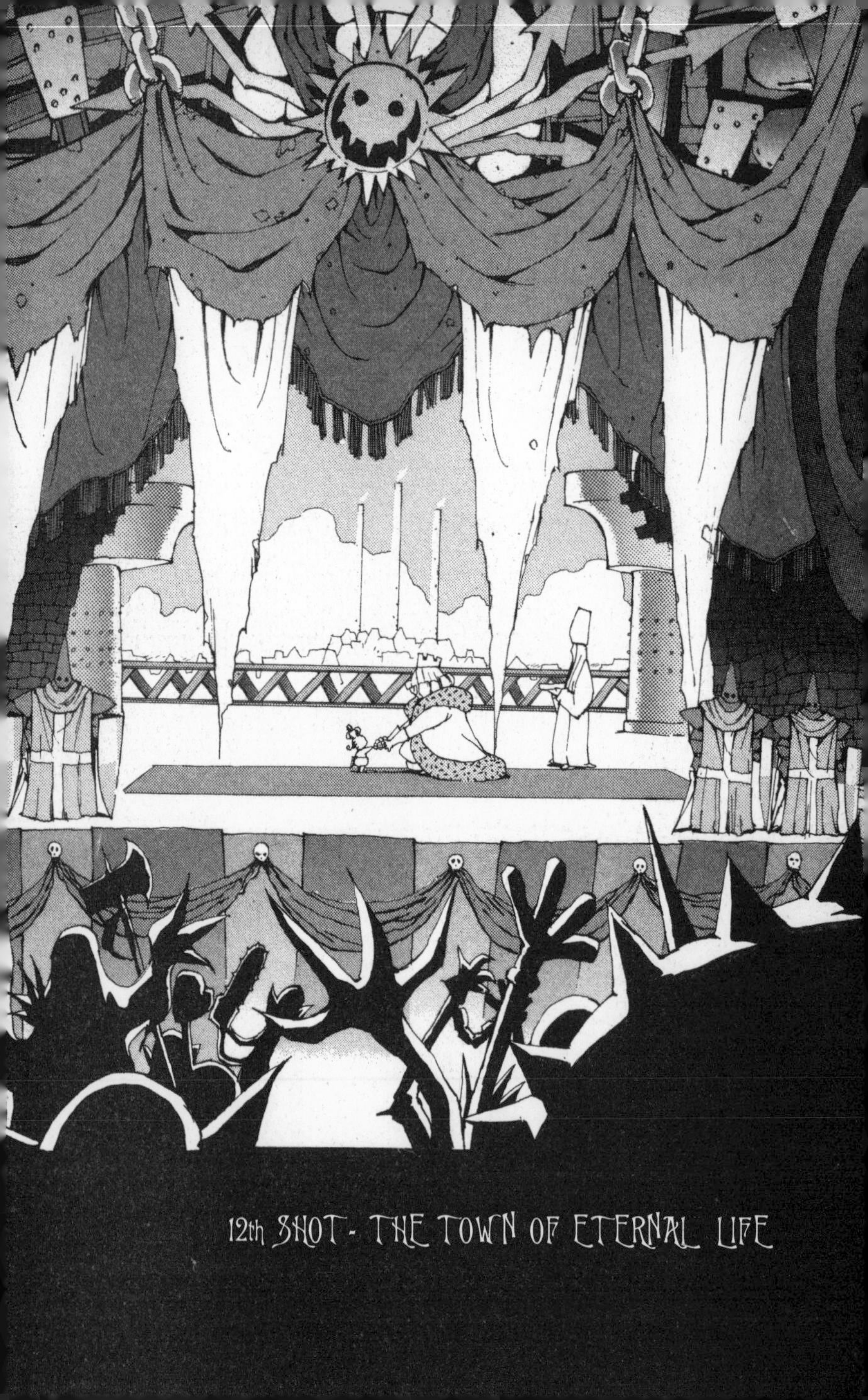
12th SHOT - THE TOWN OF ETERNAL LIFE

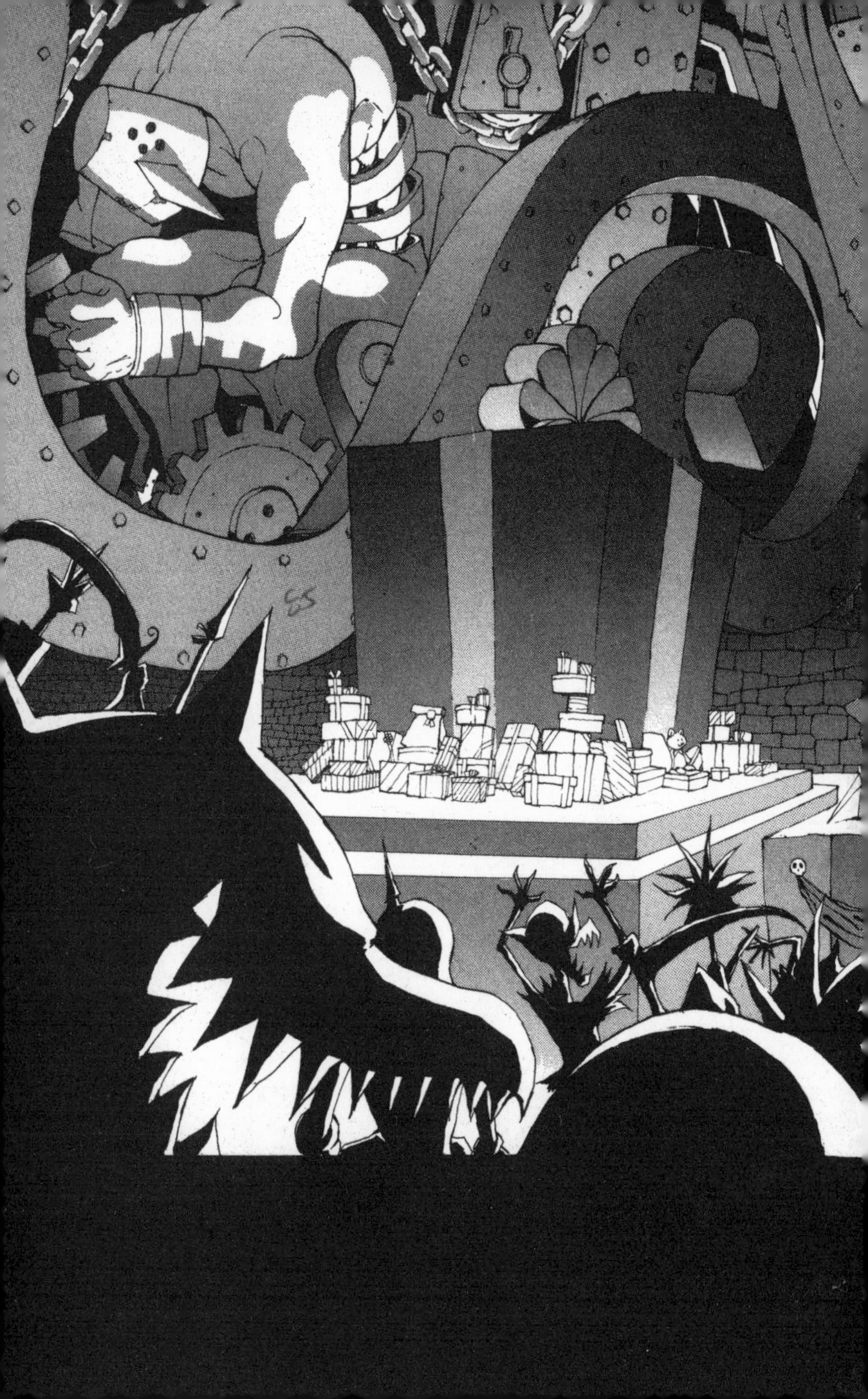

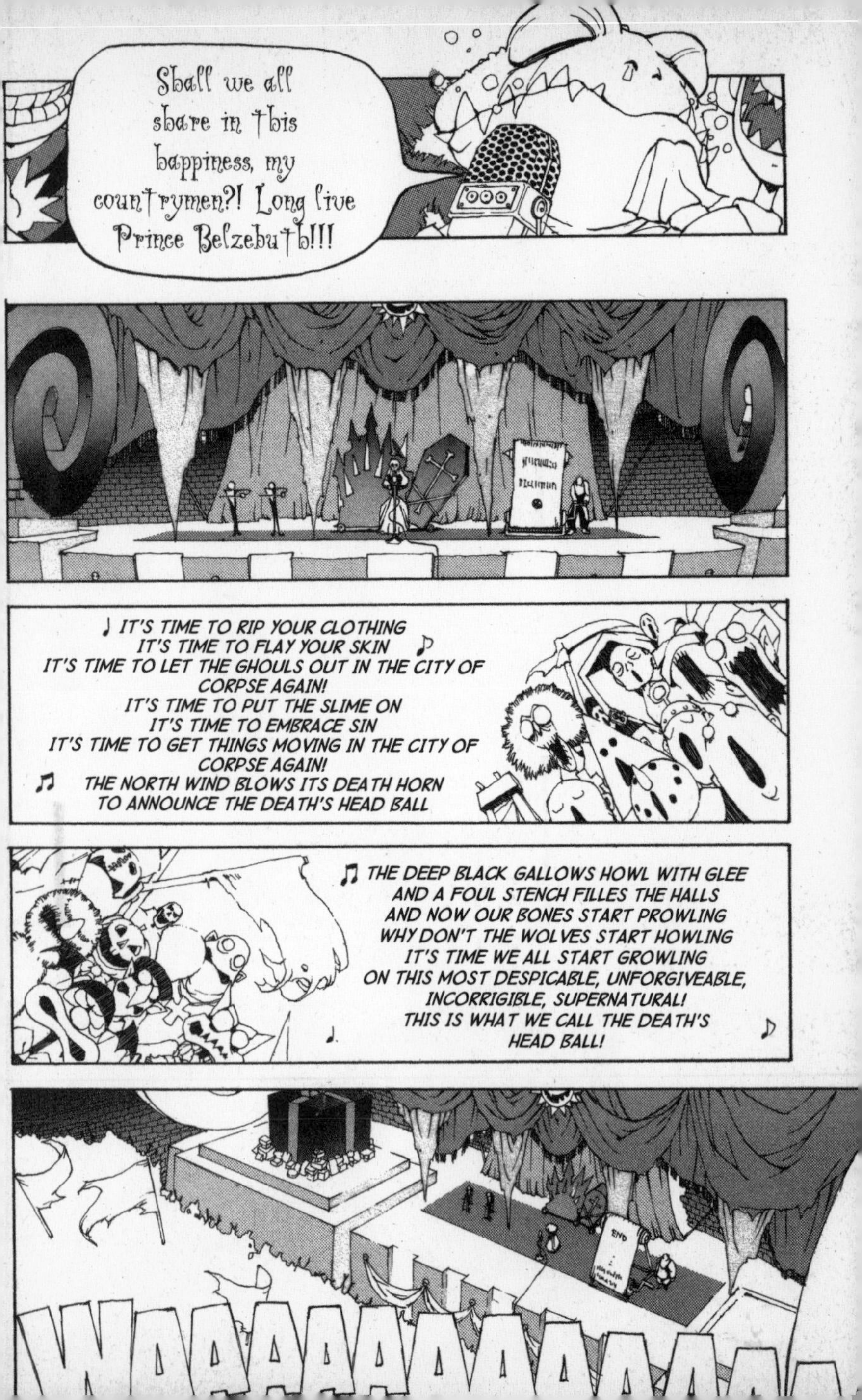
Shall we all share in this happiness, my countrymen?! Long live Prince Belzebuth!!!
♩ IT'S TIME TO RIP YOUR CLOTHING
IT'S TIME TO FLAY YOUR SKIN ♪
IT'S TIME TO LET THE GHOULS OUT IN THE CITY OF CORPSE AGAIN!
IT'S TIME TO PUT THE SLIME ON
IT'S TIME TO EMBRACE SIN
IT'S TIME TO GET THINGS MOVING IN THE CITY OF CORPSE AGAIN!
♫ THE NORTH WIND BLOWS ITS DEATH HORN
TO ANNOUNCE THE DEATH'S HEAD BALL
♫ THE DEEP BLACK GALLOWS HOWL WITH GLEE
AND A FOUL STENCH FILLES THE HALLS
AND NOW OUR BONES START PROWLING
WHY DON'T THE WOLVES START HOWLING
IT'S TIME WE ALL START GROWLING
ON THIS MOST DESPICABLE, UNFORGIVEABLE, INCORRIGIBLE, SUPERNATURAL!
THIS IS WHAT WE CALL THE DEATH'S HEAD BALL! ♩ ♪
END
WAAAAAAAAAAA

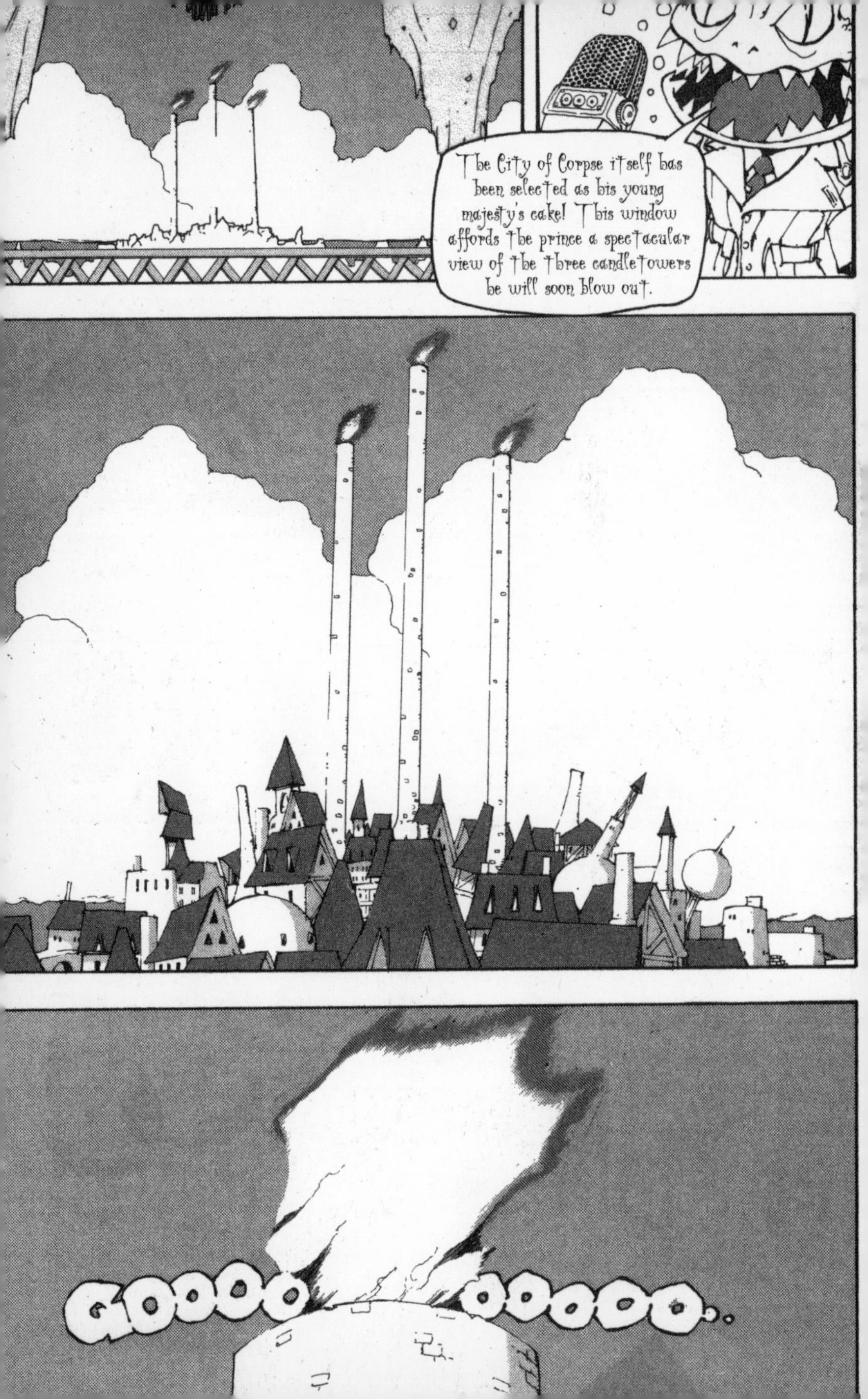

The City of Corpse itself has been selected as his young majesty's cake! This window affords the prince a spectacular view of the three candletowers he will soon blow out.
GOOOO OOOOOO..

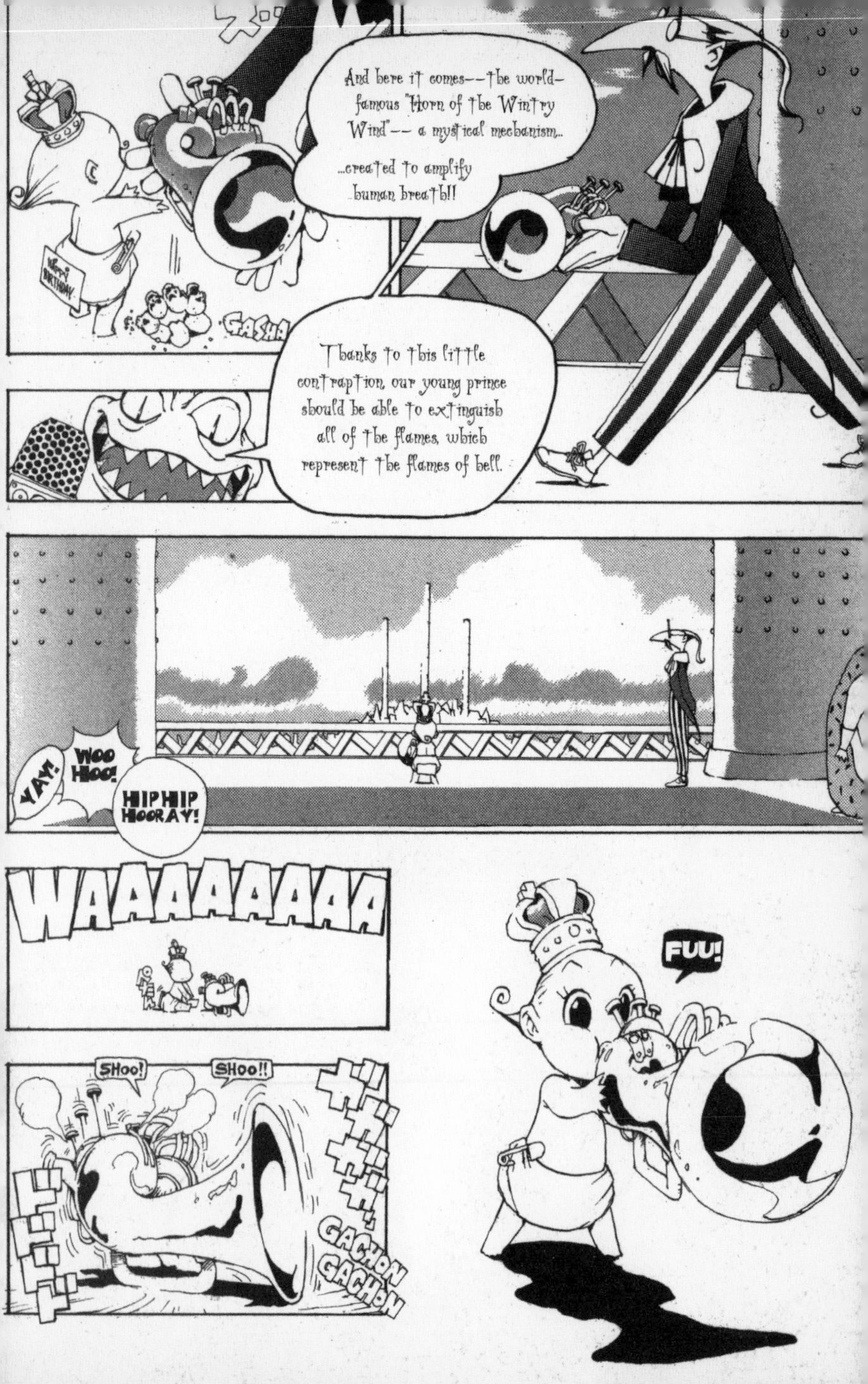
And here it comes--the world-famous "Horn of the Wintry Wind"-- a mystical mechanism...
...created to amplify human breath!!
GASHA
Thanks to this little contraption, our young prince should be able to extinguish all of the flames, which represent the flames of hell.
WOO HOO!
YAY!
HIP HIP HOORAY!
FUU!
WAAAAAAAA
SHOO!!
SHOO!
GACHON GACHON

Although some expected a disturbance on this occasion as the self-professed "King of Bandits" had announced an intention to steal the rosary beads at the ceremony, they appear for now to be safe and sound...

OH, CRUMBS.

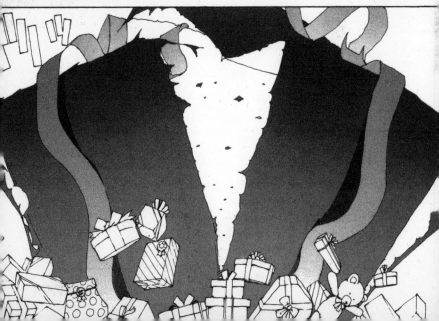

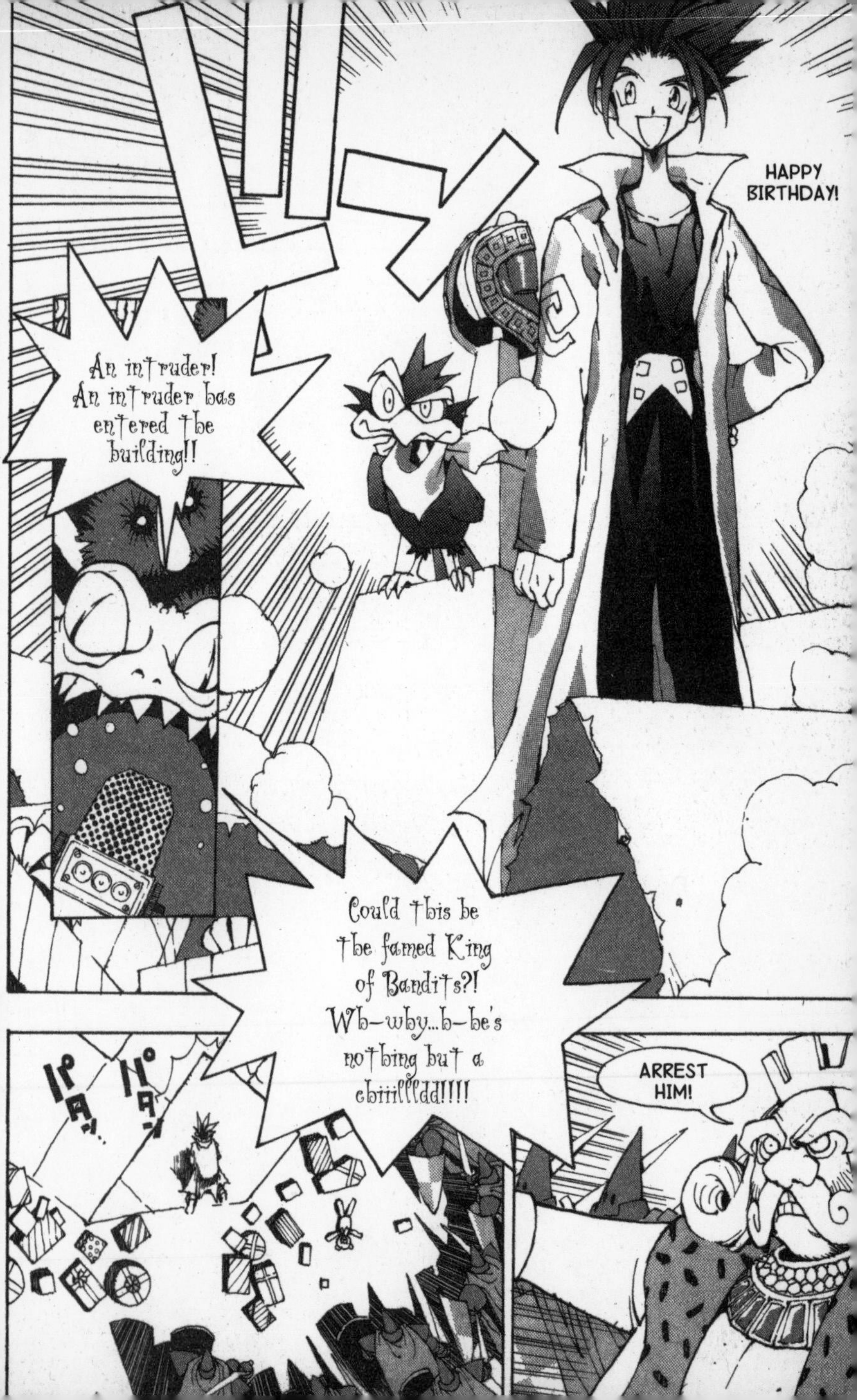
HAPPY BIRTHDAY!
An intruder! An intruder has entered the building!!
Could this be the famed King of Bandits?! Wh-why...h-he's nothing but a chiiilldd!!!!
ARREST HIM!

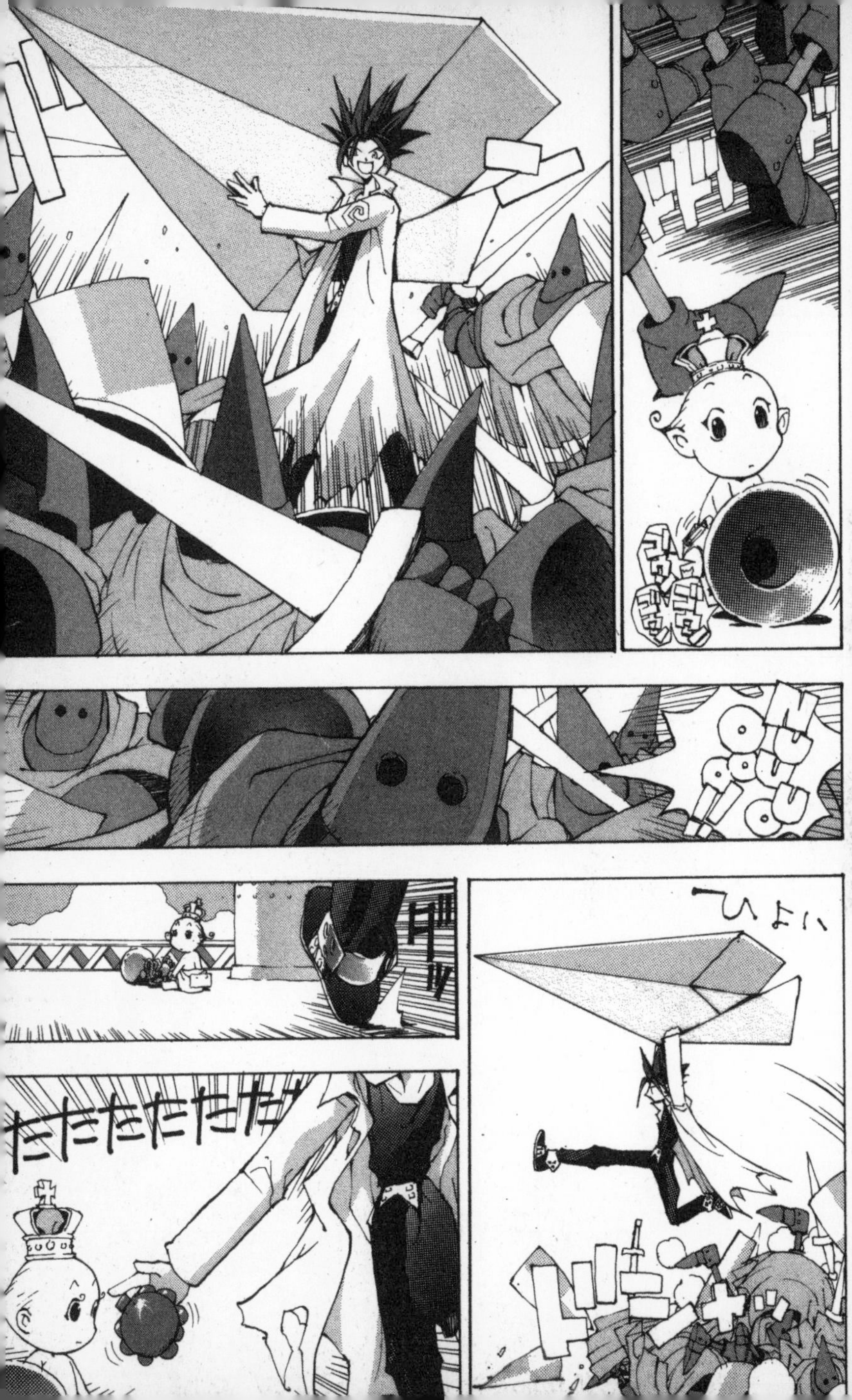
ダッ
ひょい
たたたたたたっ

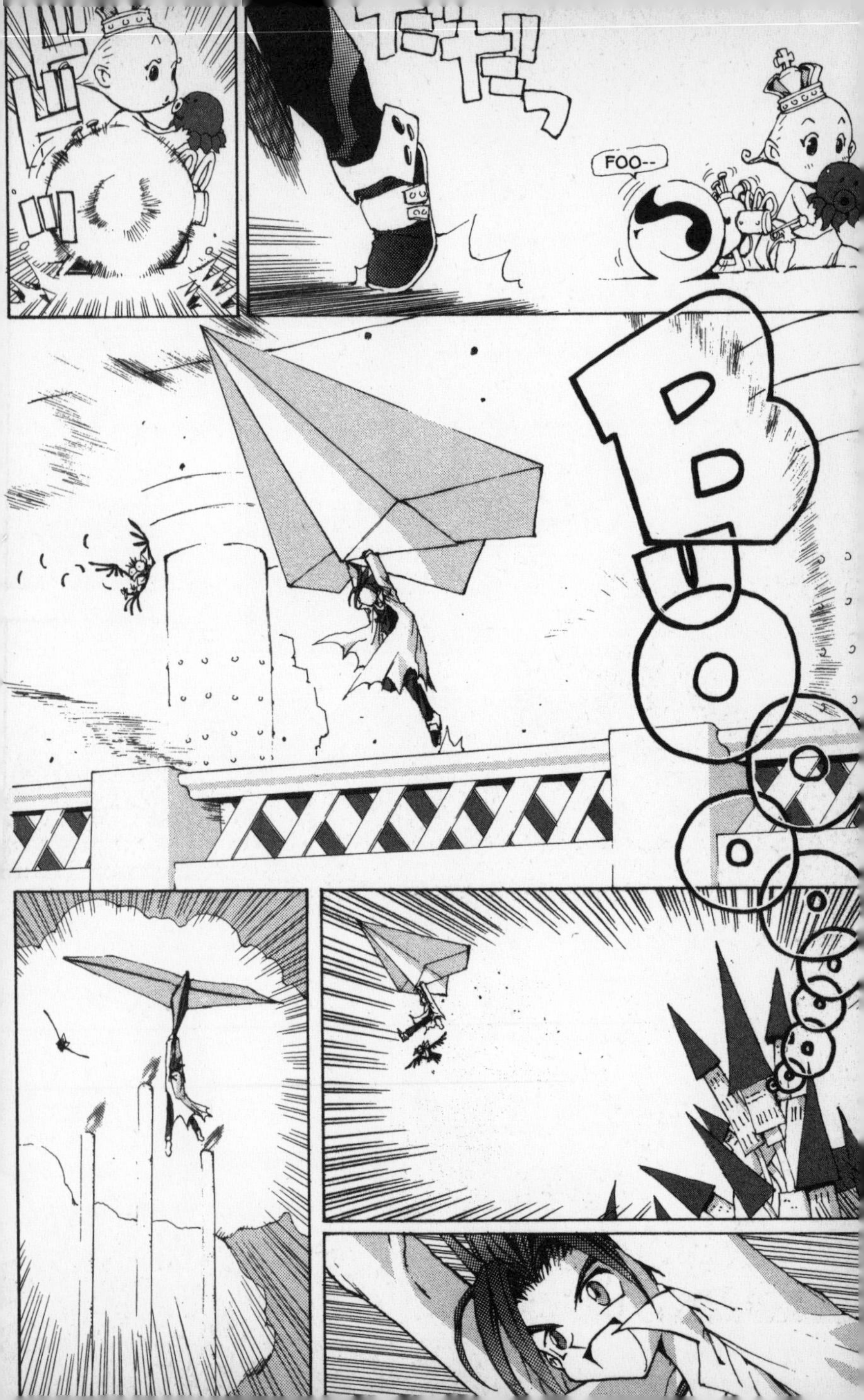
FOO--

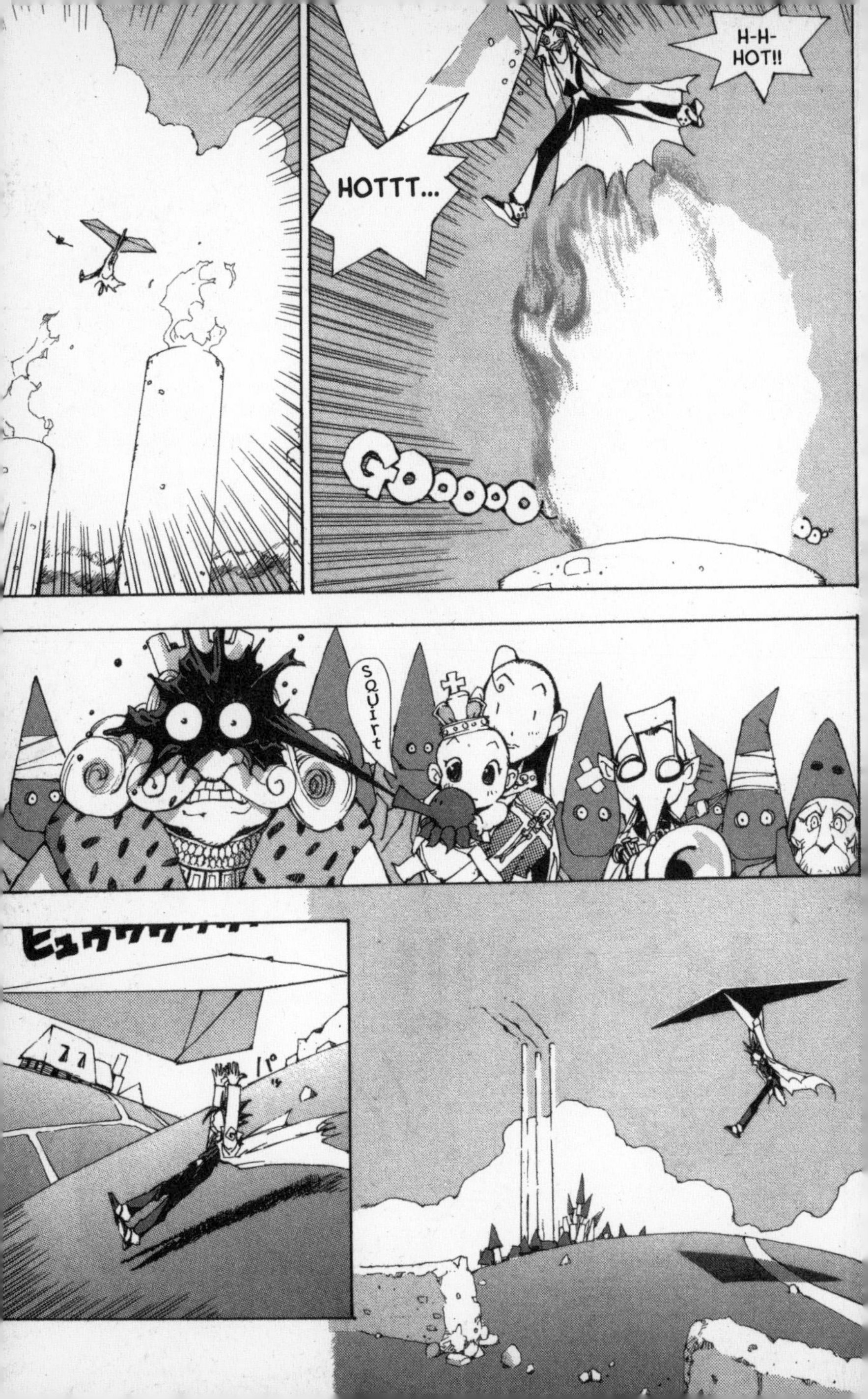
H-H-HOT!!
HOTTT...
GOoooo
SQUirt
パ

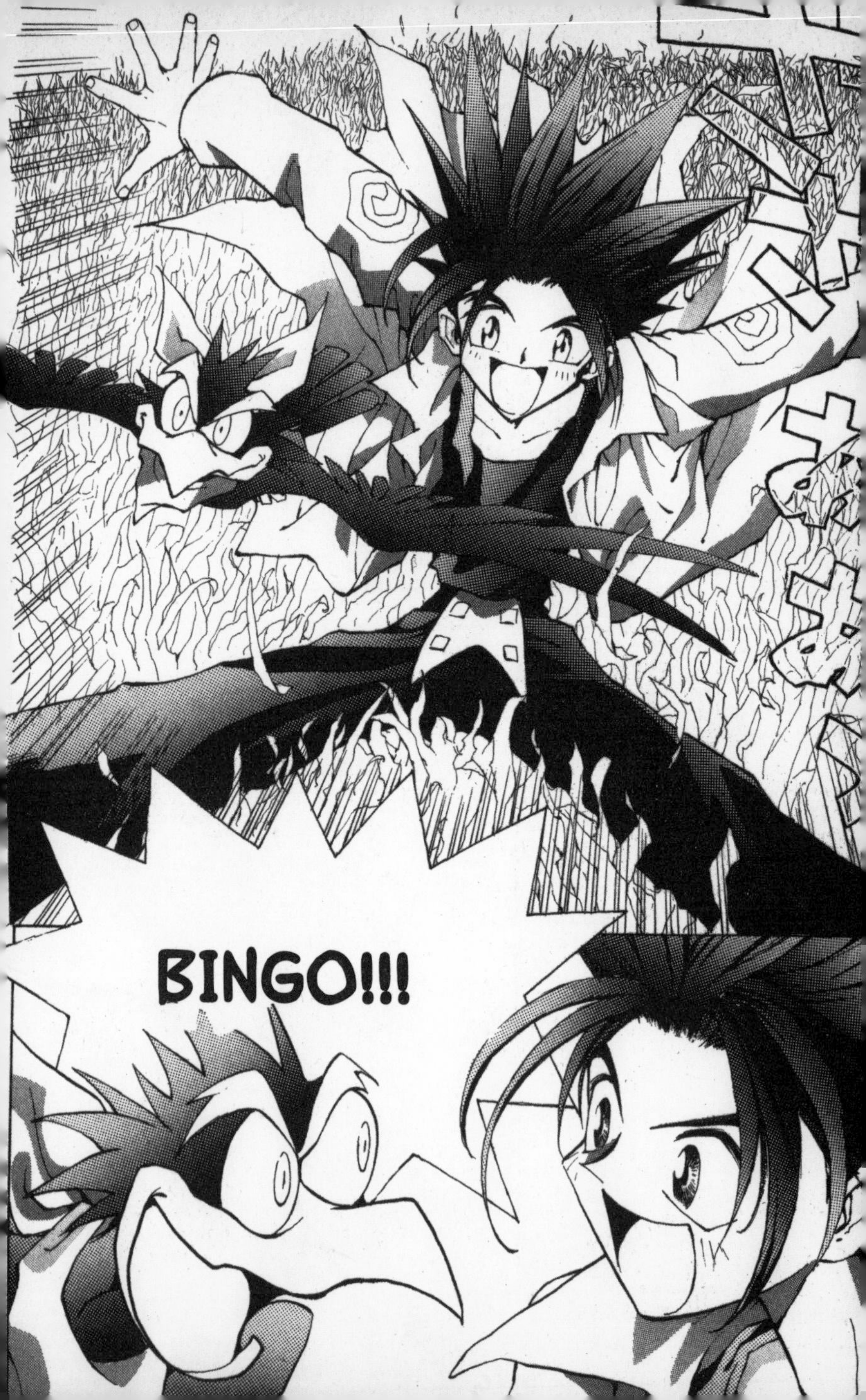
BINGO!!!

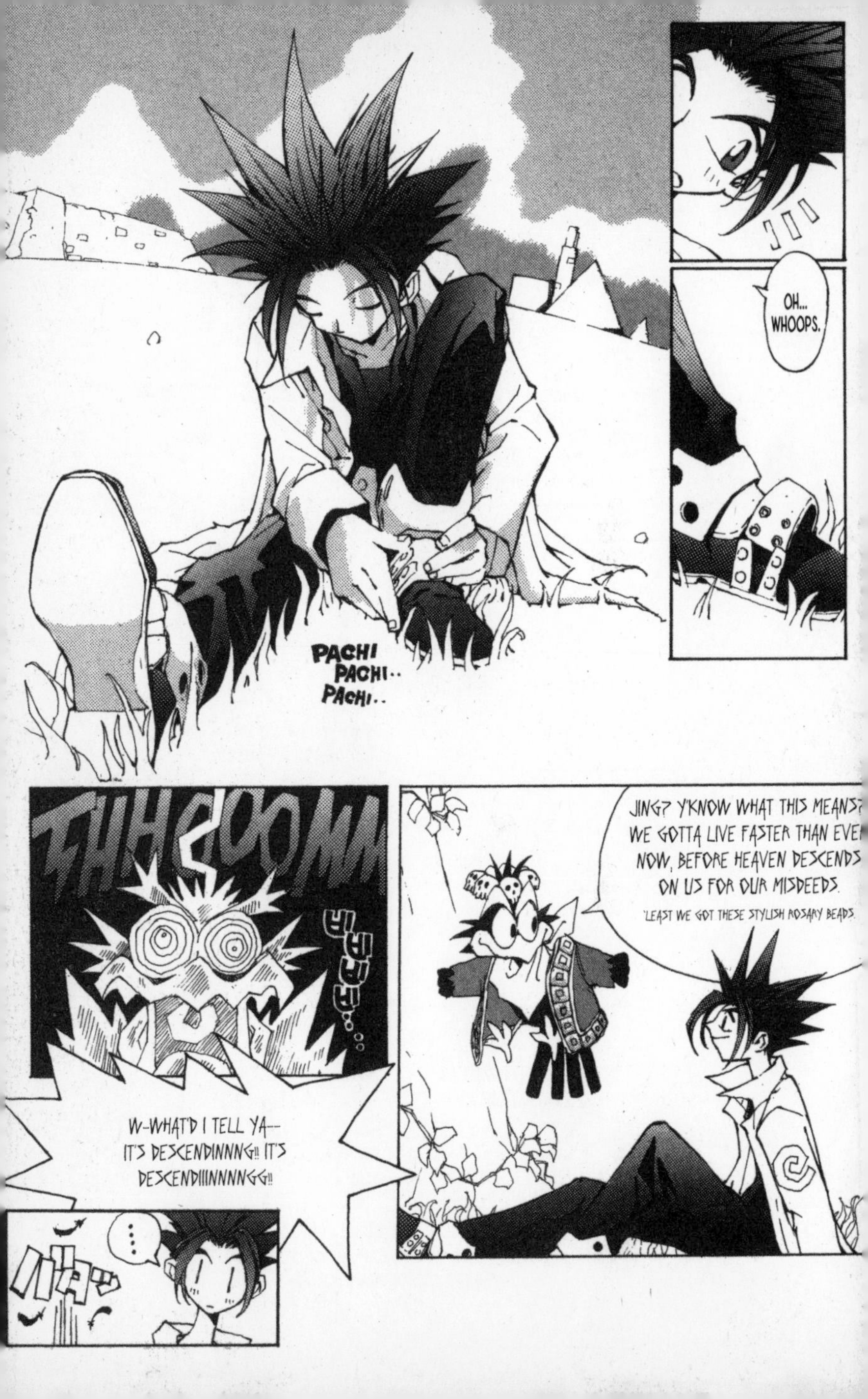
OH... WHOOPS.
PACHI PACHI.. PACHI..
JING? Y'KNOW WHAT THIS MEANS? WE GOTTA LIVE FASTER THAN EVE NOW, BEFORE HEAVEN DESCENDS ON US FOR OUR MISDEEDS.
'LEAST WE GOT THESE STYLISH ROSARY BEADS.
W-WHAT'D I TELL YA-- IT'S DESCENDINNNG!! IT'S DESCENDIIIINNNNGG!!
....

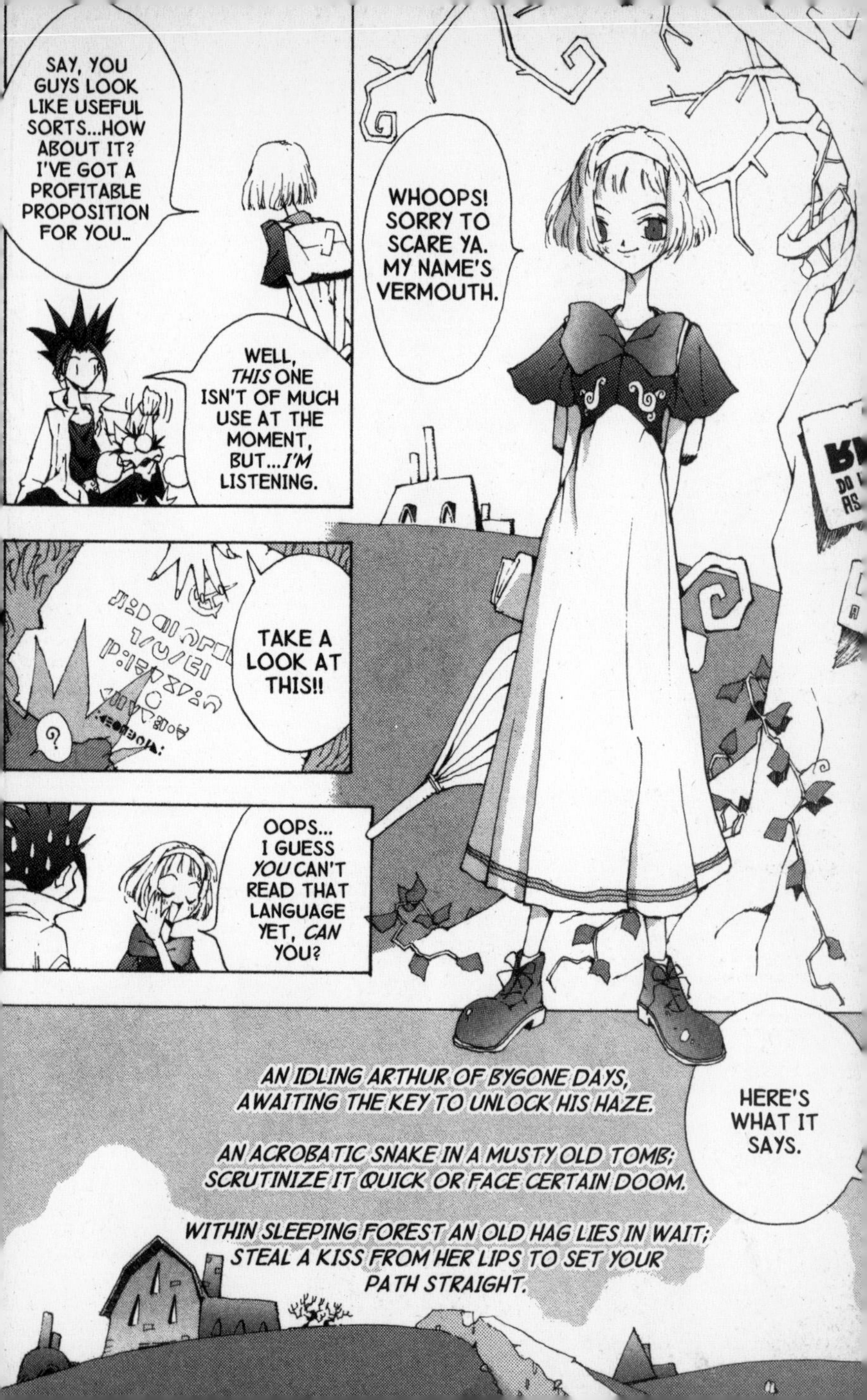
WHOOPS! SORRY TO SCARE YA. MY NAME'S VERMOUTH.
SAY, YOU GUYS LOOK LIKE USEFUL SORTS...HOW ABOUT IT? I'VE GOT A PROFITABLE PROPOSITION FOR YOU...
WELL, *THIS* ONE ISN'T OF MUCH USE AT THE MOMENT, BUT...*I'M* LISTENING.
TAKE A LOOK AT THIS!!
OOPS... I GUESS *YOU* CAN'T READ THAT LANGUAGE YET, *CAN* YOU?
HERE'S WHAT IT SAYS.
AN IDLING ARTHUR OF BYGONE DAYS, AWAITING THE KEY TO UNLOCK HIS HAZE.
AN ACROBATIC SNAKE IN A MUSTY OLD TOMB; SCRUTINIZE IT QUICK OR FACE CERTAIN DOOM.
WITHIN SLEEPING FOREST AN OLD HAG LIES IN WAIT; STEAL A KISS FROM HER LIPS TO SET YOUR PATH STRAIGHT.

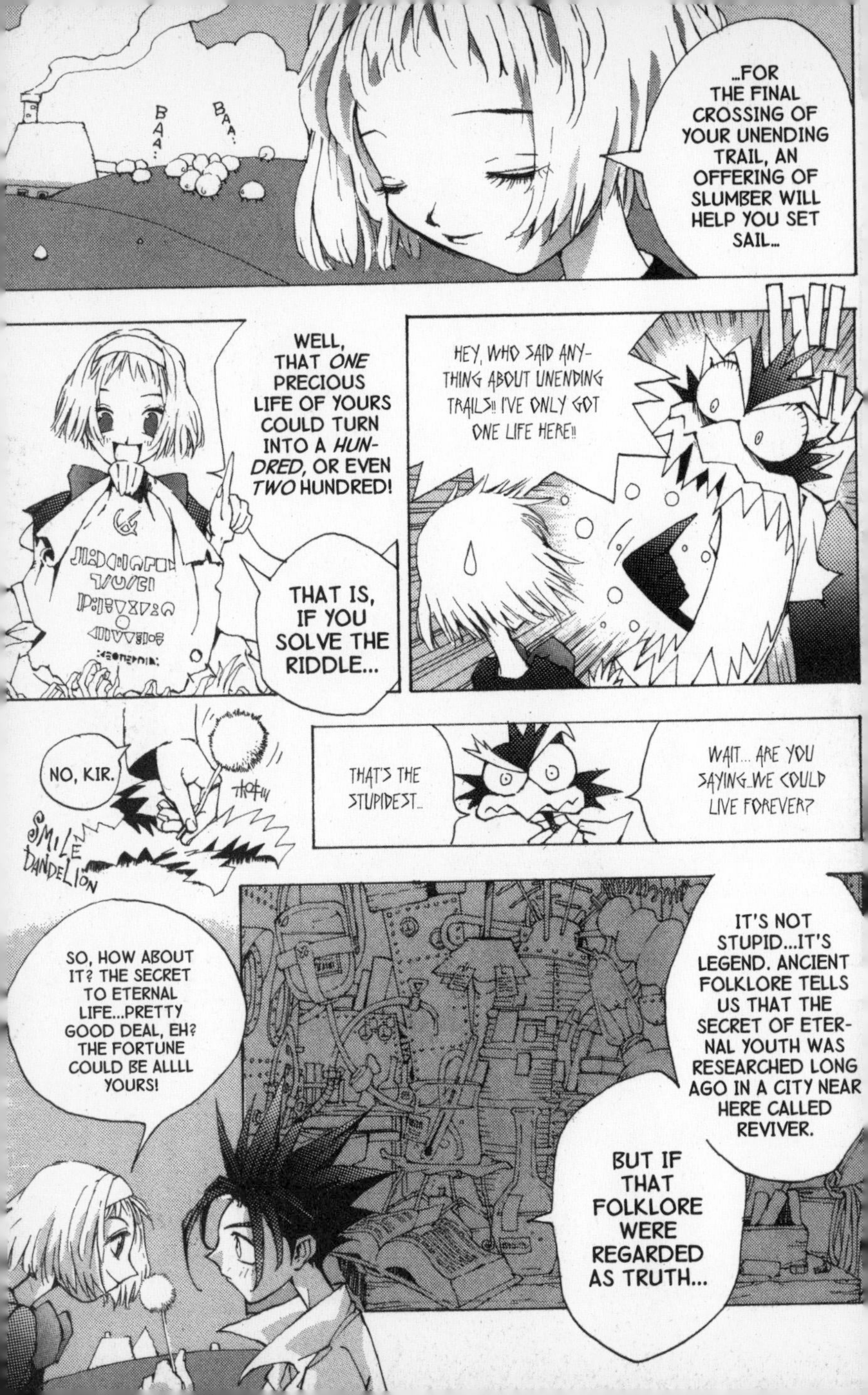

...FOR THE FINAL CROSSING OF YOUR UNENDING TRAIL, AN OFFERING OF SLUMBER WILL HELP YOU SET SAIL...
BAA...
BAA...
HEY, WHO SAID ANY-THING ABOUT UNENDING TRAILS!! I'VE ONLY GOT ONE LIFE HERE!!
WELL, THAT *ONE* PRECIOUS LIFE OF YOURS COULD TURN INTO A *HUN-DRED*, OR EVEN *TWO* HUNDRED!
THAT IS, IF YOU SOLVE THE RIDDLE...
WAIT... ARE YOU SAYING..WE COULD LIVE FOREVER?
THAT'S THE STUPIDEST...
NO, KIR.
SMILE DANDELION
IT'S NOT STUPID...IT'S LEGEND. ANCIENT FOLKLORE TELLS US THAT THE SECRET OF ETER-NAL YOUTH WAS RESEARCHED LONG AGO IN A CITY NEAR HERE CALLED REVIVER.
SO, HOW ABOUT IT? THE SECRET TO ETERNAL LIFE...PRETTY GOOD DEAL, EH? THE FORTUNE COULD BE ALLLL YOURS!
BUT IF THAT FOLKLORE WERE REGARDED AS TRUTH...

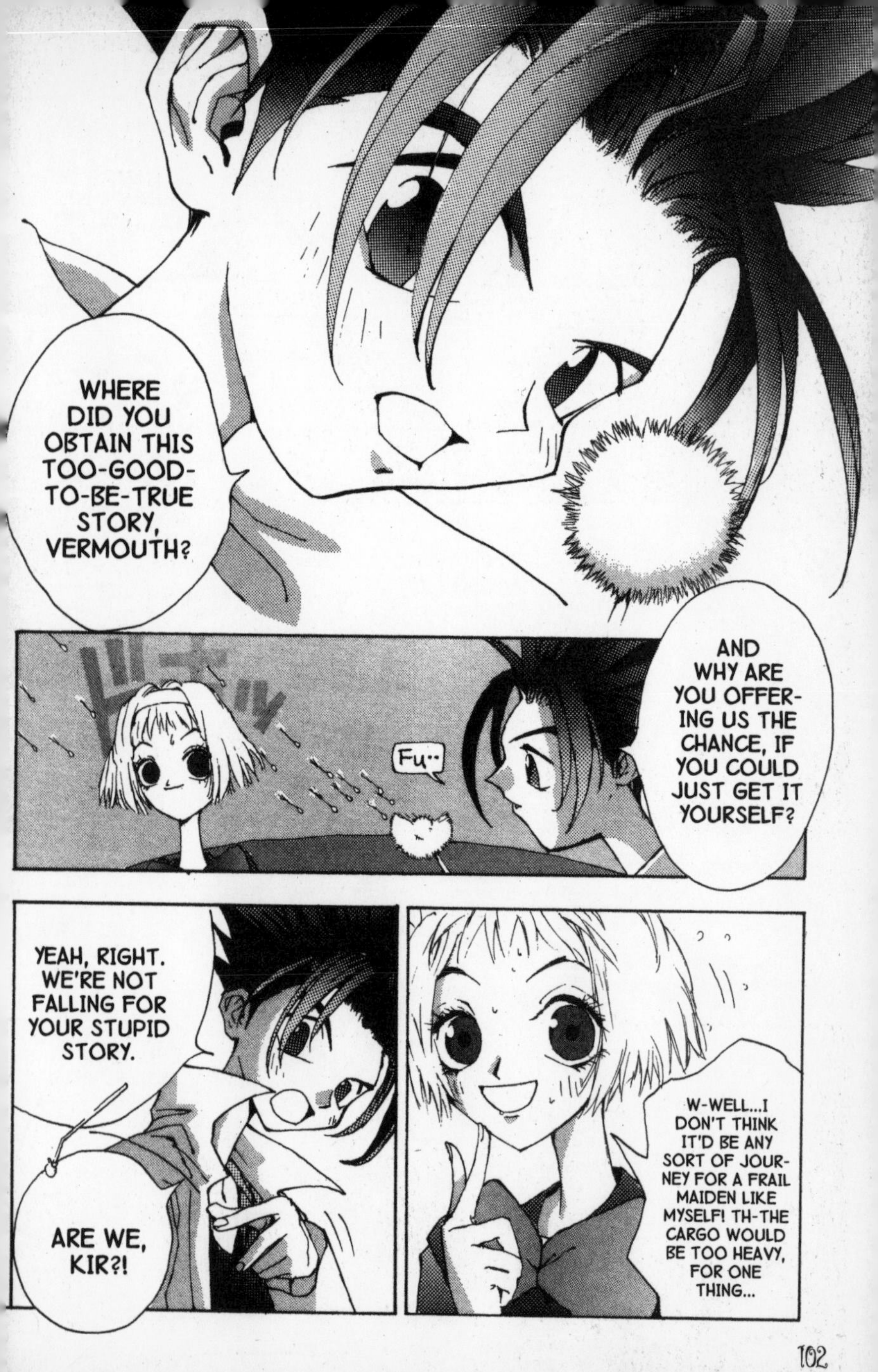
WHERE DID YOU OBTAIN THIS TOO-GOOD-TO-BE-TRUE STORY, VERMOUTH?
AND WHY ARE YOU OFFERING US THE CHANCE, IF YOU COULD JUST GET IT YOURSELF?
Fu..
W-WELL...I DON'T THINK IT'D BE ANY SORT OF JOURNEY FOR A FRAIL MAIDEN LIKE MYSELF! TH-THE CARGO WOULD BE TOO HEAVY, FOR ONE THING...
YEAH, RIGHT. WE'RE NOT FALLING FOR YOUR STUPID STORY.
ARE WE, KIR?!

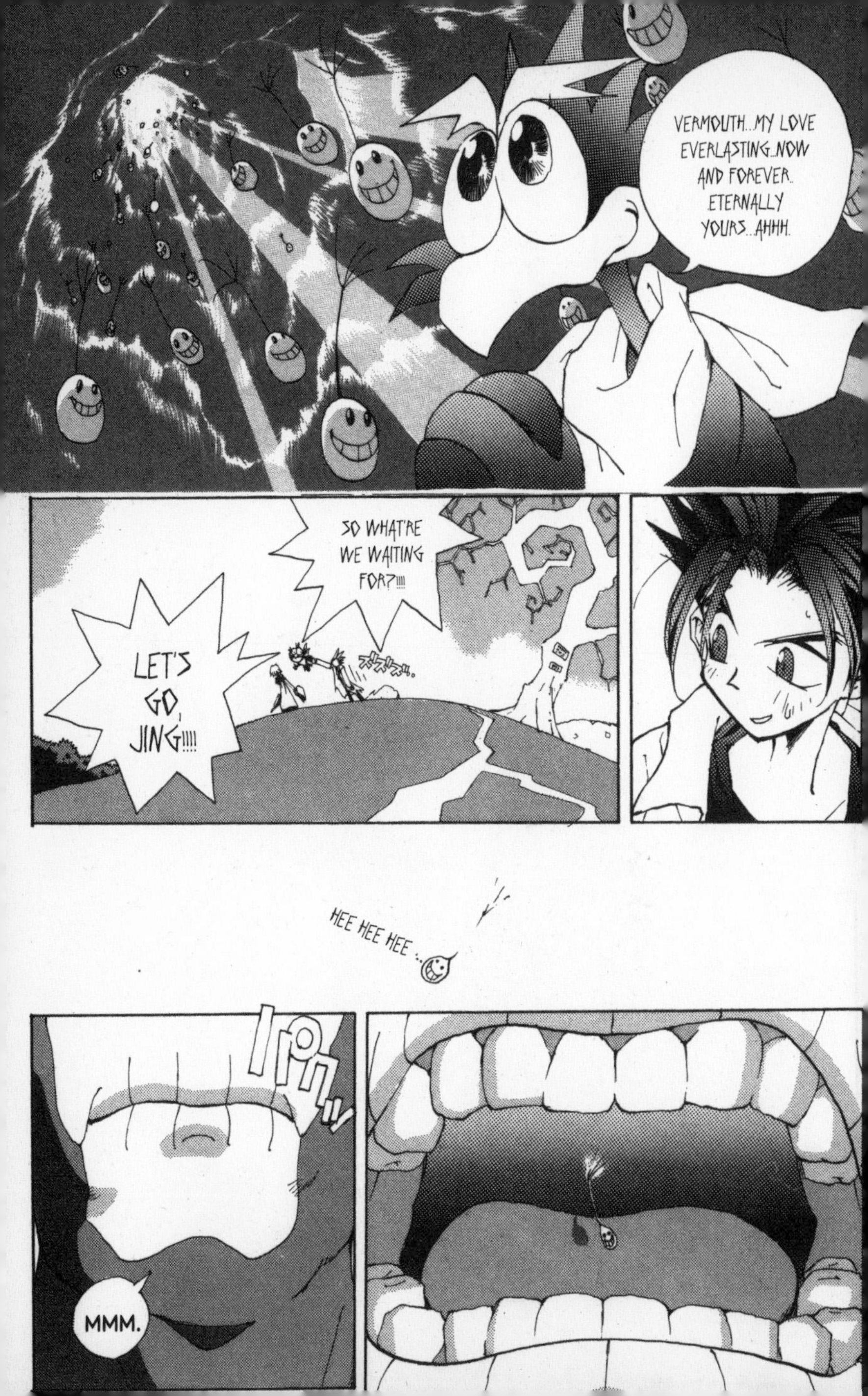
VERMOUTH...MY LOVE EVERLASTING...NOW AND FOREVER... ETERNALLY YOURS...AHHH.
SO WHAT'RE WE WAITING FOR?!!!!
LET'S GO, JING!!!!
HEE HEE HEE...
MMM.

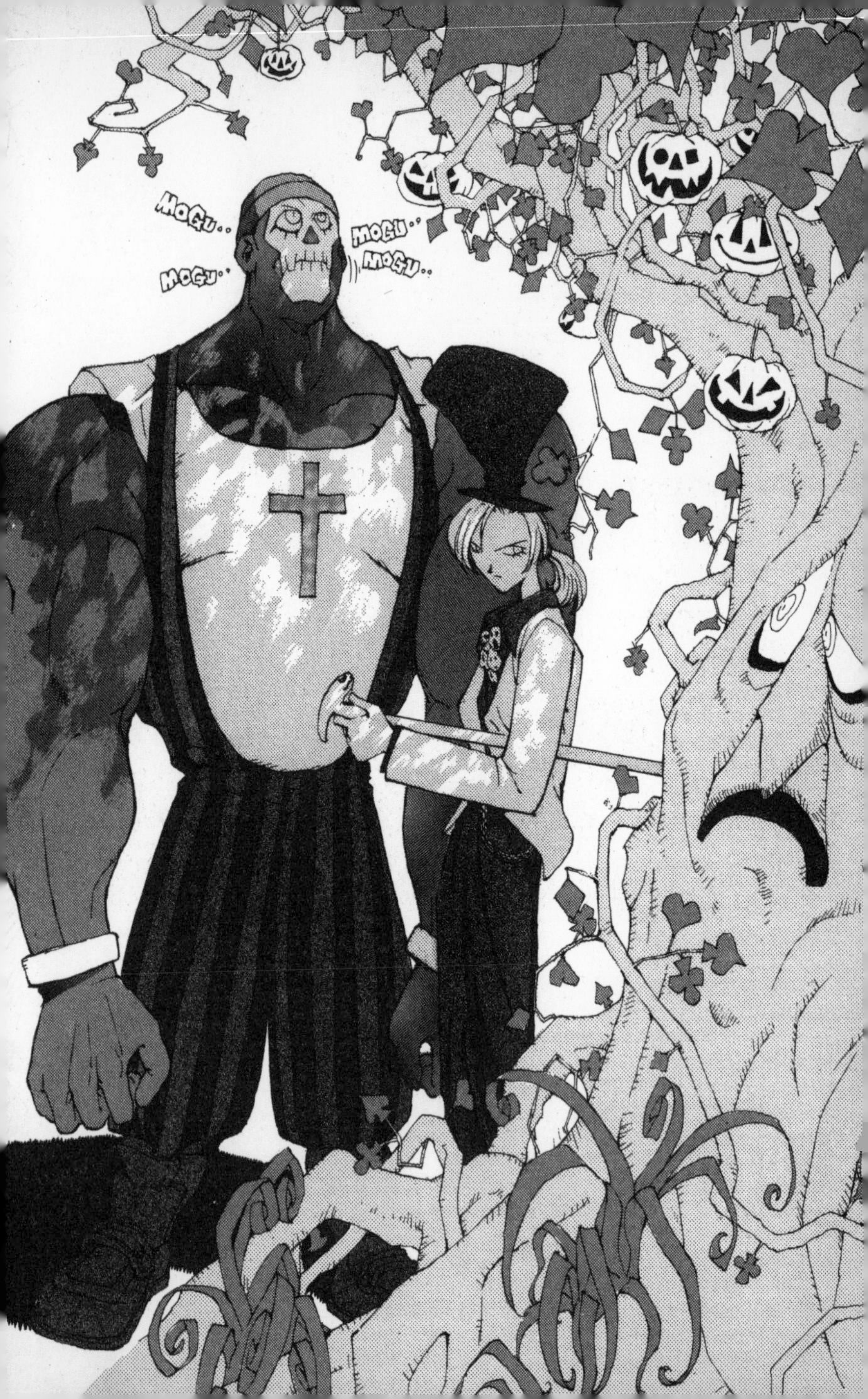
MOGU..
MOGU..
MOGU..
MOGU..

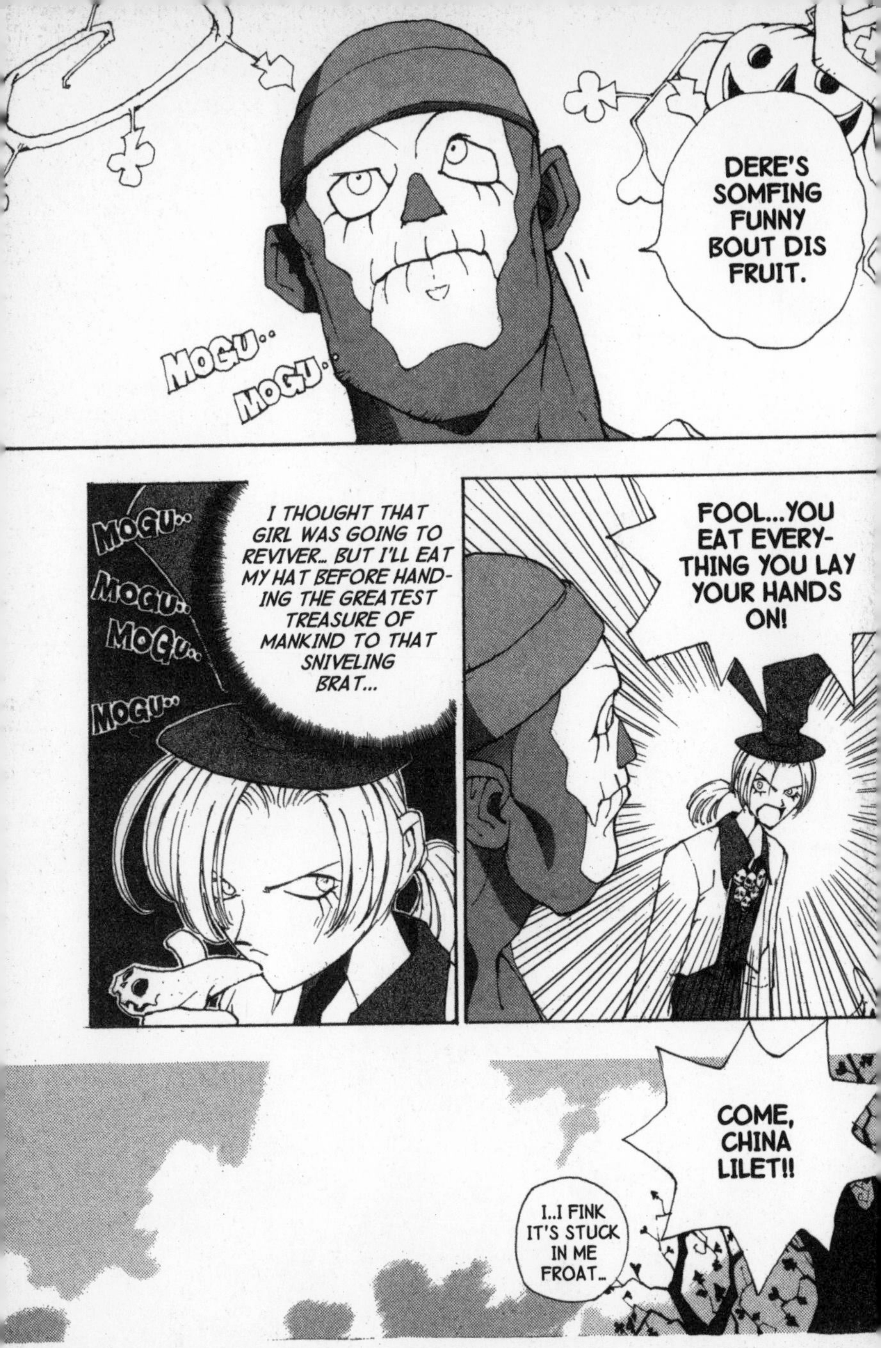
DERE'S SOMFING FUNNY BOUT DIS FRUIT.
MOGU.. MOGU..
FOOL...YOU EAT EVERY-THING YOU LAY YOUR HANDS ON!
I THOUGHT THAT GIRL WAS GOING TO REVIVER... BUT I'LL EAT MY HAT BEFORE HAND-ING THE GREATEST TREASURE OF MANKIND TO THAT SNIVELING BRAT...
MOGU.. MOGU.. MOGU.. MOGU..
COME, CHINA LILET!!
I..I FINK IT'S STUCK IN ME FROAT..

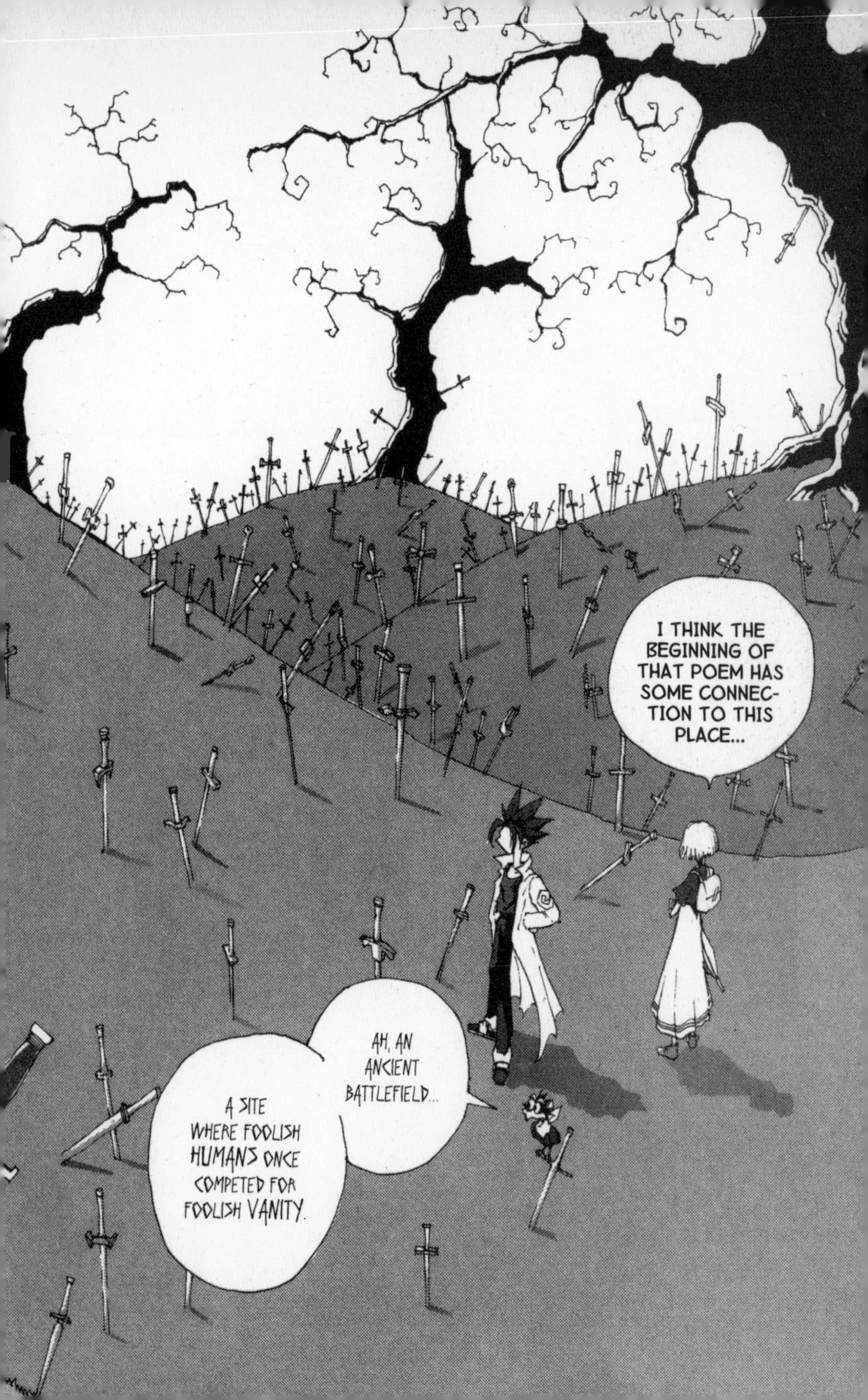
I THINK THE BEGINNING OF THAT POEM HAS SOME CONNECTION TO THIS PLACE...
AH, AN ANCIENT BATTLEFIELD...
A SITE WHERE FOOLISH HUMANS ONCE COMPETED FOR FOOLISH VANITY.

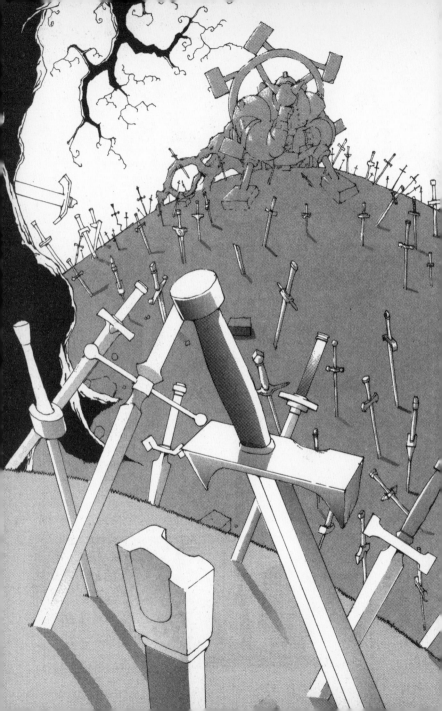

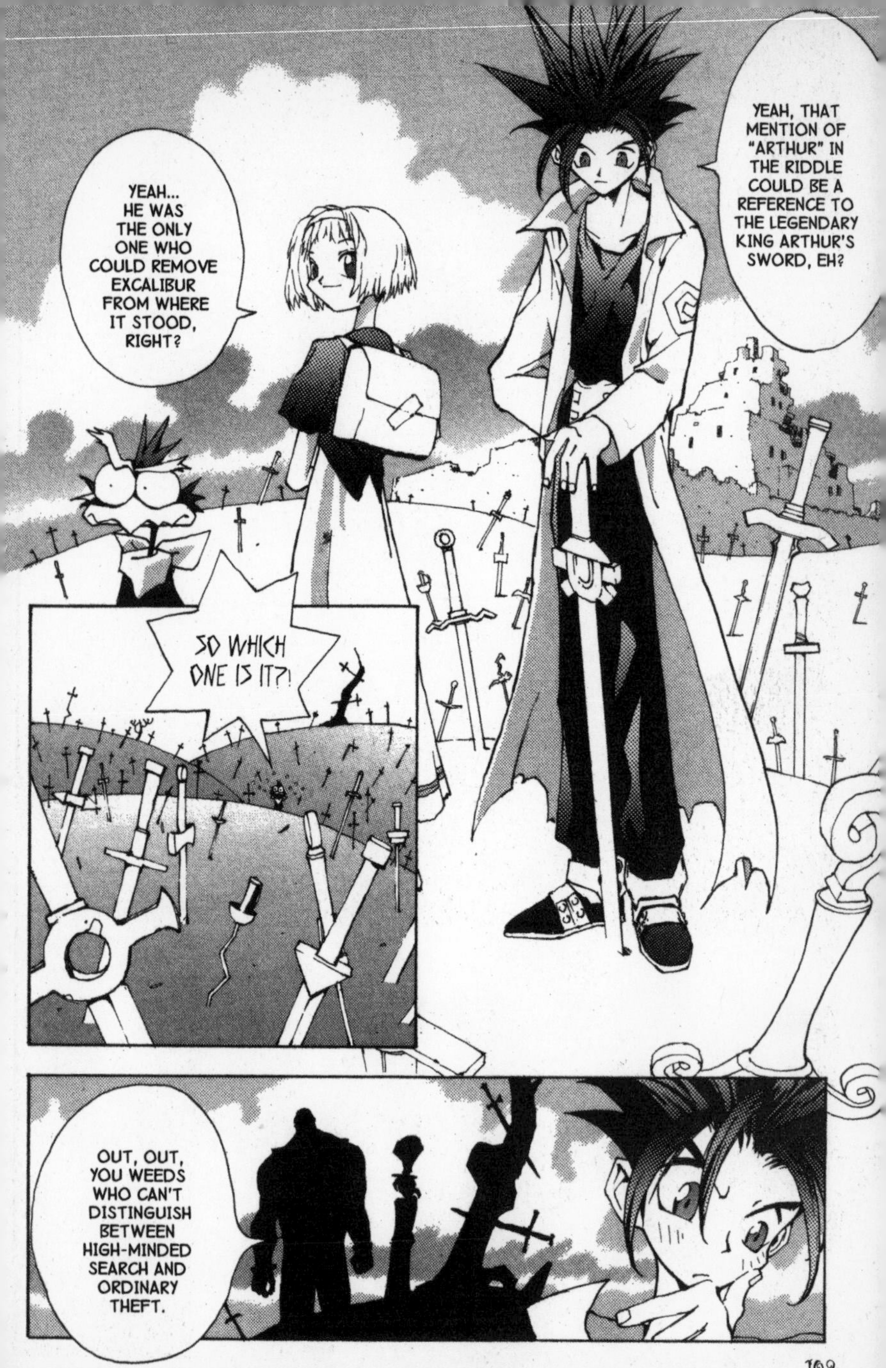
YEAH, THAT MENTION OF "ARTHUR" IN THE RIDDLE COULD BE A REFERENCE TO THE LEGENDARY KING ARTHUR'S SWORD, EH?
YEAH... HE WAS THE ONLY ONE WHO COULD REMOVE EXCALIBUR FROM WHERE IT STOOD, RIGHT?
SO WHICH ONE IS IT?!
OUT, OUT, YOU WEEDS WHO CAN'T DISTINGUISH BETWEEN HIGH-MINDED SEARCH AND ORDINARY THEFT.

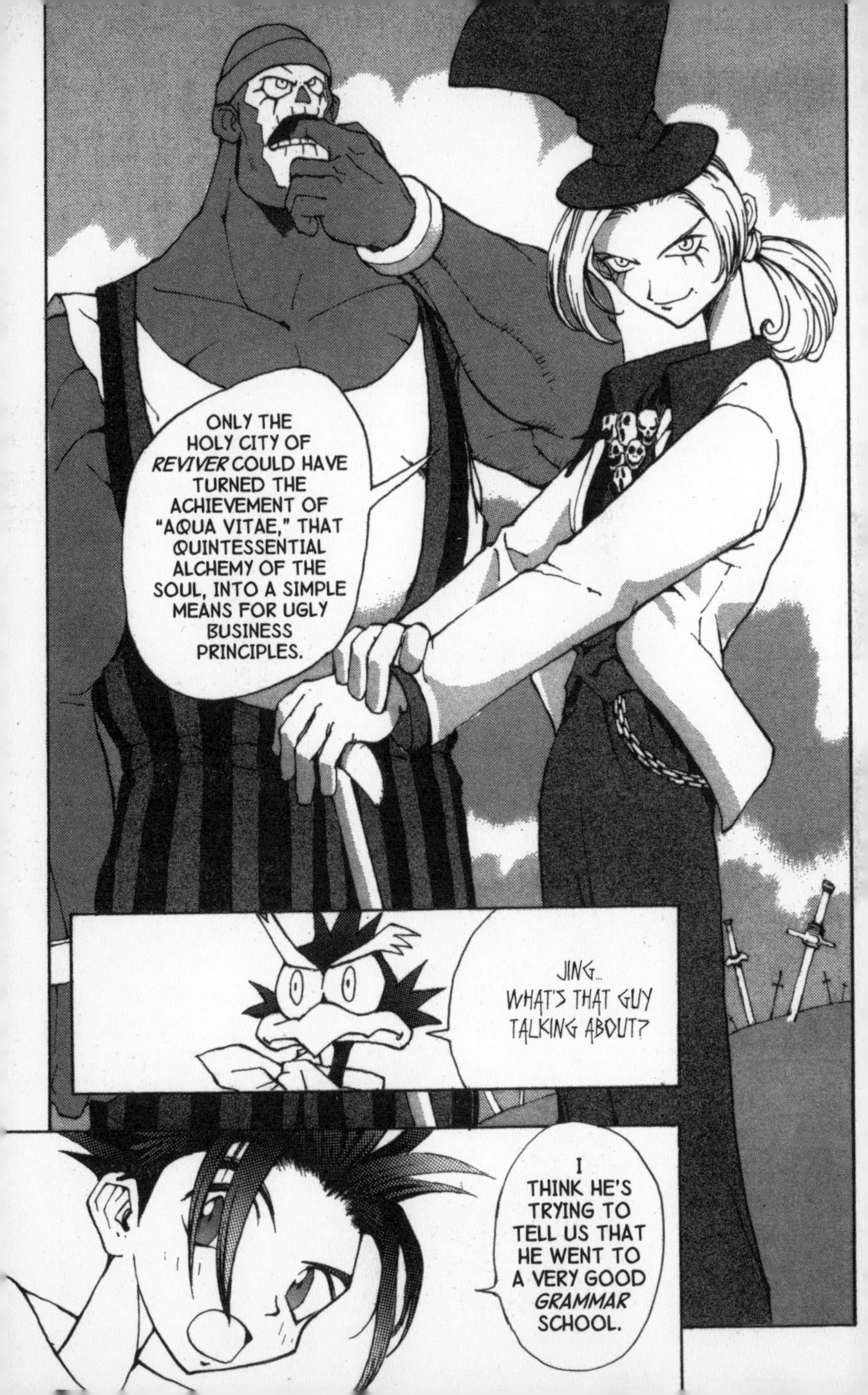
ONLY THE HOLY CITY OF *REVIVER* COULD HAVE TURNED THE ACHIEVEMENT OF "AQUA VITAE," THAT QUINTESSENTIAL ALCHEMY OF THE SOUL, INTO A SIMPLE MEANS FOR UGLY BUSINESS PRINCIPLES.
JING... WHAT'S THAT GUY TALKING ABOUT?
I THINK HE'S TRYING TO TELL US THAT HE WENT TO A VERY GOOD *GRAMMAR* SCHOOL.

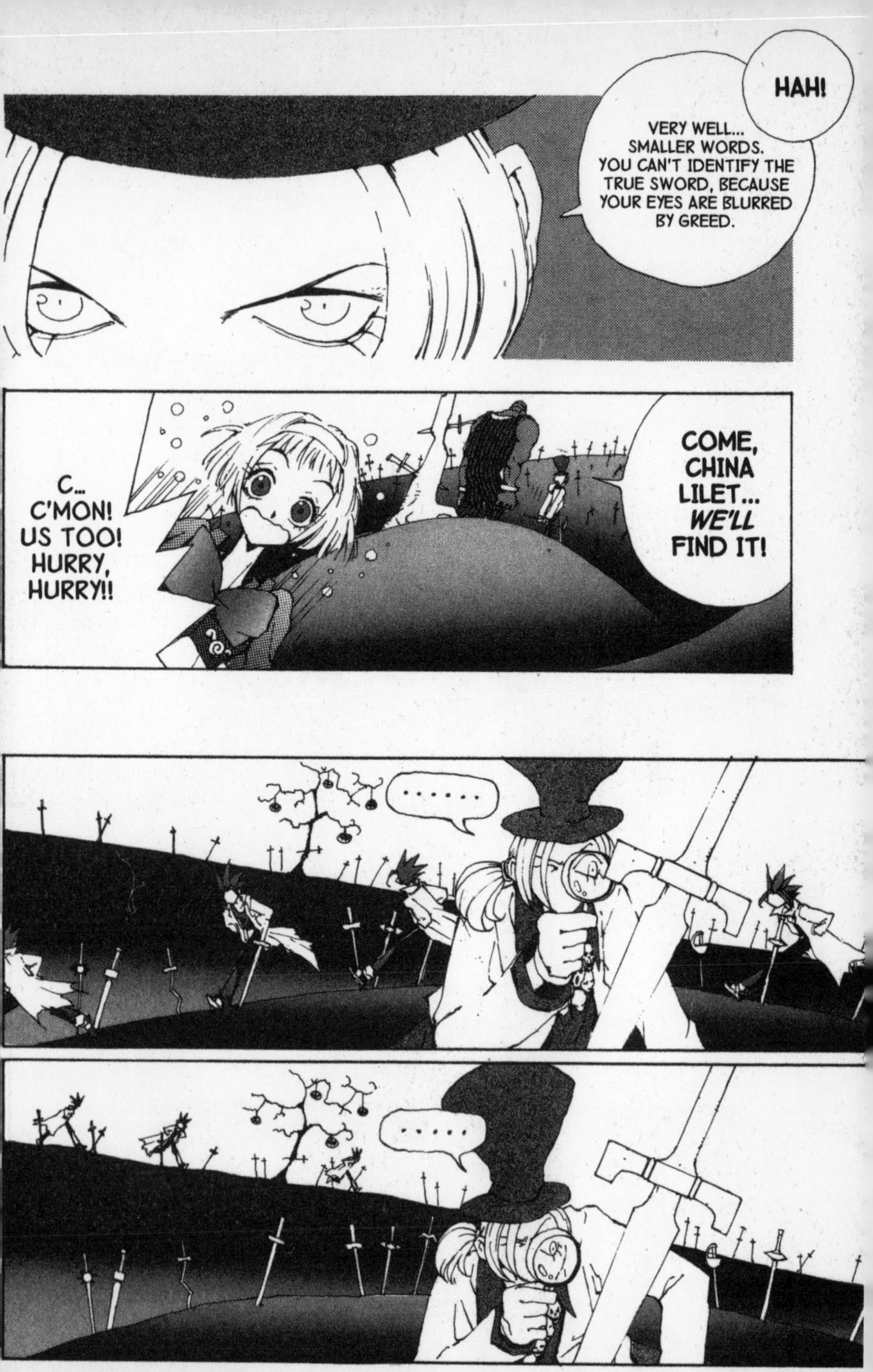
HAH!
VERY WELL... SMALLER WORDS. YOU CAN'T IDENTIFY THE TRUE SWORD, BECAUSE YOUR EYES ARE BLURRED BY GREED.
COME, CHINA LILET... *WE'LL* FIND IT!
C... C'MON! US TOO! HURRY, HURRY!!
......
.....

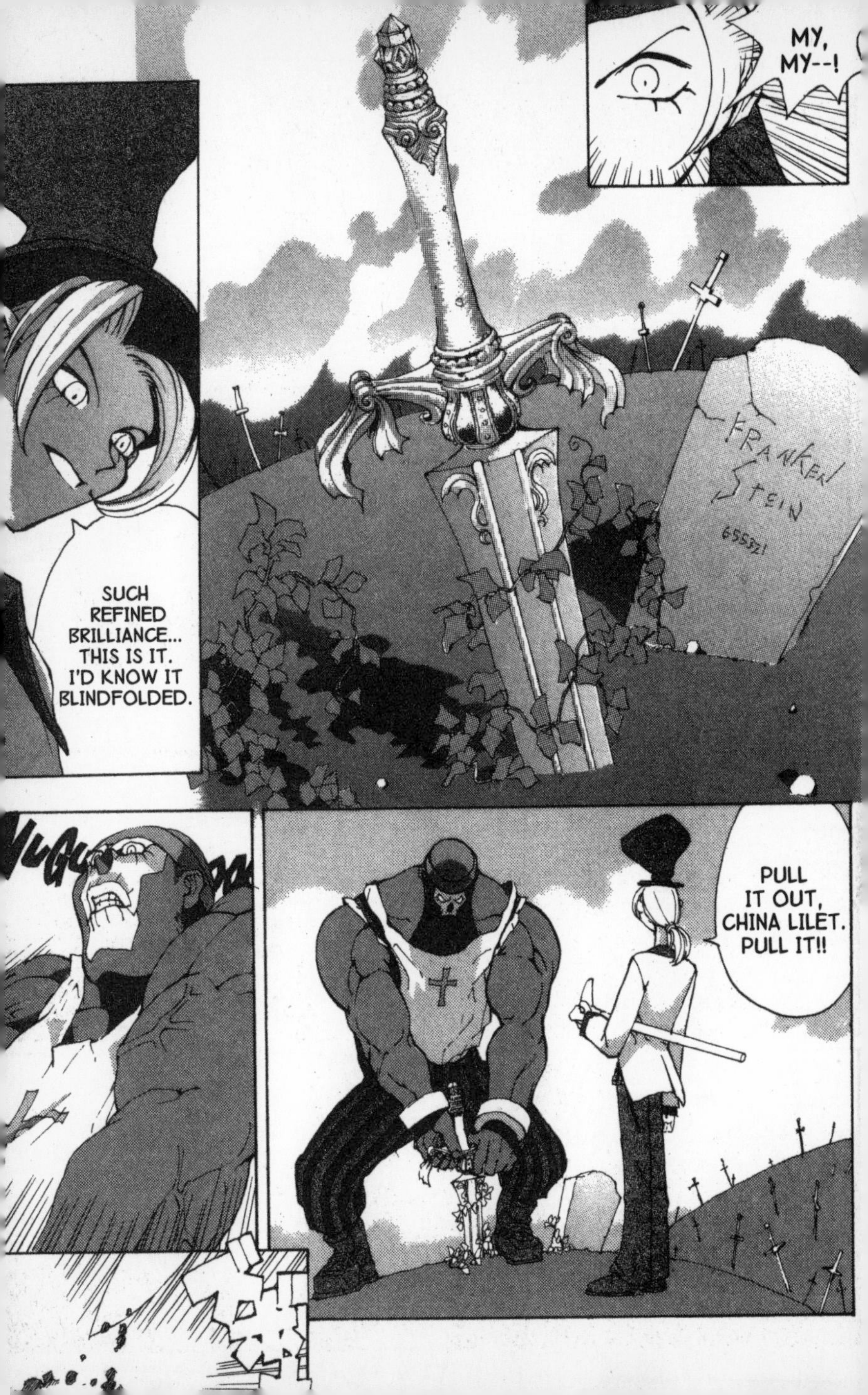
MY, MY--!
FRANKEN STEIN
65521
SUCH REFINED BRILLIANCE... THIS IS IT. I'D KNOW IT BLINDFOLDED.
PULL IT OUT, CHINA LILET. PULL IT!!
NUGU

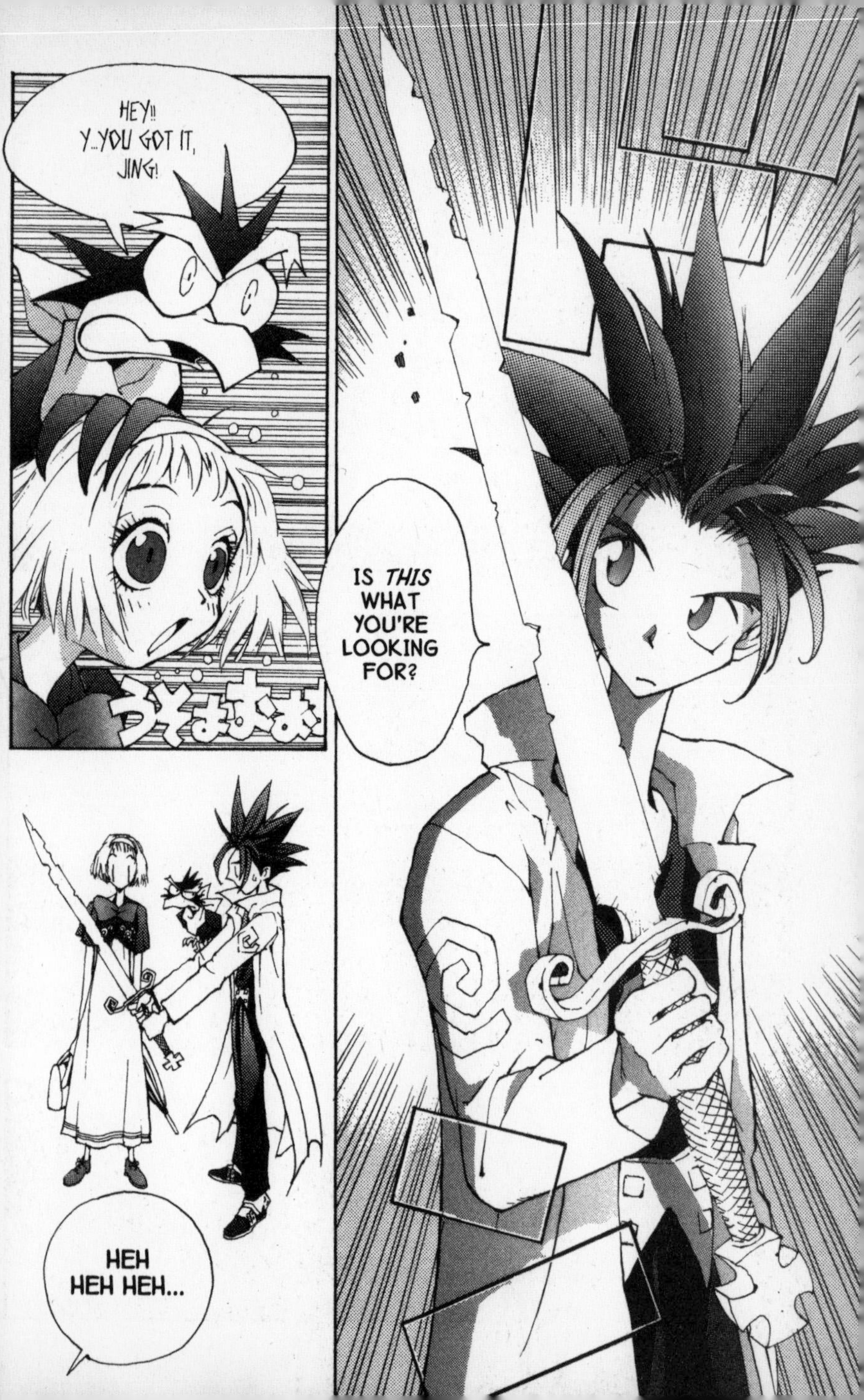
IS *THIS* WHAT YOU'RE LOOKING FOR?
HEY!! Y...YOU GOT IT, JING!
HEH HEH HEH...

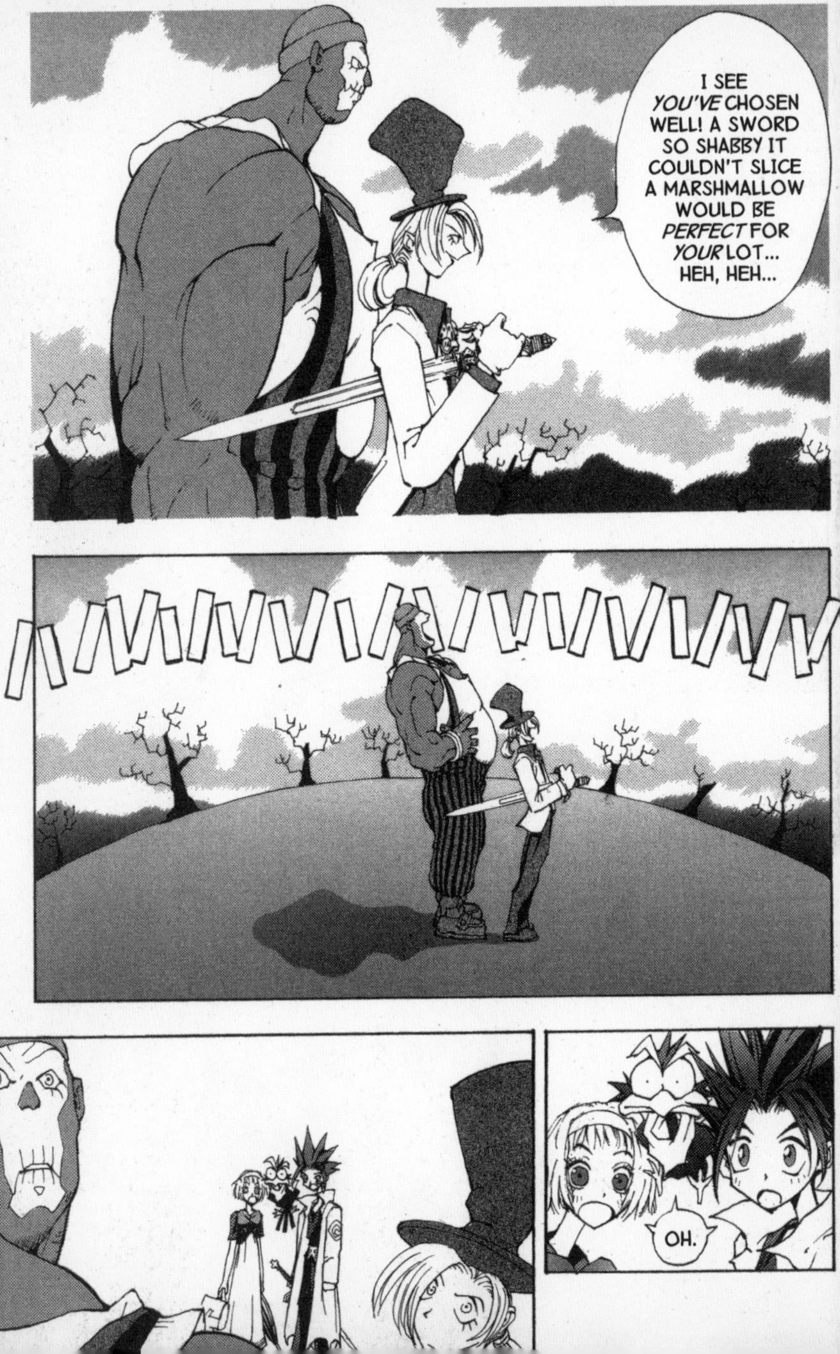
I SEE *YOU'VE* CHOSEN WELL! A SWORD SO SHABBY IT COULDN'T SLICE A MARSHMALLOW WOULD BE *PERFECT* FOR *YOUR* LOT... HEH, HEH...
OH.

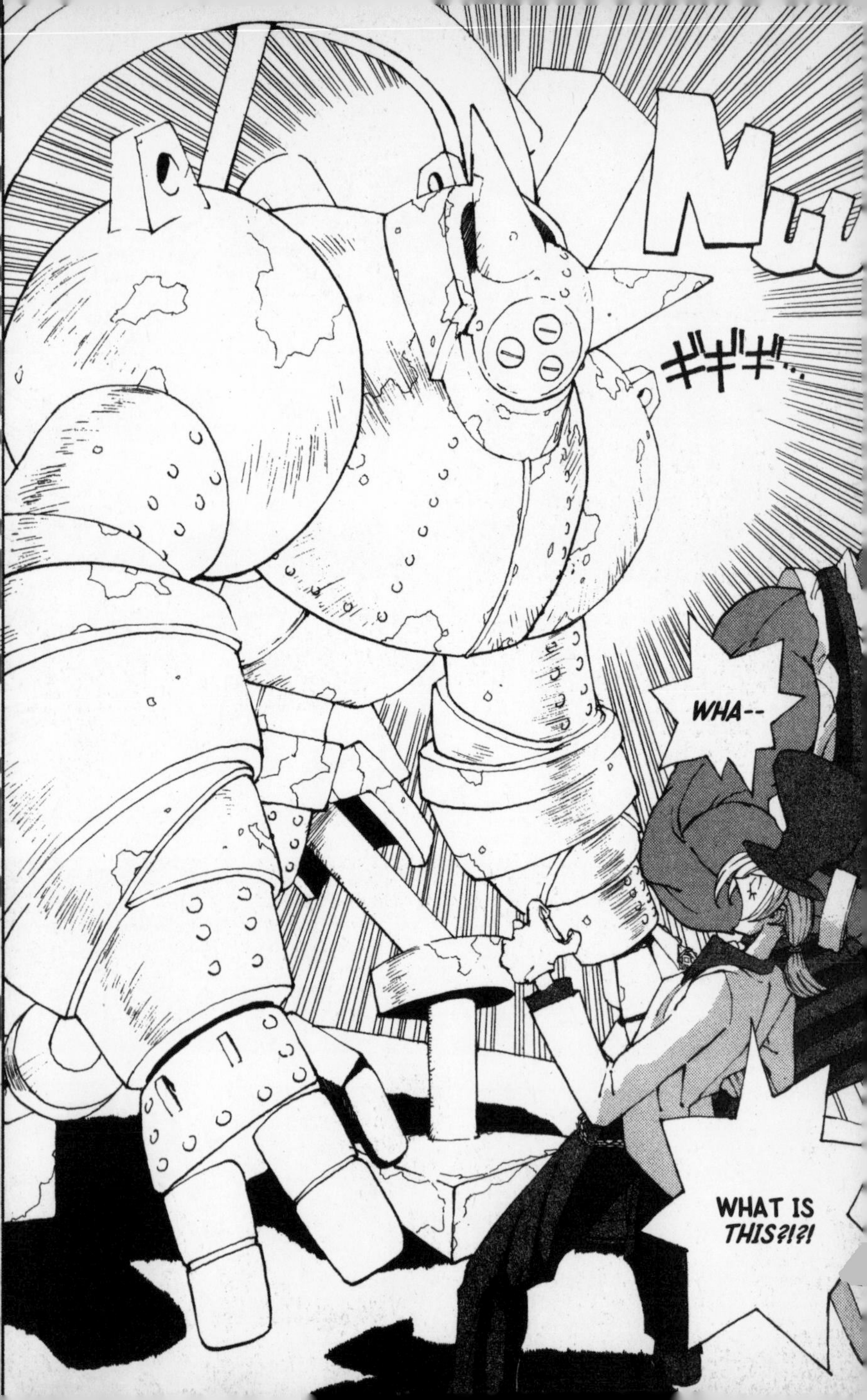
ギギギ...
WHA--
WHAT IS THIS?!?!

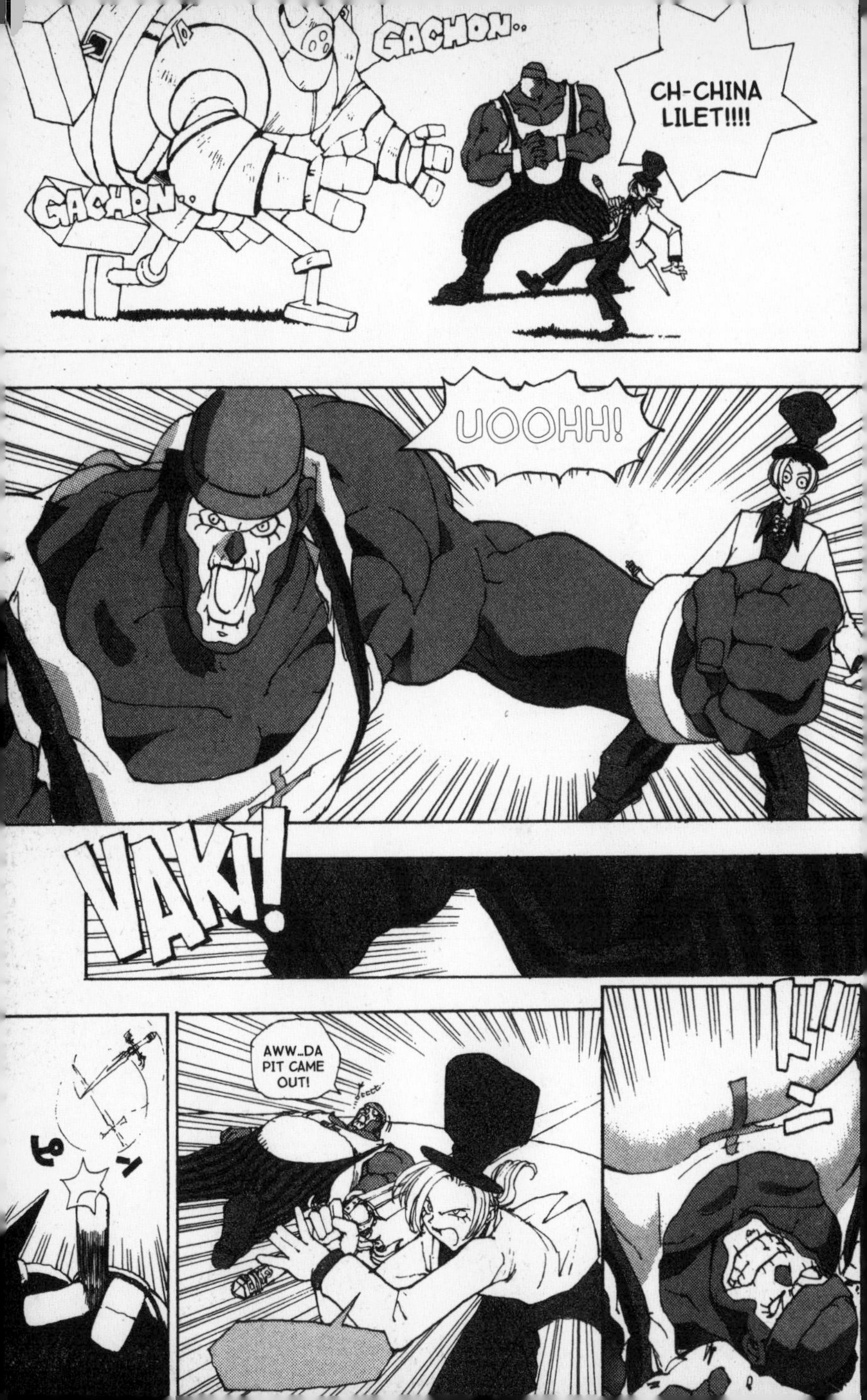
CH-CHINA LILET!!!!
GACHON..
GACHON..
UOOHH!
VAK!
AWW..DA PIT CAME OUT!

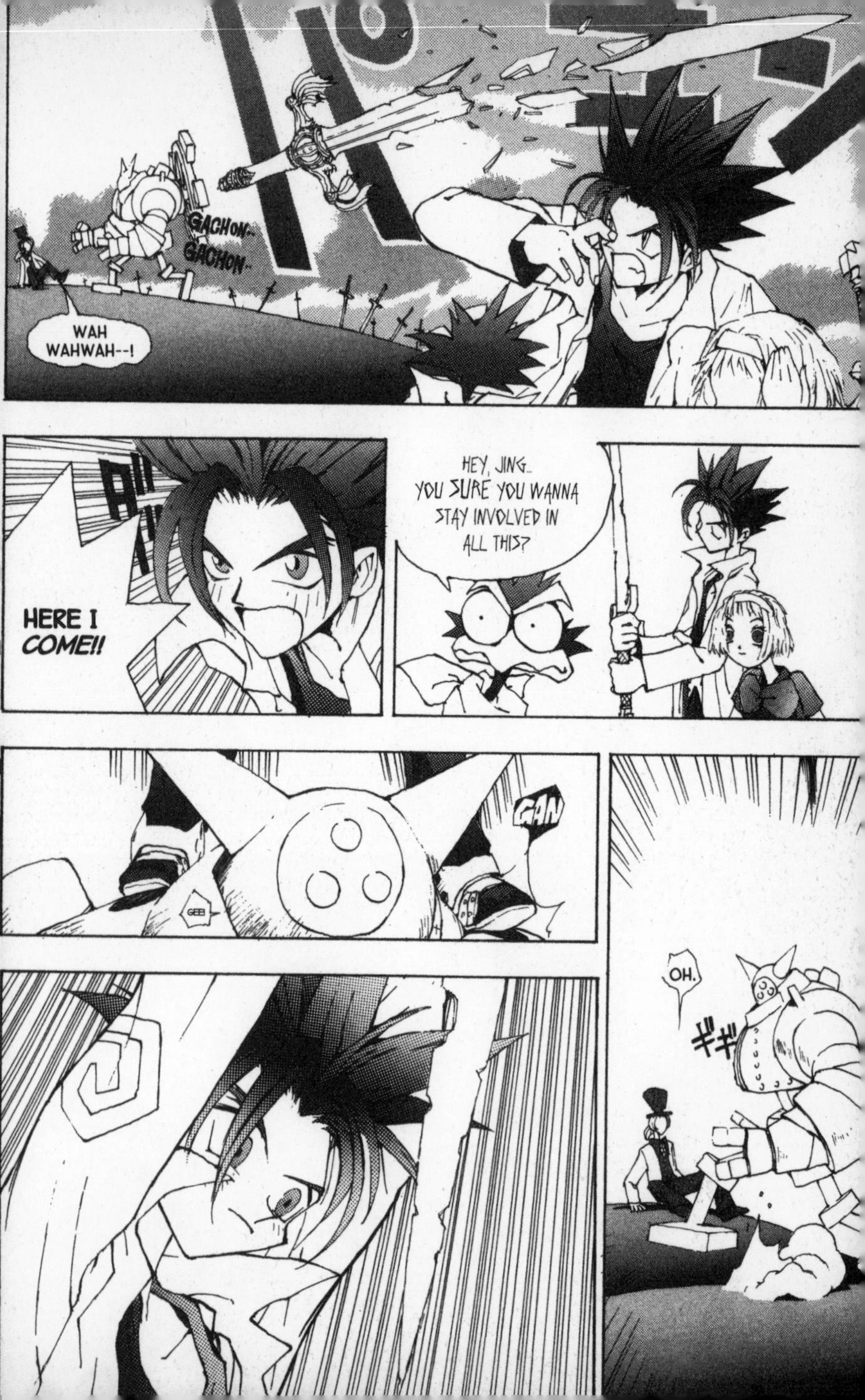
GACHON--
GACHON--
WAH WAHWAH--!
HEY, JING... YOU SURE YOU WANNA STAY INVOLVED IN ALL THIS?
HERE I COME!!
GAN
GEE!
OH.
ギギ

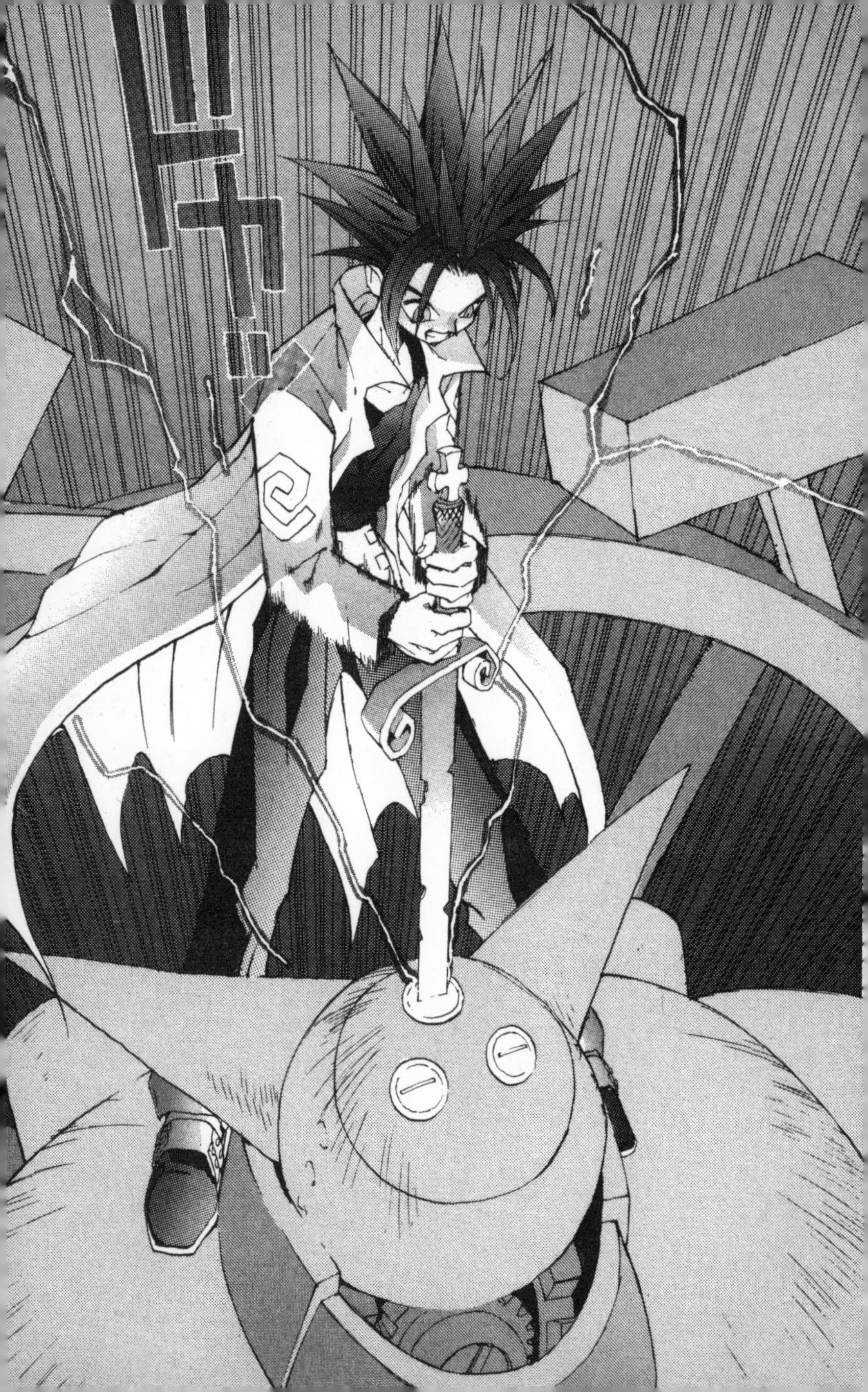
ドカ

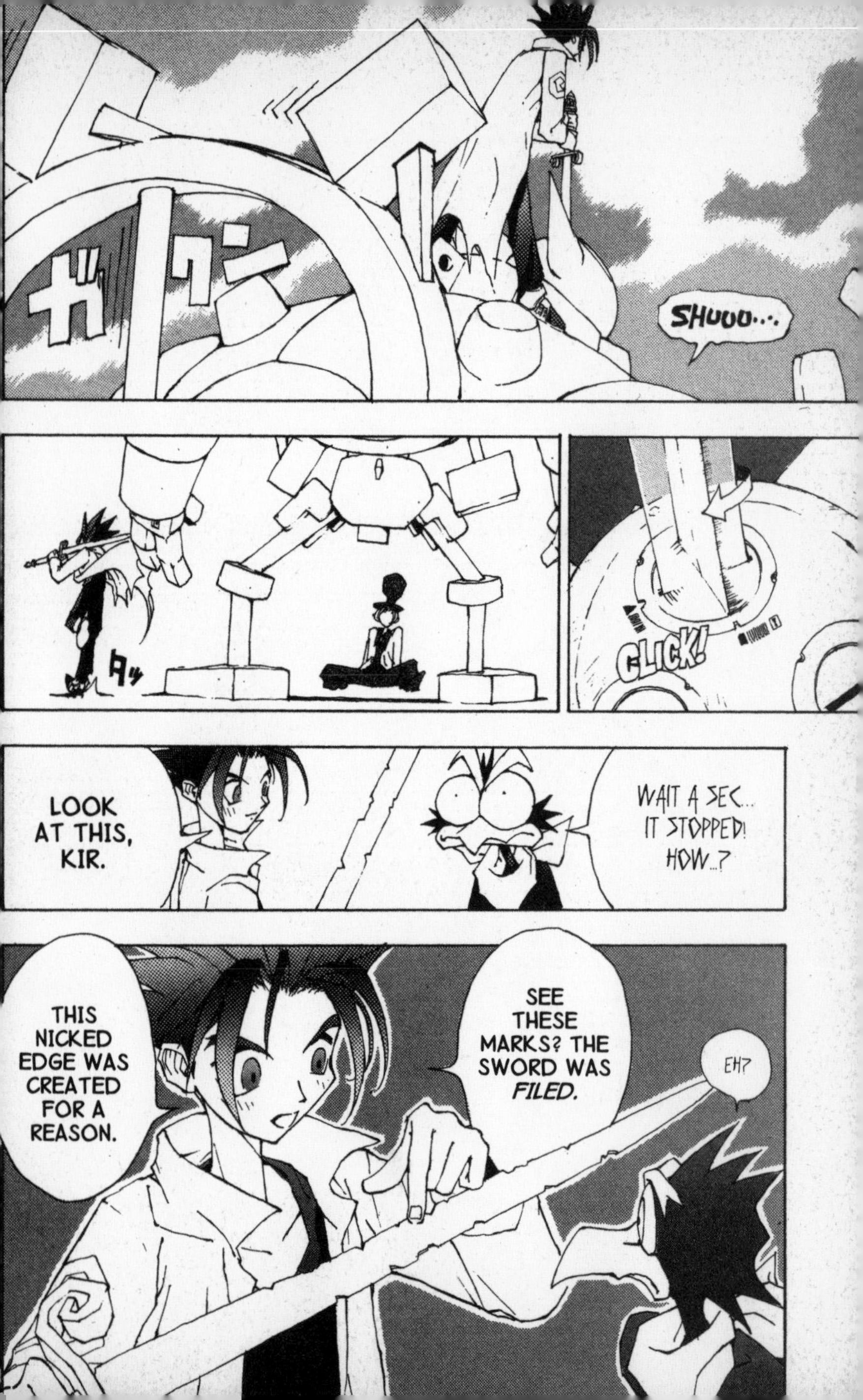
ガクン
SHUUU....
CLICK!
タッ
WAIT A SEC... IT STOPPED! HOW...?
LOOK AT THIS, KIR.
EH?
SEE THESE MARKS? THE SWORD WAS *FILED.*
THIS NICKED EDGE WAS CREATED FOR A REASON.

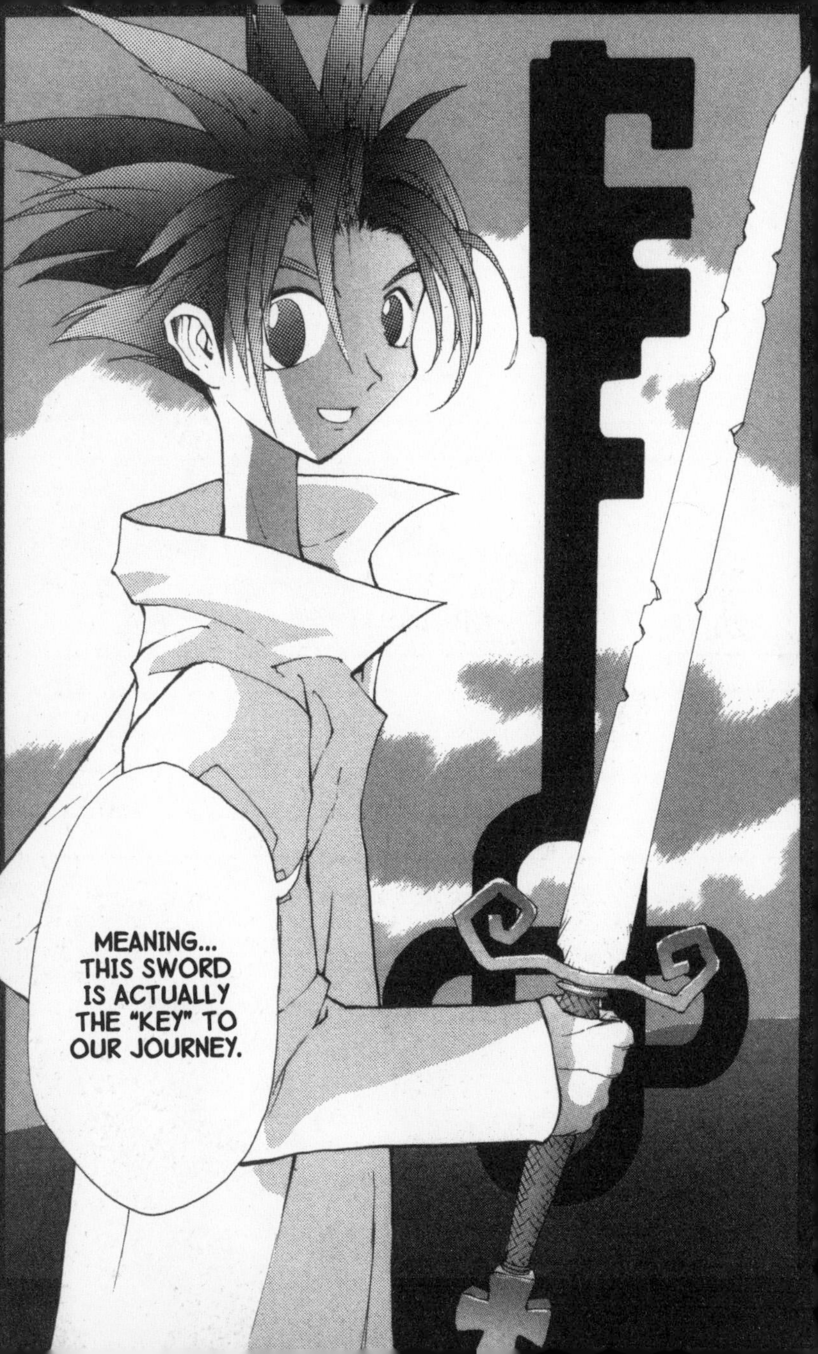
MEANING... THIS SWORD IS ACTUALLY THE "KEY" TO OUR JOURNEY.

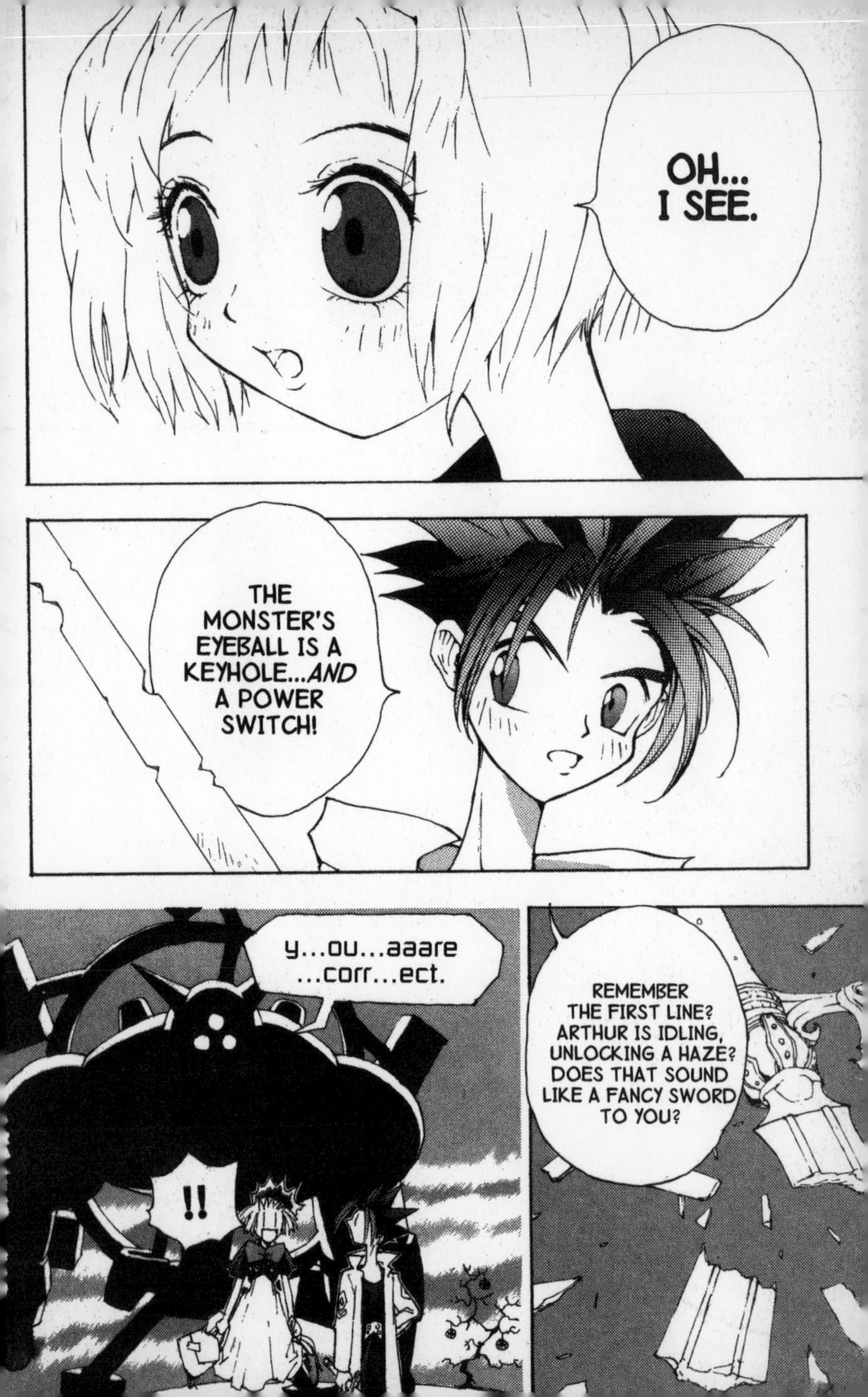
OH... I SEE.
THE MONSTER'S EYEBALL IS A KEYHOLE...*AND* A POWER SWITCH!
REMEMBER THE FIRST LINE? ARTHUR IS IDLING, UNLOCKING A HAZE? DOES THAT SOUND LIKE A FANCY SWORD TO YOU?
y...ou...aaare ...corr...ect.
!!

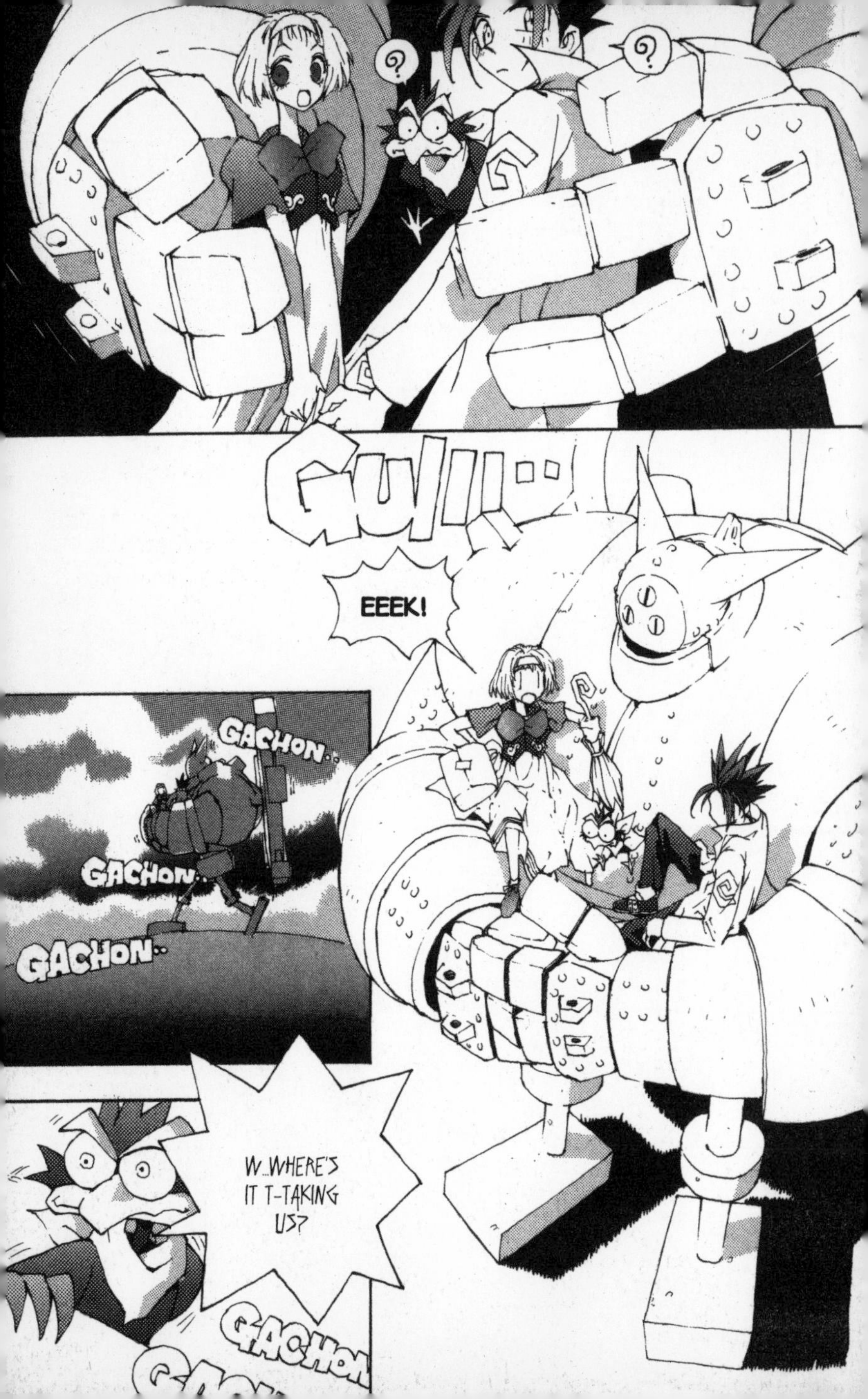
GUIII..
EEEK!
GACHON..
GACHON..
GACHON..
W...WHERE'S IT T-TAKING US?
GACHON

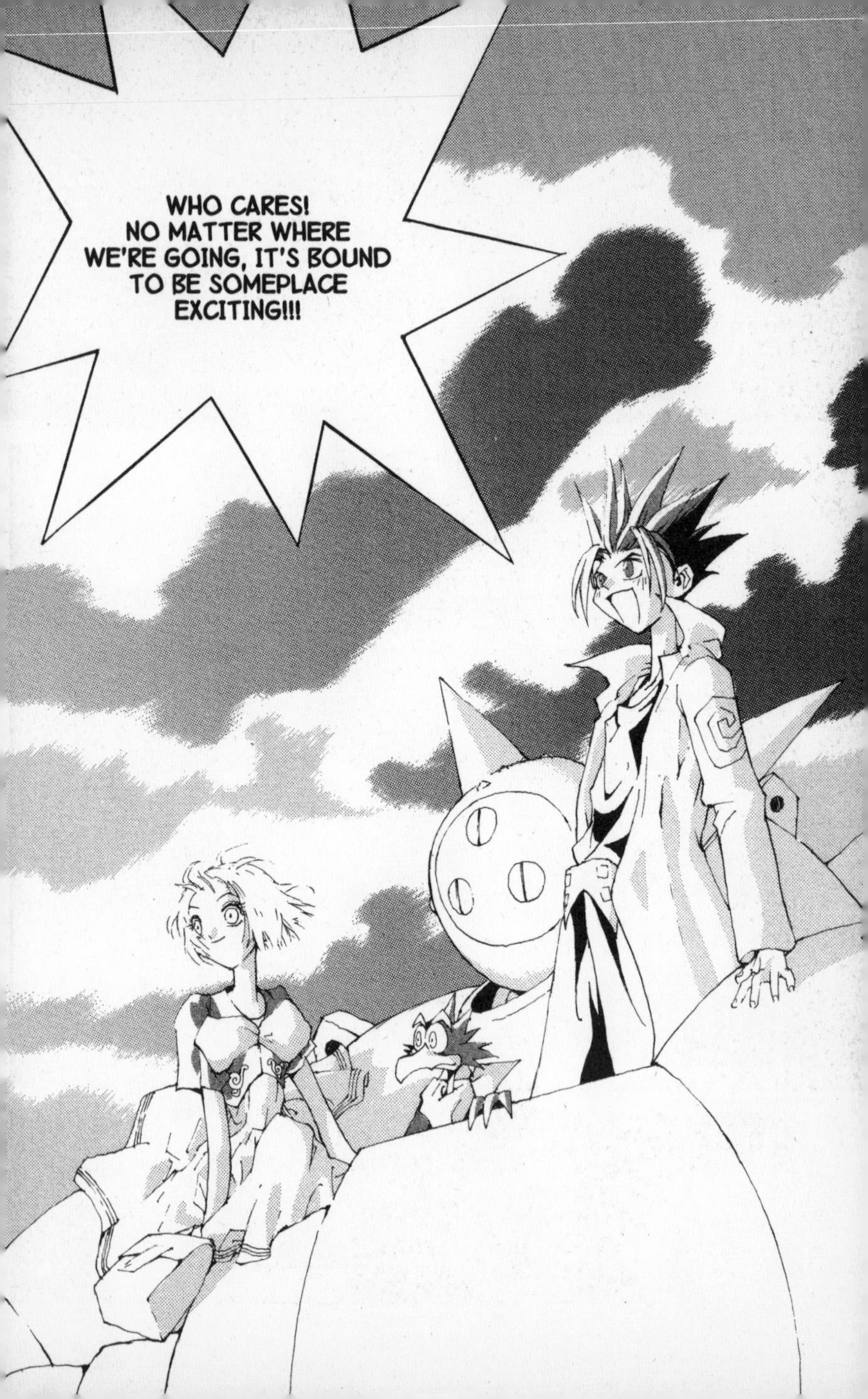
WHO CARES! NO MATTER WHERE WE'RE GOING, IT'S BOUND TO BE SOMEPLACE EXCITING!!!

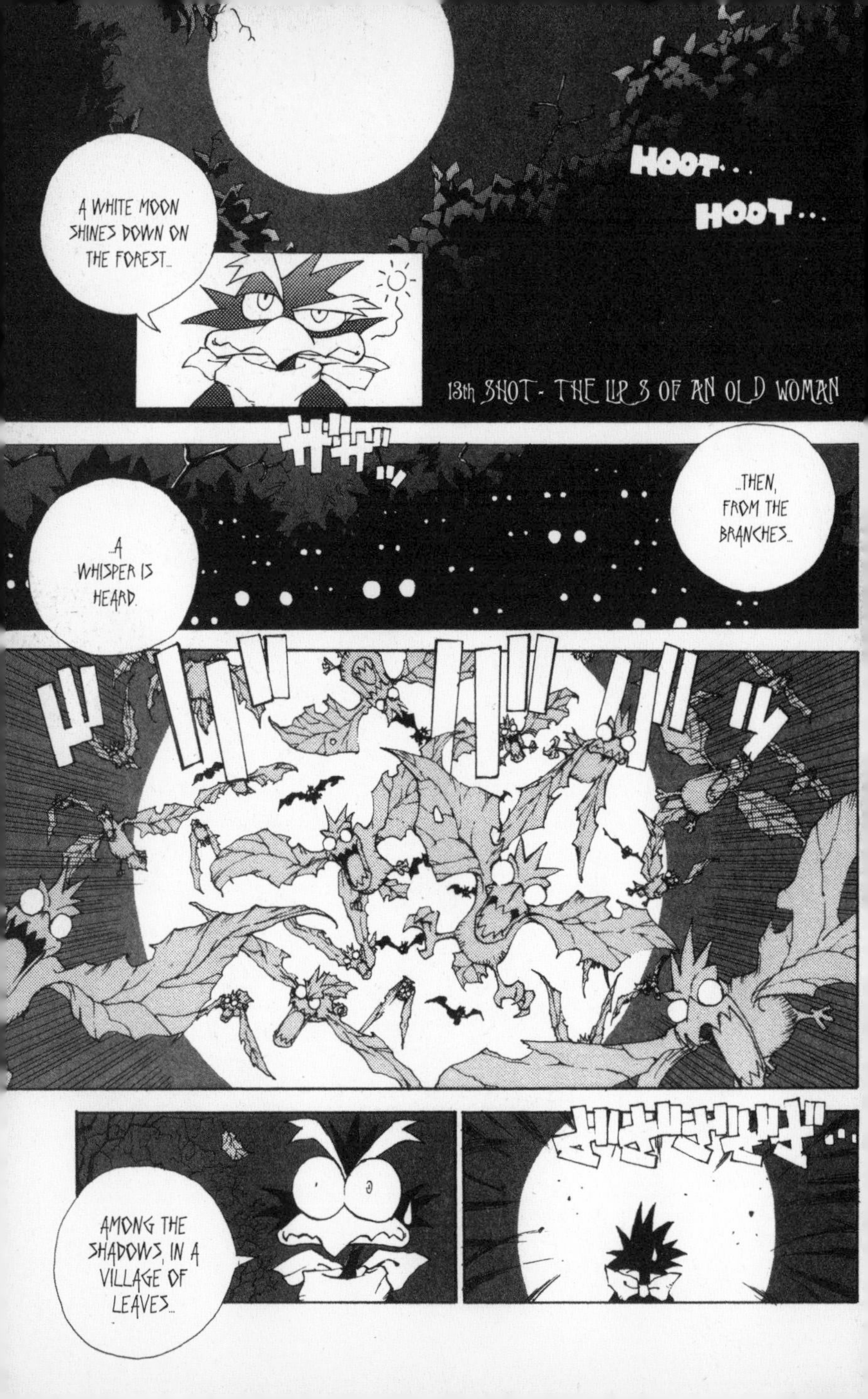
HOOT...
HOOT...
A WHITE MOON SHINES DOWN ON THE FOREST...
13th SHOT - THE LIPS OF AN OLD WOMAN
...THEN, FROM THE BRANCHES...
...A WHISPER IS HEARD.
AMONG THE SHADOWS, IN A VILLAGE OF LEAVES...

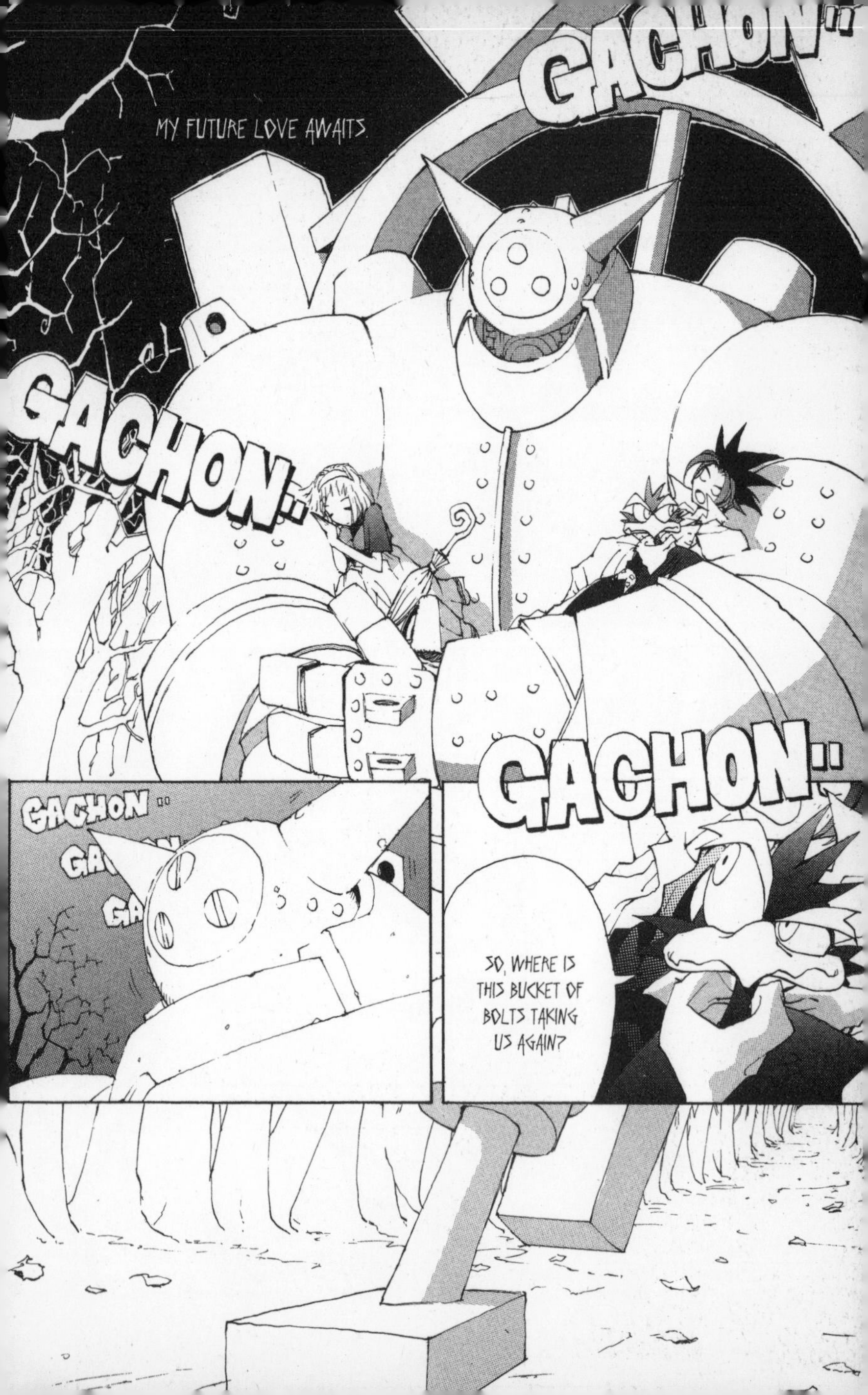
GACHON
MY FUTURE LOVE AWAITS.
GACHON
GACHON
SO, WHERE IS THIS BUCKET OF BOLTS TAKING US AGAIN?
GACHON
GA
GA

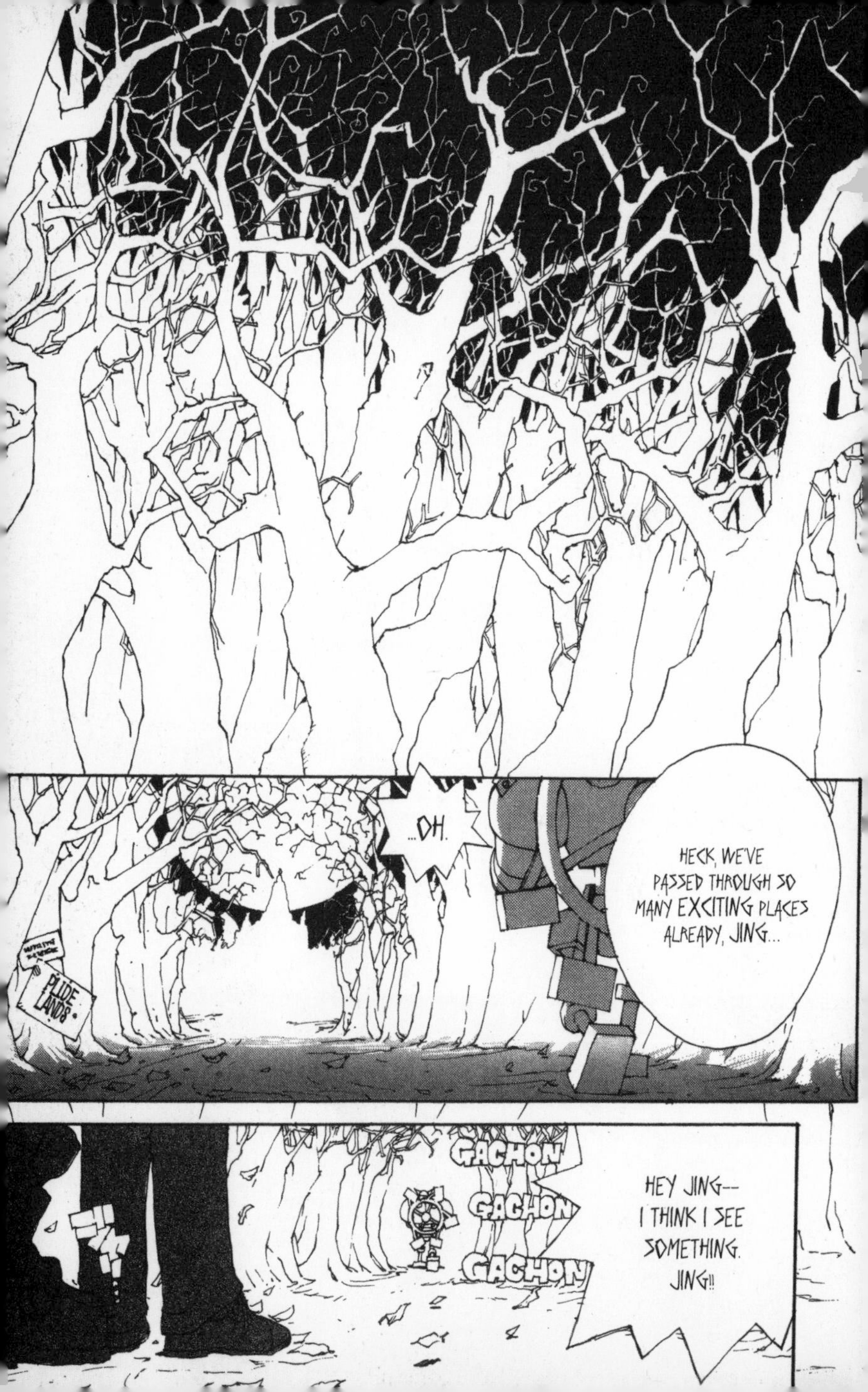
HECK, WE'VE PASSED THROUGH SO MANY EXCITING PLACES ALREADY, JING...
...OH.
PLIDE LANDS
HEY JING-- I THINK I SEE SOMETHING. JING!!
GACHON
GACHON
GACHON

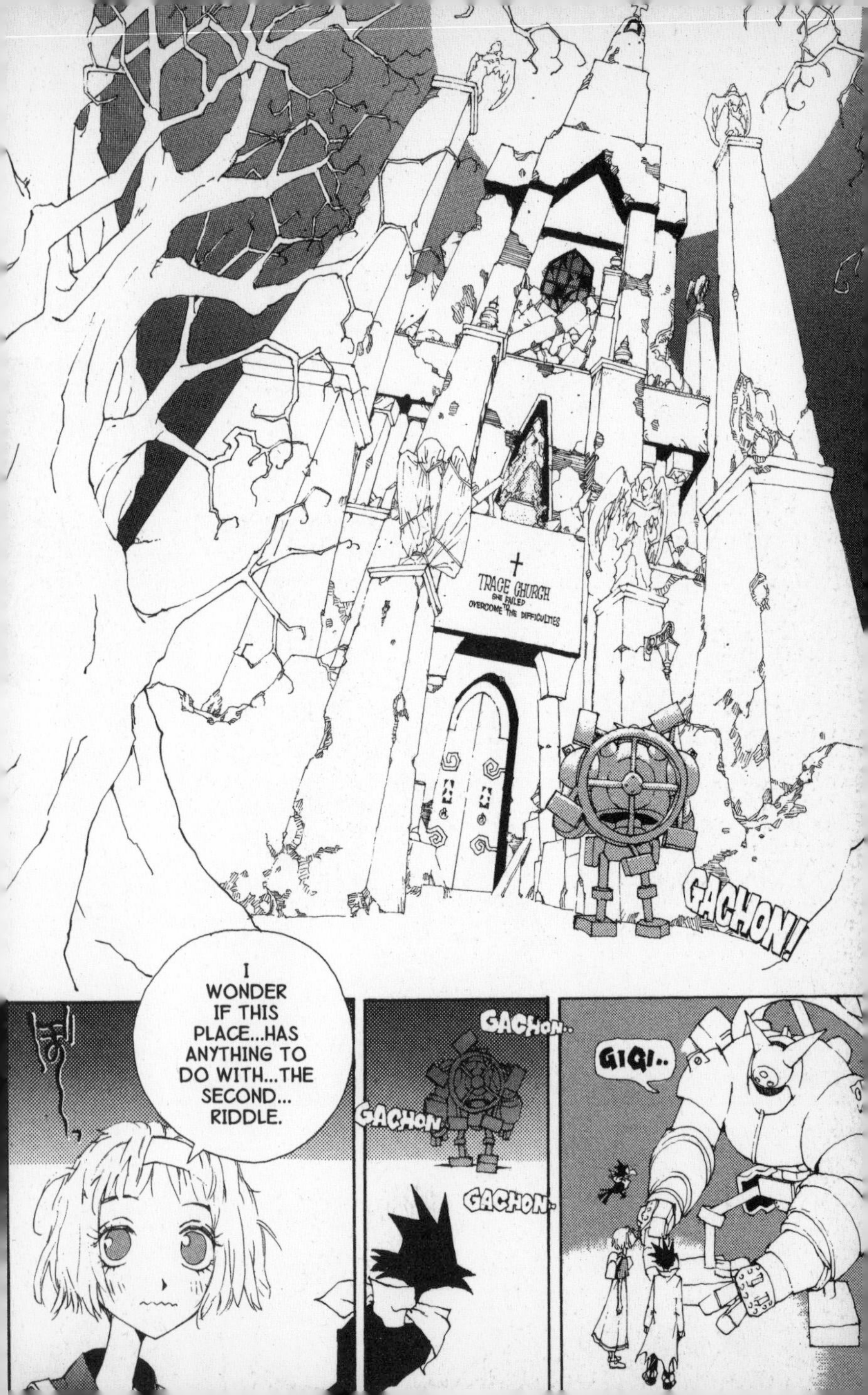
TRACE CHURCH
SHE FAILED TO OVERCOME THE DIFFICULTIES
GACHON!
GIQI..
GACHON..
GACHON
GACHON..
I WONDER IF THIS PLACE...HAS ANYTHING TO DO WITH...THE SECOND... RIDDLE.

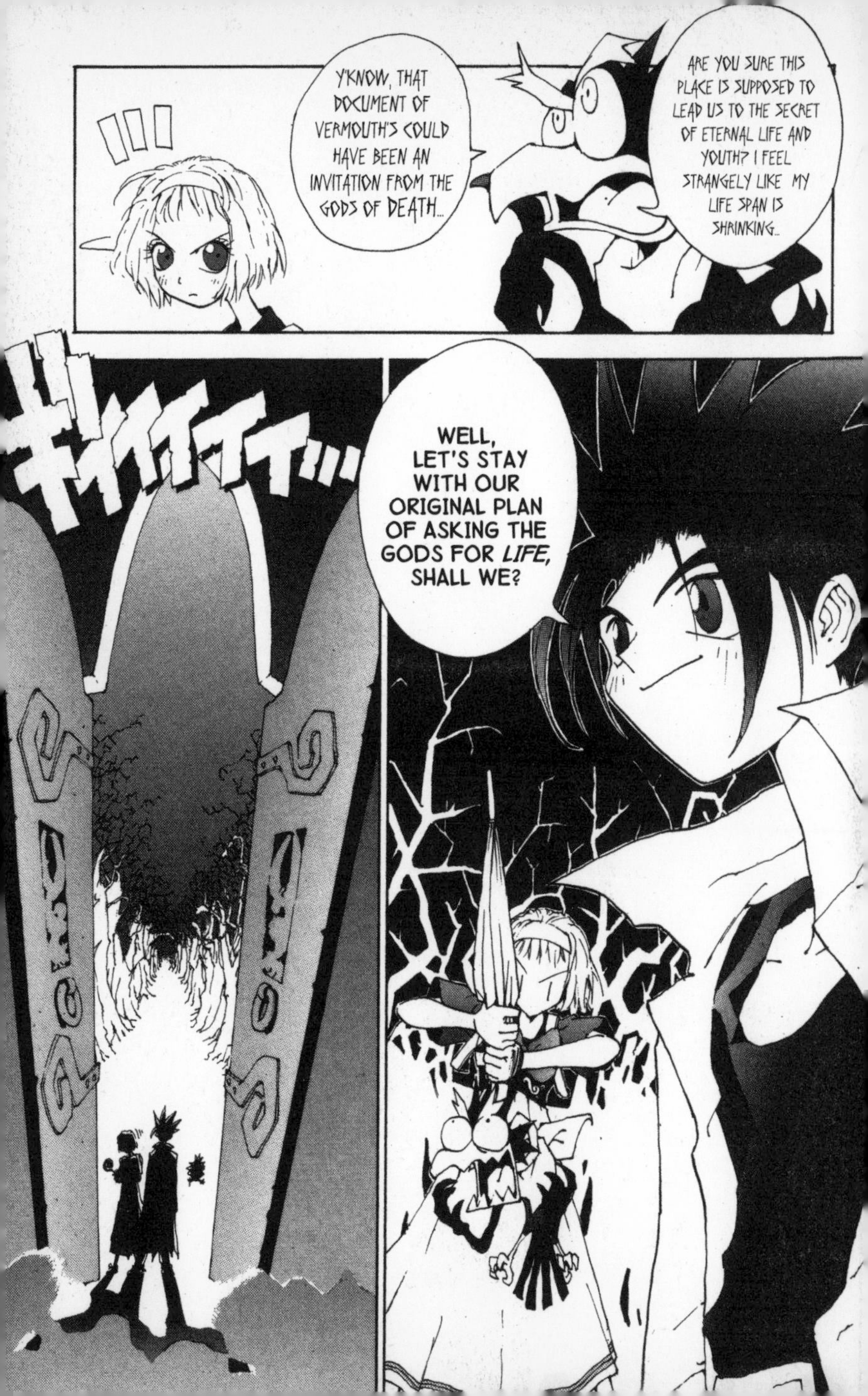
ARE YOU SURE THIS PLACE IS SUPPOSED TO LEAD US TO THE SECRET OF ETERNAL LIFE AND YOUTH? I FEEL STRANGELY LIKE MY LIFE SPAN IS SHRINKING...
Y'KNOW, THAT DOCUMENT OF VERMOUTH'S COULD HAVE BEEN AN INVITATION FROM THE GODS OF DEATH...
WELL, LET'S STAY WITH OUR ORIGINAL PLAN OF ASKING THE GODS FOR *LIFE*, SHALL WE?

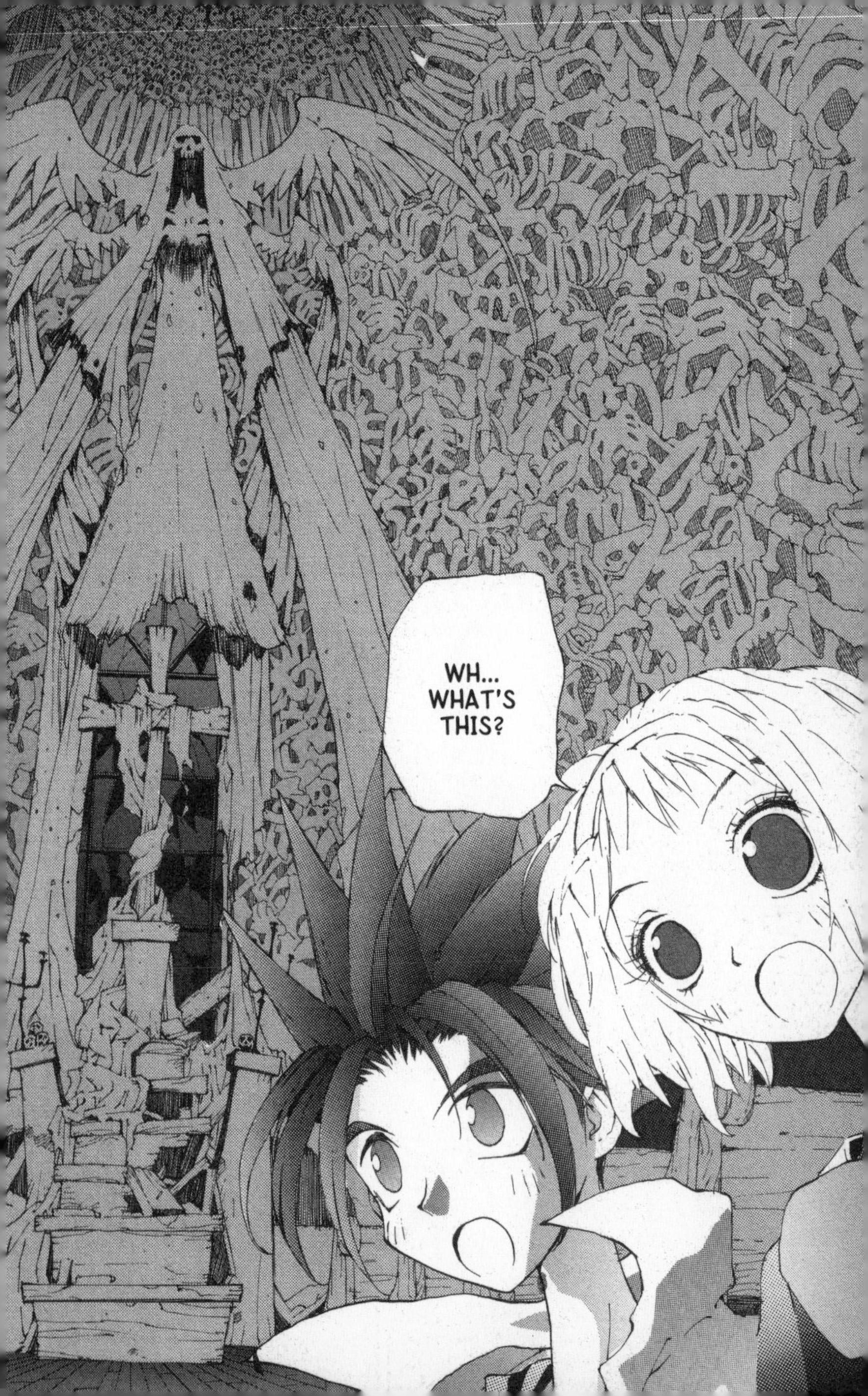
WH... WHAT'S THIS?

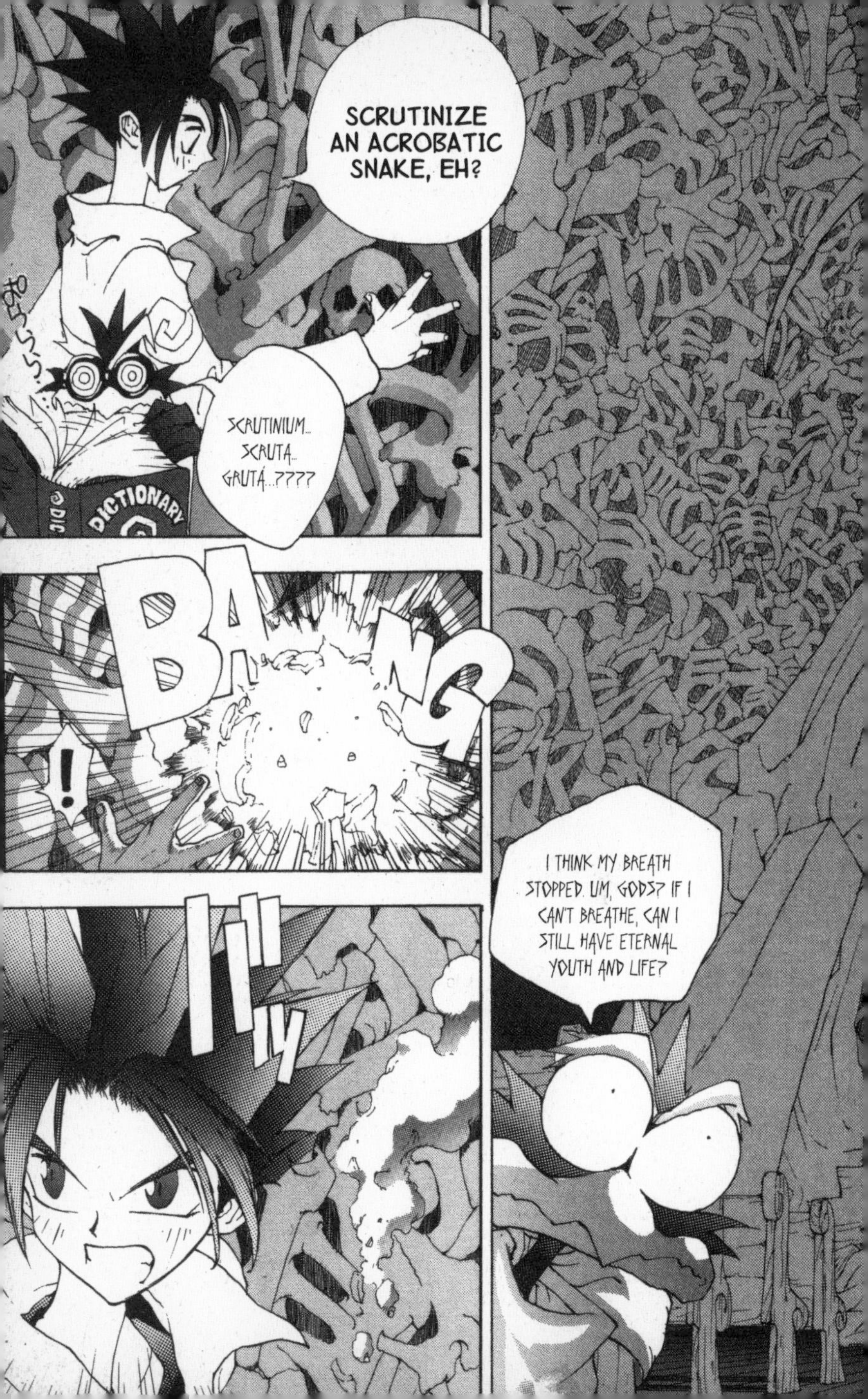
I THINK MY BREATH STOPPED. UM, GODS? IF I CAN'T BREATHE, CAN I STILL HAVE ETERNAL YOUTH AND LIFE?
SCRUTINIZE AN ACROBATIC SNAKE, EH?
SCRUTINIUM... SCRUTA... GRUTA...????
DICTIONARY
BANG
!

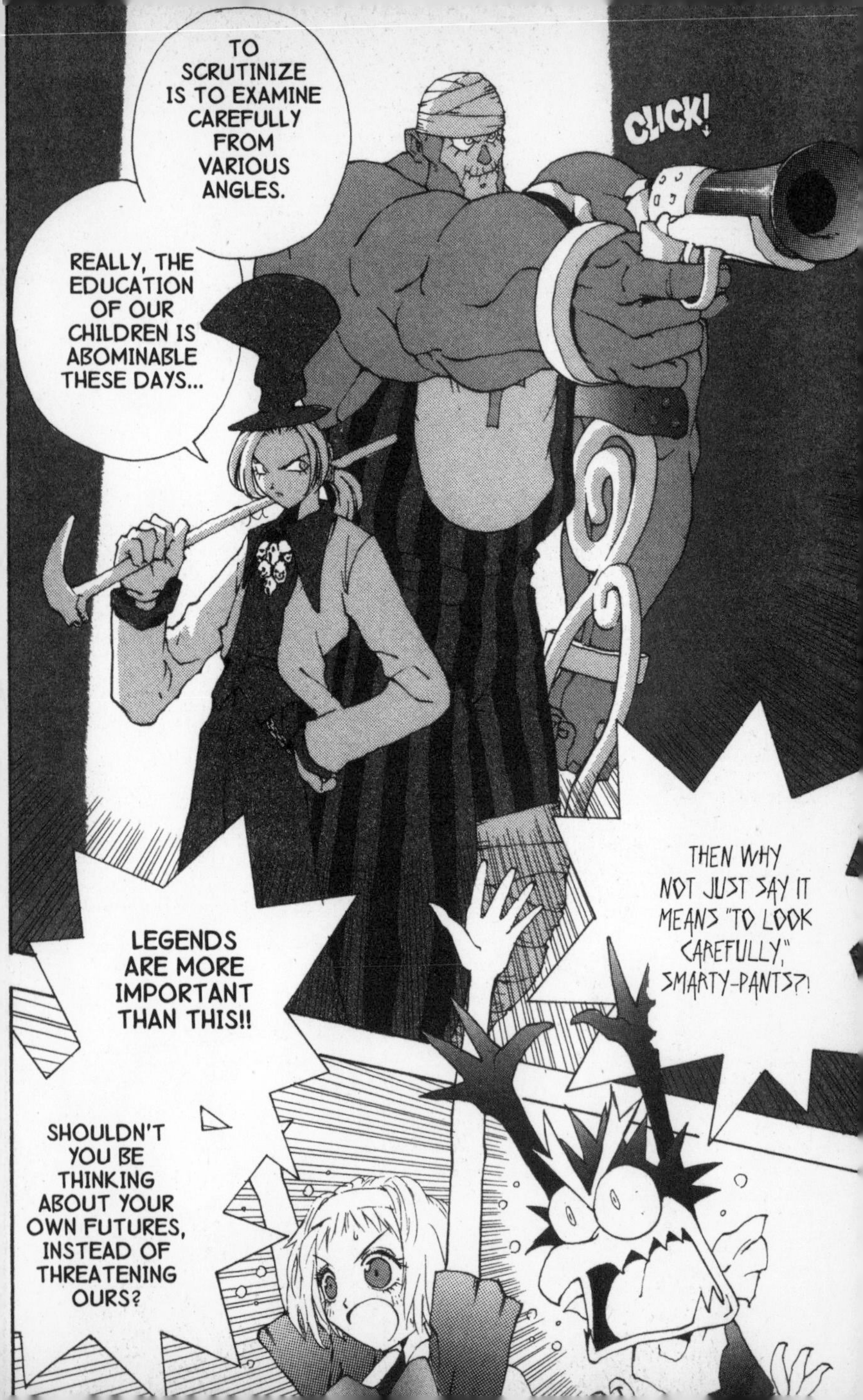
CLICK!
TO SCRUTINIZE IS TO EXAMINE CAREFULLY FROM VARIOUS ANGLES.
REALLY, THE EDUCATION OF OUR CHILDREN IS ABOMINABLE THESE DAYS...
THEN WHY NOT JUST SAY IT MEANS "TO LOOK CAREFULLY," SMARTY-PANTS?!
LEGENDS ARE MORE IMPORTANT THAN THIS!!
SHOULDN'T YOU BE THINKING ABOUT YOUR OWN FUTURES, INSTEAD OF THREATENING OURS?

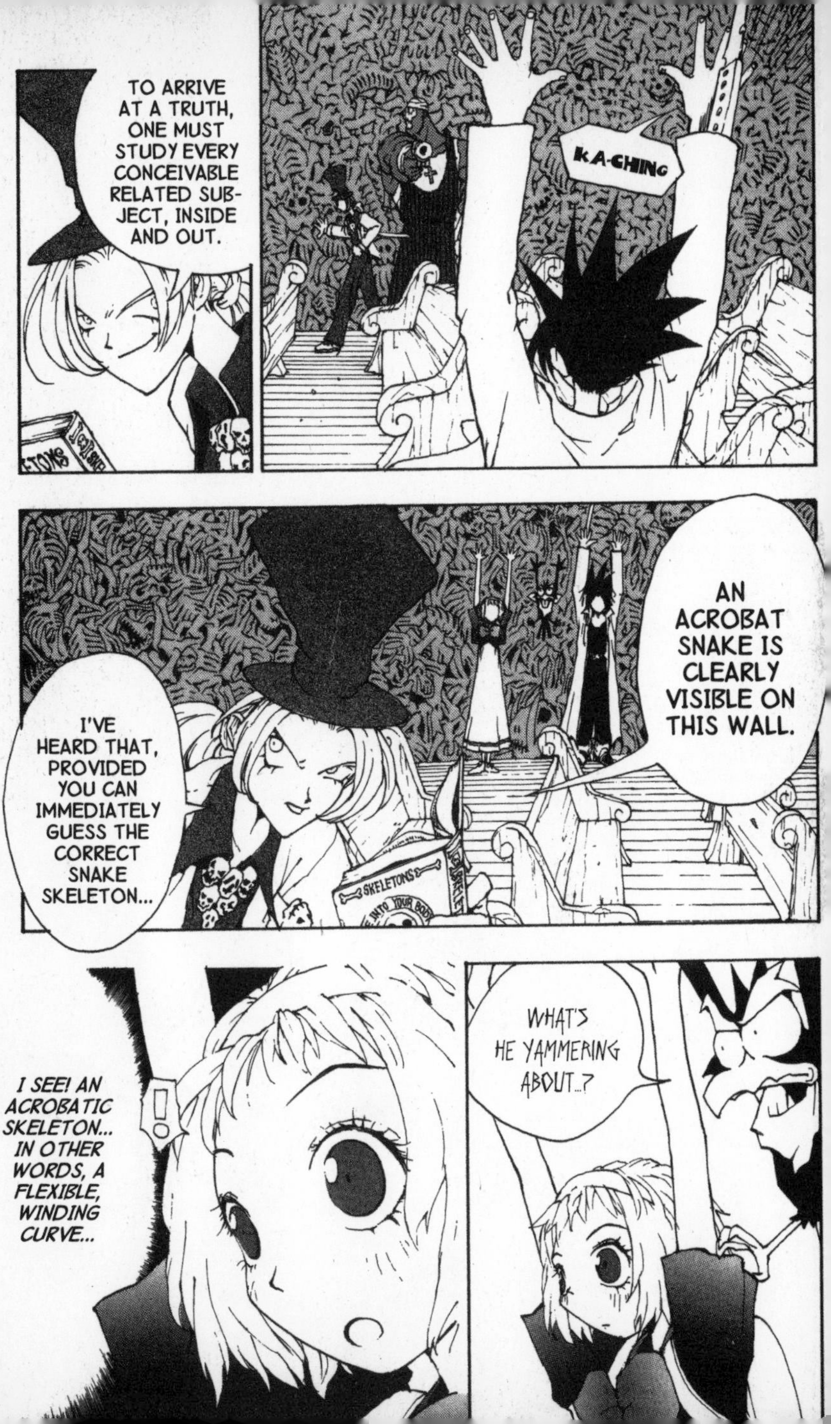
KA-CHING
TO ARRIVE AT A TRUTH, ONE MUST STUDY EVERY CONCEIVABLE RELATED SUB-JECT, INSIDE AND OUT.
AN ACROBAT SNAKE IS CLEARLY VISIBLE ON THIS WALL.
I'VE HEARD THAT, PROVIDED YOU CAN IMMEDIATELY GUESS THE CORRECT SNAKE SKELETON...
SKELETONS
WHAT'S HE YAMMERING ABOUT..?
!
I SEE! AN ACROBATIC SKELETON... IN OTHER WORDS, A FLEXIBLE, WINDING CURVE...

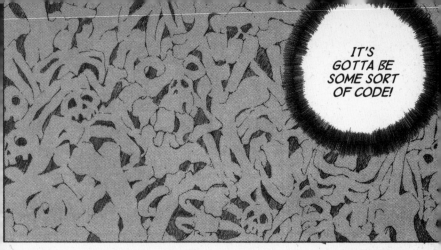

IT'S GOTTA BE SOME SORT OF CODE!

IT SHOULD BE A CRIME...LITTLE BOYS GROW UP SO EASILY, BUT TO PROPERLY EDUCATE THEM IS SO DIFFICULT!

...THIS IS IT...THE CORRECT SHAPE OF THE BONES...I-I'LL MAKE A NOTE OF IT.

ALL RIGHT...

GARI! GARI!

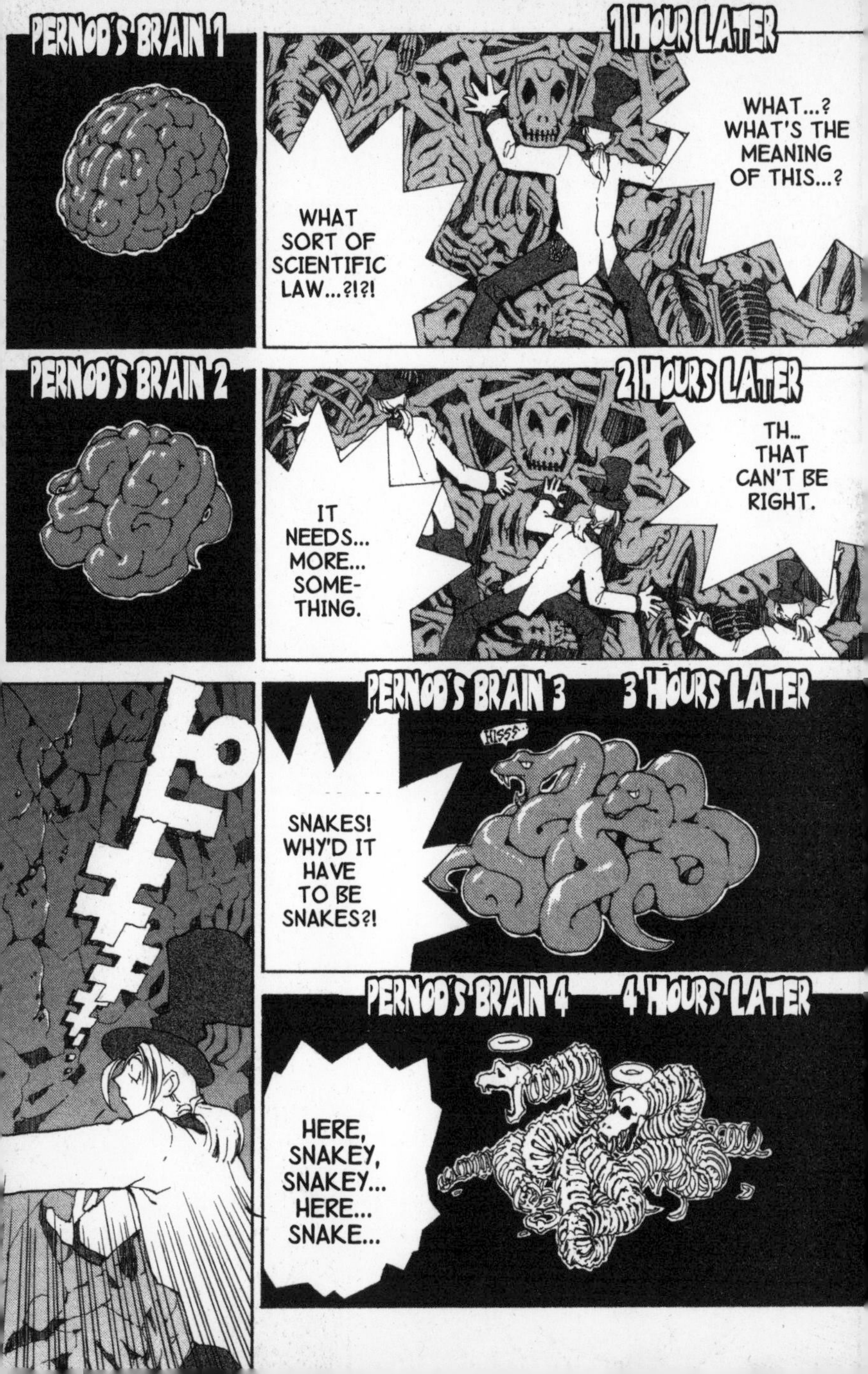
1 HOUR LATER
WHAT...? WHAT'S THE MEANING OF THIS...?
WHAT SORT OF SCIENTIFIC LAW...?!?!
PERNOD'S BRAIN 1
2 HOURS LATER
TH... THAT CAN'T BE RIGHT.
IT NEEDS... MORE... SOME-THING.
PERNOD'S BRAIN 2
PERNOD'S BRAIN 3
3 HOURS LATER
HISSS
SNAKES! WHY'D IT HAVE TO BE SNAKES?!
PERNOD'S BRAIN 4
4 HOURS LATER
HERE, SNAKEY, SNAKEY... HERE... SNAKE...

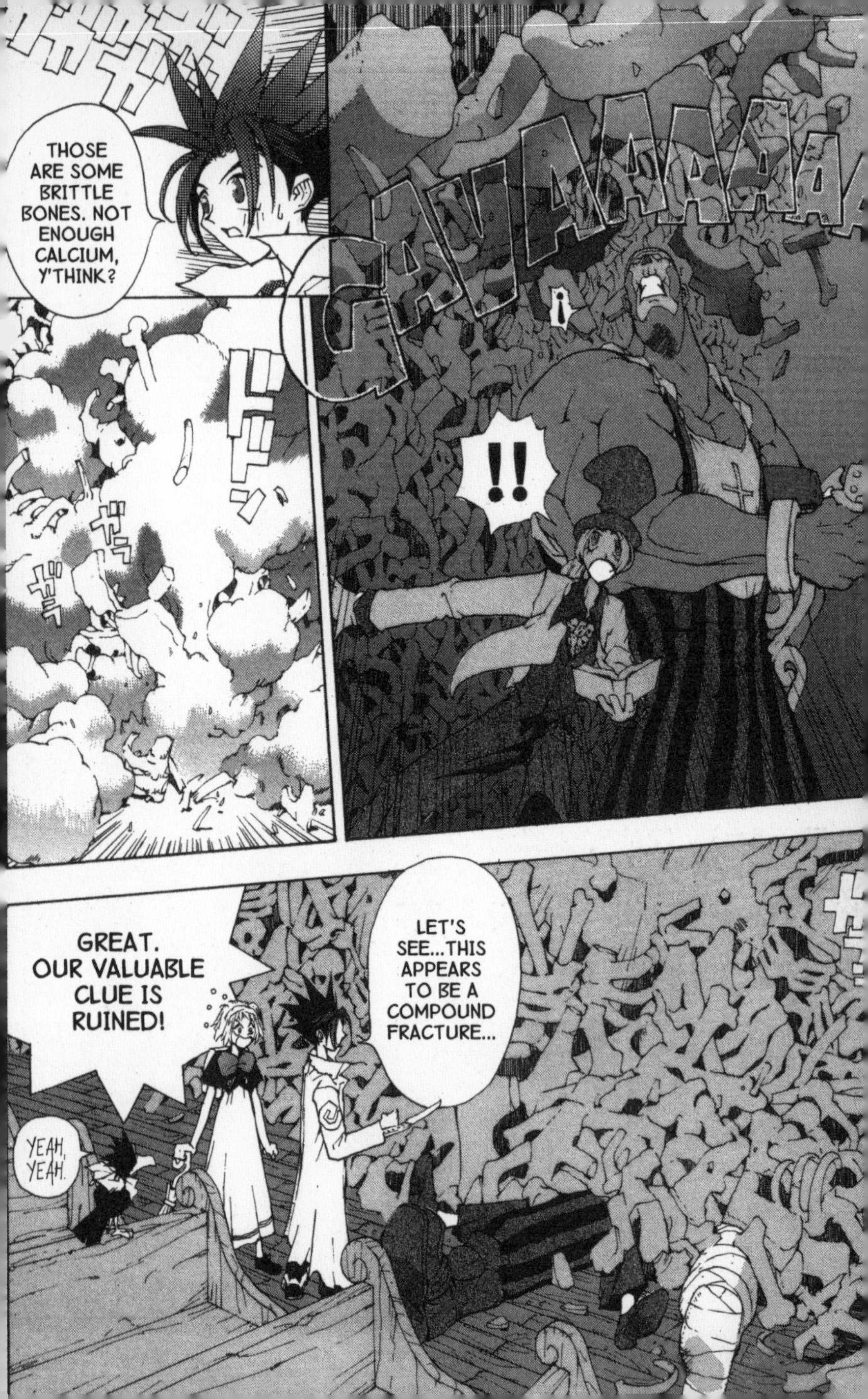
GAAAAAAAA
!!
THOSE ARE SOME BRITTLE BONES. NOT ENOUGH CALCIUM, Y'THINK?
LET'S SEE...THIS APPEARS TO BE A COMPOUND FRACTURE...
GREAT. OUR VALUABLE CLUE IS RUINED!
YEAH, YEAH.

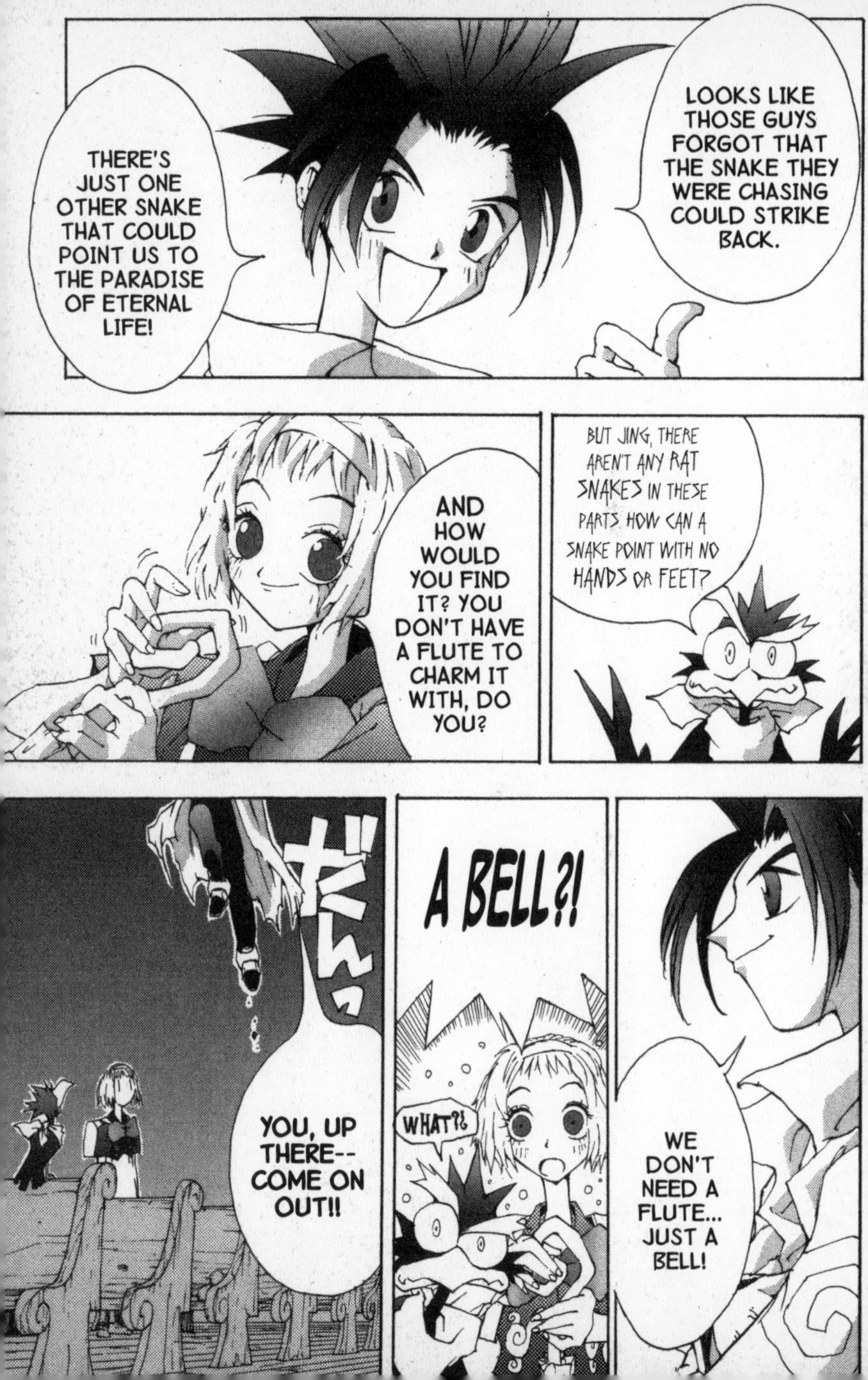
LOOKS LIKE THOSE GUYS FORGOT THAT THE SNAKE THEY WERE CHASING COULD STRIKE BACK.
THERE'S JUST ONE OTHER SNAKE THAT COULD POINT US TO THE PARADISE OF ETERNAL LIFE!
BUT JING, THERE AREN'T ANY RAT SNAKES IN THESE PARTS. HOW CAN A SNAKE POINT WITH NO HANDS OR FEET?
AND HOW WOULD YOU FIND IT? YOU DON'T HAVE A FLUTE TO CHARM IT WITH, DO YOU?
WE DON'T NEED A FLUTE... JUST A BELL!
A BELL?!
WHAT?!
だんっ
YOU, UP THERE-- COME ON OUT!!

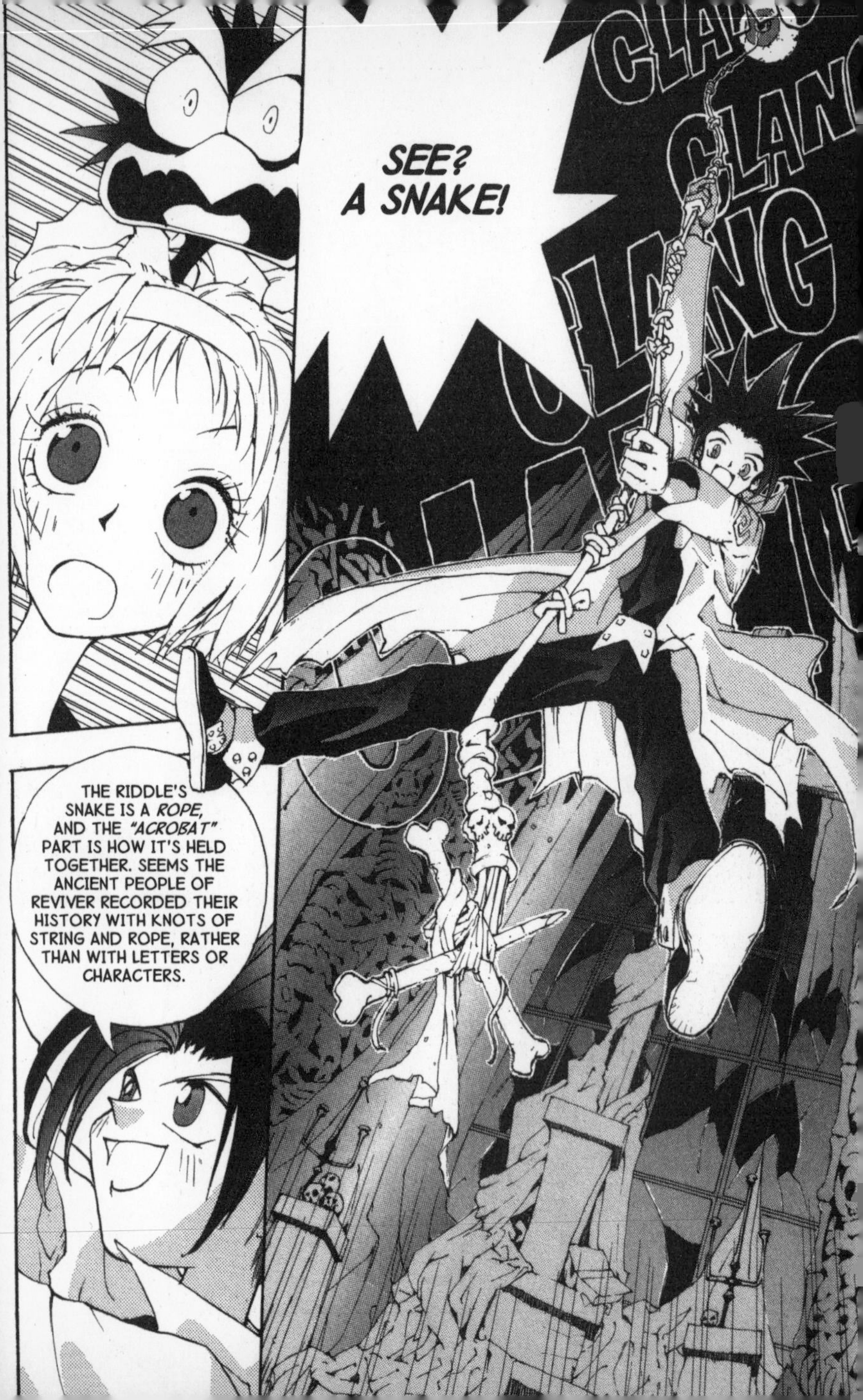
CLANG
CLANG
SEE? A SNAKE!
THE RIDDLE'S SNAKE IS A *ROPE*, AND THE *"ACROBAT"* PART IS HOW IT'S HELD TOGETHER. SEEMS THE ANCIENT PEOPLE OF REVIVER RECORDED THEIR HISTORY WITH KNOTS OF STRING AND ROPE, RATHER THAN WITH LETTERS OR CHARACTERS.

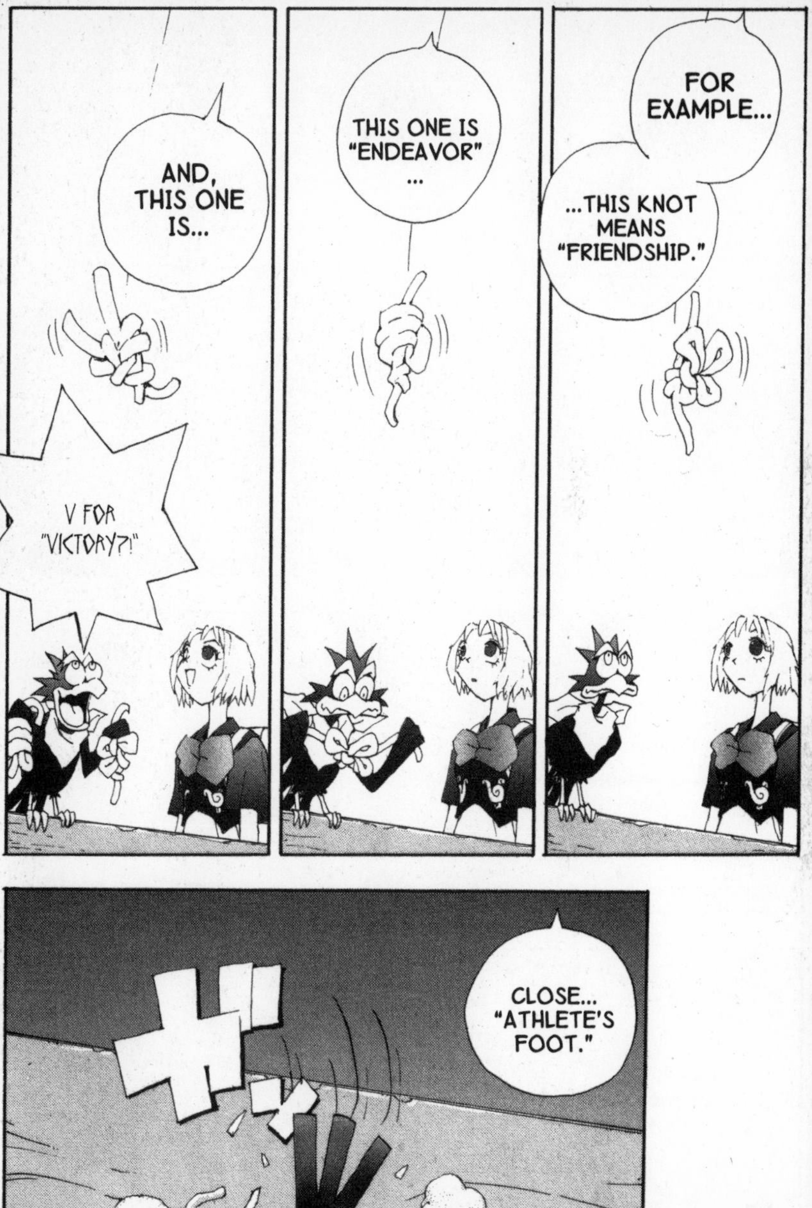
FOR EXAMPLE...
...THIS KNOT MEANS "FRIENDSHIP."
THIS ONE IS "ENDEAVOR" ...
AND, THIS ONE IS...
V FOR "VICTORY?!"
CLOSE... "ATHLETE'S FOOT."

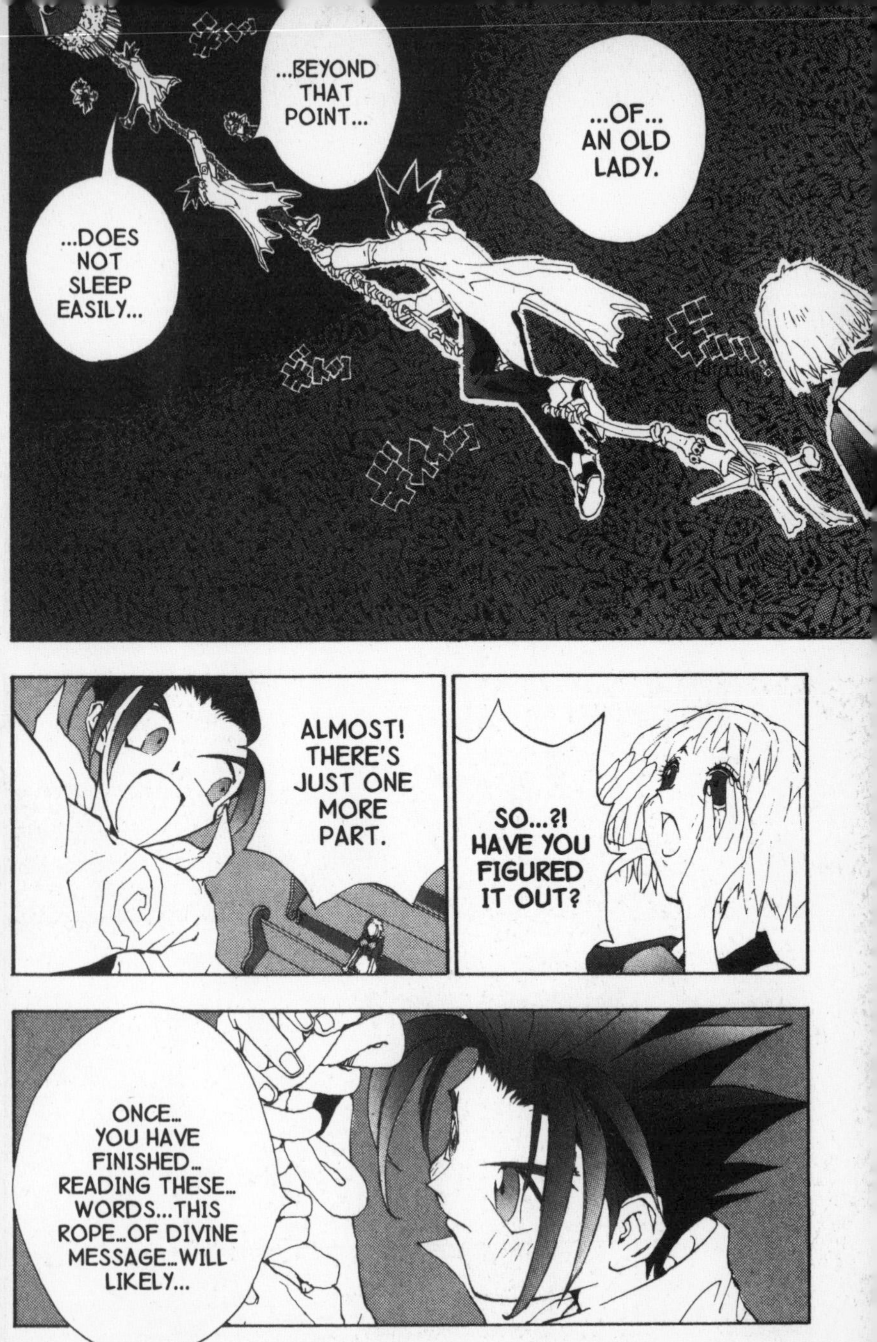
...OF... AN OLD LADY.
...BEYOND THAT POINT...
...DOES NOT SLEEP EASILY...
SO...?! HAVE YOU FIGURED IT OUT?
ALMOST! THERE'S JUST ONE MORE PART.
ONCE... YOU HAVE FINISHED... READING THESE... WORDS...THIS ROPE...OF DIVINE MESSAGE...WILL LIKELY...

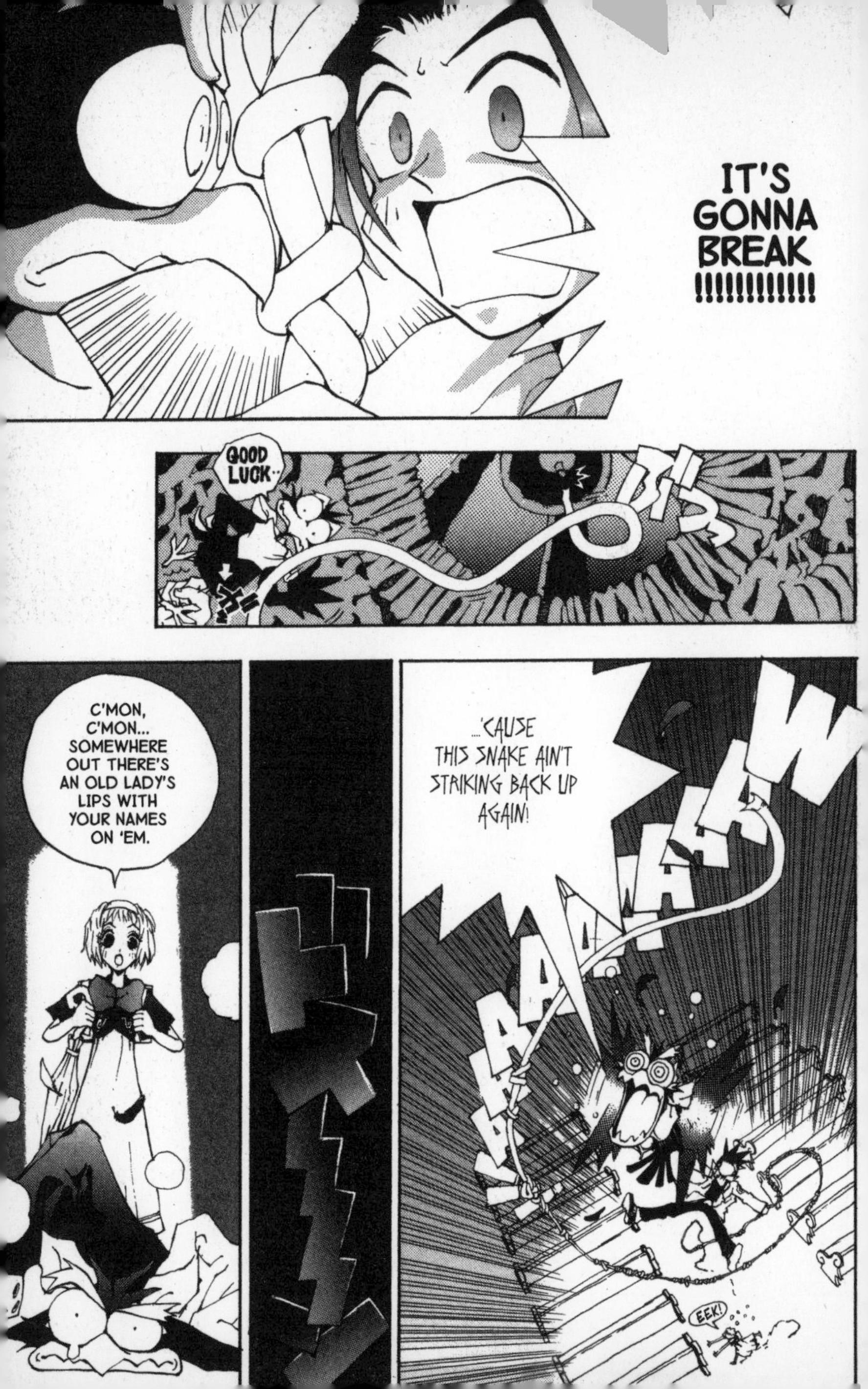
IT'S GONNA BREAK !!!!!!!!!!!!
GOOD LUCK..
...'CAUSE THIS SNAKE AIN'T STRIKING BACK UP AGAIN!
EEK!
C'MON, C'MON... SOMEWHERE OUT THERE'S AN OLD LADY'S LIPS WITH YOUR NAMES ON 'EM.

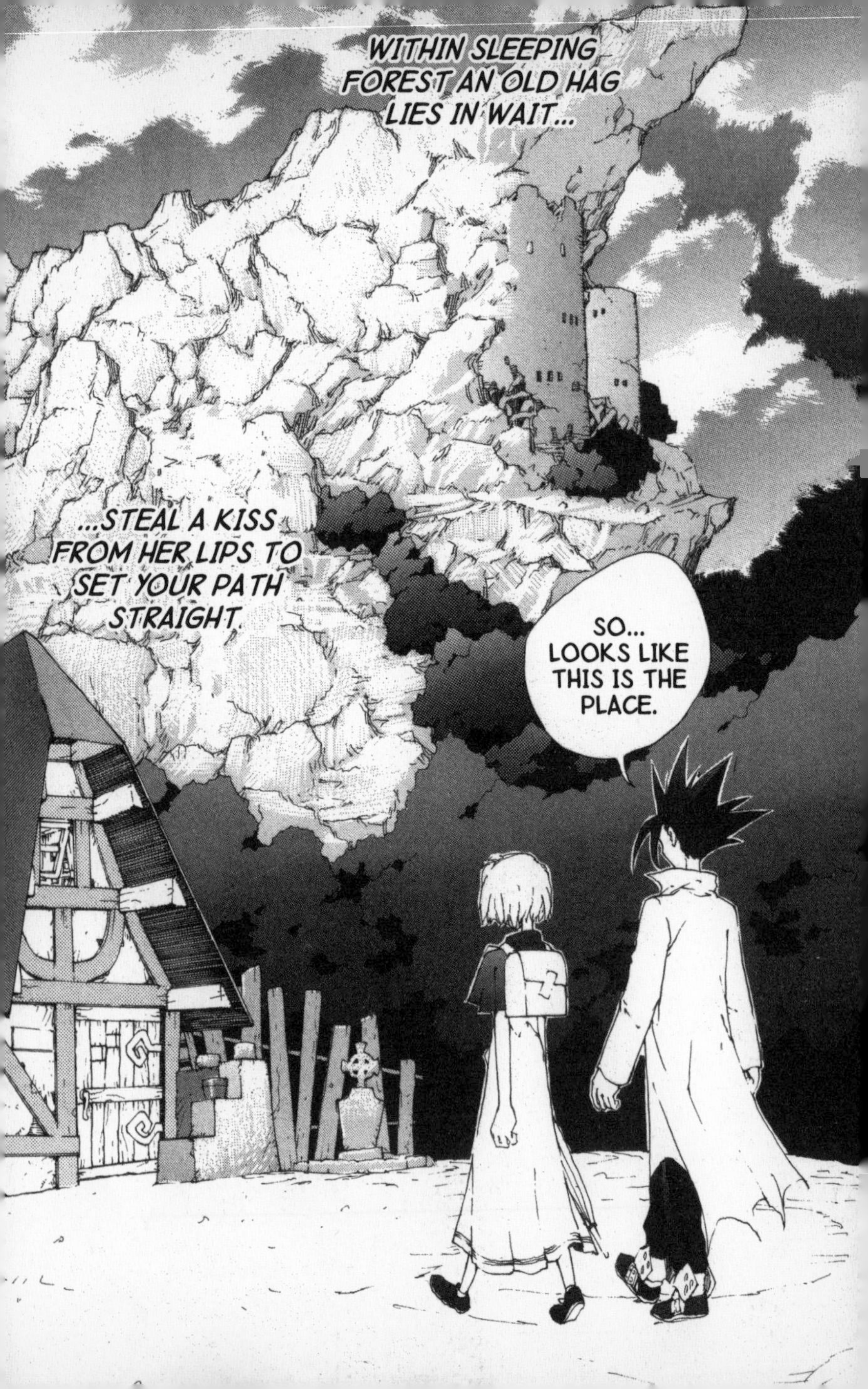
WITHIN SLEEPING FOREST AN OLD HAG LIES IN WAIT...
...STEAL A KISS FROM HER LIPS TO SET YOUR PATH STRAIGHT.
SO... LOOKS LIKE THIS IS THE PLACE.

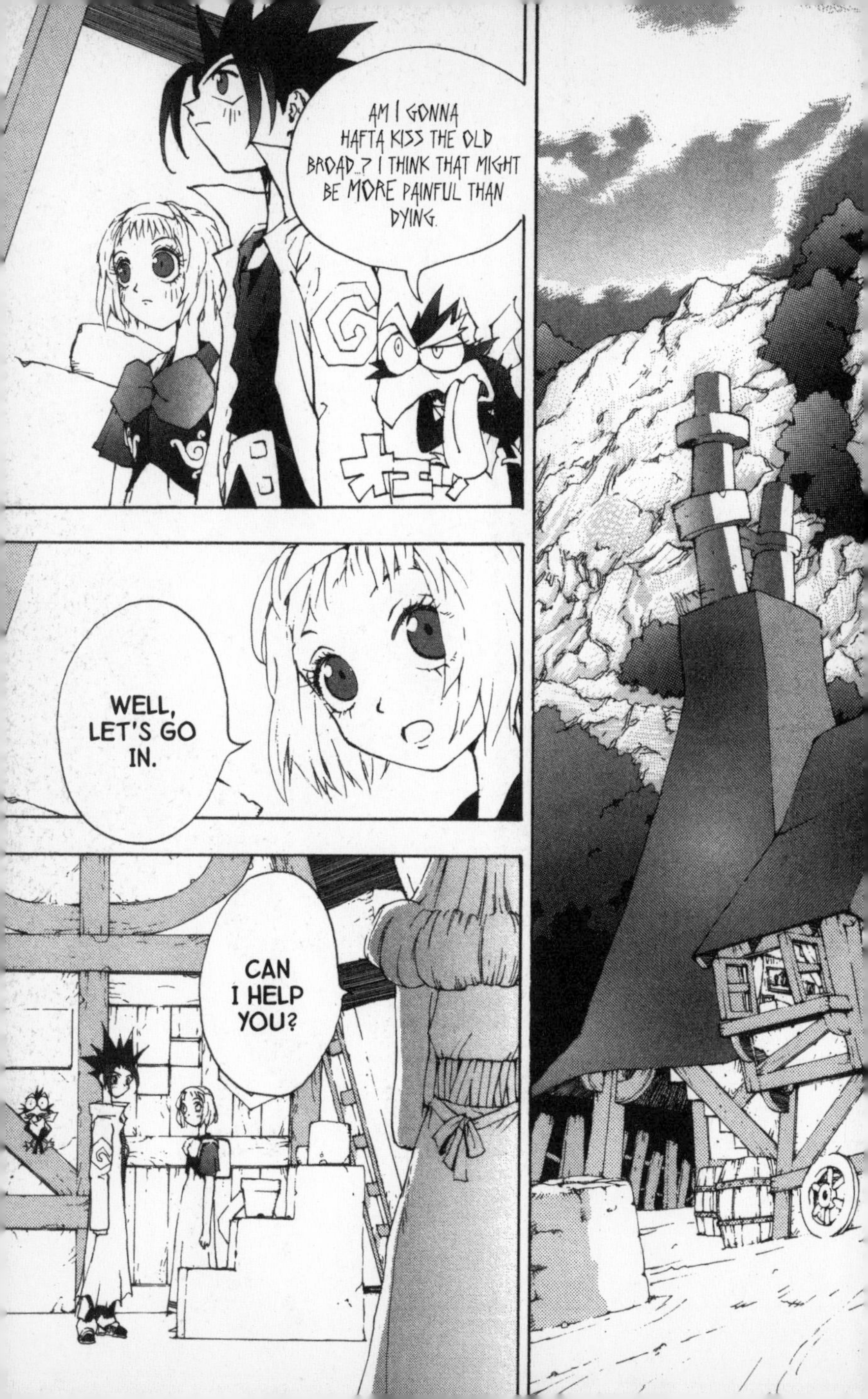
AM I GONNA HAFTA KISS THE OLD BROAD...? I THINK THAT MIGHT BE MORE PAINFUL THAN DYING.
オエッ
WELL, LET'S GO IN.
CAN I HELP YOU?

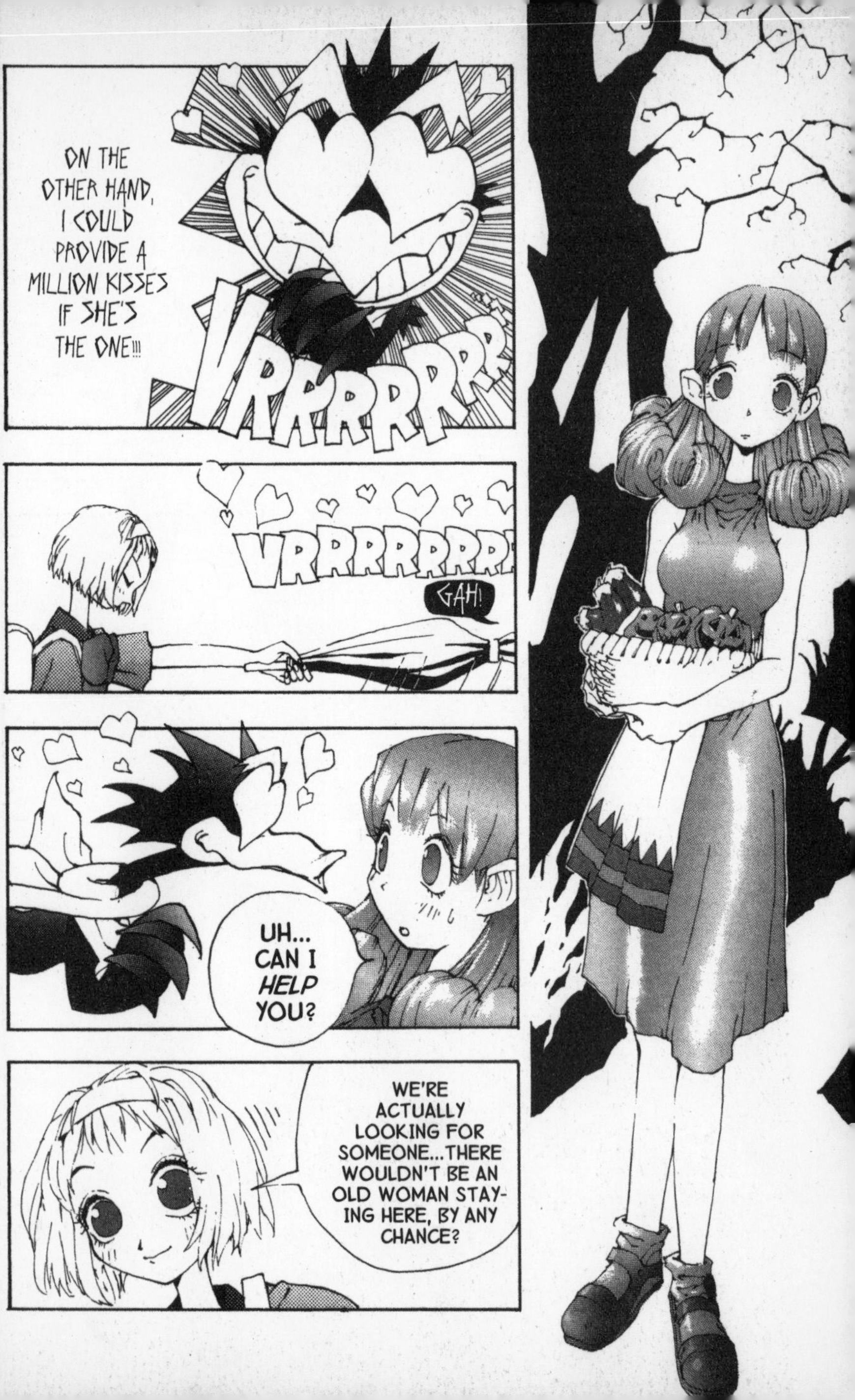
ON THE OTHER HAND, I COULD PROVIDE A MILLION KISSES IF SHE'S THE ONE!!!
VRRRRRRRR
VRRRRRRRRR
GAH!
UH... CAN I *HELP* YOU?
WE'RE ACTUALLY LOOKING FOR SOMEONE...THERE WOULDN'T BE AN OLD WOMAN STAY-ING HERE, BY ANY CHANCE?

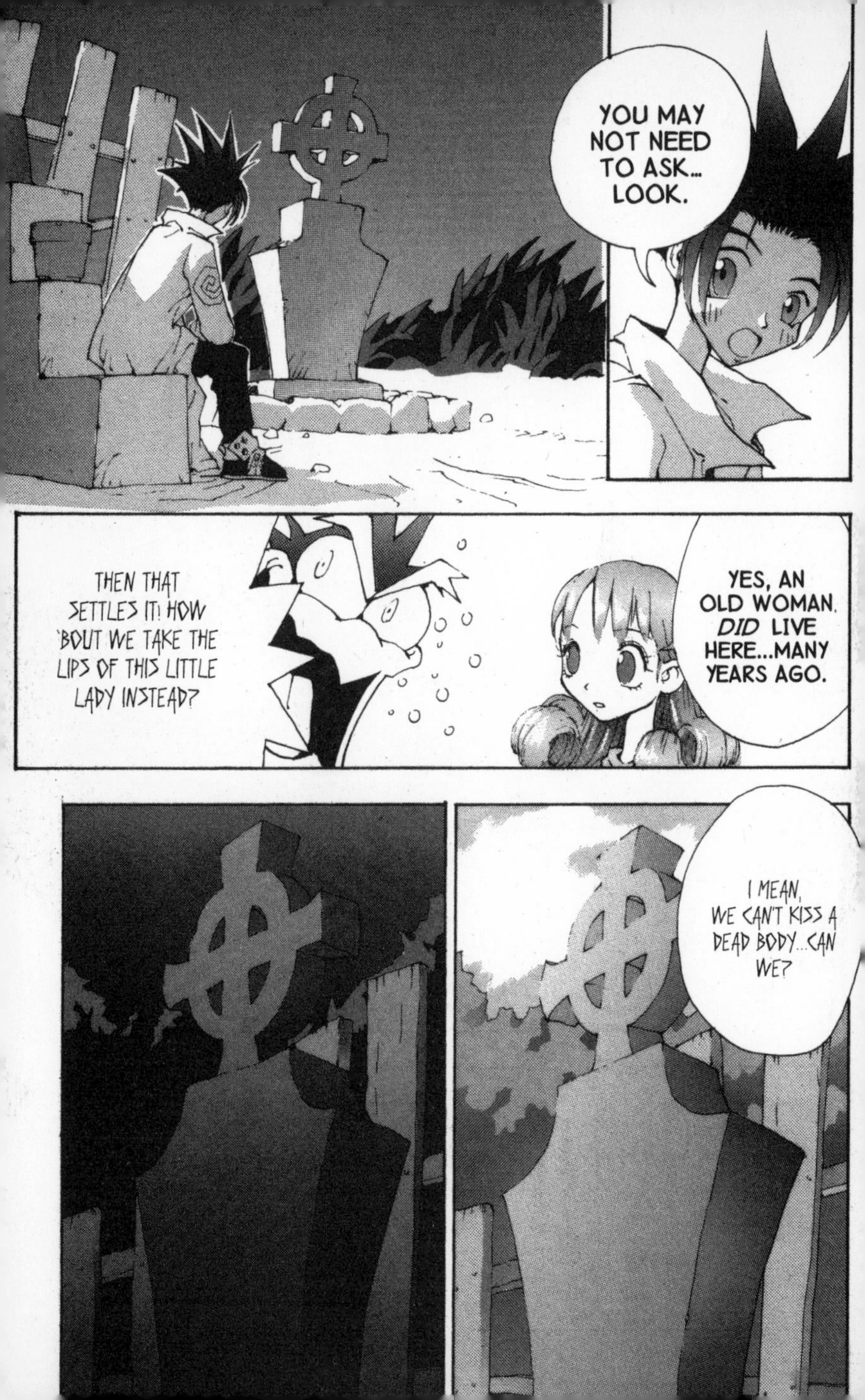
YOU MAY NOT NEED TO ASK... LOOK.
YES, AN OLD WOMAN *DID* LIVE HERE...MANY YEARS AGO.
THEN THAT SETTLES IT! HOW 'BOUT WE TAKE THE LIPS OF THIS LITTLE LADY INSTEAD?
I MEAN, WE CAN'T KISS A DEAD BODY...CAN WE?

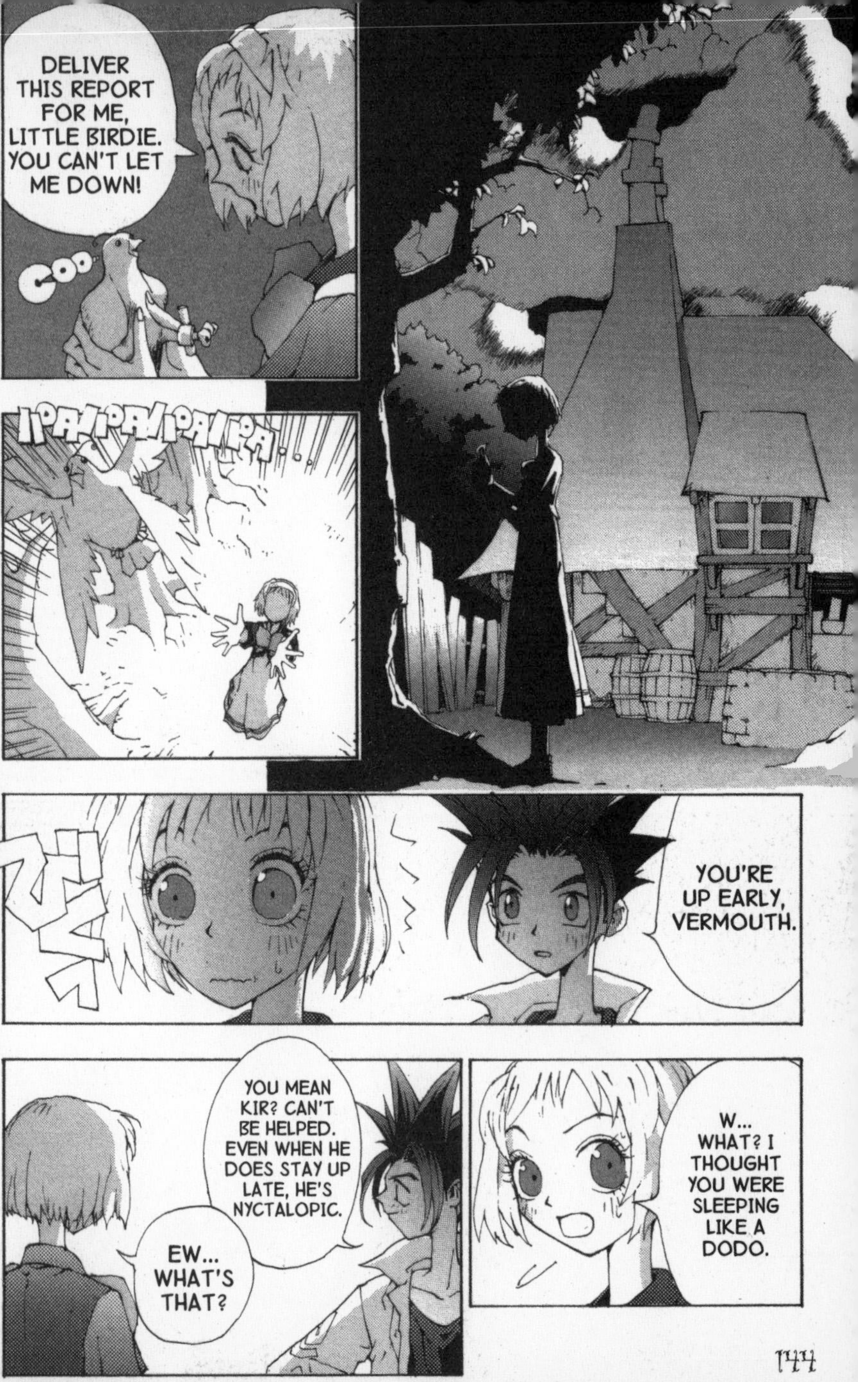
DELIVER THIS REPORT FOR ME, LITTLE BIRDIE. YOU CAN'T LET ME DOWN!
COO
YOU'RE UP EARLY, VERMOUTH.
W... WHAT? I THOUGHT YOU WERE SLEEPING LIKE A DODO.
YOU MEAN KIR? CAN'T BE HELPED. EVEN WHEN HE DOES STAY UP LATE, HE'S NYCTALOPIC.
EW... WHAT'S THAT?

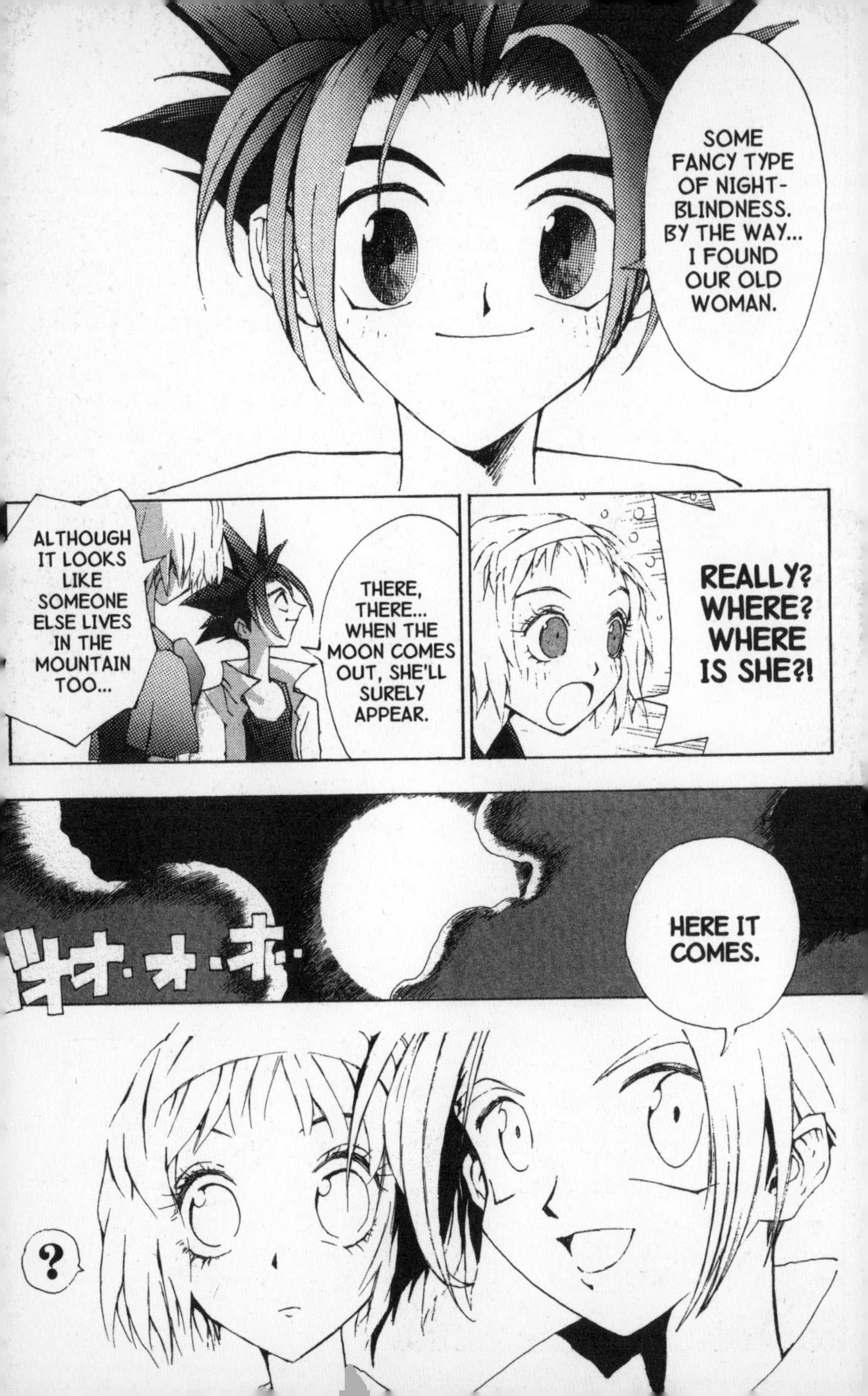
SOME FANCY TYPE OF NIGHT-BLINDNESS. BY THE WAY... I FOUND OUR OLD WOMAN.
REALLY? WHERE? WHERE IS SHE?!
THERE, THERE... WHEN THE MOON COMES OUT, SHE'LL SURELY APPEAR.
ALTHOUGH IT LOOKS LIKE SOMEONE ELSE LIVES IN THE MOUNTAIN TOO...
HERE IT COMES.
?

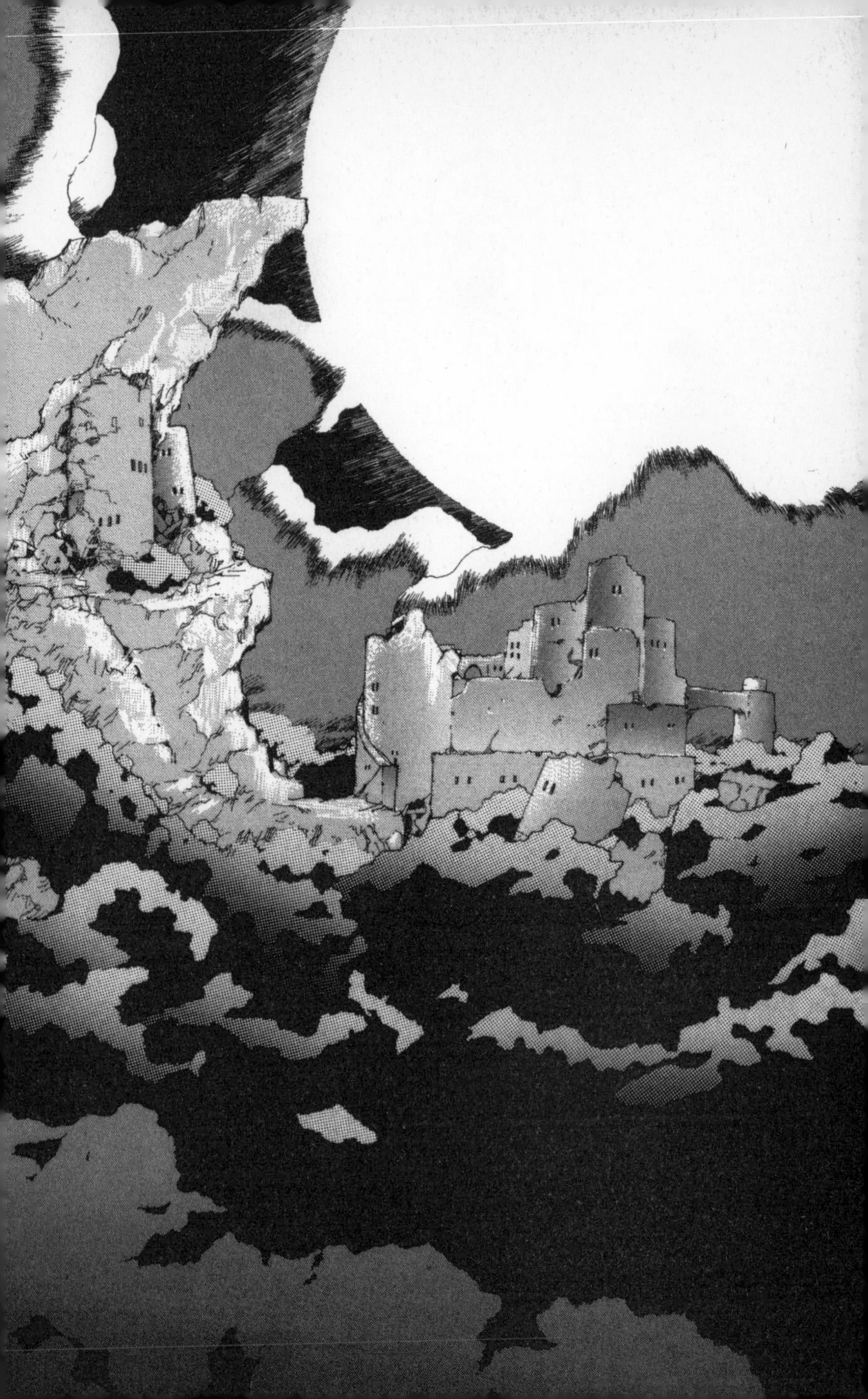

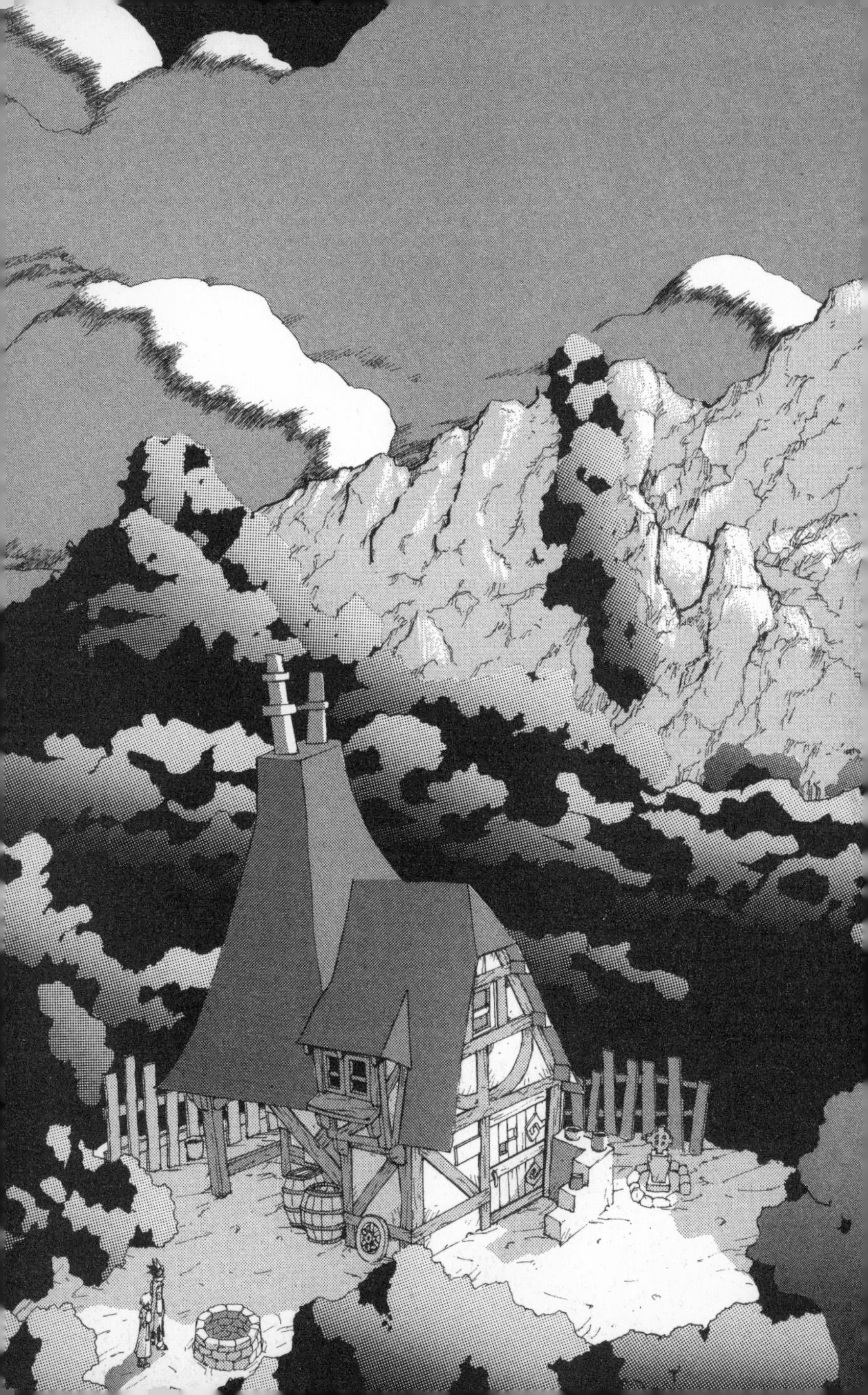

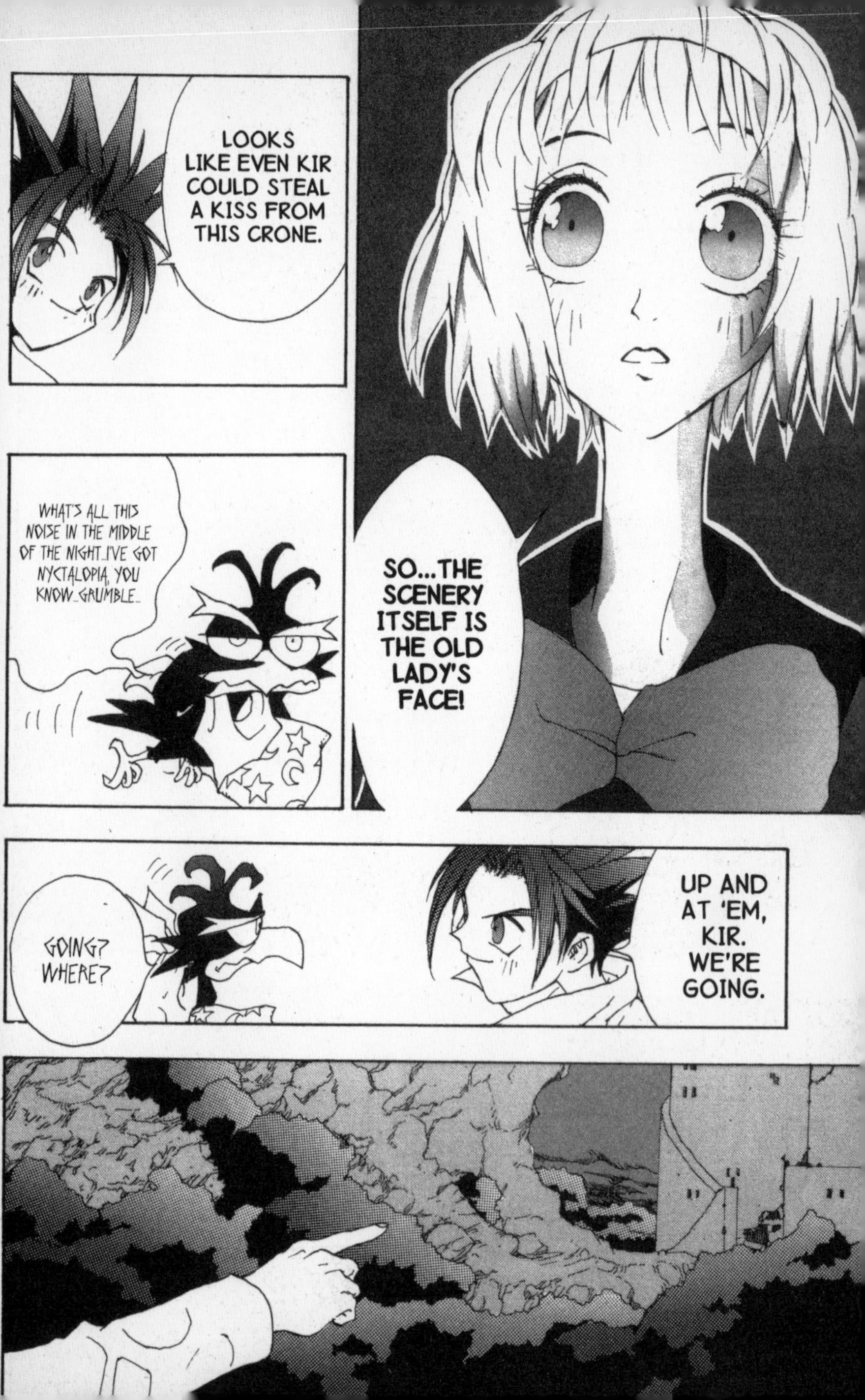
SO...THE SCENERY ITSELF IS THE OLD LADY'S FACE!
LOOKS LIKE EVEN KIR COULD STEAL A KISS FROM THIS CRONE.
WHAT'S ALL THIS NOISE IN THE MIDDLE OF THE NIGHT...I'VE GOT NYCTALOPIA, YOU KNOW...GRUMBLE...
UP AND AT 'EM, KIR. WE'RE GOING.
GOING? WHERE?

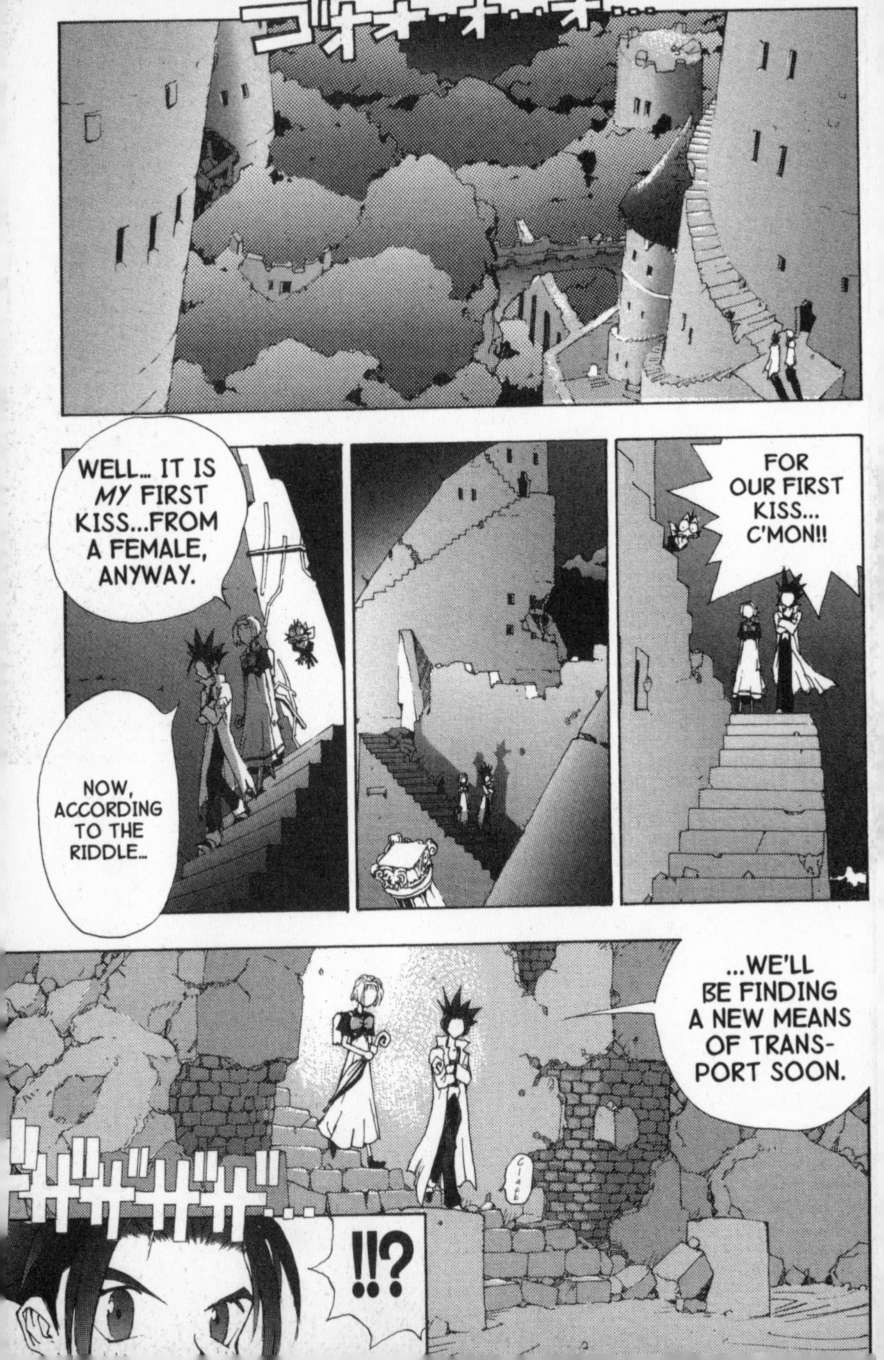
FOR OUR FIRST KISS... C'MON!!
WELL... IT IS *MY* FIRST KISS...FROM A FEMALE, ANYWAY.
NOW, ACCORDING TO THE RIDDLE...
...WE'LL BE FINDING A NEW MEANS OF TRANS-PORT SOON.
!!?

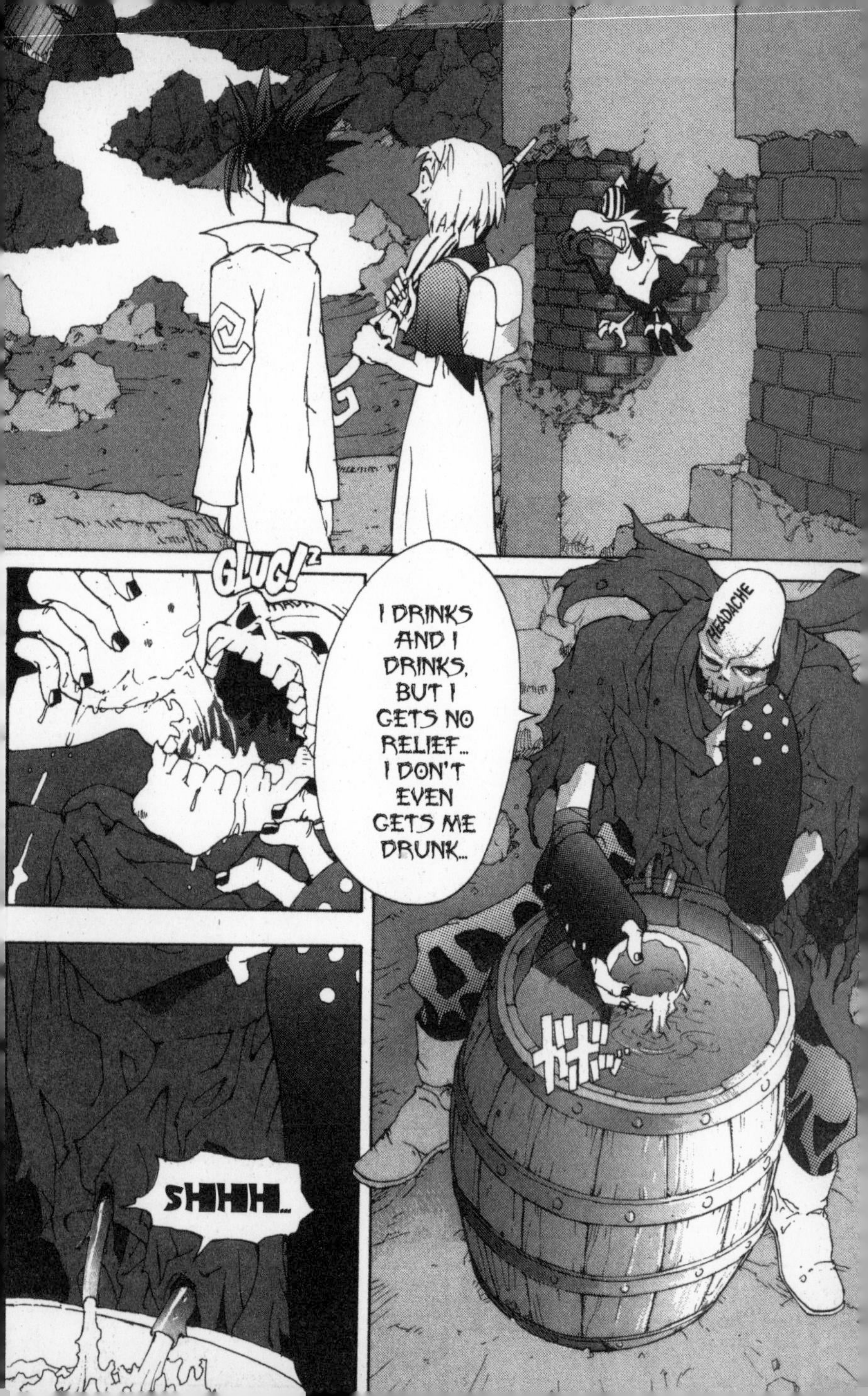
HEADACHE
I DRINKS AND I DRINKS, BUT I GETS NO RELIEF... I DON'T EVEN GETS ME DRUNK...
GLUG!
ガボッ
SHHHH...

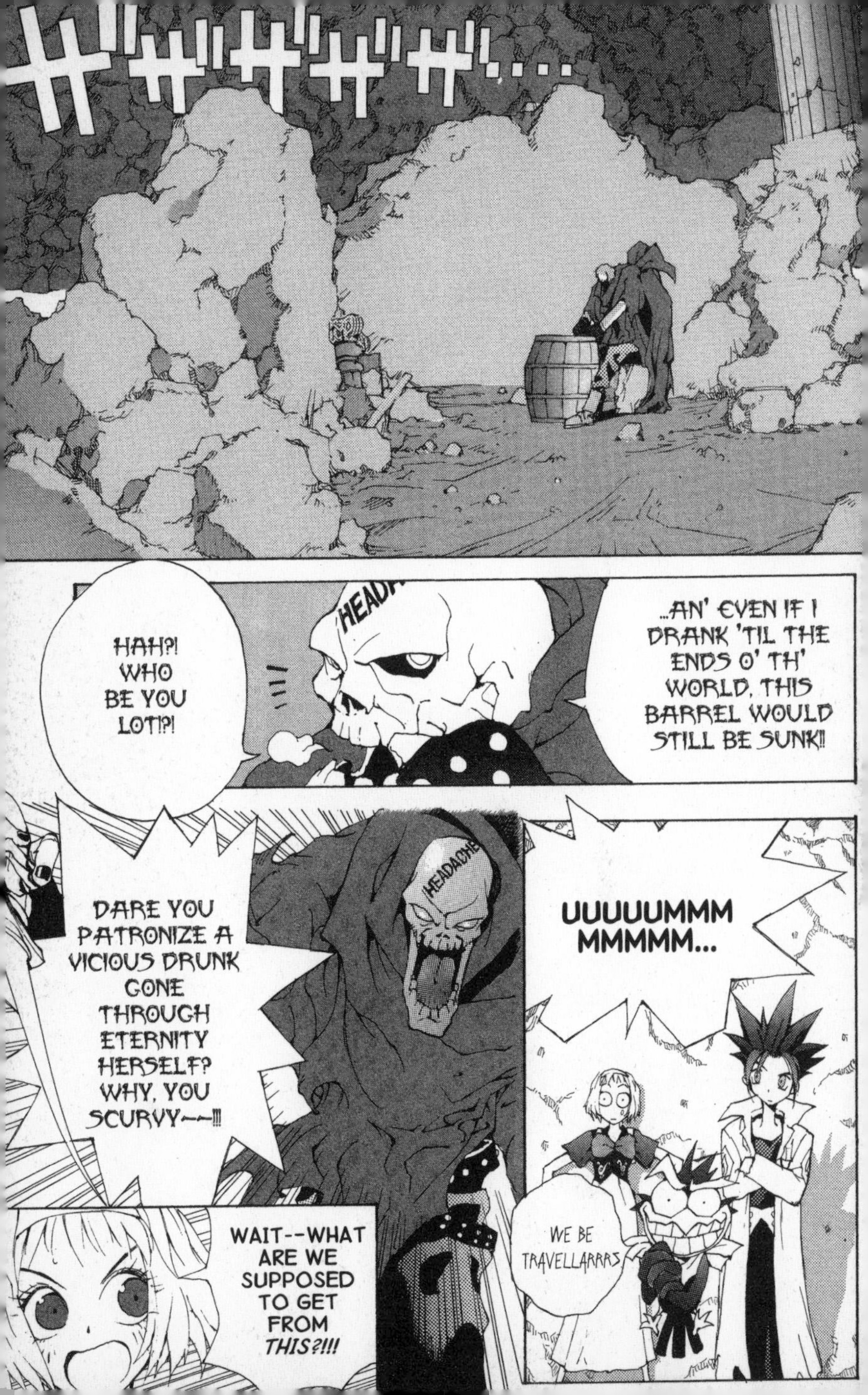
...AN' EVEN IF I DRANK 'TIL THE ENDS O' TH' WORLD, THIS BARREL WOULD STILL BE SUNK!!
HAH?! WHO BE YOU LOT?!
UUUUUMMM MMMMM...
WE BE TRAVELLARRRS
HEADACHE
DARE YOU PATRONIZE A VICIOUS DRUNK GONE THROUGH ETERNITY HERSELF? WHY, YOU SCURVY--!!!
WAIT--WHAT ARE WE SUPPOSED TO GET FROM *THIS?!!!*

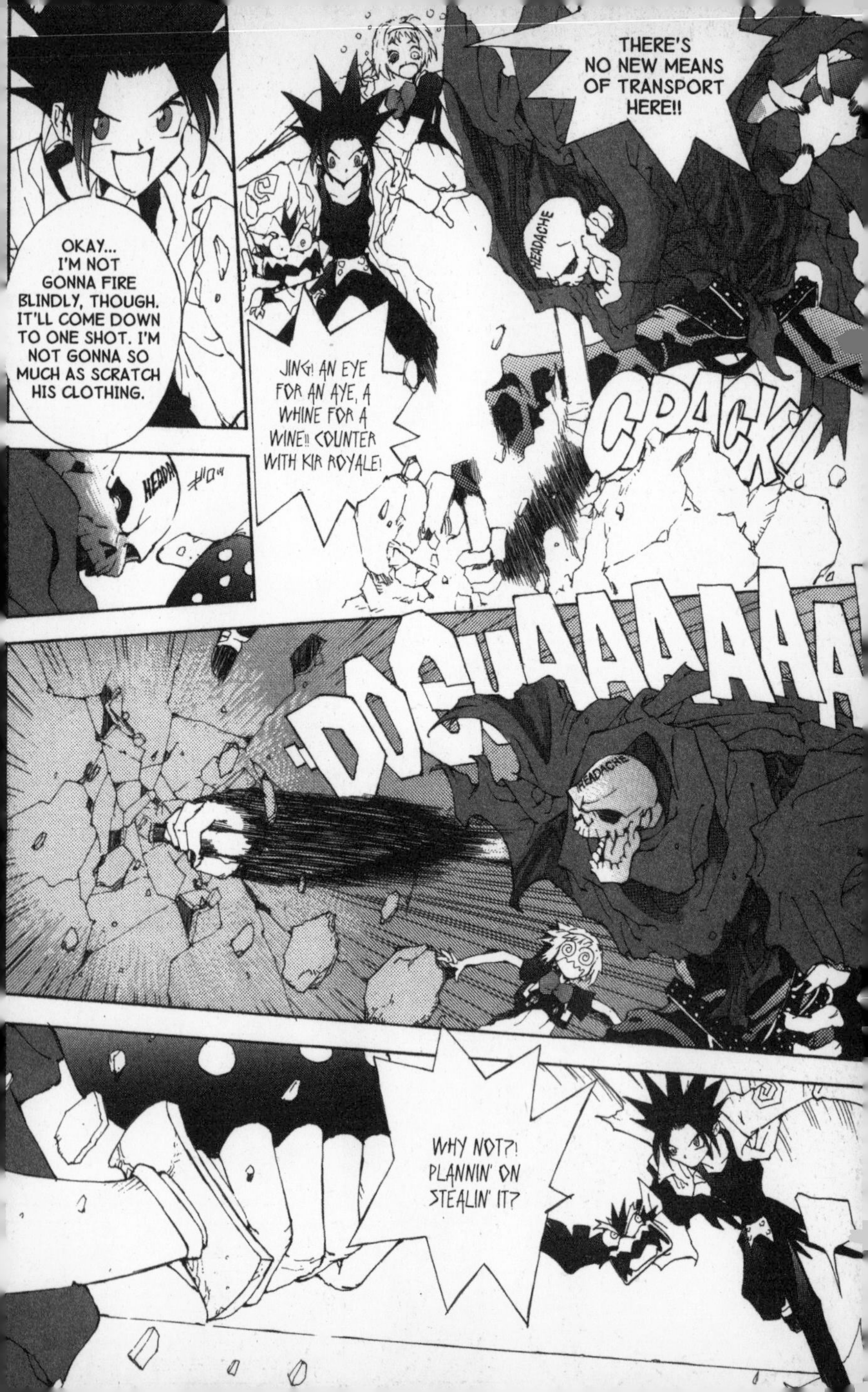
THERE'S NO NEW MEANS OF TRANSPORT HERE!!
HEADACHE
JING! AN EYE FOR AN AYE, A WHINE FOR A WINE!! COUNTER WITH KIR ROYALE!
CRACK!!
OKAY... I'M NOT GONNA FIRE BLINDLY, THOUGH. IT'LL COME DOWN TO ONE SHOT. I'M NOT GONNA SO MUCH AS SCRATCH HIS CLOTHING.
HEADA
DOGUAAAAAA
HEADACHE
WHY NOT?! PLANNIN' ON STEALIN' IT?

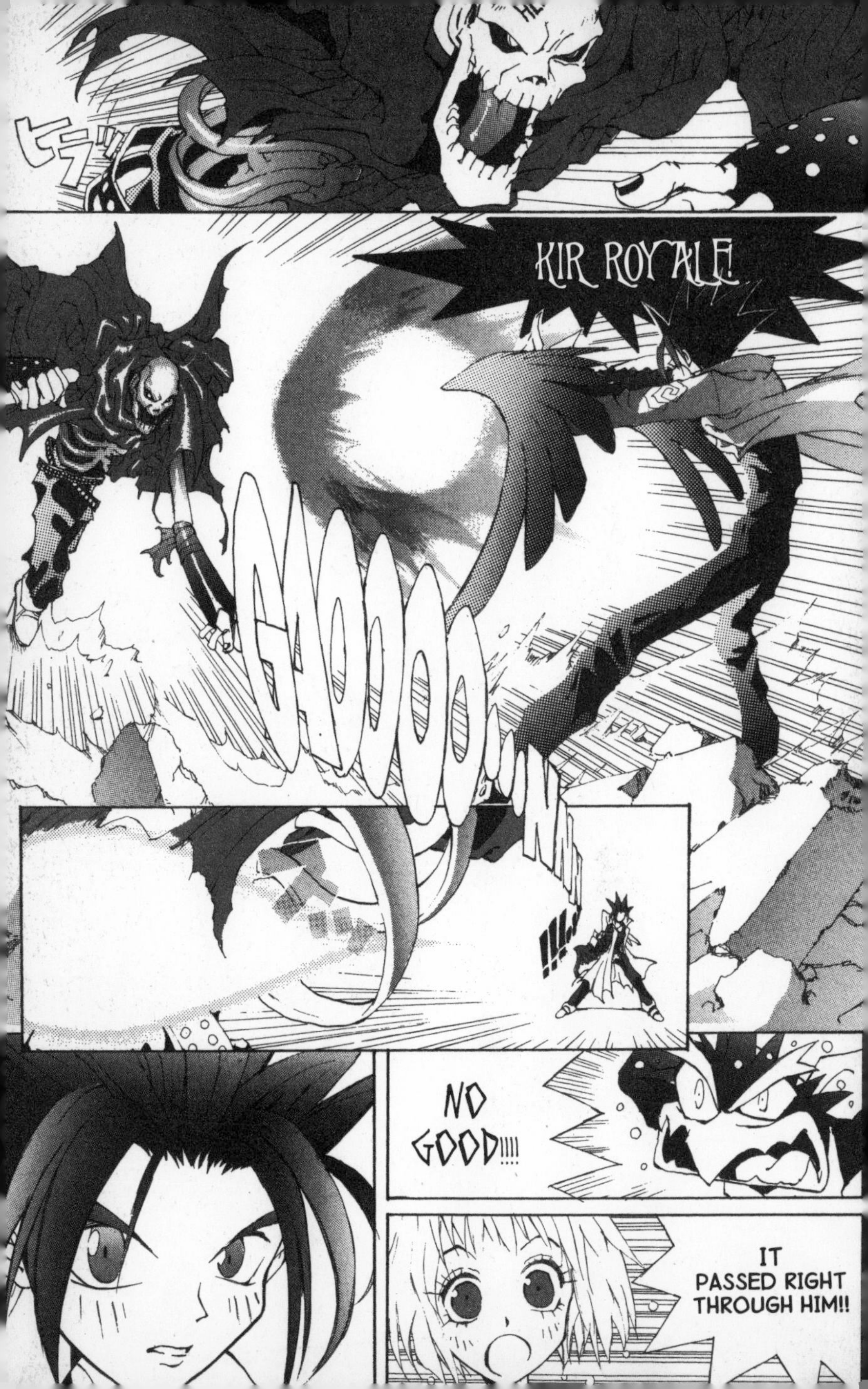

KIR ROYALE!
GAOOOO...N
NO GOOD!!!!
IT PASSED RIGHT THROUGH HIM!!

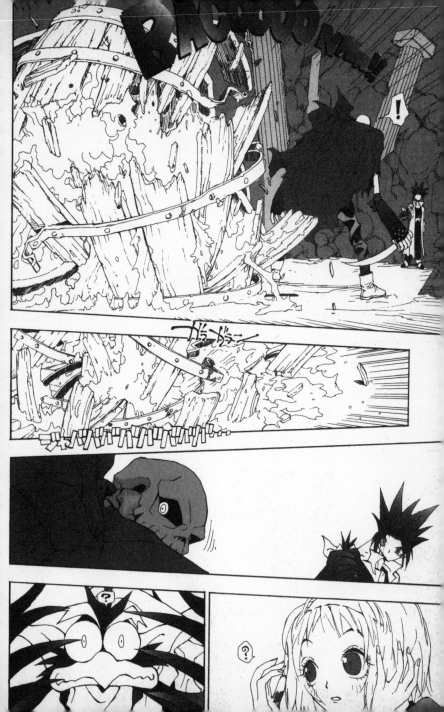

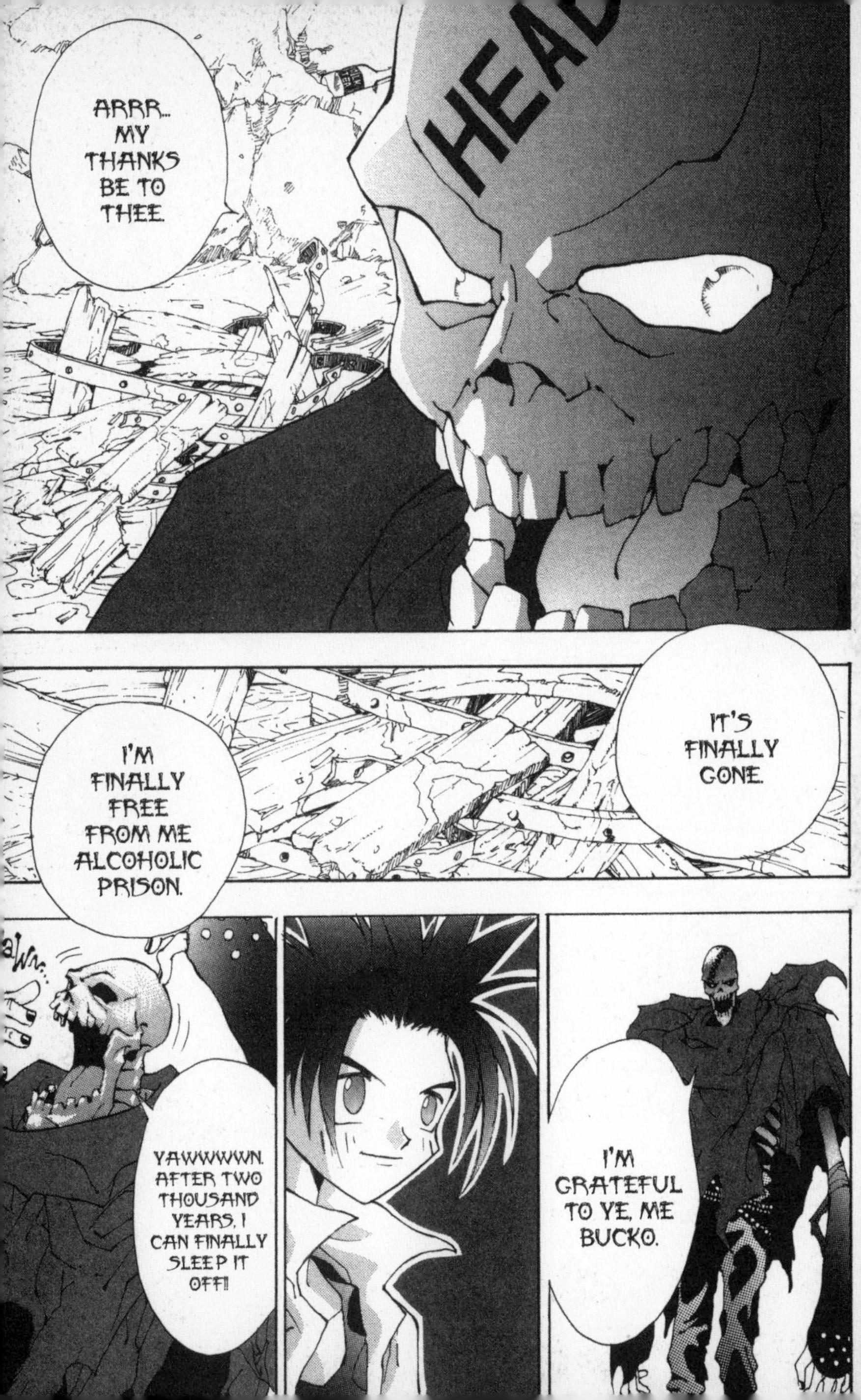
ARRR... MY THANKS BE TO THEE.
IT'S FINALLY GONE.
I'M FINALLY FREE FROM ME ALCOHOLIC PRISON.
I'M GRATEFUL TO YE, ME BUCKO.
YAWWWWN. AFTER TWO THOUSAND YEARS, I CAN FINALLY SLEEP IT OFF!!

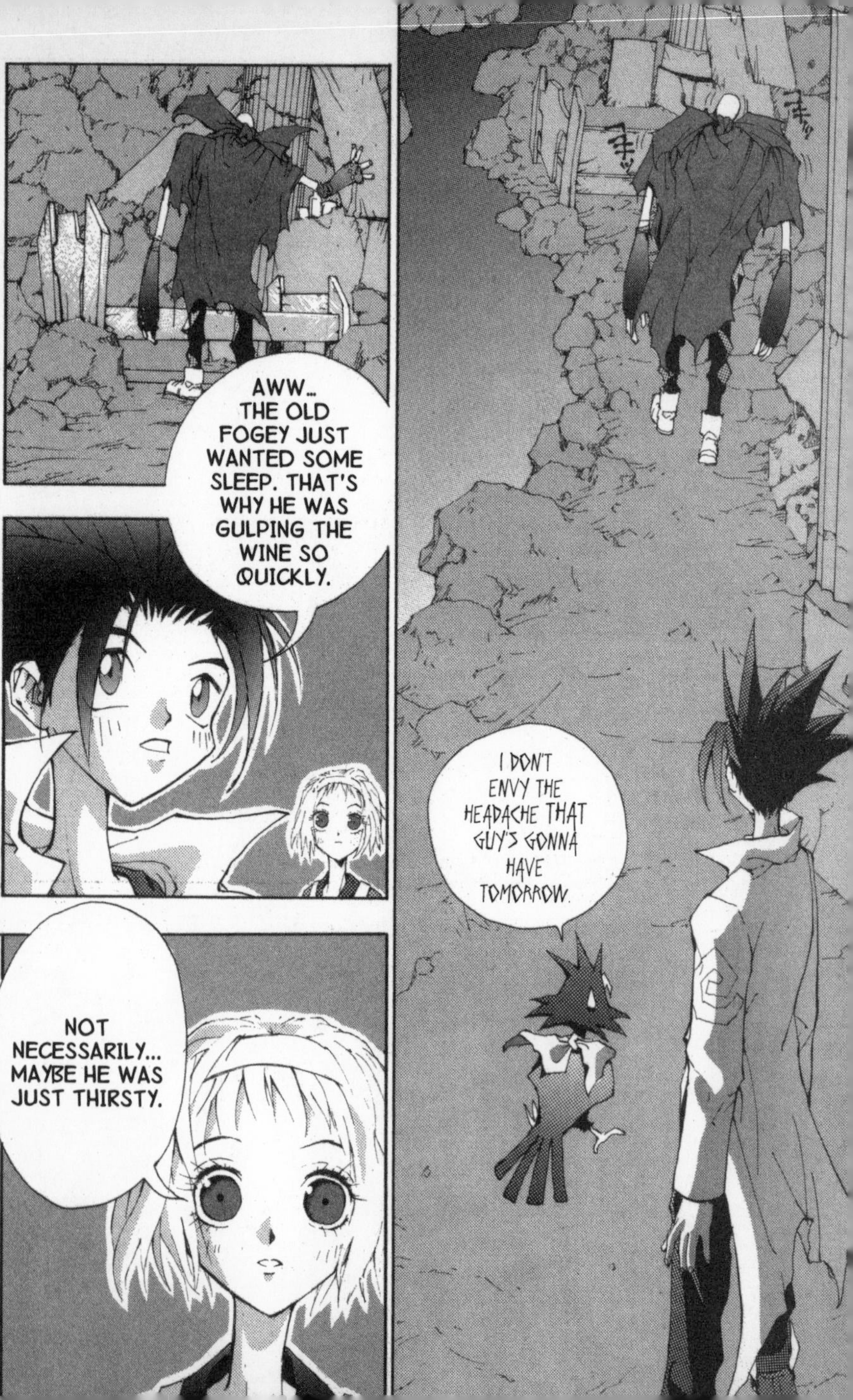
I DON'T ENVY THE HEADACHE THAT GUY'S GONNA HAVE TOMORROW.
AWW... THE OLD FOGEY JUST WANTED SOME SLEEP. THAT'S WHY HE WAS GULPING THE WINE SO QUICKLY.
NOT NECESSARILY... MAYBE HE WAS JUST THIRSTY.

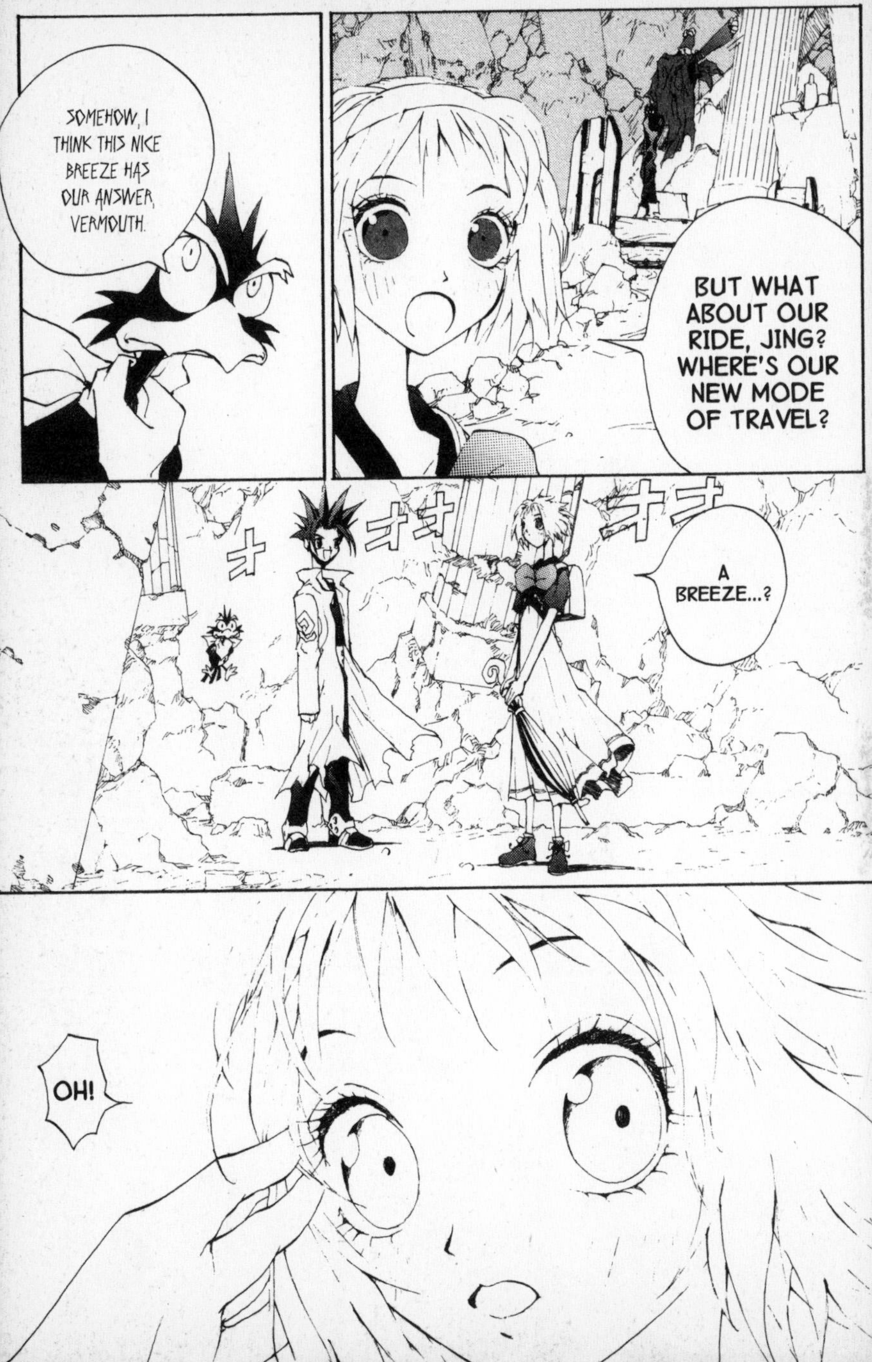
BUT WHAT ABOUT OUR RIDE, JING? WHERE'S OUR NEW MODE OF TRAVEL?
SOMEHOW, I THINK THIS NICE BREEZE HAS OUR ANSWER, VERMOUTH.
A BREEZE...?
オオ
オオ
オ
OH!

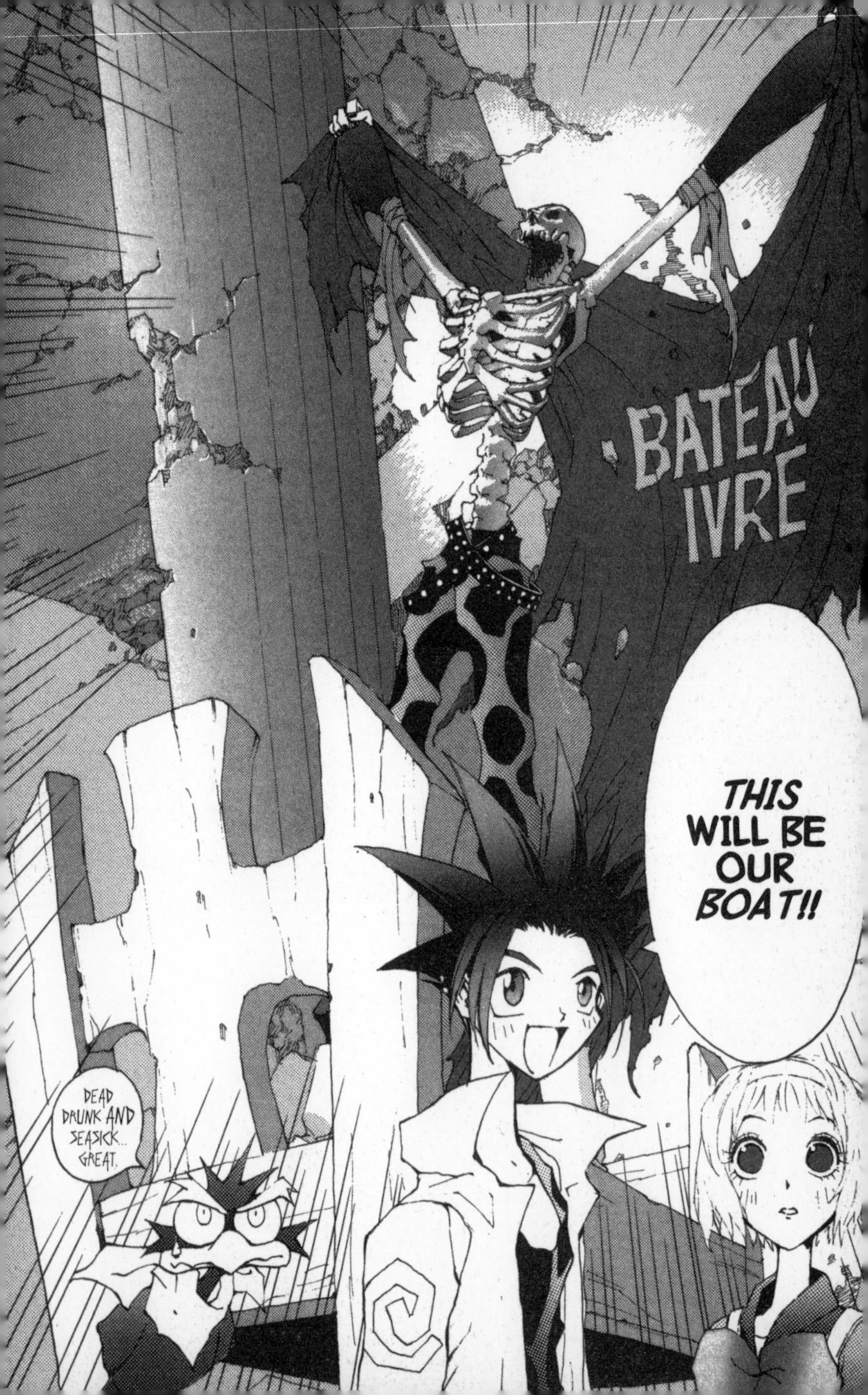
BATEAU IVRE
THIS WILL BE OUR BOAT!!
DEAD DRUNK AND SEASICK... GREAT.

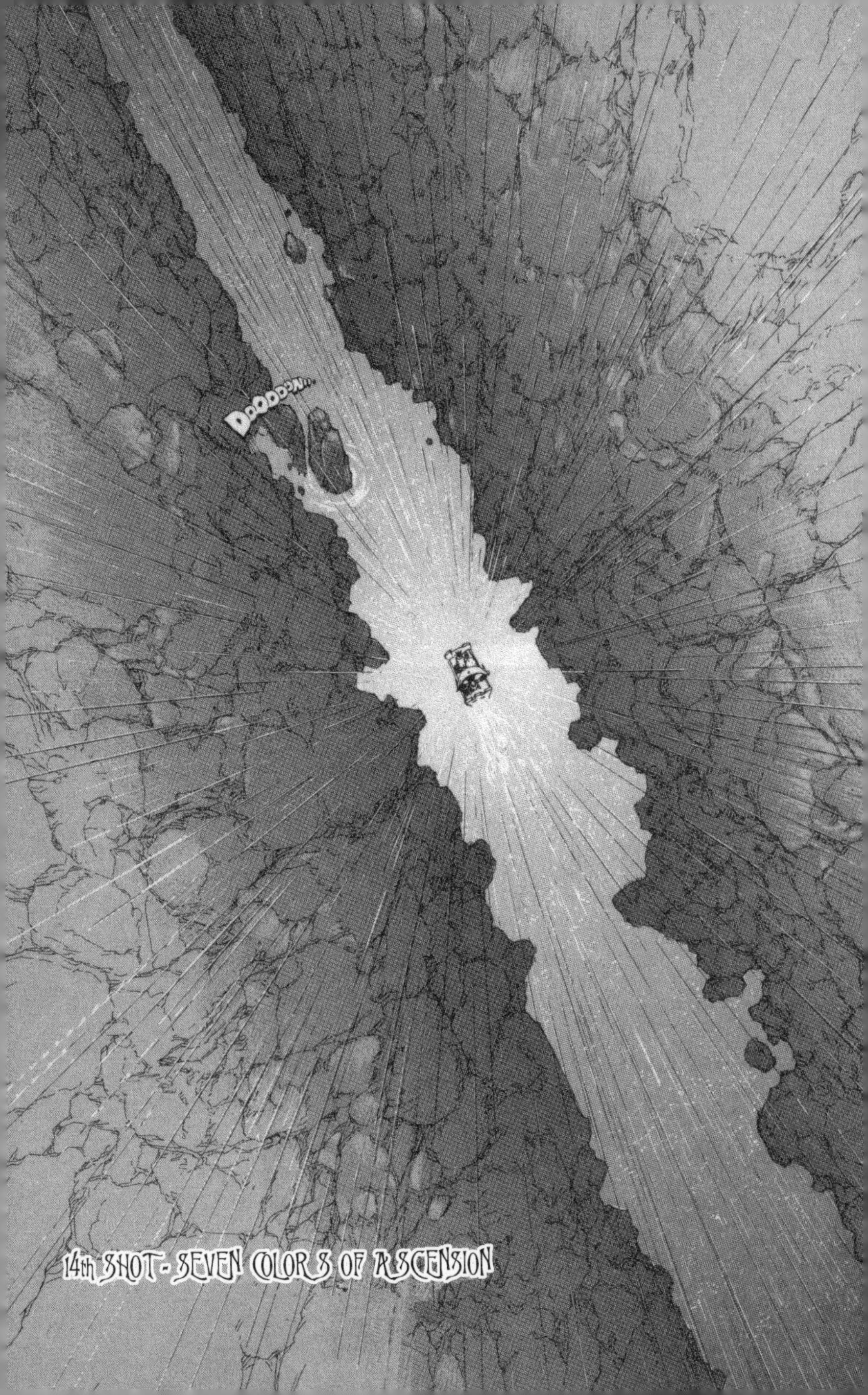
DOOOOON...
14th SHOT - SEVEN COLORS OF ASCENSION

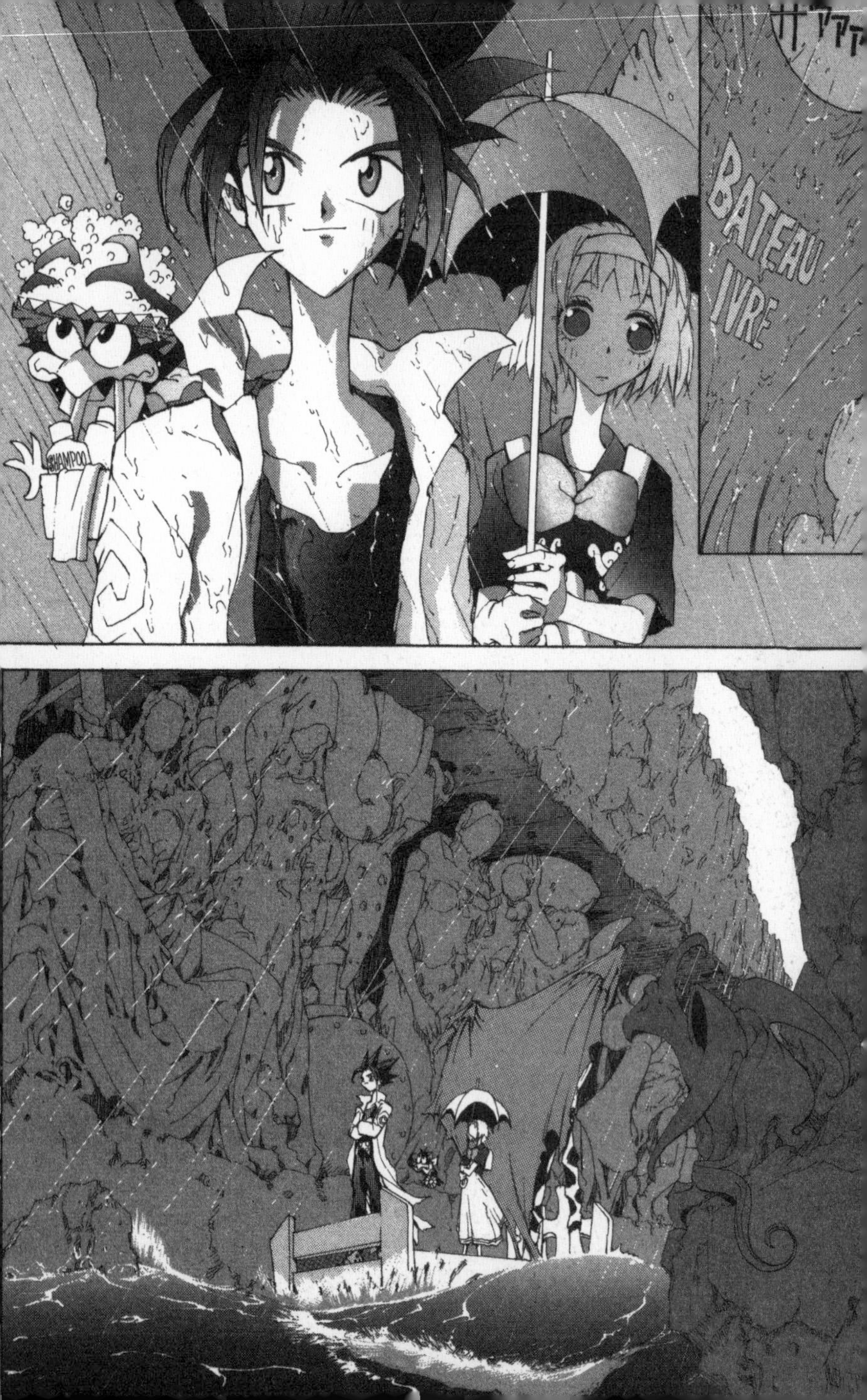
ザァァァ
BATEAU IVRE
SHAMPOO

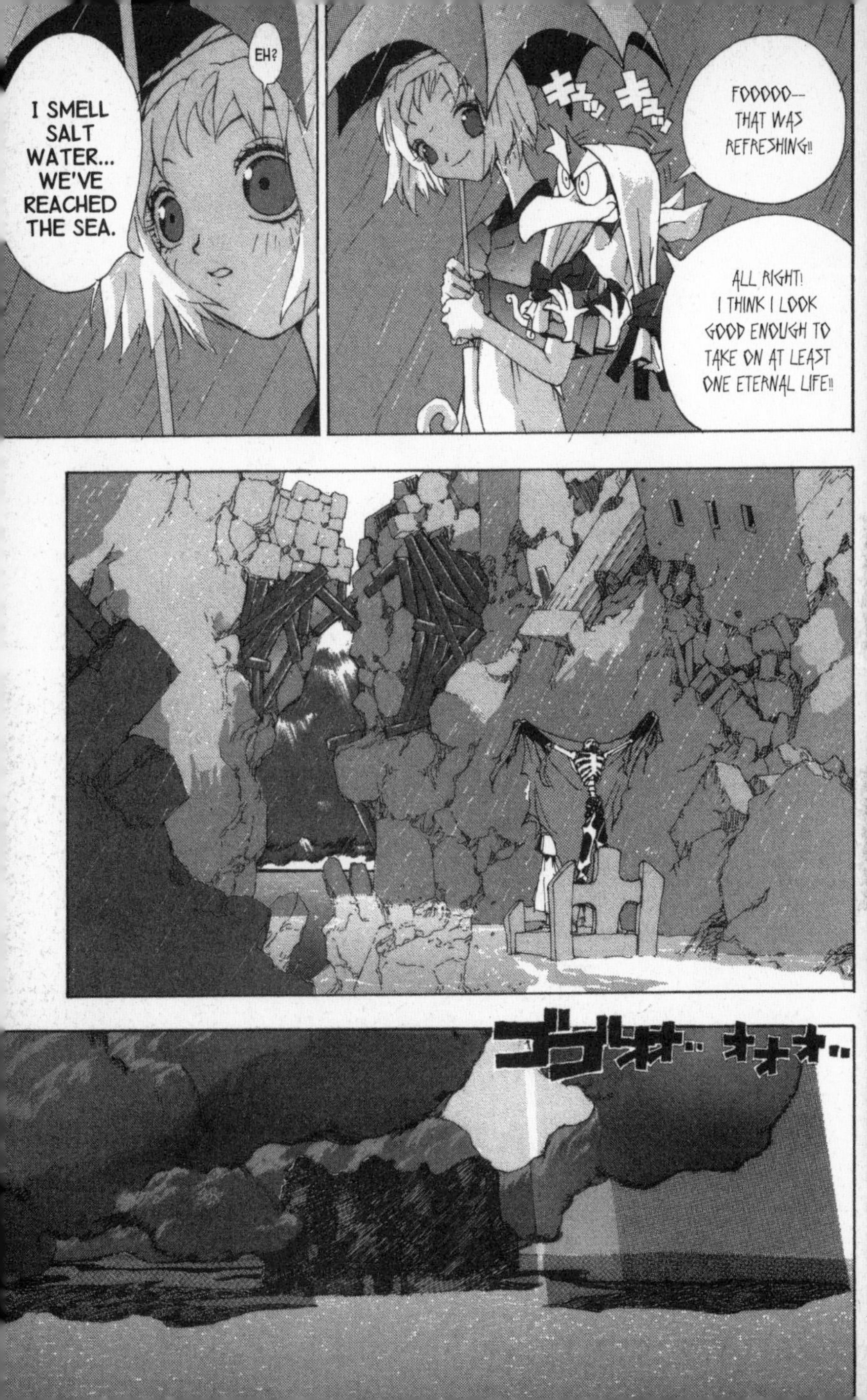

キュッ キュッ
FOOOOO--- THAT WAS REFRESHING!!
ALL RIGHT! I THINK I LOOK GOOD ENOUGH TO TAKE ON AT LEAST ONE ETERNAL LIFE!!
EH?
I SMELL SALT WATER... WE'VE REACHED THE SEA.

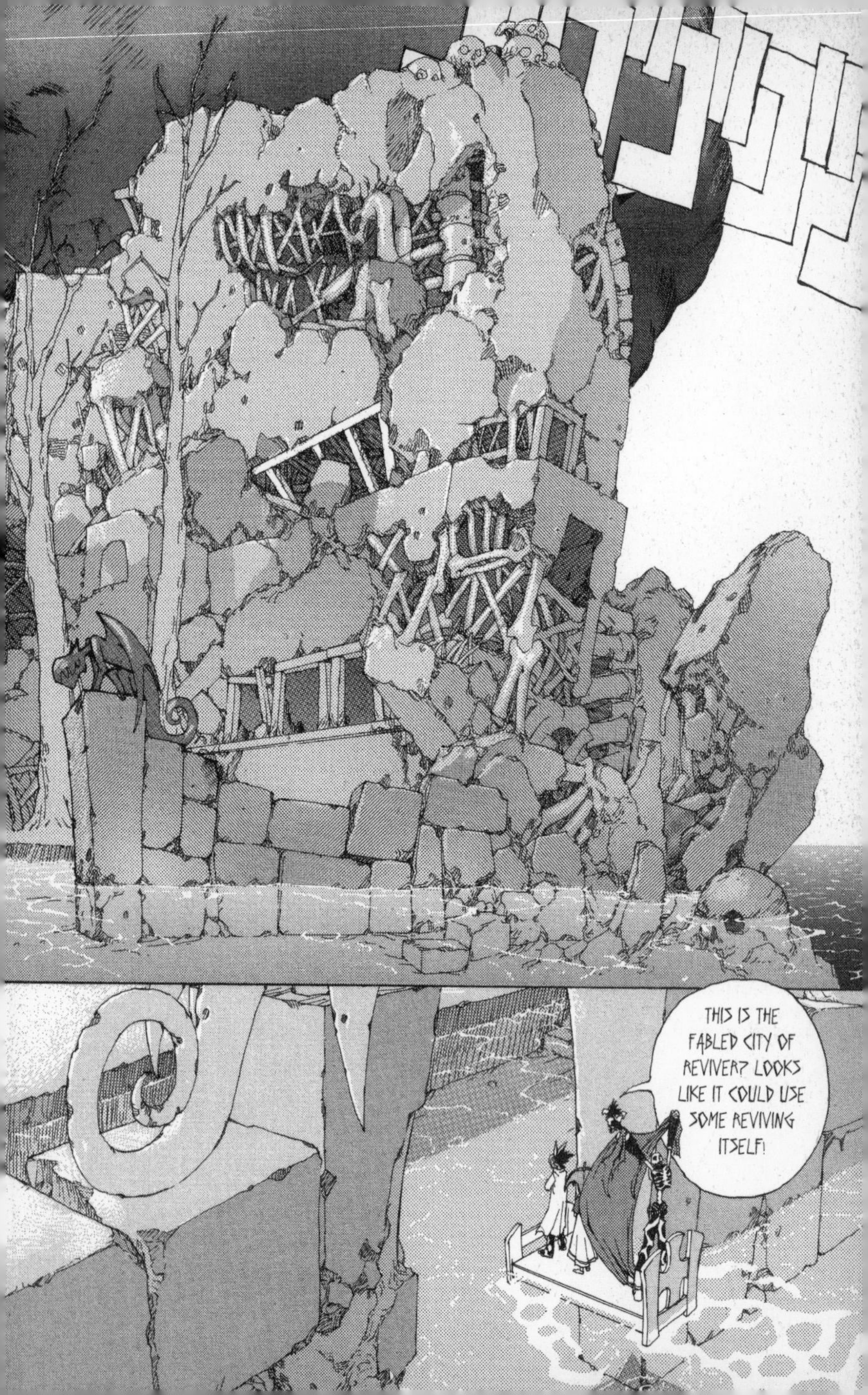
THIS IS THE FABLED CITY OF REVIVER? LOOKS LIKE IT COULD USE SOME REVIVING ITSELF!

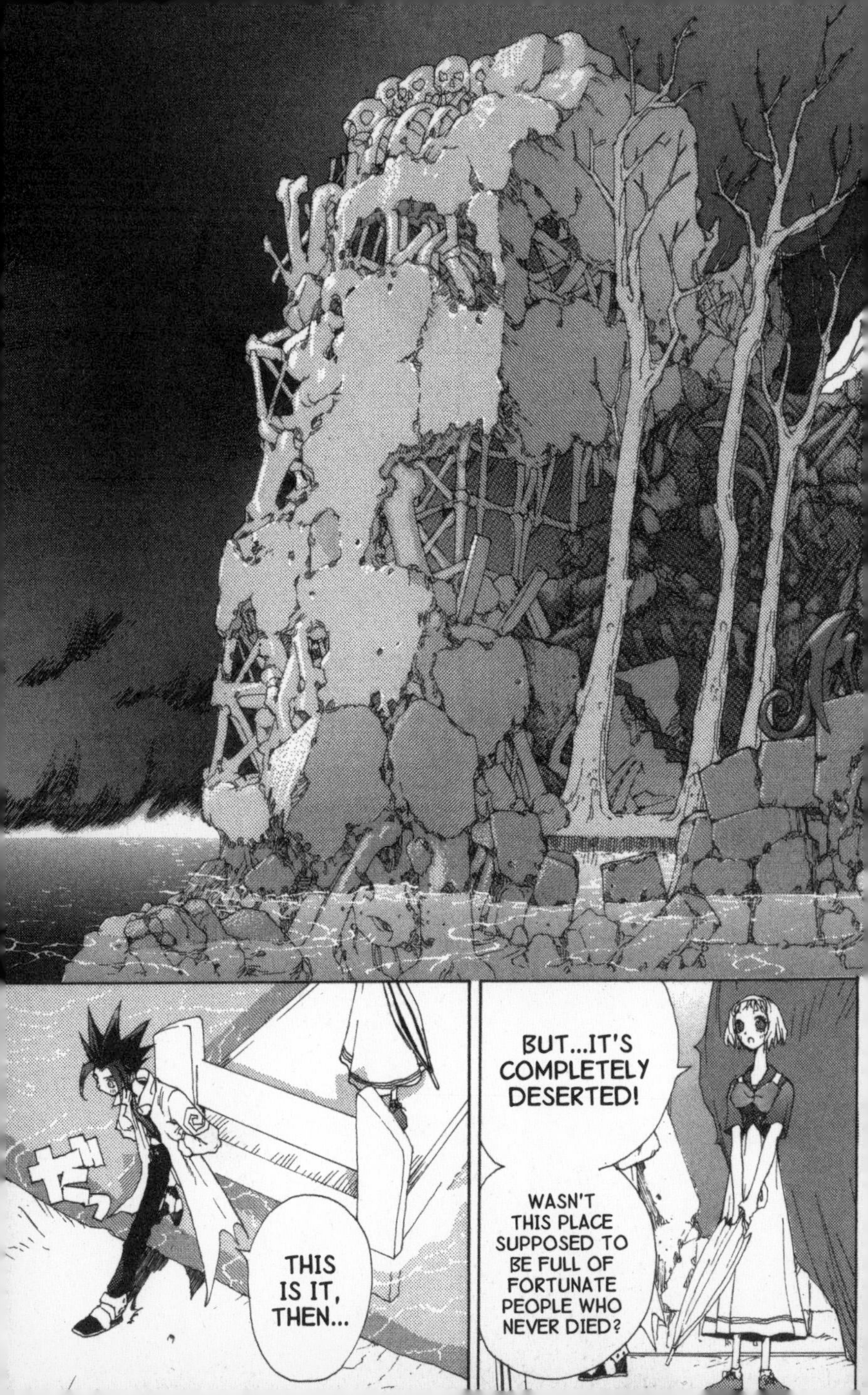
BUT...IT'S COMPLETELY DESERTED!
WASN'T THIS PLACE SUPPOSED TO BE FULL OF FORTUNATE PEOPLE WHO NEVER DIED?
THIS IS IT, THEN...

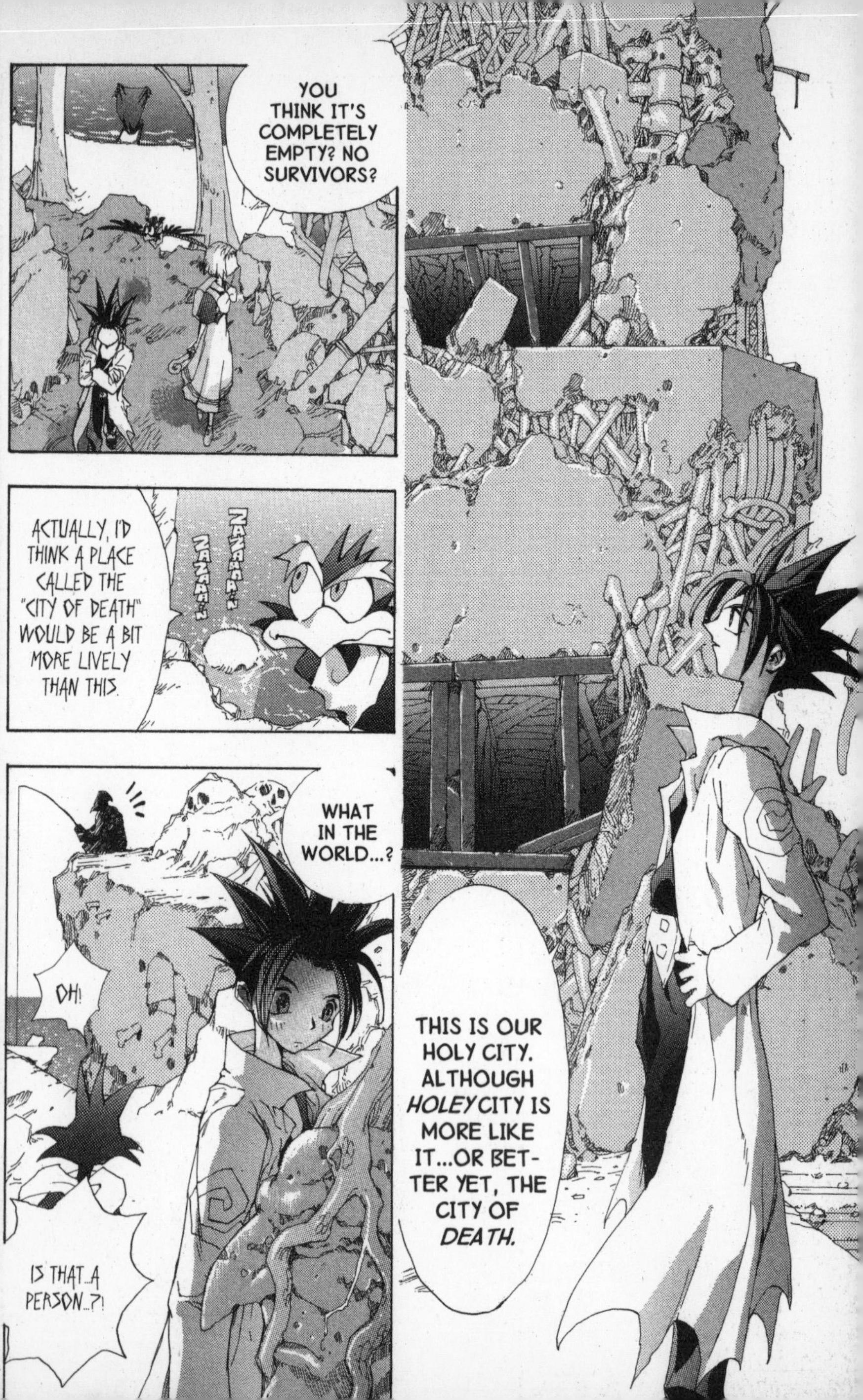
THIS IS OUR HOLY CITY. ALTHOUGH *HOLEY* CITY IS MORE LIKE IT...OR BETTER YET, THE CITY OF *DEATH*.
YOU THINK IT'S COMPLETELY EMPTY? NO SURVIVORS?
ZAZAAAN ZAZAAAN
ACTUALLY, I'D THINK A PLACE CALLED THE "CITY OF DEATH" WOULD BE A BIT MORE LIVELY THAN THIS.
WHAT IN THE WORLD...?
OH!
IS THAT...A PERSON...?!

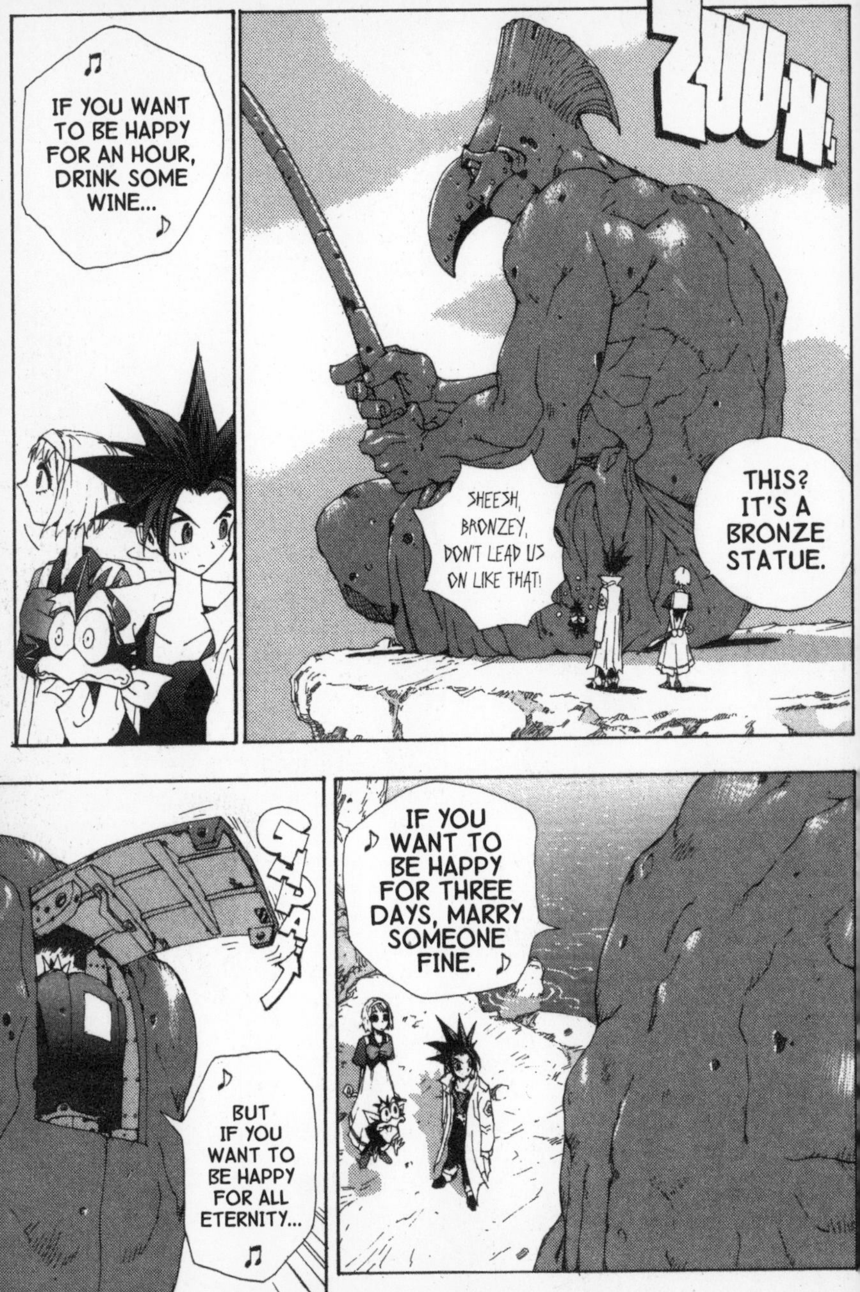
ZUU'N.
THIS? IT'S A BRONZE STATUE.
SHEESH, BRONZEY, DON'T LEAD US ON LIKE THAT!
♫ IF YOU WANT TO BE HAPPY FOR AN HOUR, DRINK SOME WINE... ♪
♪ IF YOU WANT TO BE HAPPY FOR THREE DAYS, MARRY SOMEONE FINE. ♪
♪ BUT IF YOU WANT TO BE HAPPY FOR ALL ETERNITY... ♫

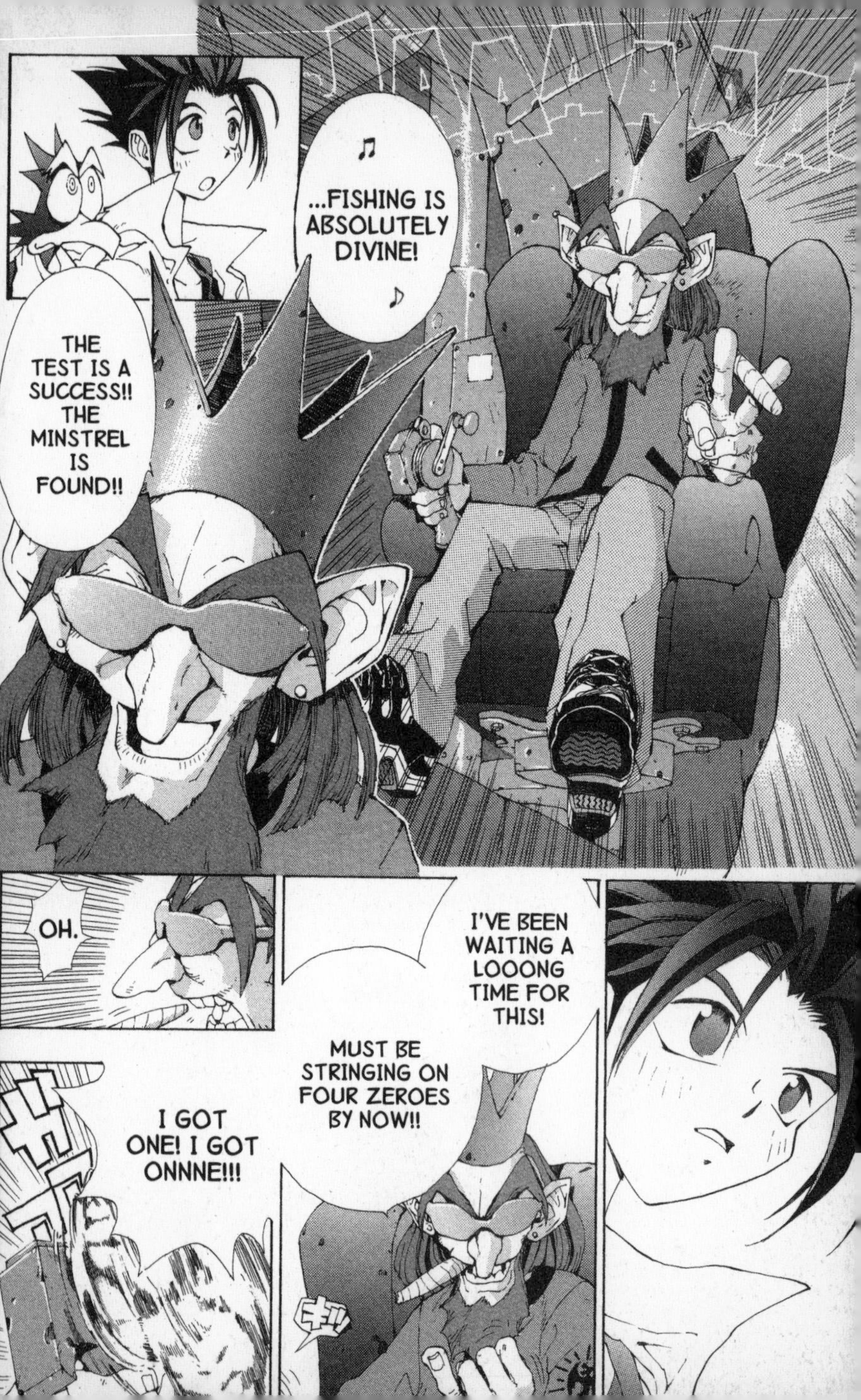
♪ ...FISHING IS ABSOLUTELY DIVINE! ♪
THE TEST IS A SUCCESS!! THE MINSTREL IS FOUND!!
I'VE BEEN WAITING A LOOONG TIME FOR THIS!
MUST BE STRINGING ON FOUR ZEROES BY NOW!!
OH.
I GOT ONE! I GOT ONNNE!!!

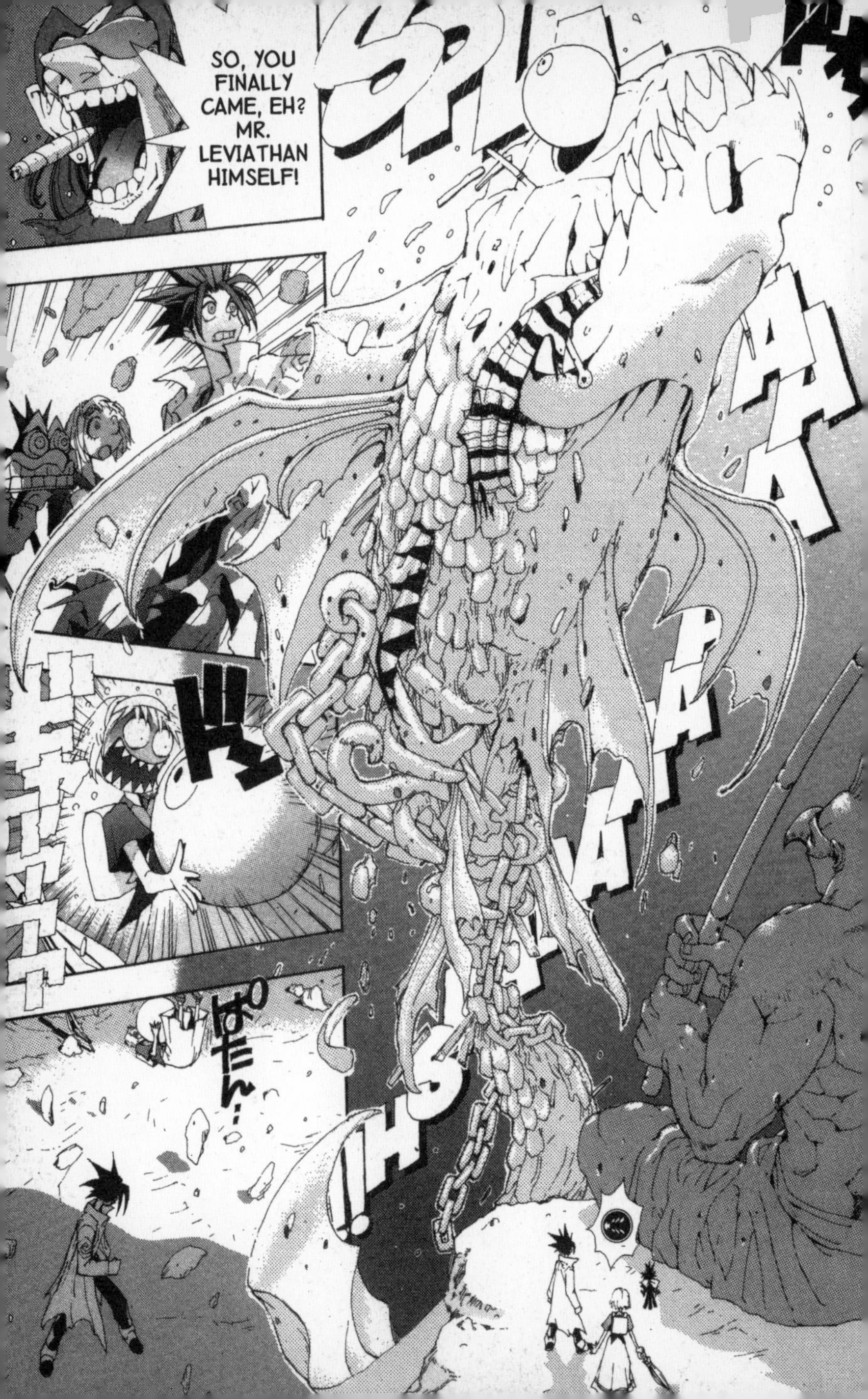
SO, YOU FINALLY CAME, EH? MR. LEVIATHAN HIMSELF!
ぱたん!

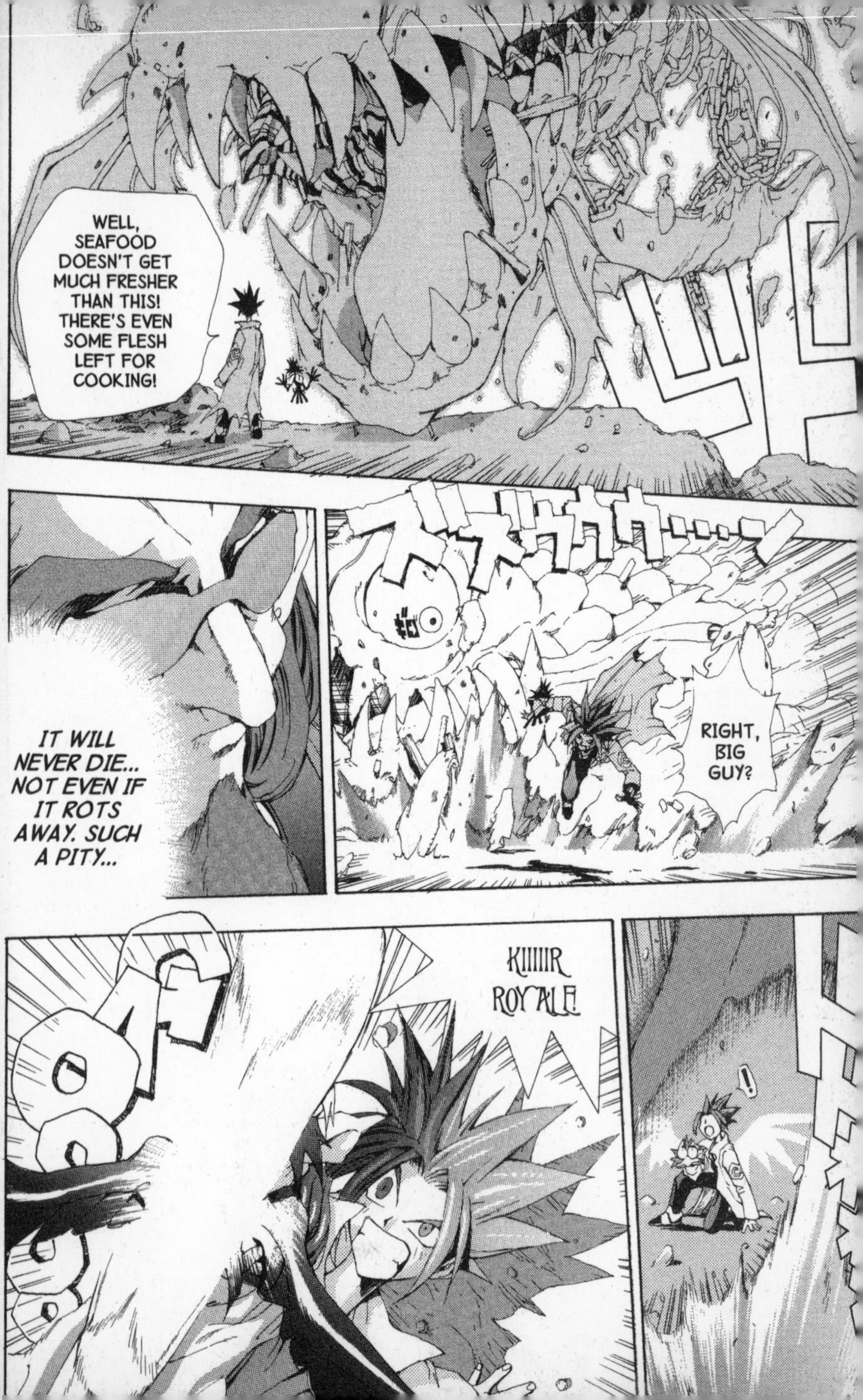
WELL, SEAFOOD DOESN'T GET MUCH FRESHER THAN THIS! THERE'S EVEN SOME FLESH LEFT FOR COOKING!
RIGHT, BIG GUY?
IT WILL NEVER DIE... NOT EVEN IF IT ROTS AWAY. SUCH A PITY...
!
KIIIIIR ROYALE!

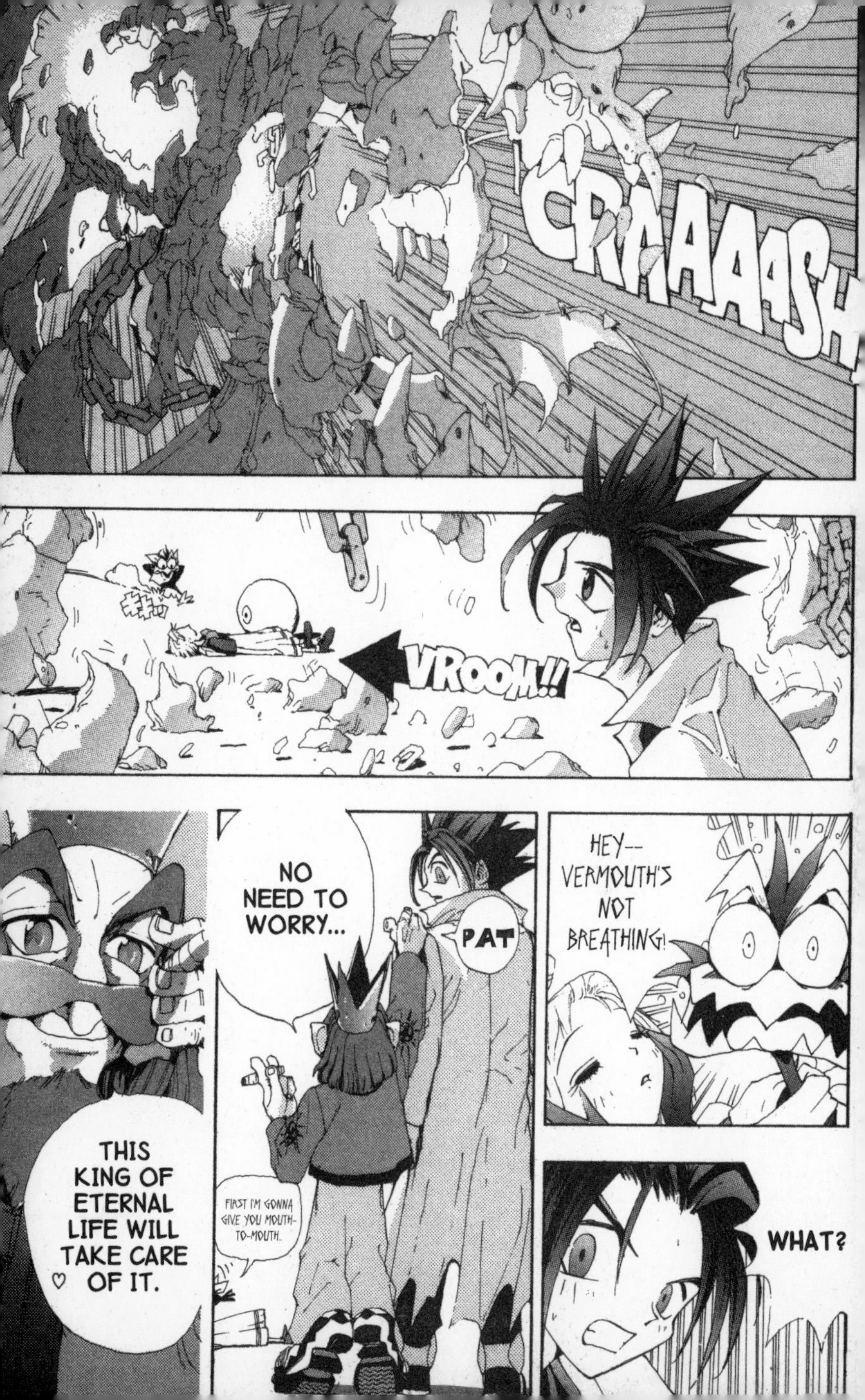
CRAAAASH
VROOM!!
HEY-- VERMOUTH'S NOT BREATHING!
NO NEED TO WORRY...
PAT
THIS KING OF ETERNAL LIFE WILL TAKE CARE OF IT. ♡
FIRST I'M GONNA GIVE YOU MOUTH-TO-MOUTH...
WHAT?

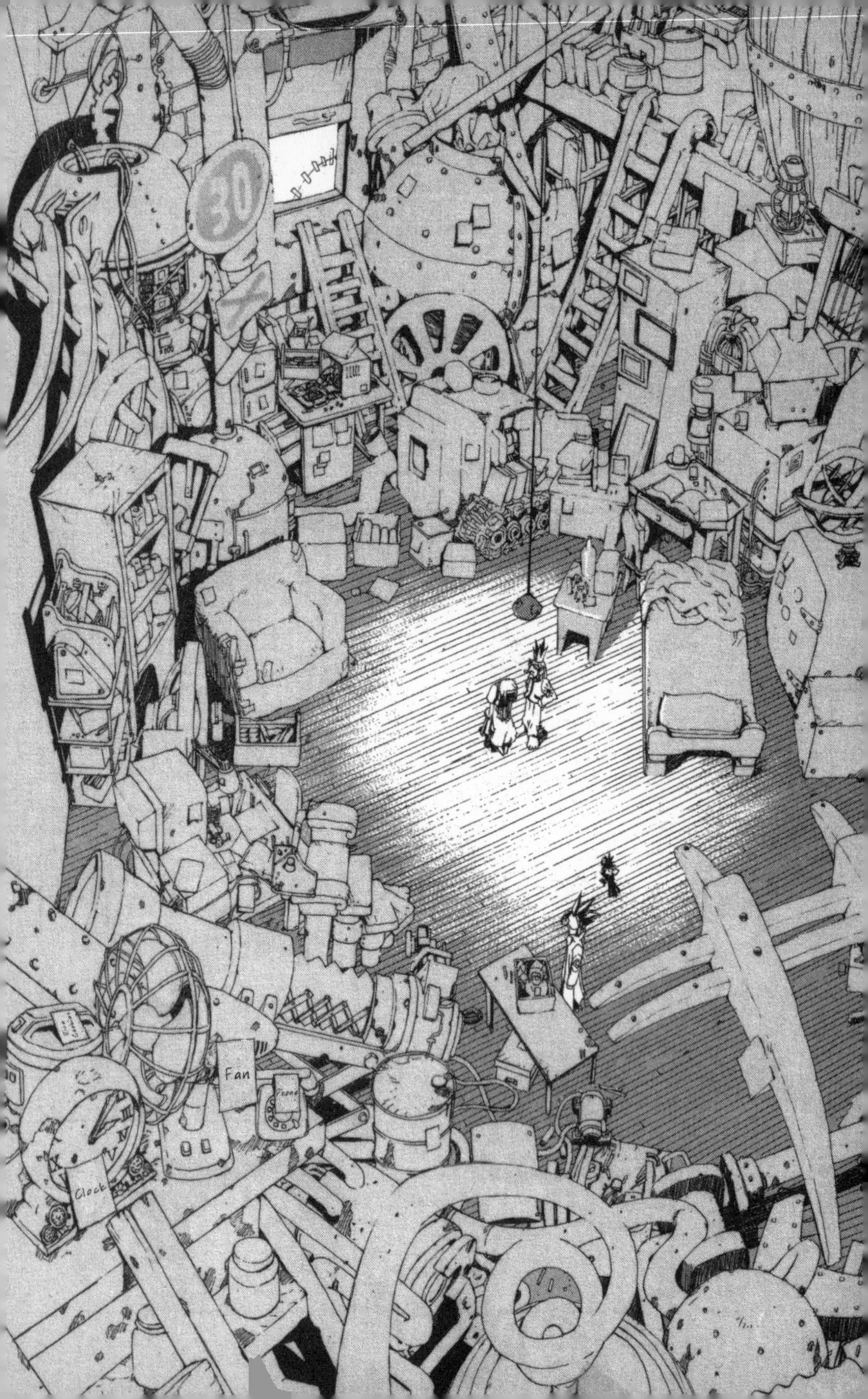
30
Phone
Fan
Rice Cooker
Clock

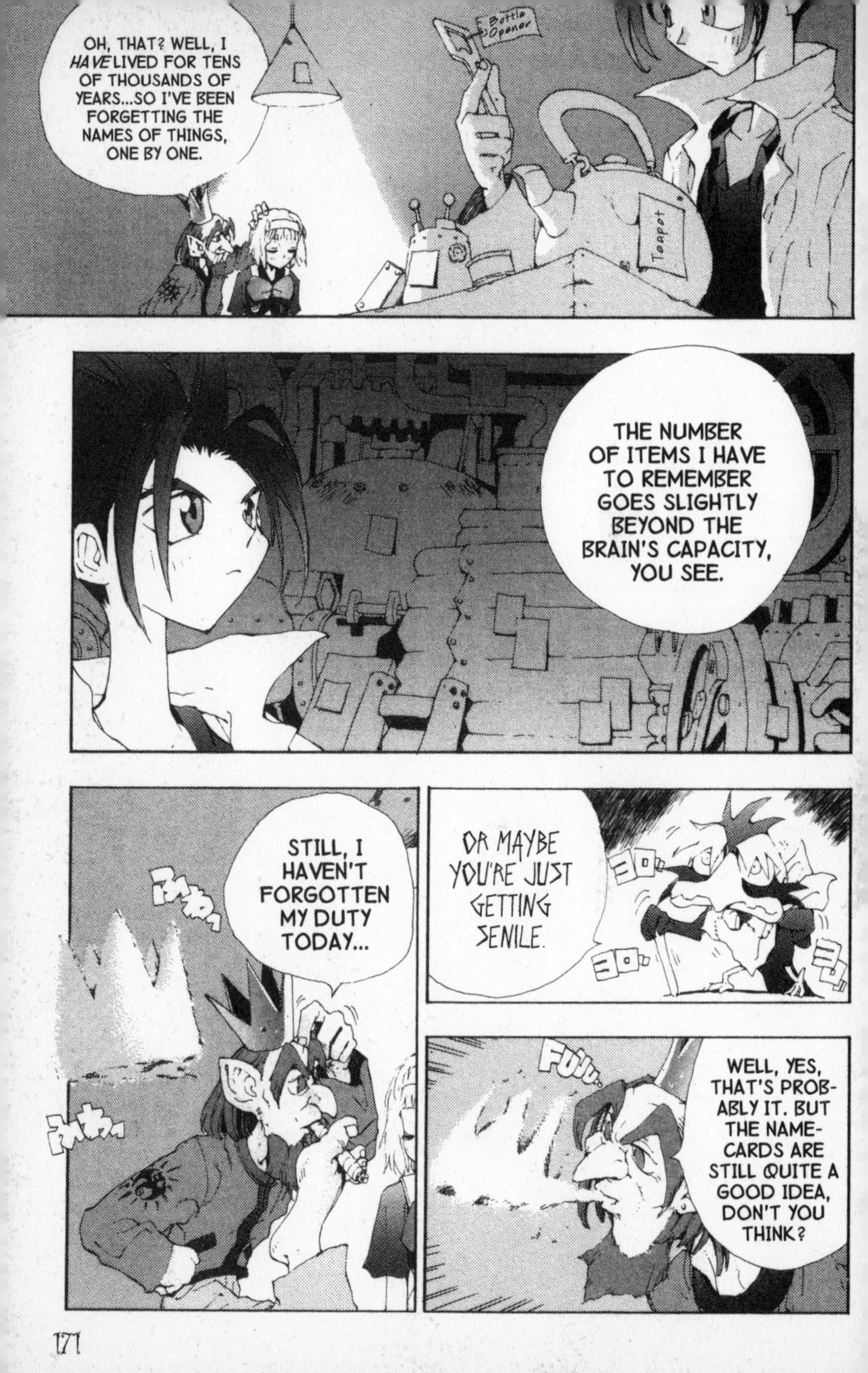
OH, THAT? WELL, I *HAVE* LIVED FOR TENS OF THOUSANDS OF YEARS...SO I'VE BEEN FORGETTING THE NAMES OF THINGS, ONE BY ONE.
Bottle Opener
Teapot
THE NUMBER OF ITEMS I HAVE TO REMEMBER GOES SLIGHTLY BEYOND THE BRAIN'S CAPACITY, YOU SEE.
OR MAYBE YOU'RE JUST GETTING SENILE.
FUU
WELL, YES, THAT'S PROBABLY IT. BUT THE NAME-CARDS ARE STILL QUITE A GOOD IDEA, DON'T YOU THINK?
STILL, I HAVEN'T FORGOTTEN MY DUTY TODAY...

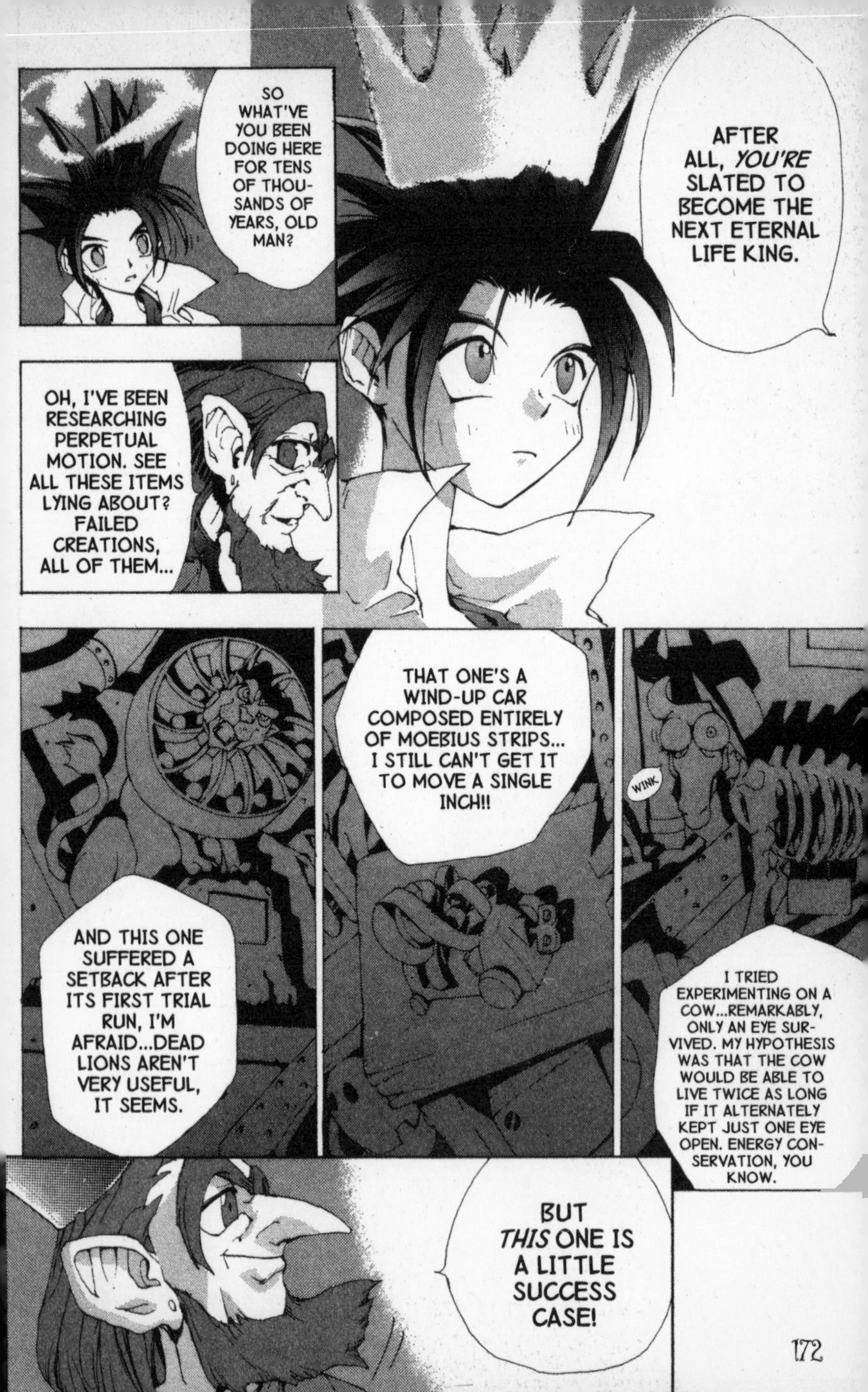
AFTER ALL, *YOU'RE* SLATED TO BECOME THE NEXT ETERNAL LIFE KING.
SO WHAT'VE YOU BEEN DOING HERE FOR TENS OF THOU-SANDS OF YEARS, OLD MAN?
OH, I'VE BEEN RESEARCHING PERPETUAL MOTION. SEE ALL THESE ITEMS LYING ABOUT? FAILED CREATIONS, ALL OF THEM...
WINK
I TRIED EXPERIMENTING ON A COW...REMARKABLY, ONLY AN EYE SUR-VIVED. MY HYPOTHESIS WAS THAT THE COW WOULD BE ABLE TO LIVE TWICE AS LONG IF IT ALTERNATELY KEPT JUST ONE EYE OPEN. ENERGY CON-SERVATION, YOU KNOW.
THAT ONE'S A WIND-UP CAR COMPOSED ENTIRELY OF MOEBIUS STRIPS... I STILL CAN'T GET IT TO MOVE A SINGLE INCH!!
AND THIS ONE SUFFERED A SETBACK AFTER ITS FIRST TRIAL RUN, I'M AFRAID...DEAD LIONS AREN'T VERY USEFUL, IT SEEMS.
BUT *THIS* ONE IS A LITTLE SUCCESS CASE!

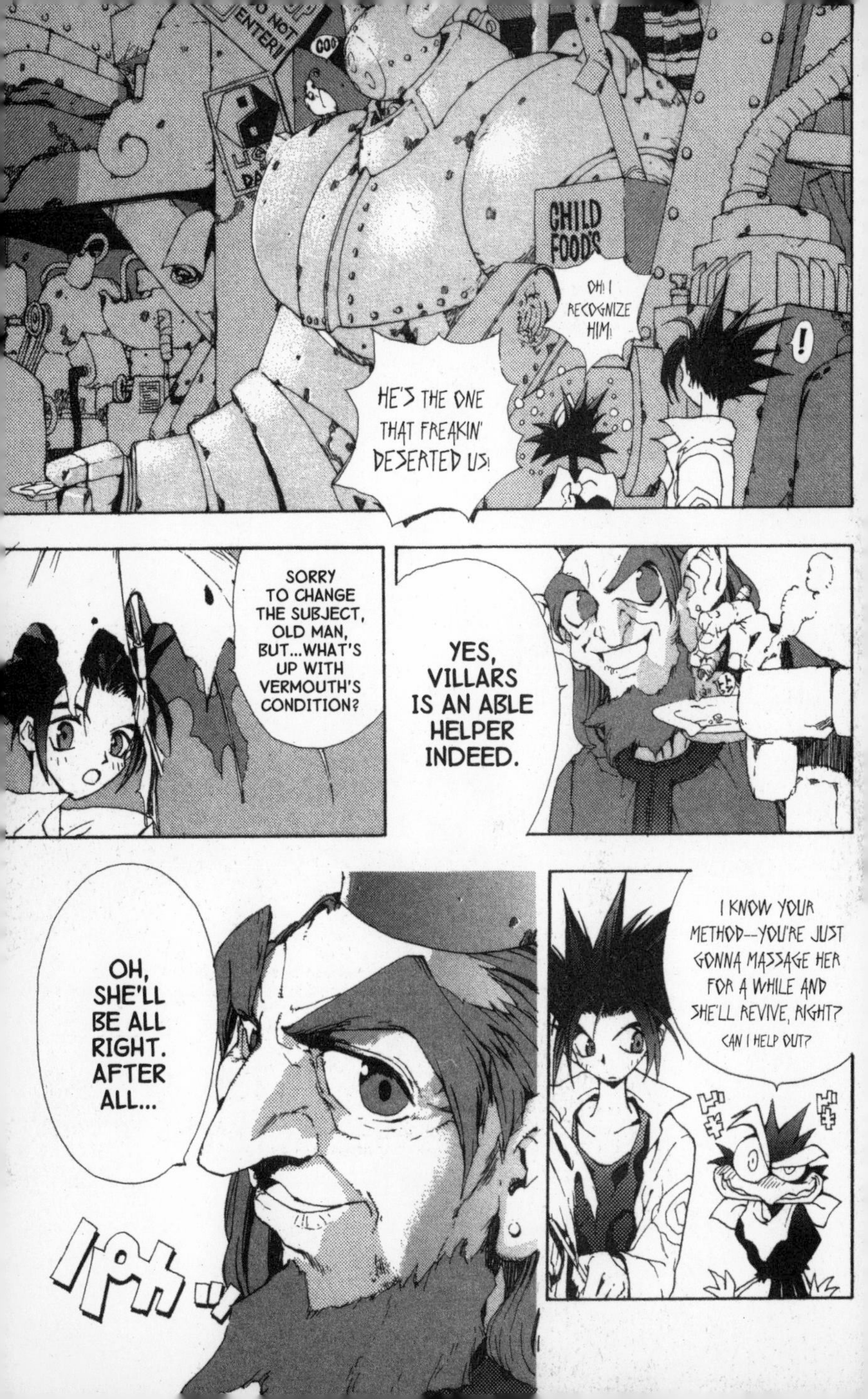
DO NOT ENTER!!
CHILD FOOD'S
OH! I RECOGNIZE HIM!
!
HE'S THE ONE THAT FREAKIN' DESERTED US!
YES, VILLARS IS AN ABLE HELPER INDEED.
SORRY TO CHANGE THE SUBJECT, OLD MAN, BUT...WHAT'S UP WITH VERMOUTH'S CONDITION?
I KNOW YOUR METHOD--YOU'RE JUST GONNA MASSAGE HER FOR A WHILE AND SHE'LL REVIVE, RIGHT?
CAN I HELP OUT?
OH, SHE'LL BE ALL RIGHT. AFTER ALL...

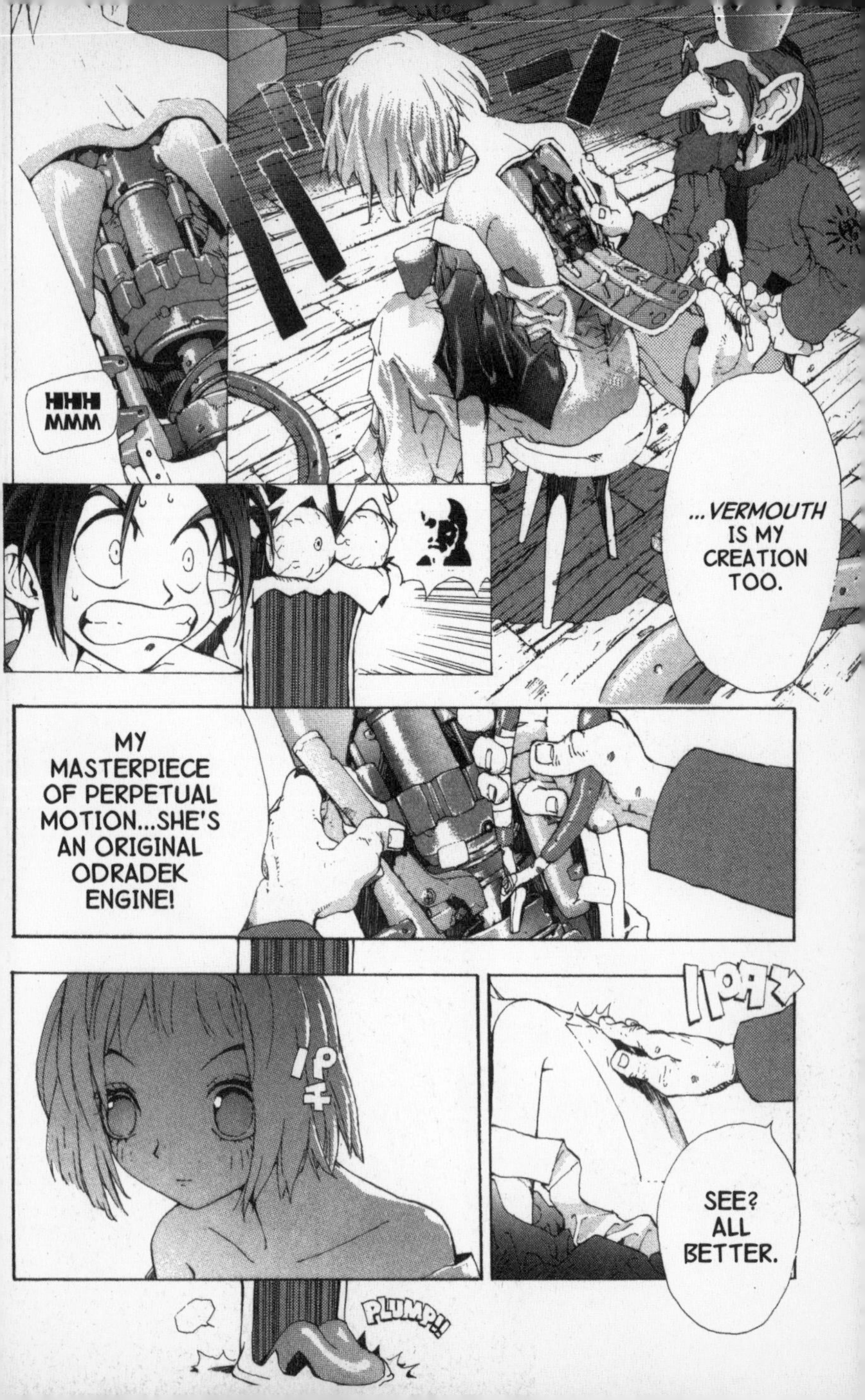
...VERMOUTH IS MY CREATION TOO.
HHH MMM
MY MASTERPIECE OF PERPETUAL MOTION...SHE'S AN ORIGINAL ODRADEK ENGINE!
SEE? ALL BETTER.
PLUMP!!

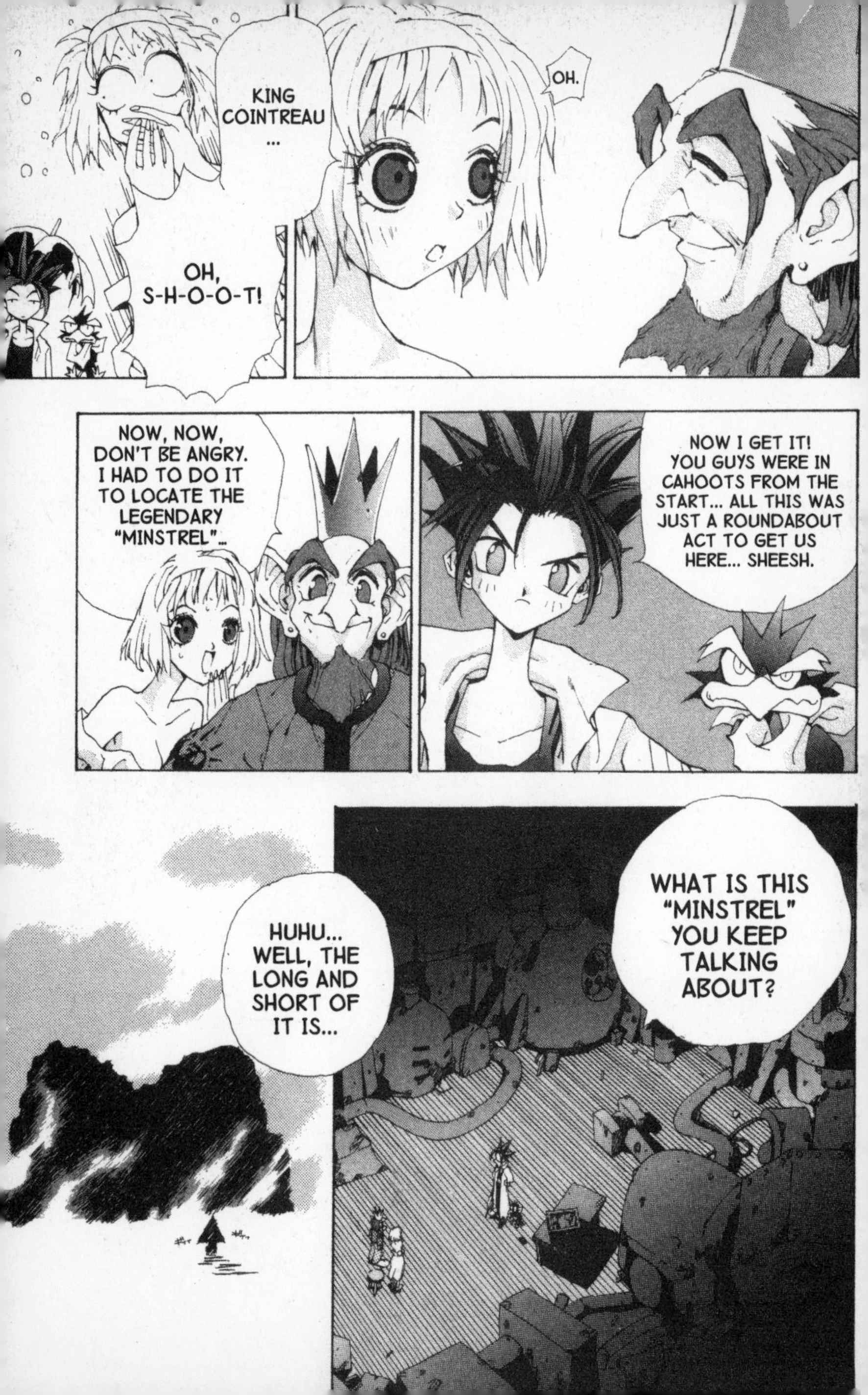
OH.
KING COINTREAU ...
OH, S-H-O-O-T!
NOW I GET IT! YOU GUYS WERE IN CAHOOTS FROM THE START... ALL THIS WAS JUST A ROUNDABOUT ACT TO GET US HERE... SHEESH.
NOW, NOW, DON'T BE ANGRY. I HAD TO DO IT TO LOCATE THE LEGENDARY "MINSTREL"...
WHAT IS THIS "MINSTREL" YOU KEEP TALKING ABOUT?
HUHU... WELL, THE LONG AND SHORT OF IT IS...

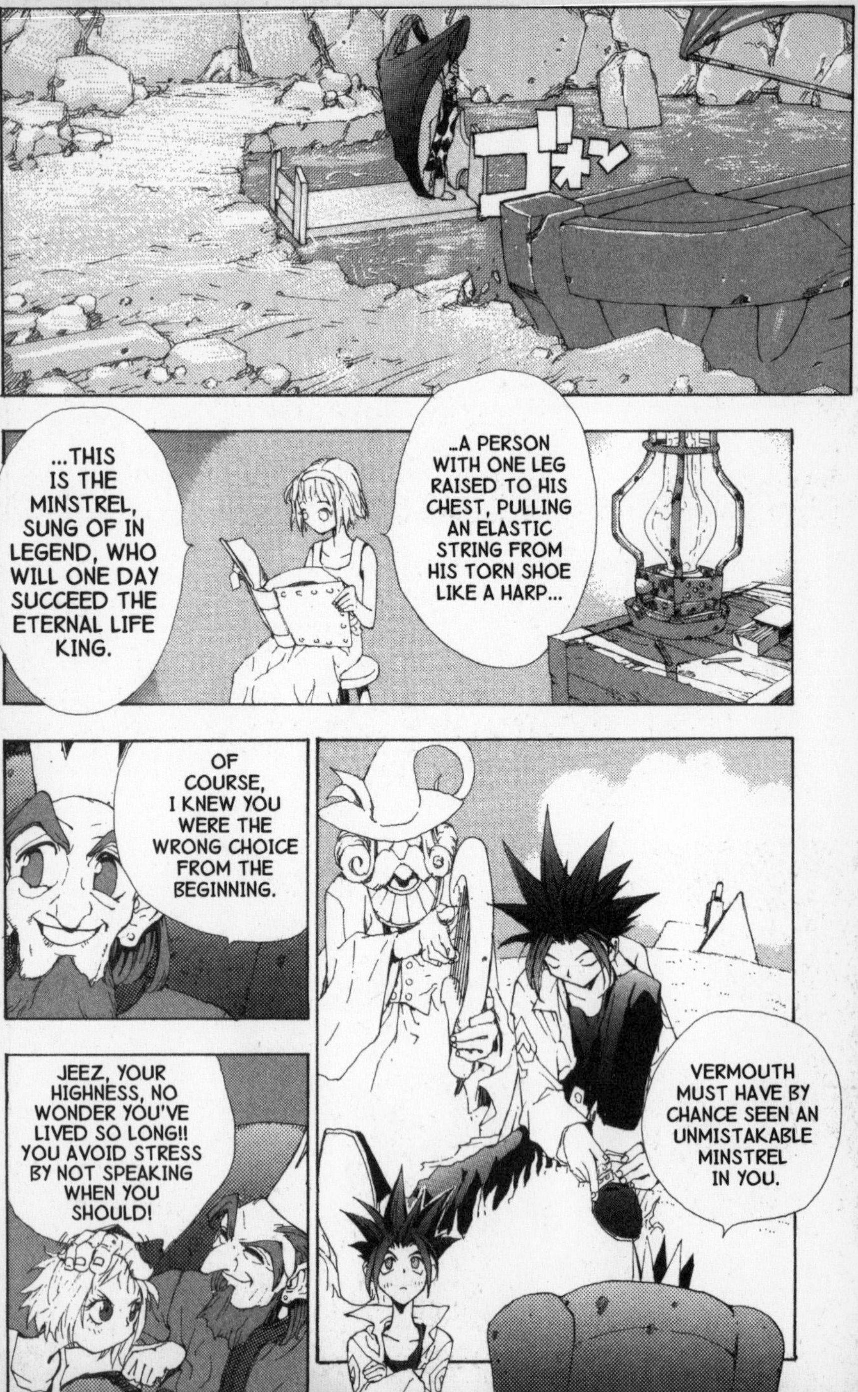
ゴォン
...A PERSON WITH ONE LEG RAISED TO HIS CHEST, PULLING AN ELASTIC STRING FROM HIS TORN SHOE LIKE A HARP...
...THIS IS THE MINSTREL, SUNG OF IN LEGEND, WHO WILL ONE DAY SUCCEED THE ETERNAL LIFE KING.
VERMOUTH MUST HAVE BY CHANCE SEEN AN UNMISTAKABLE MINSTREL IN YOU.
OF COURSE, I KNEW YOU WERE THE WRONG CHOICE FROM THE BEGINNING.
JEEZ, YOUR HIGHNESS, NO WONDER YOU'VE LIVED SO LONG!! YOU AVOID STRESS BY NOT SPEAKING WHEN YOU SHOULD!

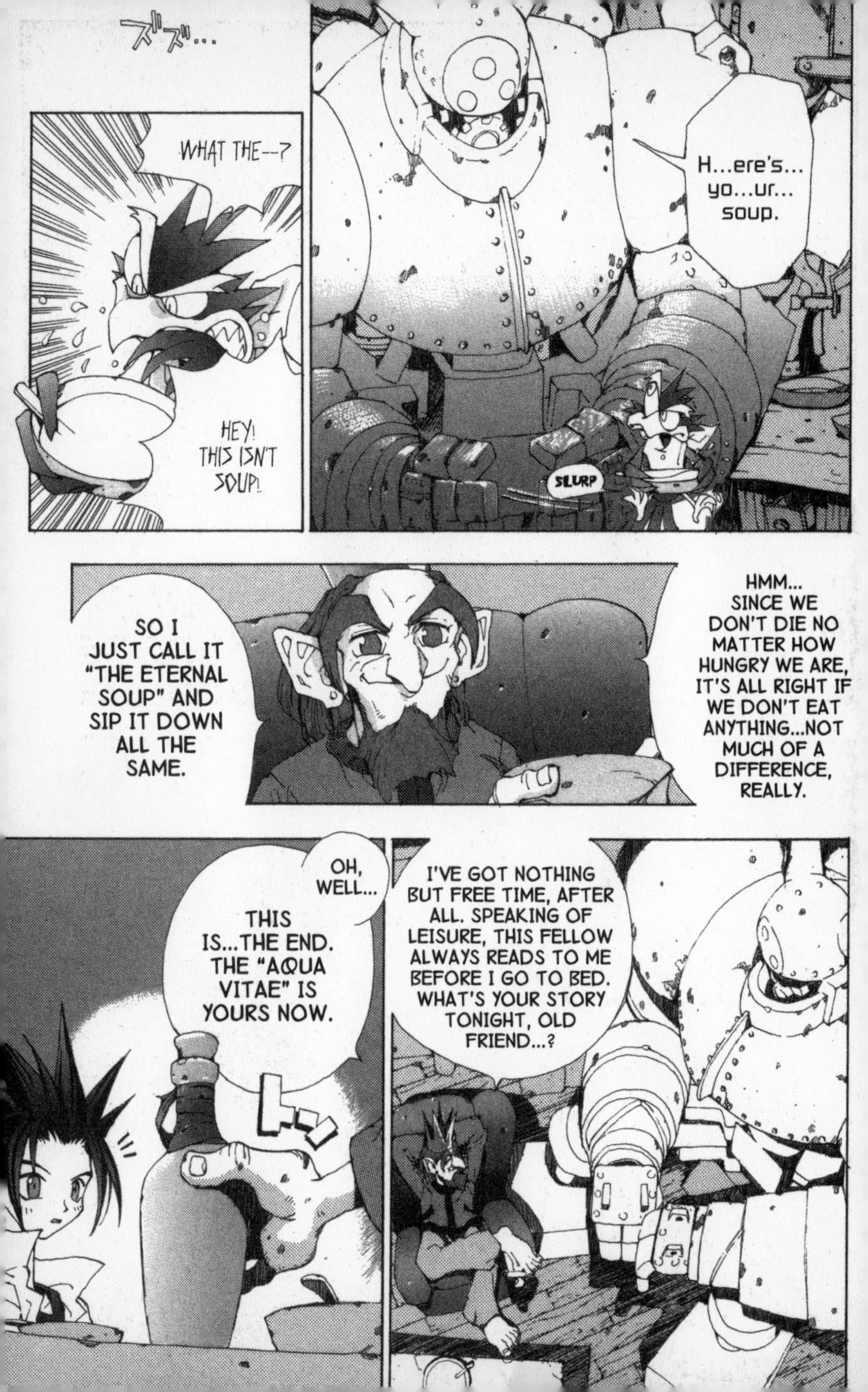
ズズ...
H...ere's... yo...ur... soup.
SLURP
WHAT THE--?
HEY! THIS ISN'T SOUP!
HMM... SINCE WE DON'T DIE NO MATTER HOW HUNGRY WE ARE, IT'S ALL RIGHT IF WE DON'T EAT ANYTHING...NOT MUCH OF A DIFFERENCE, REALLY.
SO I JUST CALL IT "THE ETERNAL SOUP" AND SIP IT DOWN ALL THE SAME.
I'VE GOT NOTHING BUT FREE TIME, AFTER ALL. SPEAKING OF LEISURE, THIS FELLOW ALWAYS READS TO ME BEFORE I GO TO BED. WHAT'S YOUR STORY TONIGHT, OLD FRIEND...?
OH, WELL...
THIS IS...THE END. THE "AQUA VITAE" IS YOURS NOW.
トン

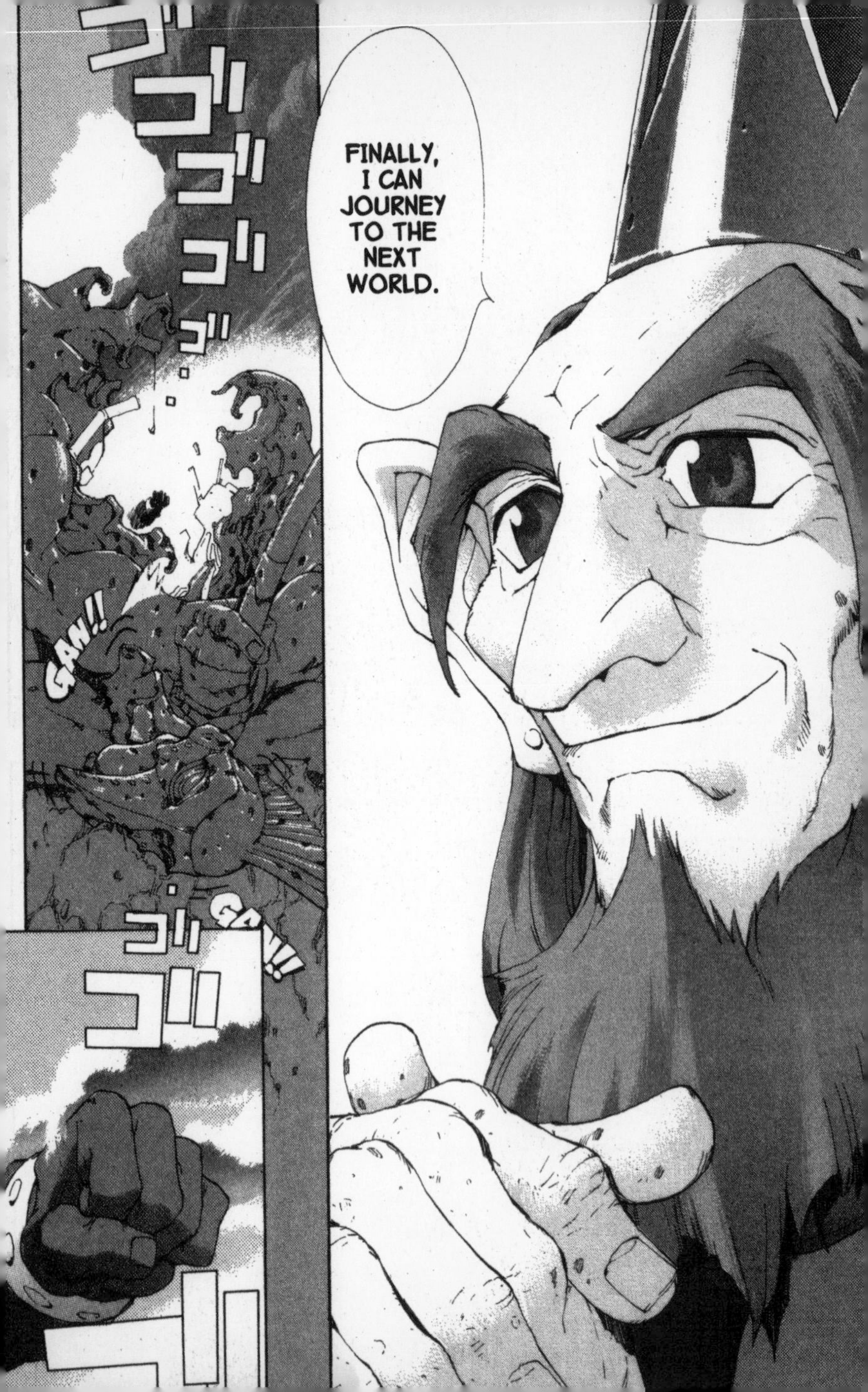
FINALLY, I CAN JOURNEY TO THE NEXT WORLD.
ゴゴゴゴゴ
GAN!!
GAN!!
ゴゴ

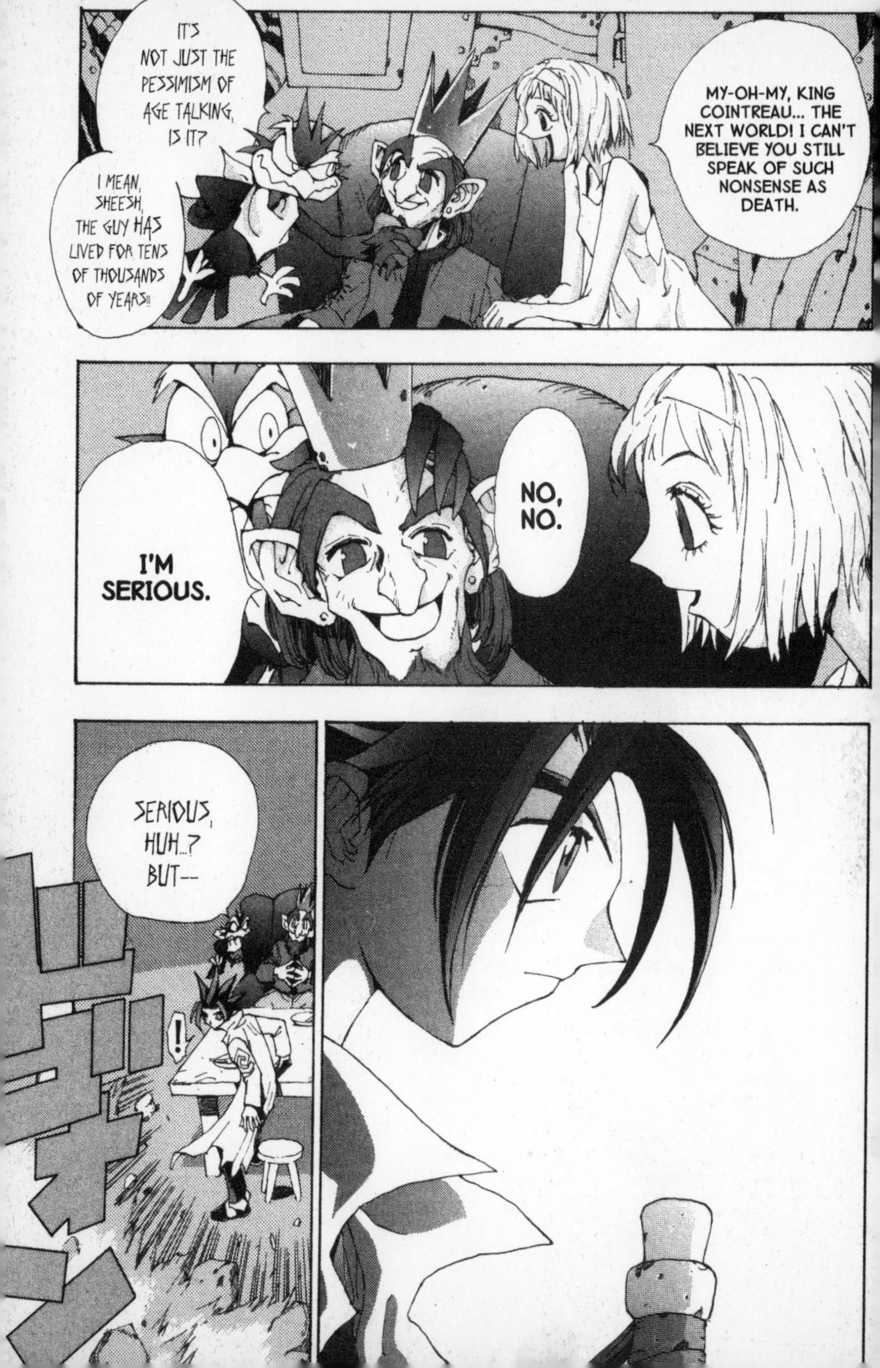
MY-OH-MY, KING COINTREAU... THE NEXT WORLD! I CAN'T BELIEVE YOU STILL SPEAK OF SUCH NONSENSE AS DEATH.
IT'S NOT JUST THE PESSIMISM OF AGE TALKING, IS IT?
I MEAN, SHEESH, THE GUY HAS LIVED FOR TENS OF THOUSANDS OF YEARS!!
NO, NO.
I'M SERIOUS.
SERIOUS, HUH...? BUT--
!

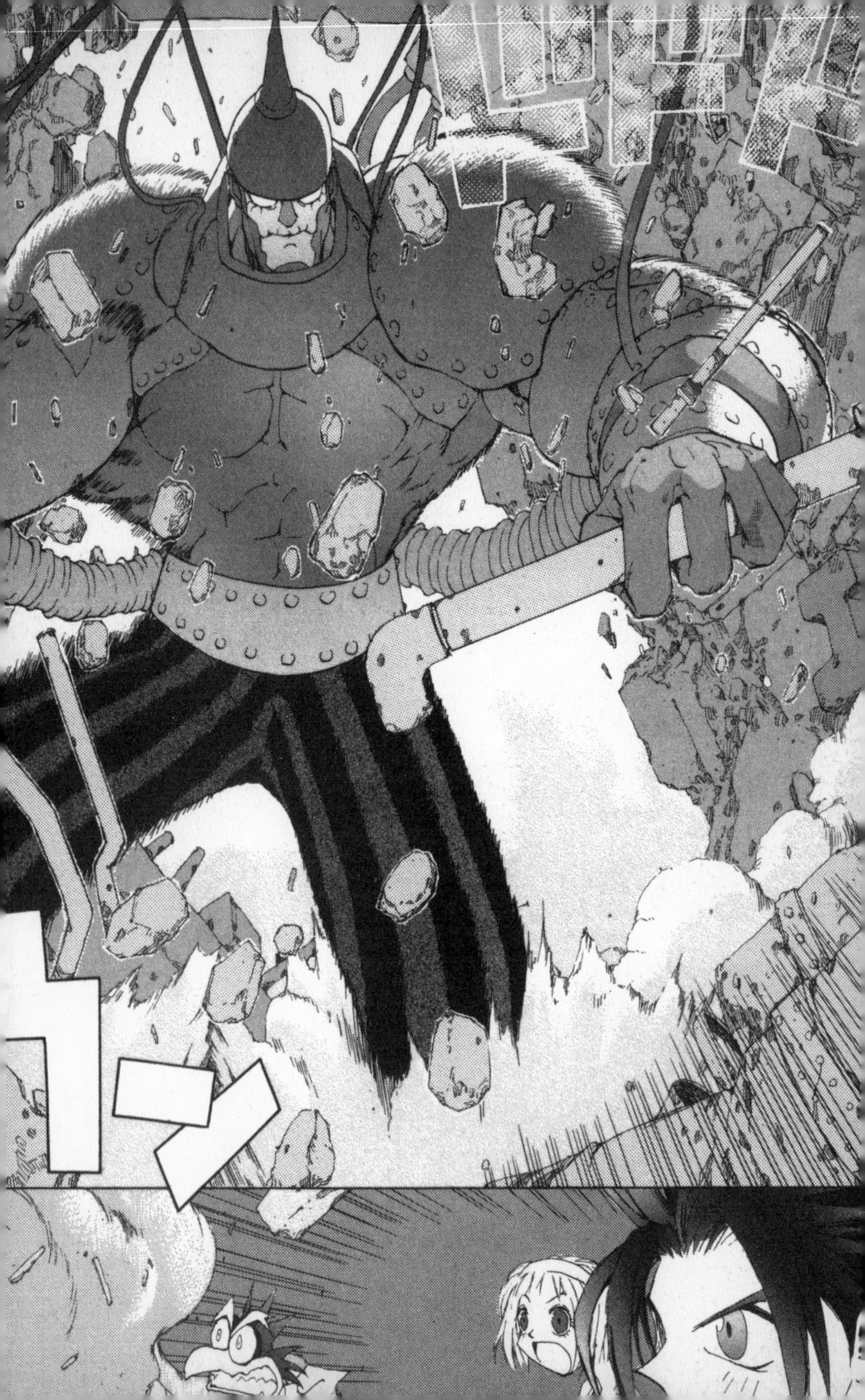

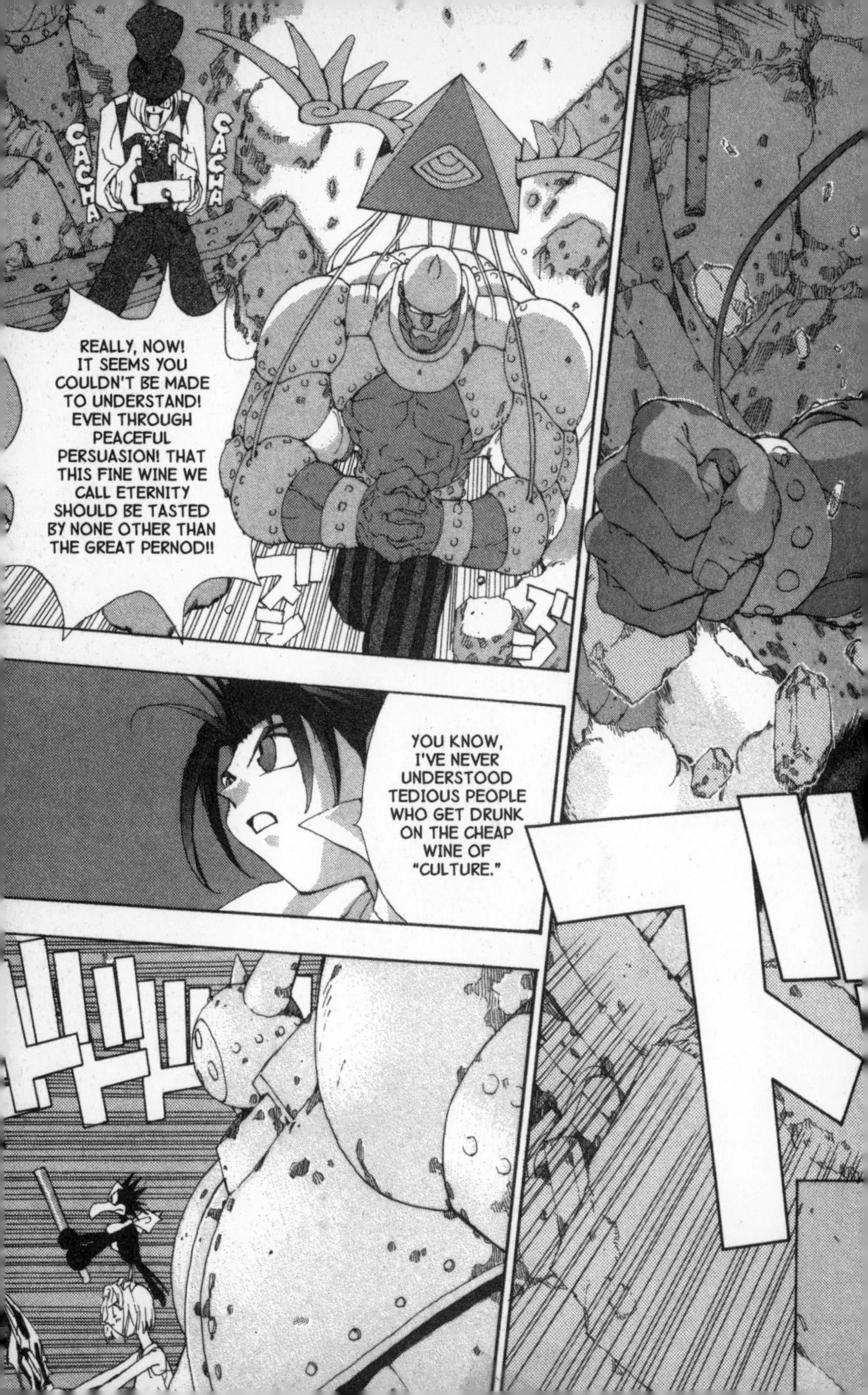
CACHA
CACHA
REALLY, NOW! IT SEEMS YOU COULDN'T BE MADE TO UNDERSTAND! EVEN THROUGH PEACEFUL PERSUASION! THAT THIS FINE WINE WE CALL ETERNITY SHOULD BE TASTED BY NONE OTHER THAN THE GREAT PERNOD!!
YOU KNOW, I'VE NEVER UNDERSTOOD TEDIOUS PEOPLE WHO GET DRUNK ON THE CHEAP WINE OF "CULTURE."

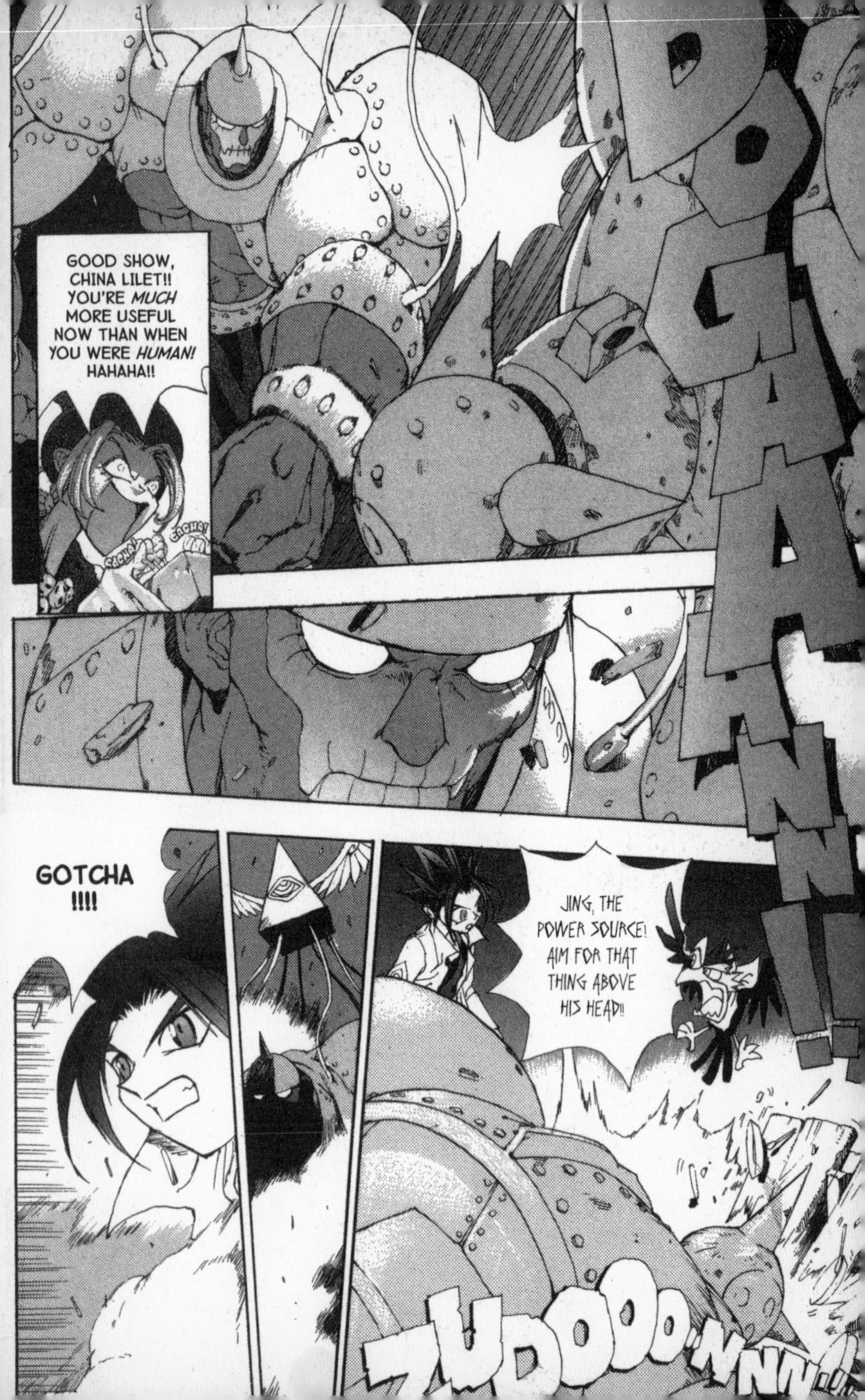
DOGAAANN!!
GOOD SHOW, CHINA LILET!! YOU'RE *MUCH* MORE USEFUL NOW THAN WHEN YOU WERE *HUMAN!* HAHAHA!!
GACHA!
GACHA!
JING, THE POWER SOURCE! AIM FOR THAT THING ABOVE HIS HEAD!!
ZUDOOO-NNN..!!
GOTCHA !!!!

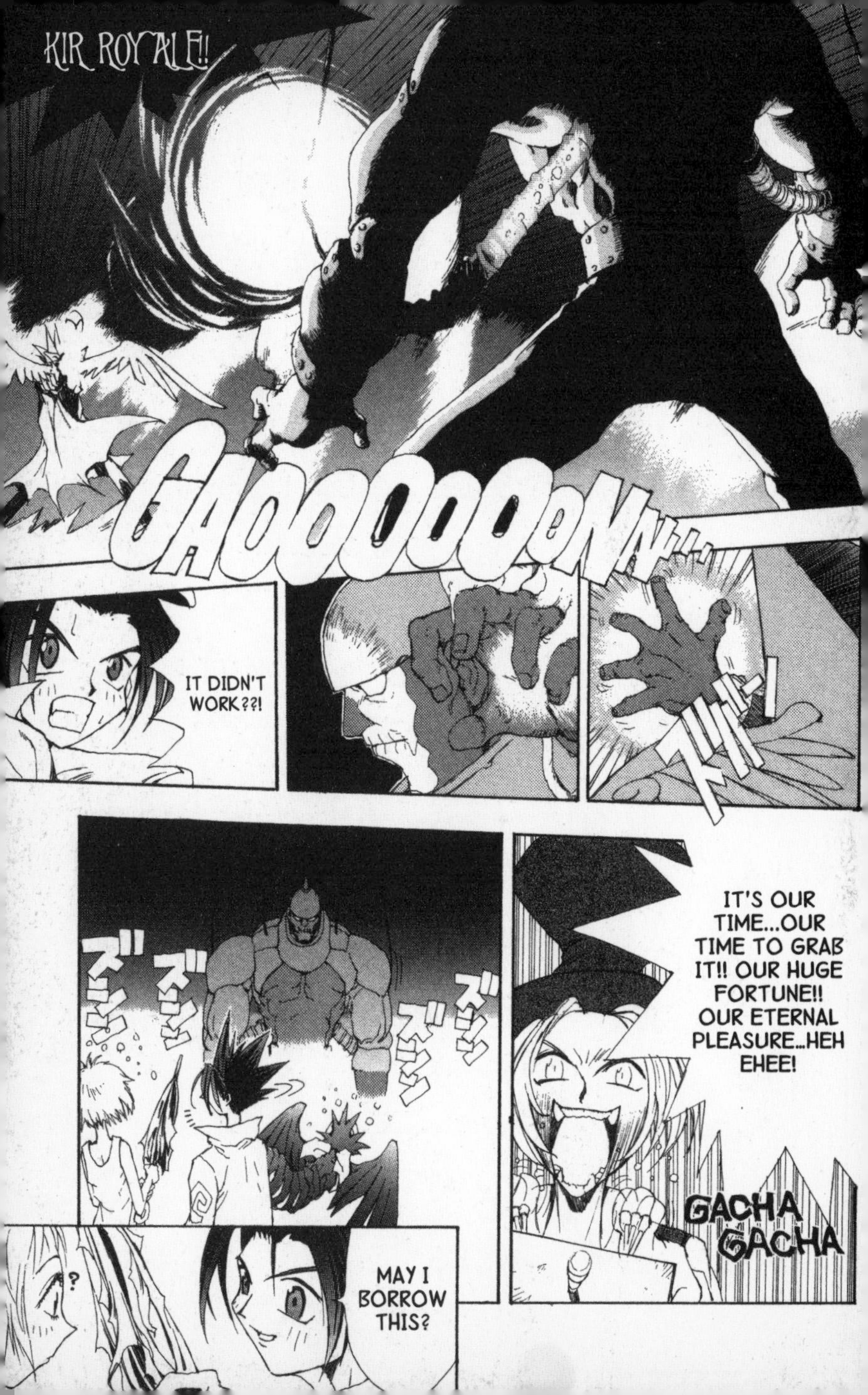
KIR ROYALE!!
GAOOOOOONN..
IT DIDN'T WORK??!
IT'S OUR TIME...OUR TIME TO GRAB IT!! OUR HUGE FORTUNE!! OUR ETERNAL PLEASURE...HEH EHEE!
GACHA GACHA
MAY I BORROW THIS?
?

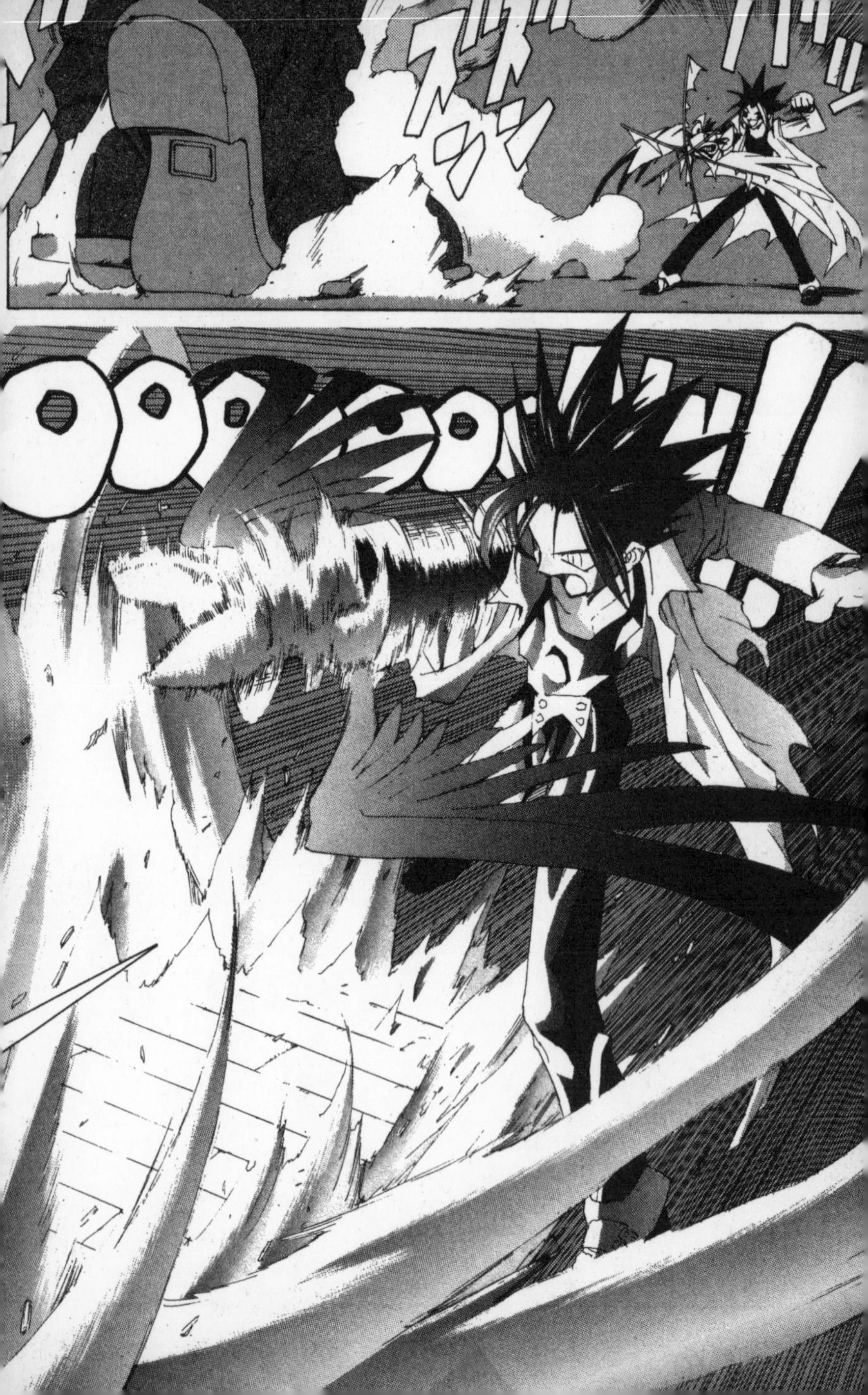

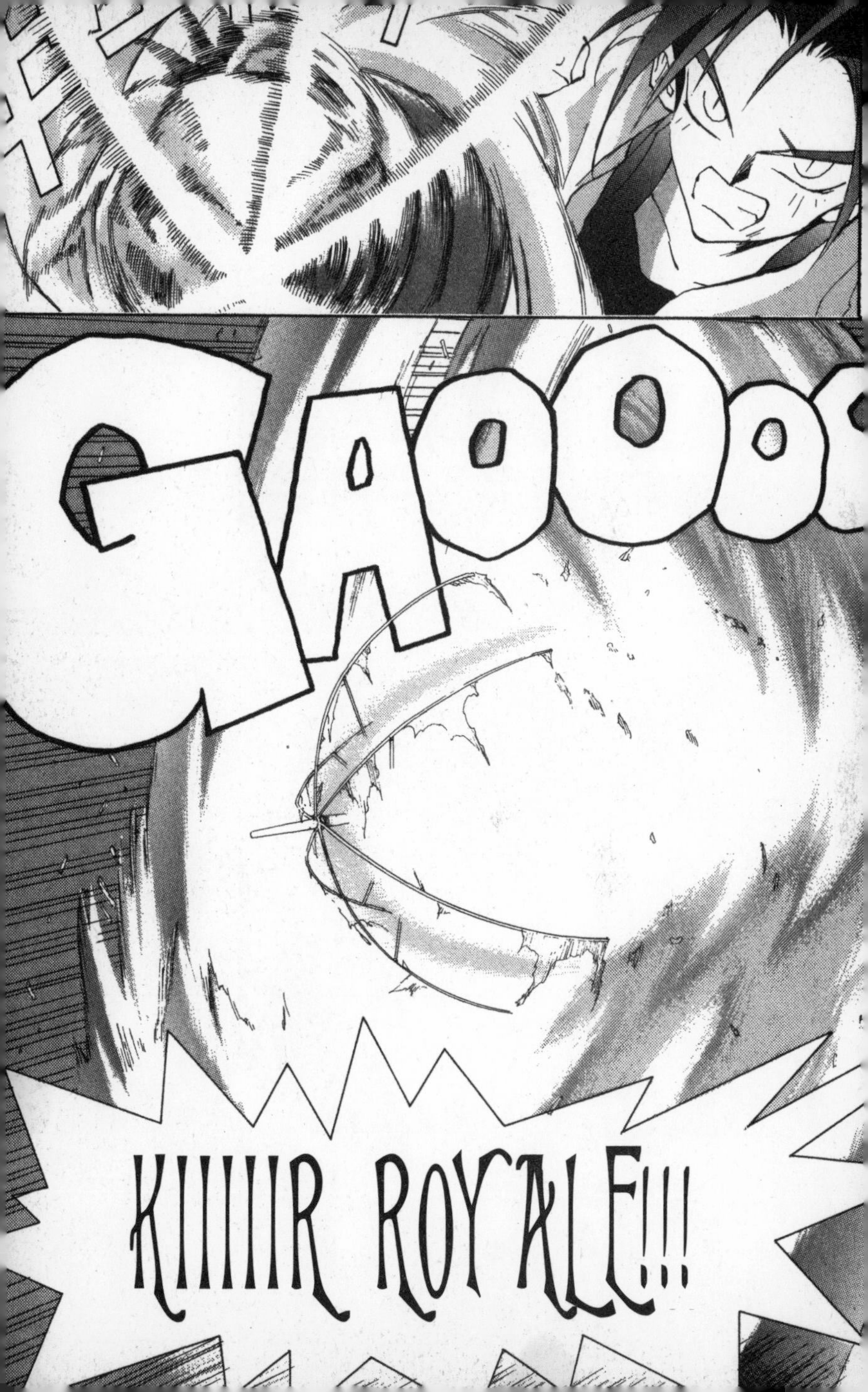
GAOOO
KIIIIR ROYALE!!!

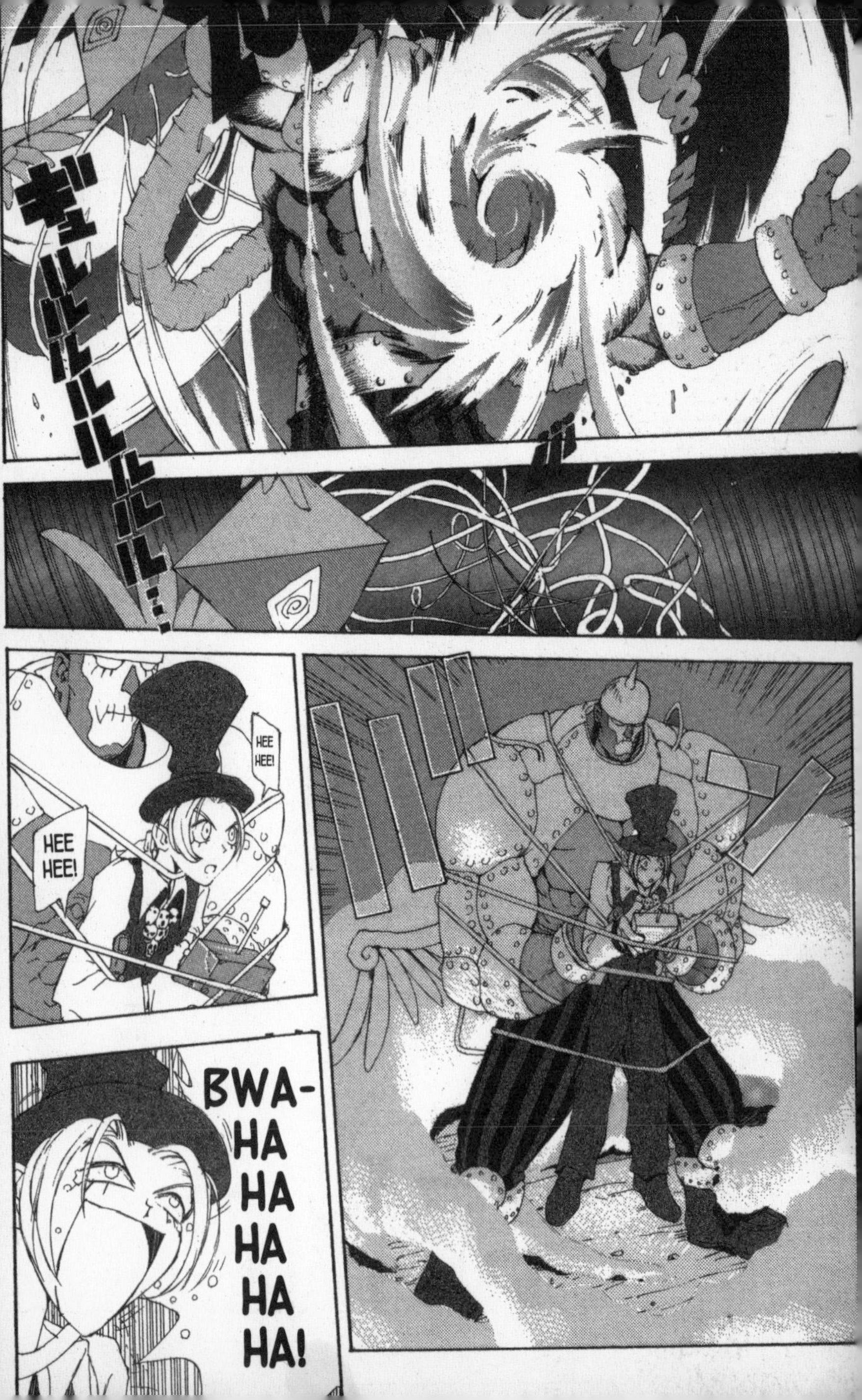
HEE HEE!
HEE HEE!
BWA-HA HA HA HA HA HA!

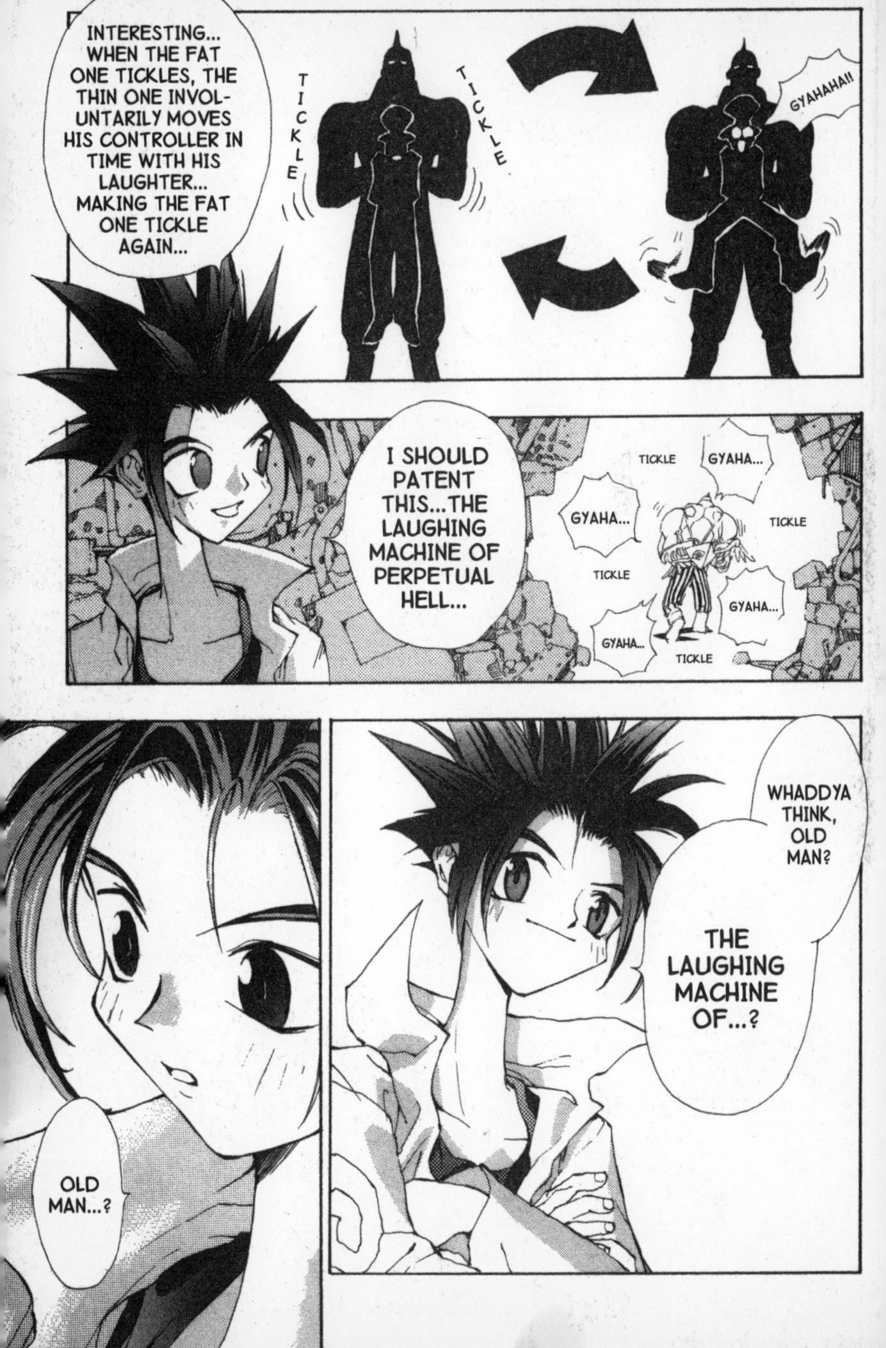
GYAHAHA!!
TICKLE
TICKLE
INTERESTING... WHEN THE FAT ONE TICKLES, THE THIN ONE INVOLUNTARILY MOVES HIS CONTROLLER IN TIME WITH HIS LAUGHTER... MAKING THE FAT ONE TICKLE AGAIN...
GYAHA...
TICKLE
TICKLE
GYAHA...
GYAHA...
TICKLE
GYAHA...
TICKLE
I SHOULD PATENT THIS...THE LAUGHING MACHINE OF PERPETUAL HELL...
WHADDYA THINK, OLD MAN?
THE LAUGHING MACHINE OF...?
OLD MAN...?

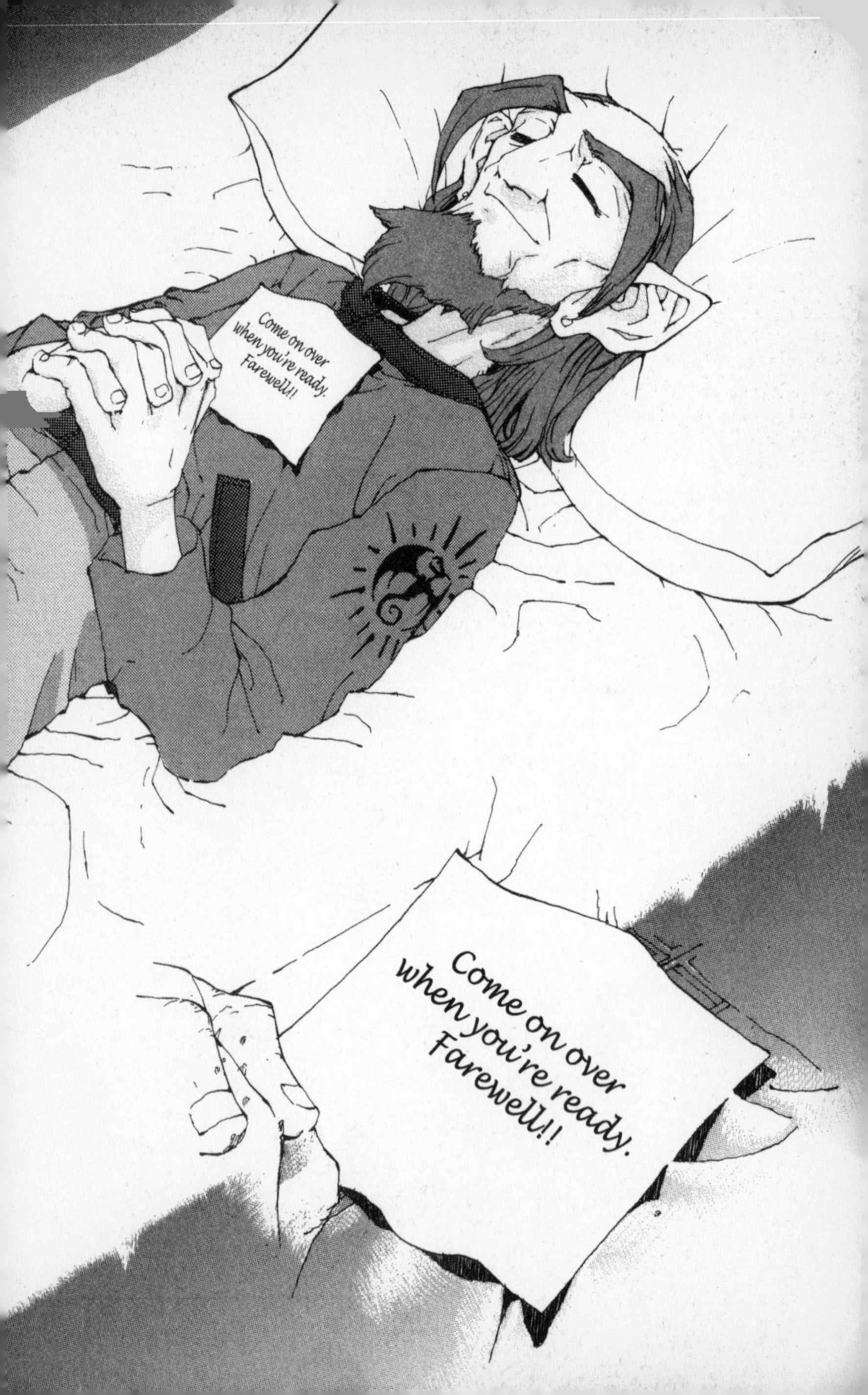
Come on over
when you're ready.
Farewell!!
Come on over
when you're ready.
Farewell!!

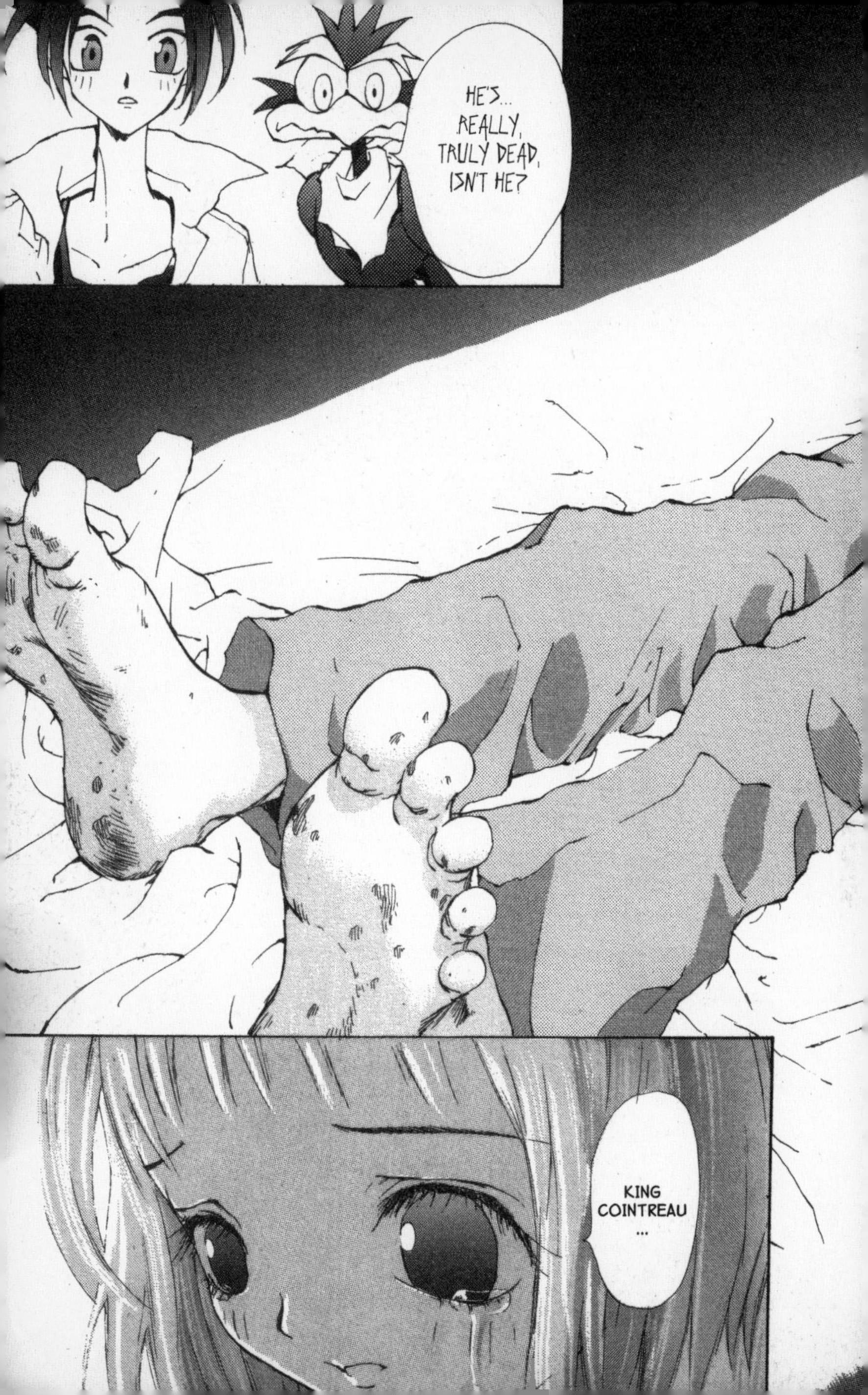
HE'S... REALLY, TRULY DEAD, ISN'T HE?
KING COINTREAU ...

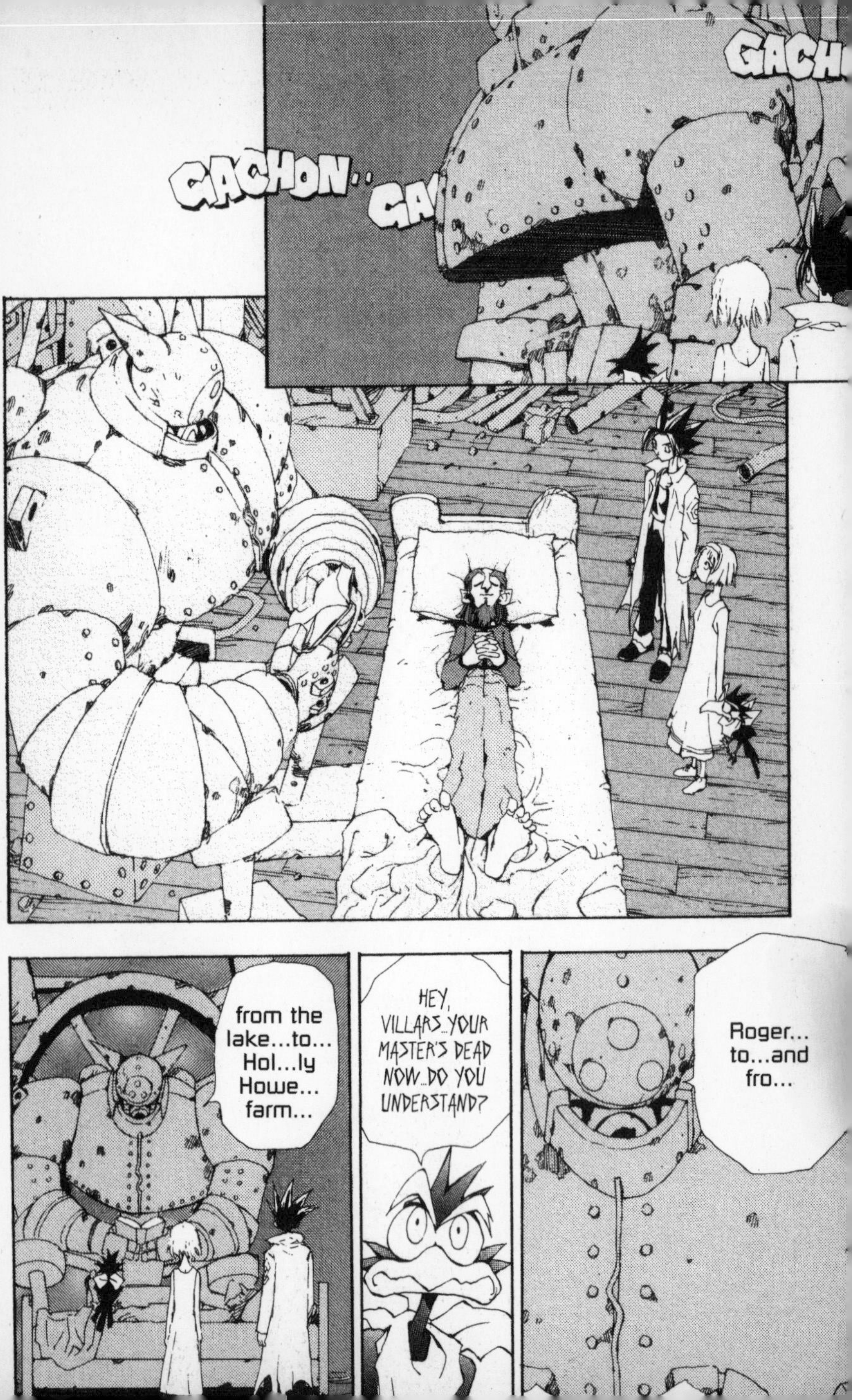
GACH
GACHON..
GA
Roger... to...and fro...
HEY, VILLARS...YOUR MASTER'S DEAD NOW...DO YOU UNDERSTAND?
from the lake...to... Hol...ly Howe... farm...

IS HE BROKEN?

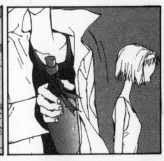

GACHA...

H-HEY, JING!!!!

YOU GONNA DRINK THAT? JUST ONE SIP FOR ME, HUH?

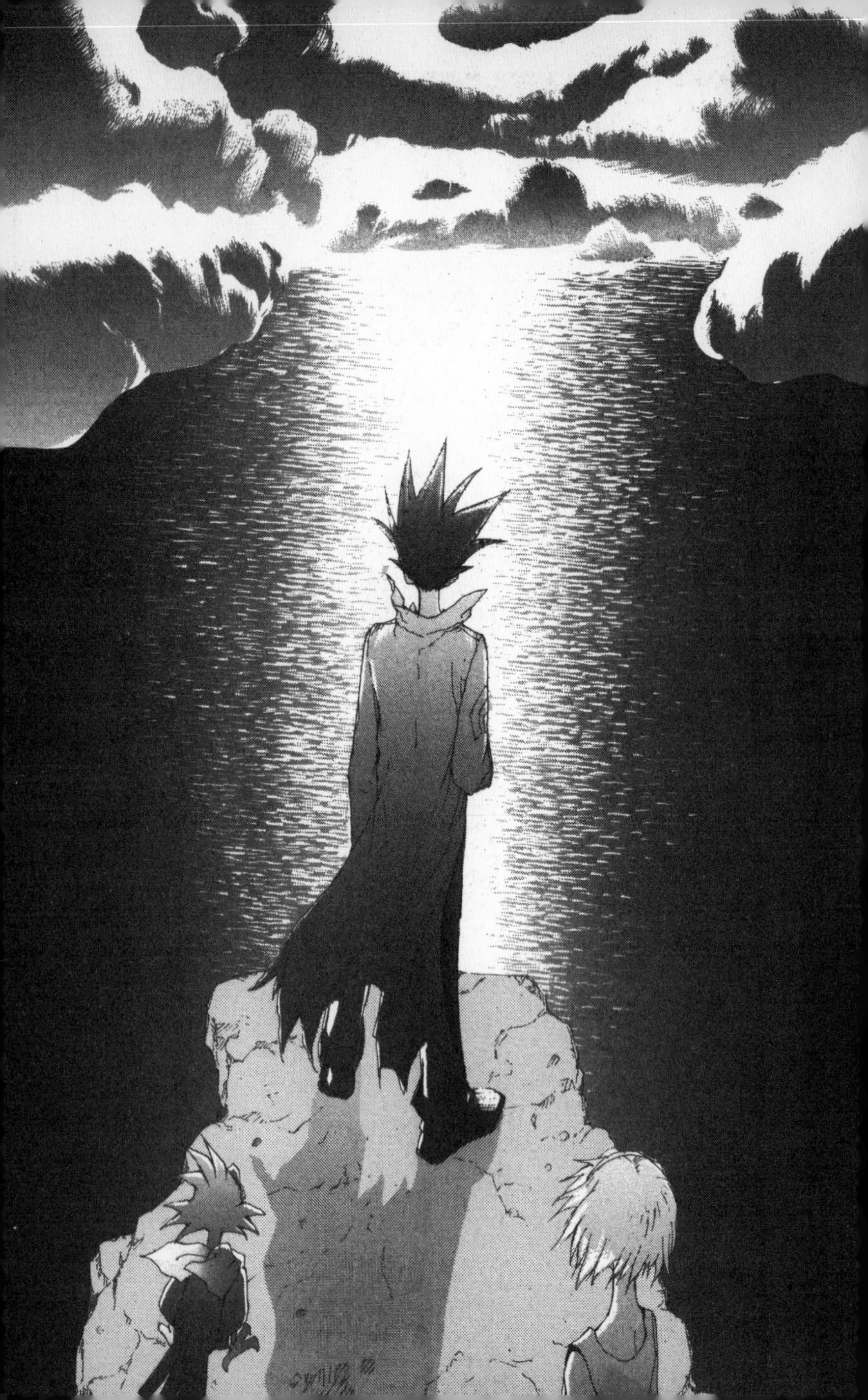

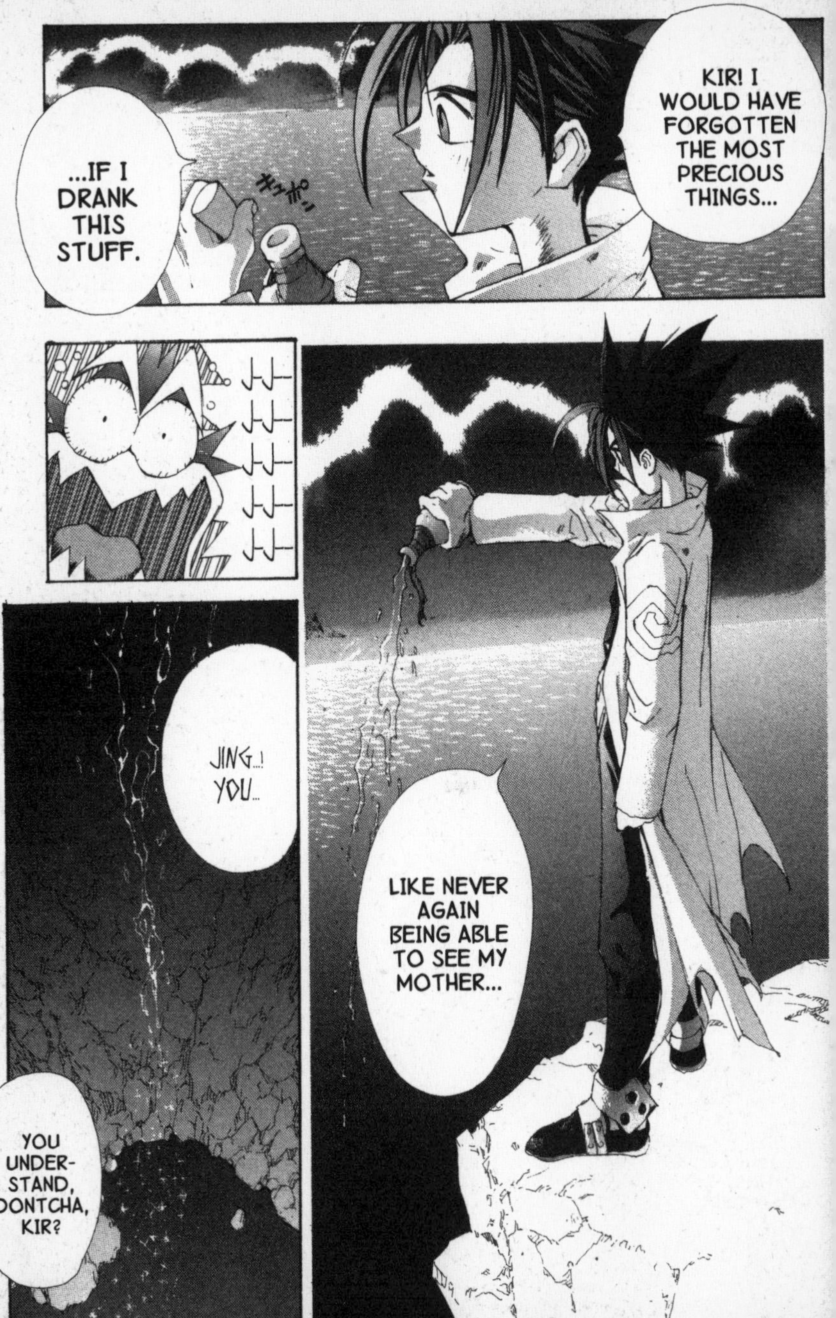
KIR! I WOULD HAVE FORGOTTEN THE MOST PRECIOUS THINGS...
...IF I DRANK THIS STUFF.
LIKE NEVER AGAIN BEING ABLE TO SEE MY MOTHER...
JING...! YOU...
YOU UNDER-STAND, DONTCHA, KIR?

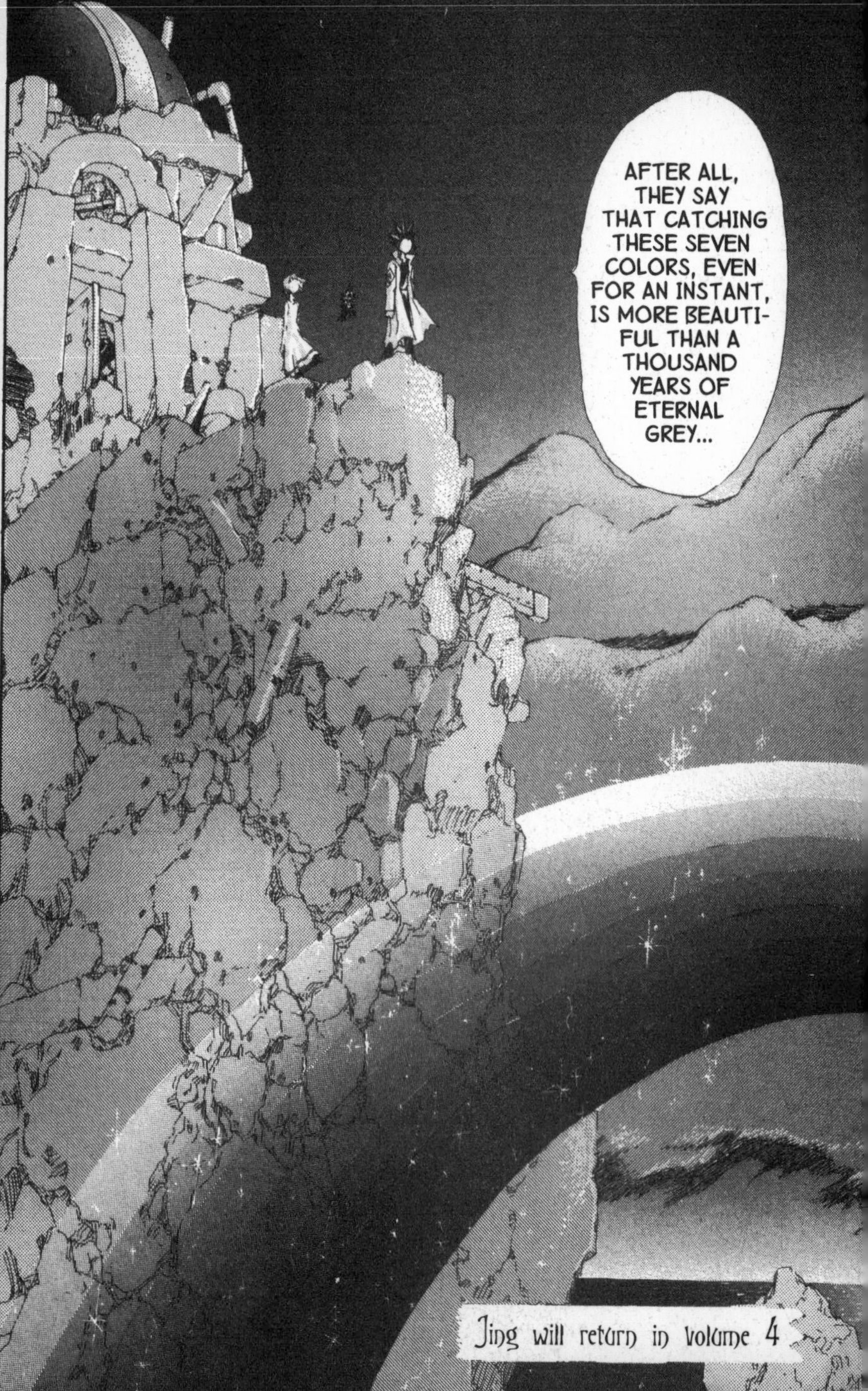
AFTER ALL, THEY SAY THAT CATCHING THESE SEVEN COLORS, EVEN FOR AN INSTANT, IS MORE BEAUTIFUL THAN A THOUSAND YEARS OF ETERNAL GREY...
Jing will return in volume 4

This logo was used on the back cover of the old edition of volume three. The cat with the spinning eyes actually appears everywhere in the "King of Bandits" series—it's the symbol of Jing.

JING, KING OF BANDITS
INITIAL SET-UP COLLECTION (3)

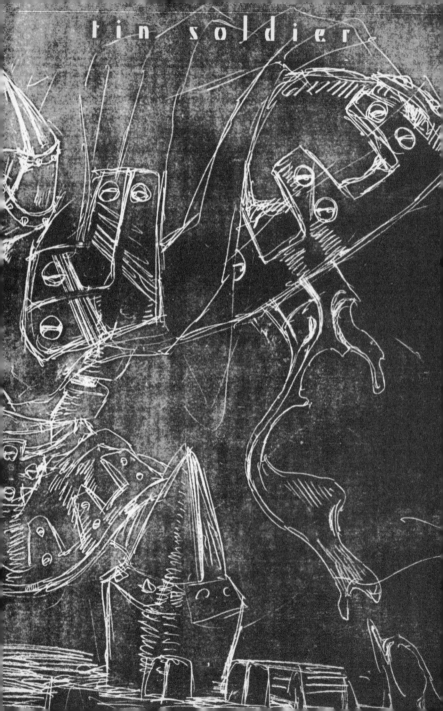

tin soldier

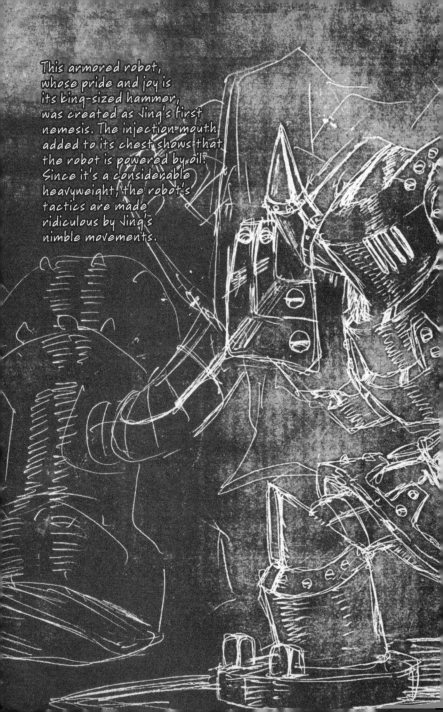

This armored robot, whose pride and joy is its king-sized hammer, was created as Jing's first nemesis. The injection-mouth added to its chest shows that the robot is powered by oil. Since it's a considerable heavyweight, the robot's tactics are made ridiculous by Jing's nimble movements.

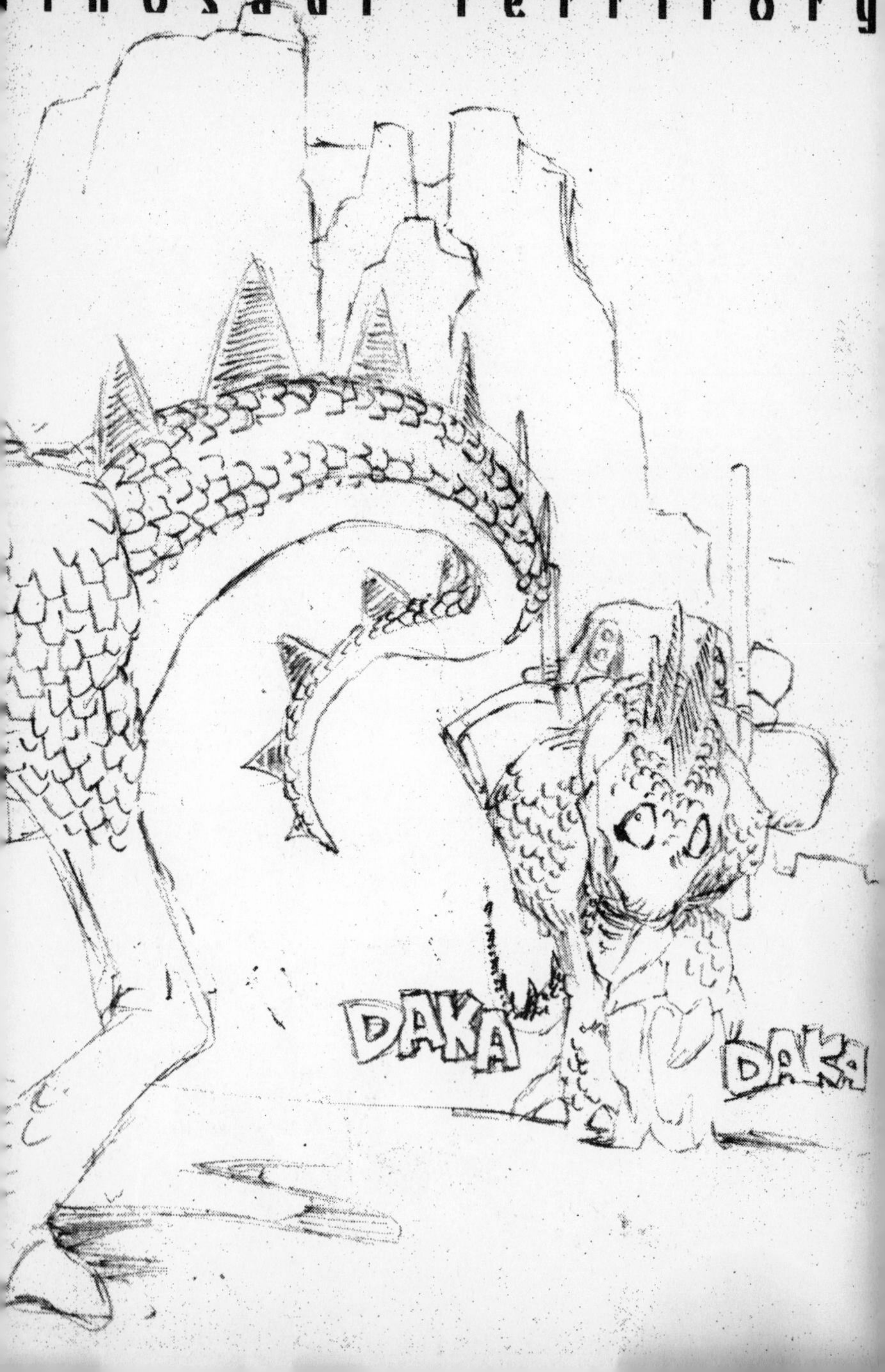
DAKA
DAKA

These animals live all around the City of Theieves.
They're mainly used as pack animals.

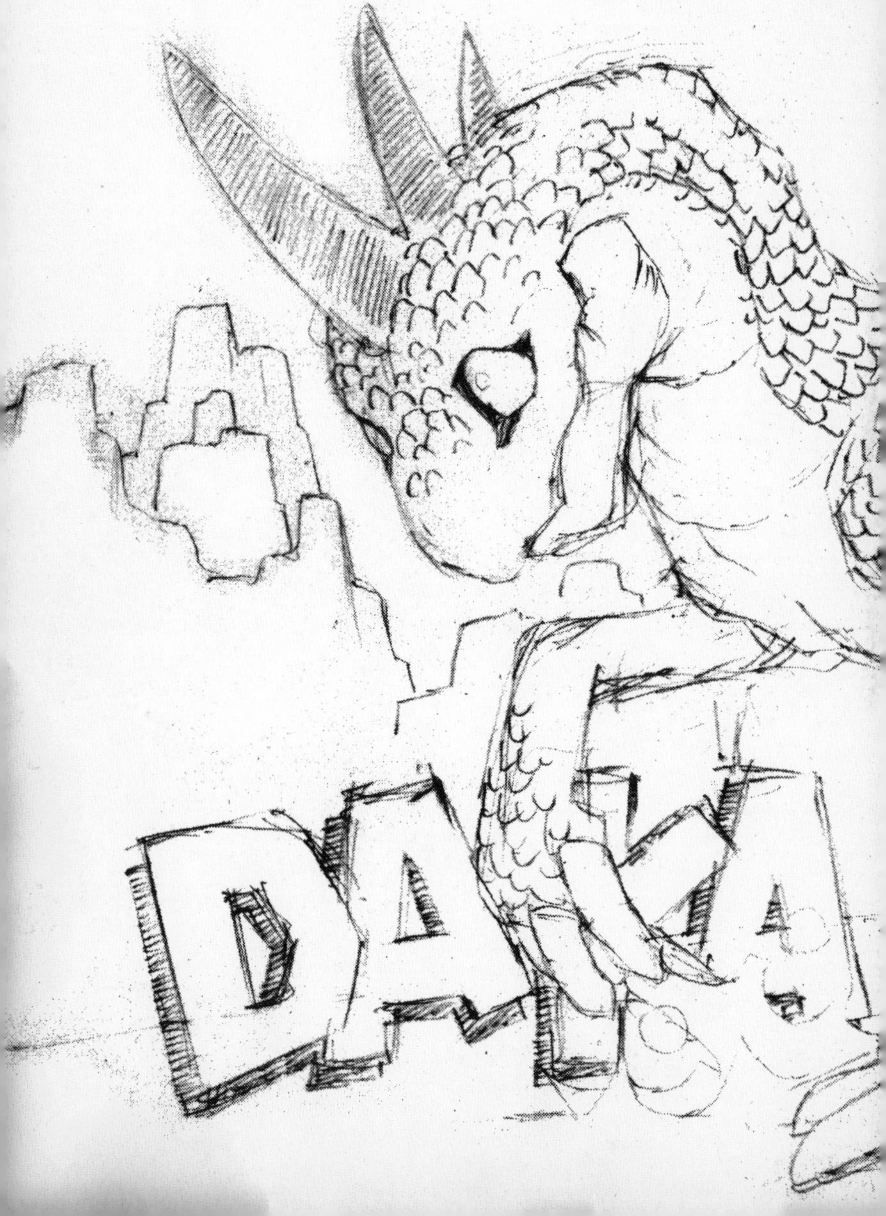

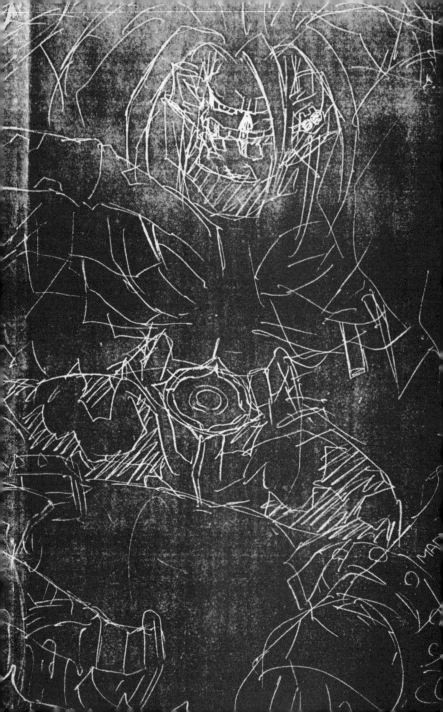

A zombie that appears on the coastal outskirts of Blue Hawaii. For the Gameboy RPG, it was named Raimi--in honor of Sam Raimi, director of that masterpiece of splatter films, "The Evil Dead."

l i v i n g d e a d a

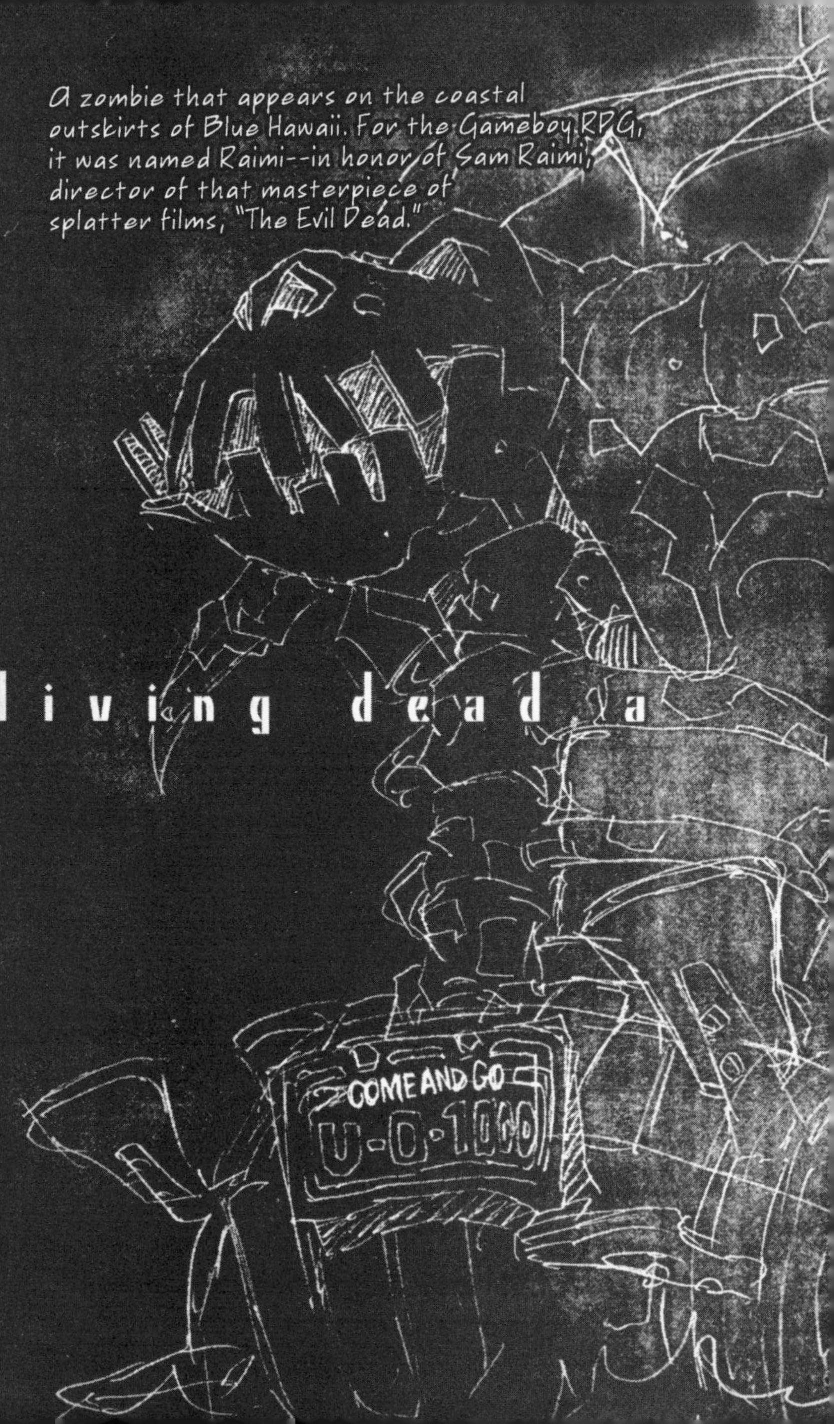
COME AND GO
U-0-1000

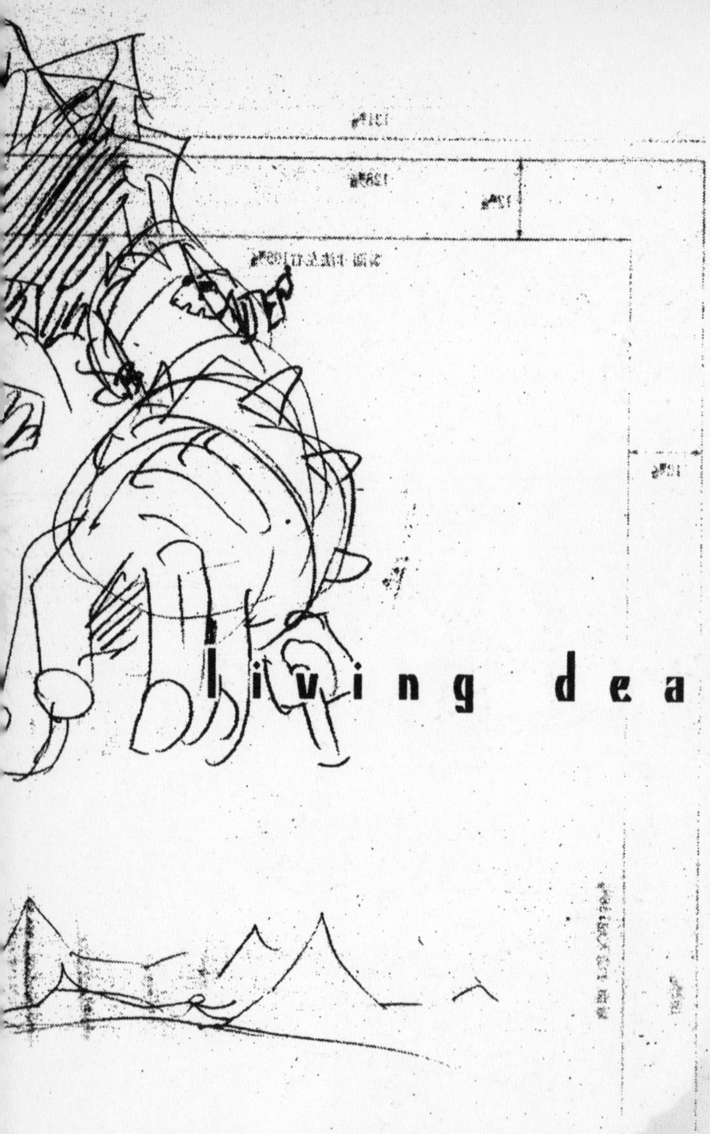

l i v i n g   d e a d   b

This feels rougher than the zombie on the previous page, but I had already decided on the zombie's current form by the time I drew this.

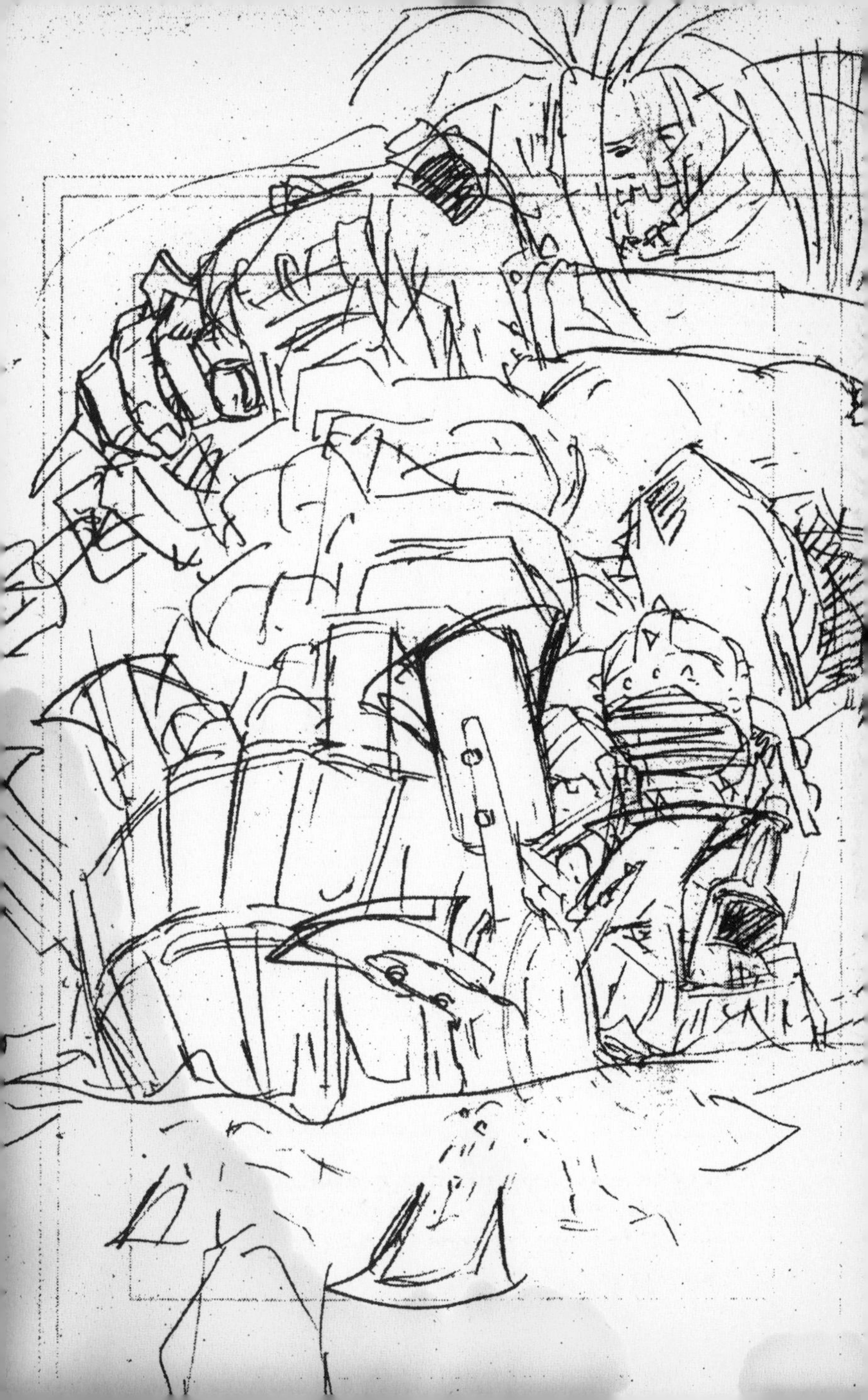

Another logo, which I designed for the back cover of volume one's old edition. This original circular, billowing logo was eliminated, making more room for the cover illustration.

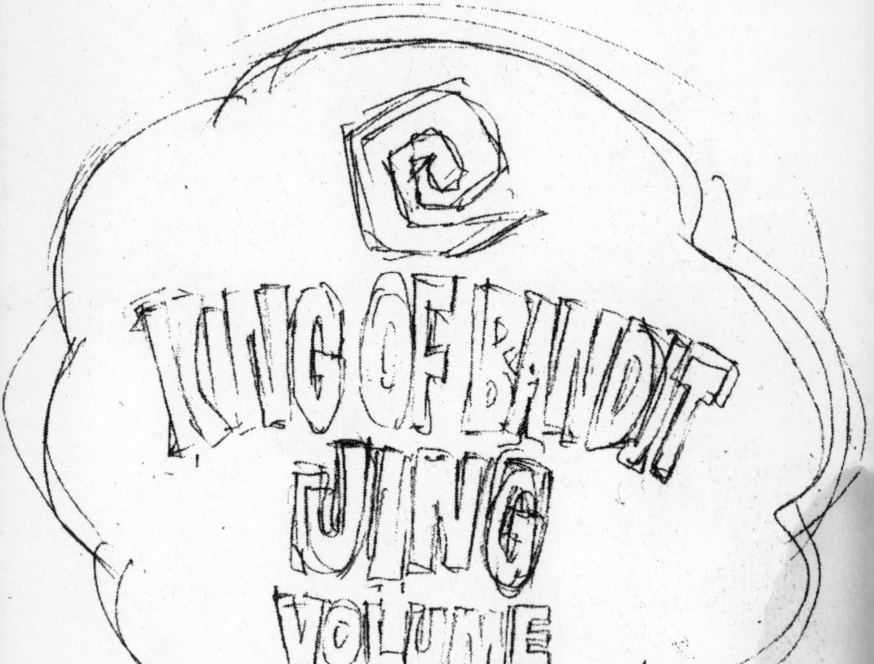
KING OF BANDIT
JING
VOLUME
1

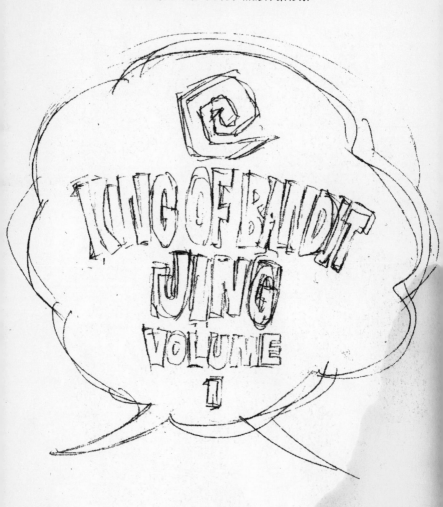

logomark

jing&bateau ivre

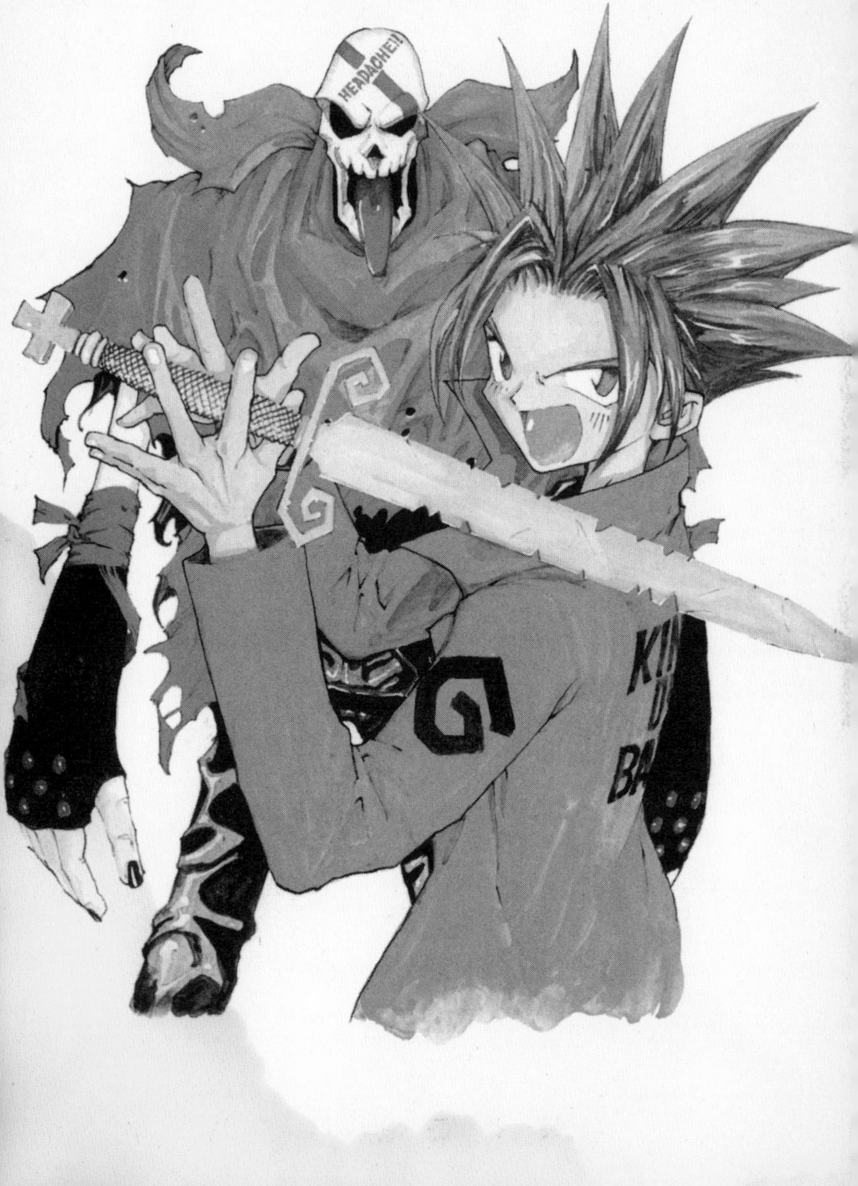
HEADACHE!!

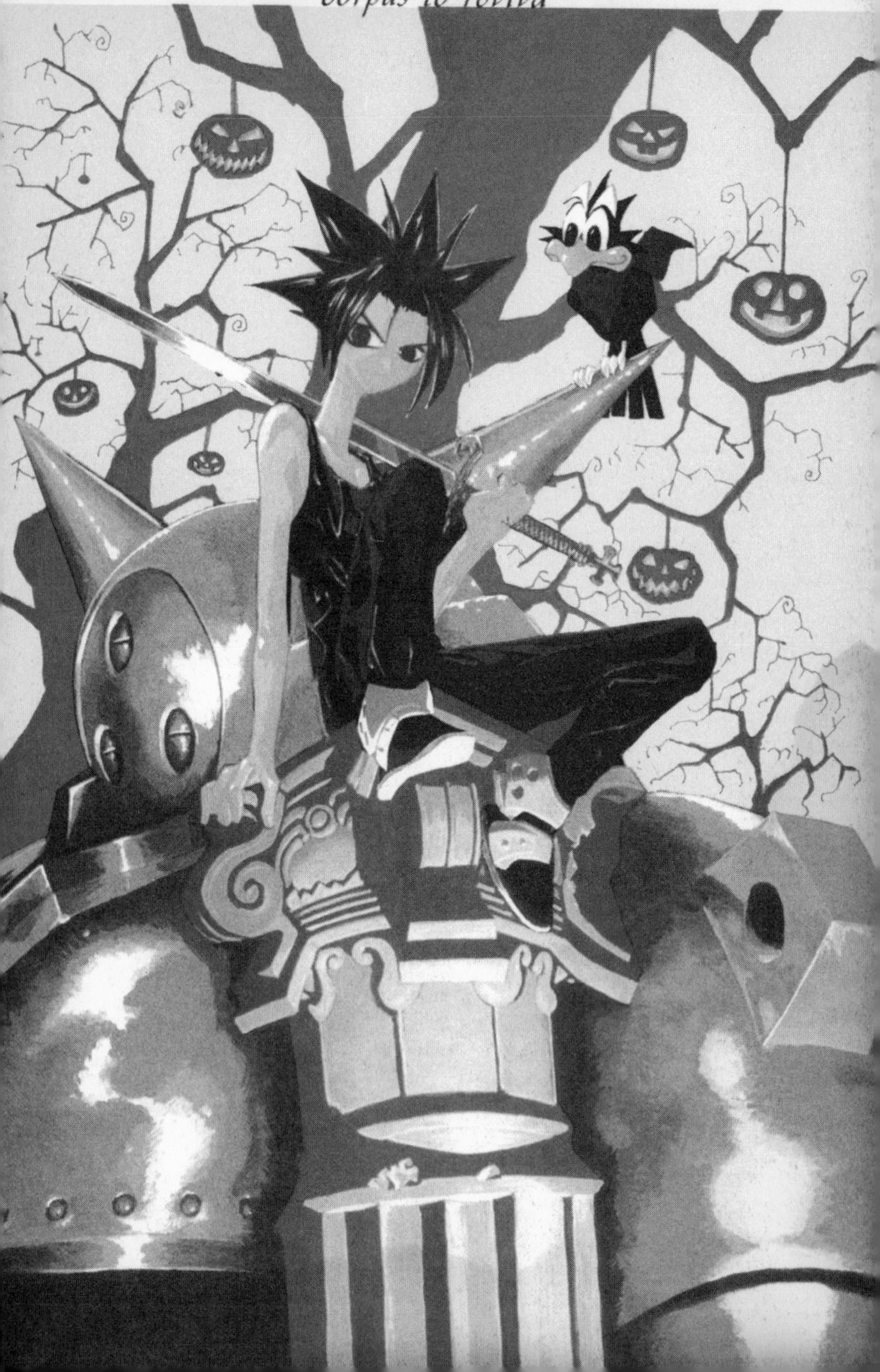

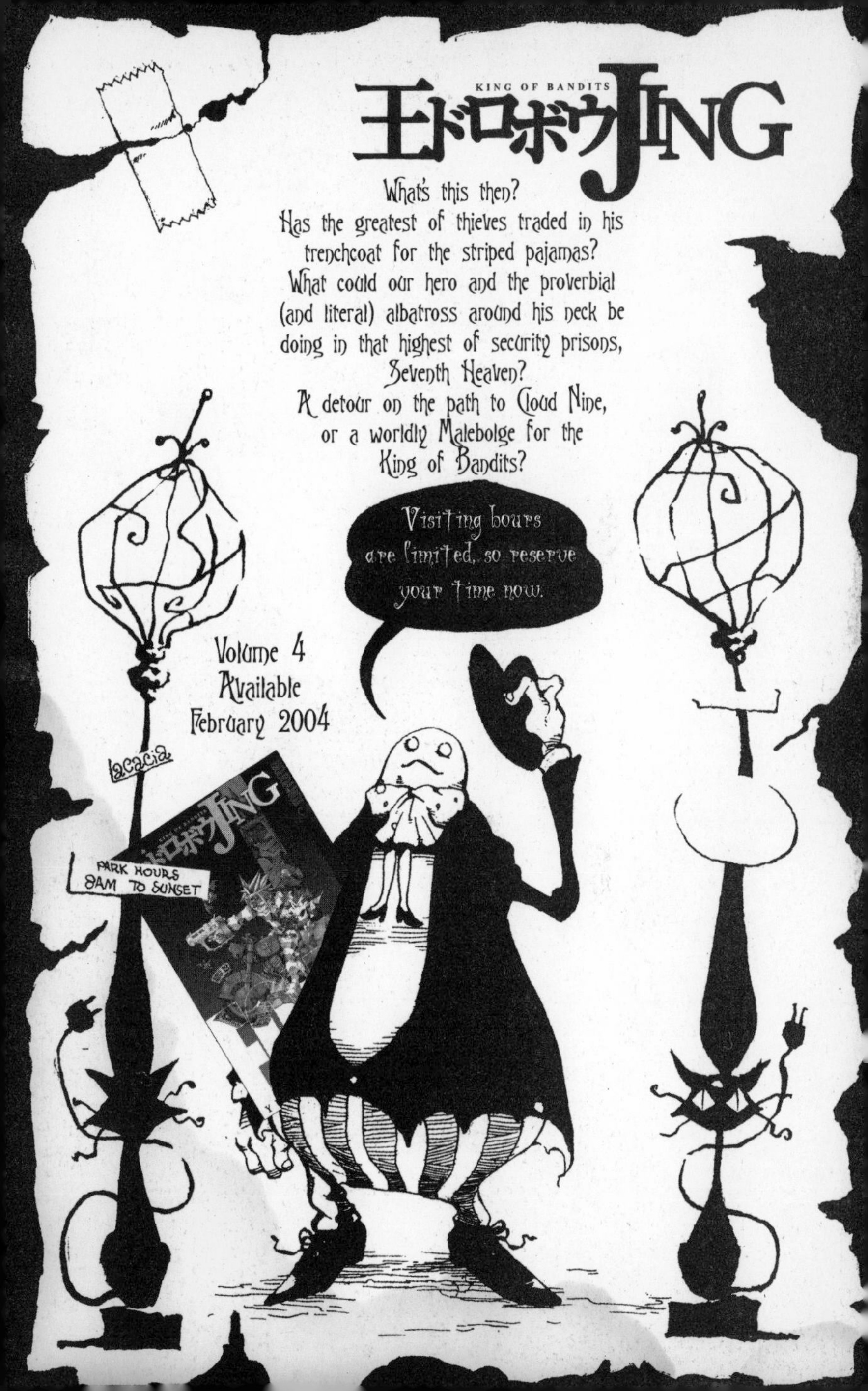
KING OF BANDITS
王ドロボウJING
What's this then?
Has the greatest of thieves traded in his trenchcoat for the striped pajamas?
What could our hero and the proverbial (and literal) albatross around his neck be doing in that highest of security prisons, Seventh Heaven?
A detour on the path to Cloud Nine, or a worldly Malebolge for the King of Bandits?
Visiting hours are limited, so reserve your time now.
Volume 4
Available
February 2004
lacacia
PARK HOURS
8AM TO SUNSET

THE FOLLOWING IS A PAID ADVERTISEMENT

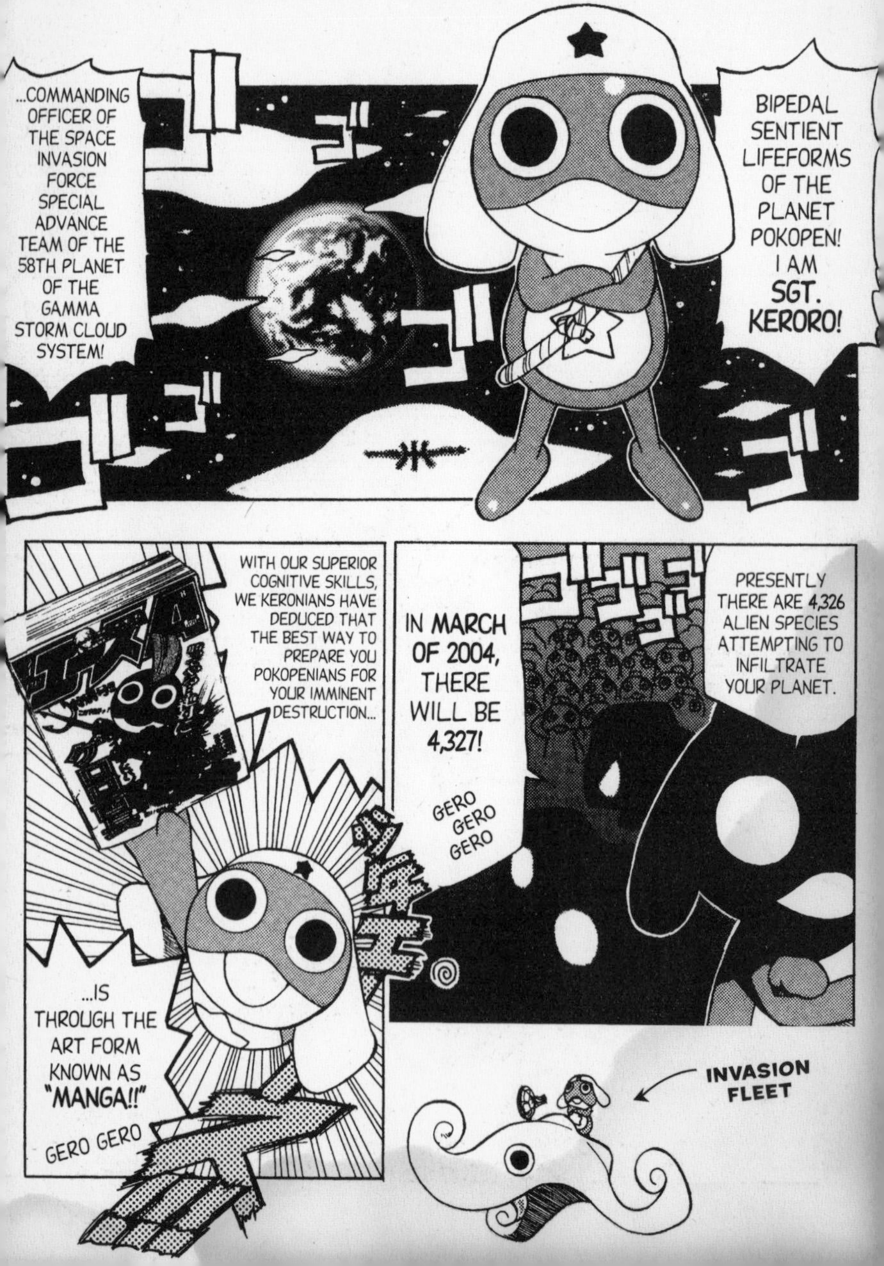
BIPEDAL SENTIENT LIFEFORMS OF THE PLANET POKOPEN! I AM SGT. KERORO!
...COMMANDING OFFICER OF THE SPACE INVASION FORCE SPECIAL ADVANCE TEAM OF THE 58TH PLANET OF THE GAMMA STORM CLOUD SYSTEM!
PRESENTLY THERE ARE 4,326 ALIEN SPECIES ATTEMPTING TO INFILTRATE YOUR PLANET.
IN MARCH OF 2004, THERE WILL BE 4,327!
GERO GERO GERO
WITH OUR SUPERIOR COGNITIVE SKILLS, WE KERONIANS HAVE DEDUCED THAT THE BEST WAY TO PREPARE YOU POKOPENIANS FOR YOUR IMMINENT DESTRUCTION...
...IS THROUGH THE ART FORM KNOWN AS "MANGA!!"
GERO GERO
INVASION FLEET

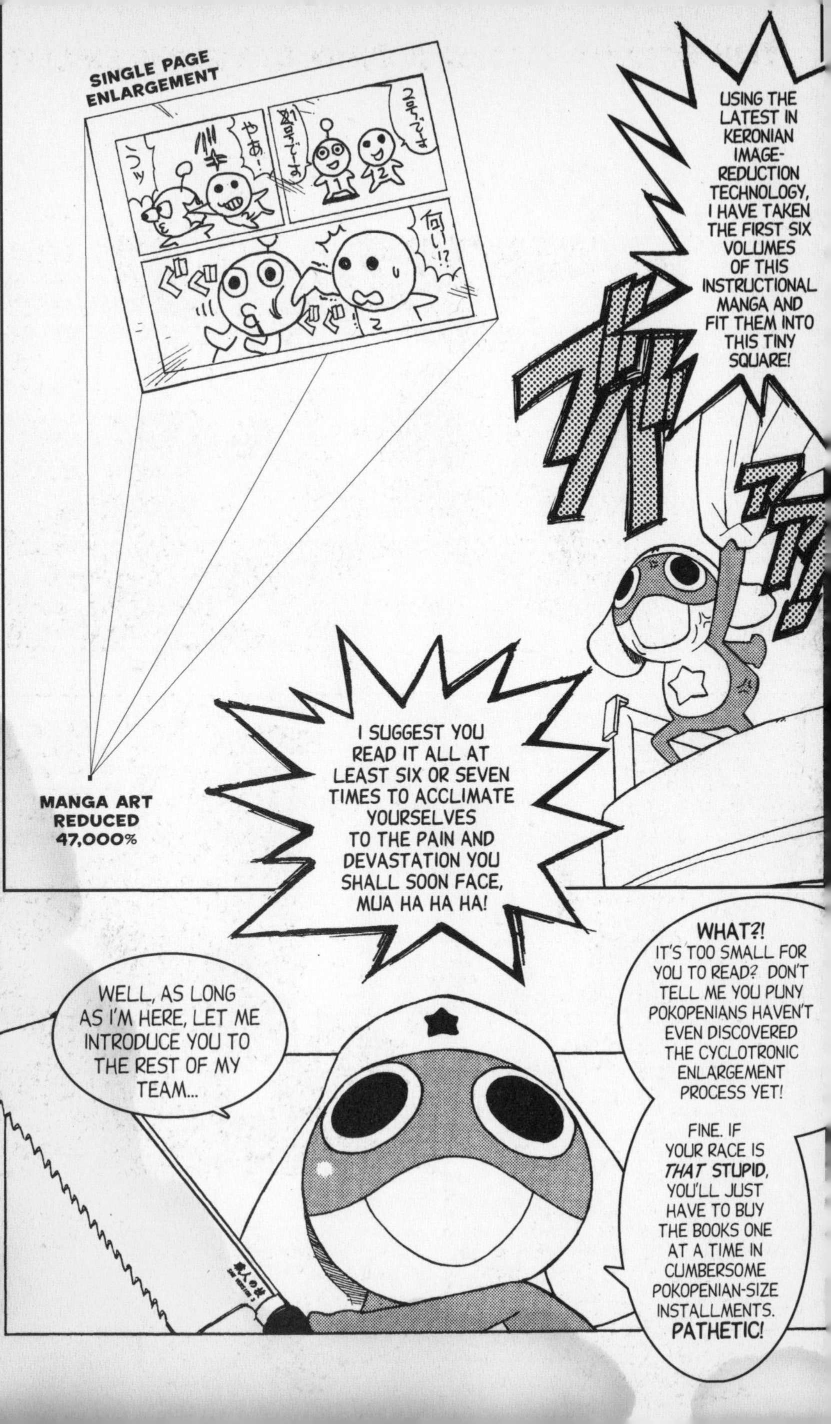
USING THE LATEST IN KERONIAN IMAGE-REDUCTION TECHNOLOGY, I HAVE TAKEN THE FIRST SIX VOLUMES OF THIS INSTRUCTIONAL MANGA AND FIT THEM INTO THIS TINY SQUARE!
I SUGGEST YOU READ IT ALL AT LEAST SIX OR SEVEN TIMES TO ACCLIMATE YOURSELVES TO THE PAIN AND DEVASTATION YOU SHALL SOON FACE, MUA HA HA HA!
SINGLE PAGE ENLARGEMENT
MANGA ART REDUCED 47,000%
WHAT?! IT'S TOO SMALL FOR YOU TO READ? DON'T TELL ME YOU PUNY POKOPENIANS HAVEN'T EVEN DISCOVERED THE CYCLOTRONIC ENLARGEMENT PROCESS YET!
FINE. IF YOUR RACE IS THAT STUPID, YOU'LL JUST HAVE TO BUY THE BOOKS ONE AT A TIME IN CUMBERSOME POKOPENIAN-SIZE INSTALLMENTS. PATHETIC!
WELL, AS LONG AS I'M HERE, LET ME INTRODUCE YOU TO THE REST OF MY TEAM...

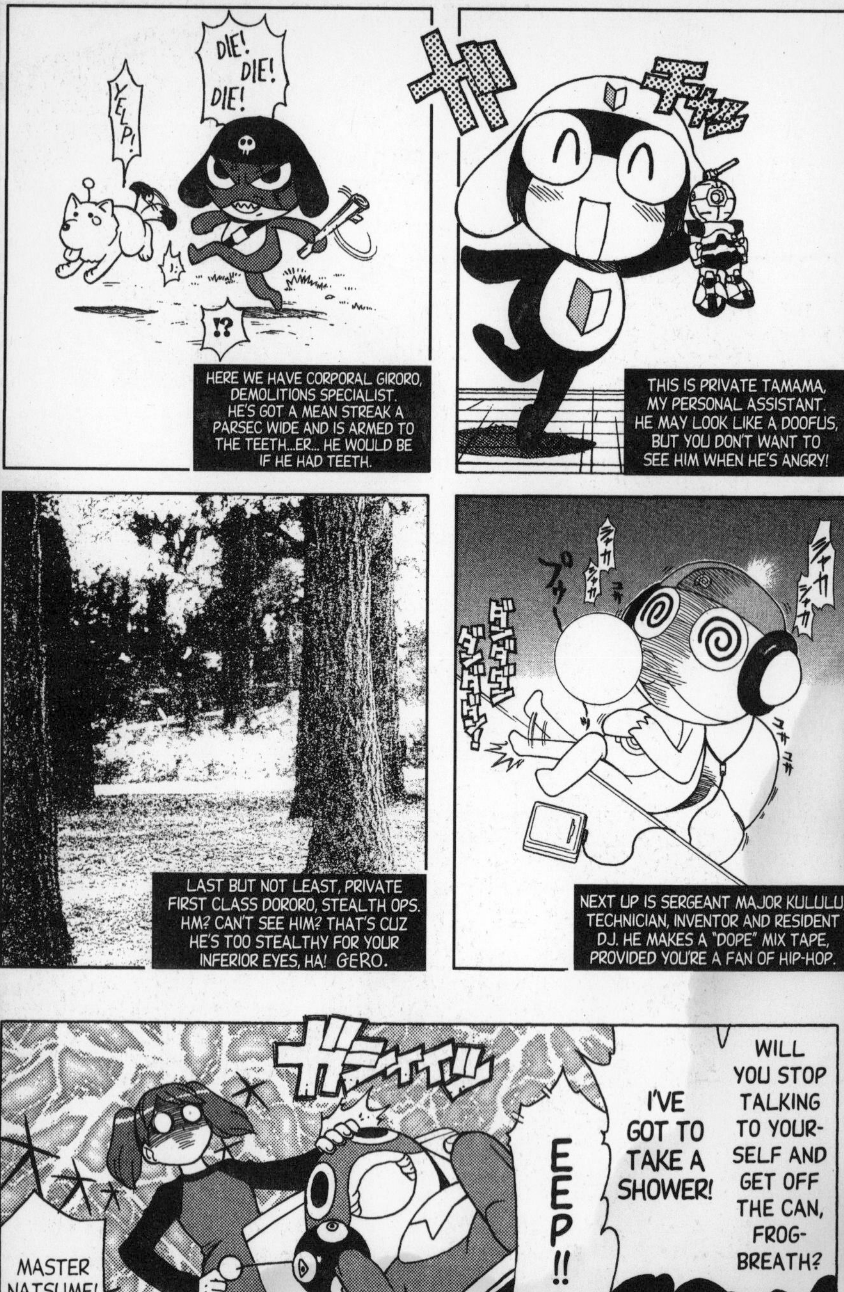
THIS IS PRIVATE TAMAMA, MY PERSONAL ASSISTANT. HE MAY LOOK LIKE A DOOFUS, BUT YOU DON'T WANT TO SEE HIM WHEN HE'S ANGRY!
DIE! DIE! DIE!
YELP!
!?
HERE WE HAVE CORPORAL GIRORO, DEMOLITIONS SPECIALIST. HE'S GOT A MEAN STREAK A PARSEC WIDE AND IS ARMED TO THE TEETH...ER... HE WOULD BE IF HE HAD TEETH.
NEXT UP IS SERGEANT MAJOR KULULU, TECHNICIAN, INVENTOR AND RESIDENT DJ. HE MAKES A "DOPE" MIX TAPE, PROVIDED YOU'RE A FAN OF HIP-HOP.
LAST BUT NOT LEAST, PRIVATE FIRST CLASS DORORO, STEALTH OPS. HM? CAN'T SEE HIM? THAT'S CUZ HE'S TOO STEALTHY FOR YOUR INFERIOR EYES, HA! GERO.
WILL YOU STOP TALKING TO YOURSELF AND GET OFF THE CAN, FROG-BREATH?
I'VE GOT TO TAKE A SHOWER!
EEP!!
MASTER NATSUME!

THE INVASION CAN WAIT!

SHOWER, EH?

CRUNCH

STUPID FROG.

TO THE WEB-CAM!!

PANTIES...

GERO

SGT FROG™
KERORO GUNSOU

COMING TO EARTH
MARCH 2004

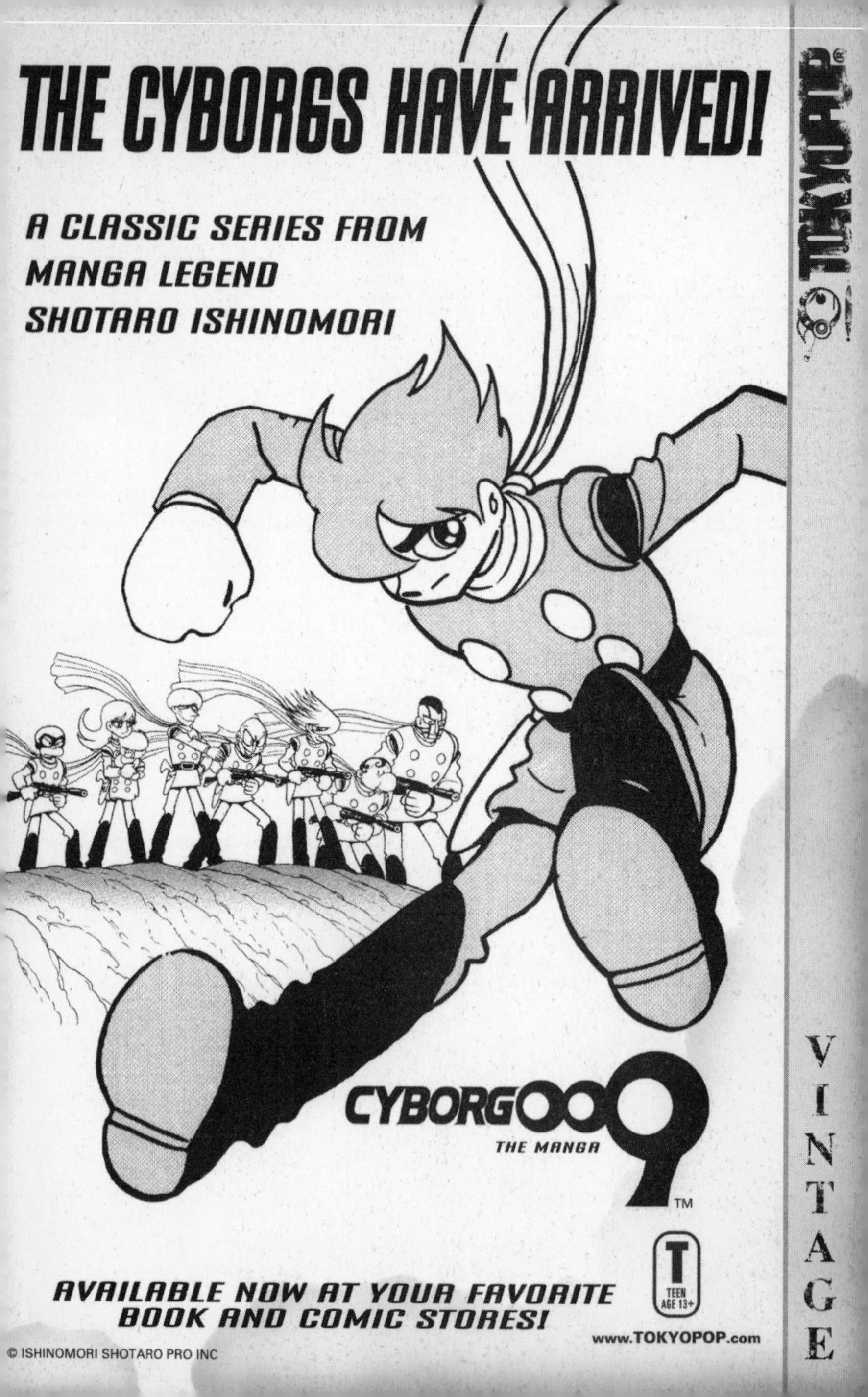
THE CYBORGS HAVE ARRIVED!
A CLASSIC SERIES FROM
MANGA LEGEND
SHOTARO ISHINOMORI
CYBORG009™
THE MANGA
T TEEN AGE 13+
AVAILABLE NOW AT YOUR FAVORITE
BOOK AND COMIC STORES!
www.TOKYOPOP.com
© ISHINOMORI SHOTARO PRO INC
TOKYOPOP®
VINTAGE